Trade Agreements at the Crossroads

This book examines trade agreements in the context of the current world economic crisis and the uncompleted World Trade Organization (WTO) Doha Round of trade negotiations. With economies shrinking and protectionism on the rise, many fear a protracted global recession. This raises important questions as to what role trade agreements – multilateral, plurilateral, and bilateral – should be playing in the current climate of uncertainty, and how best to plan for a more stable economic future. Previous assumptions are now being questioned, making this an opportune time to critically examine the WTO, free trade agreements, bilateral investment treaties, and other international economic law instruments. Furthermore, participants in international agreements are concerned with emerging issues that have the potential to strengthen or weaken the global trading system, including matters of treaty interpretation; terms of new agreements; and effects of existing provisions.

This book provides a timely addition to the international economic law literature, as its submissions have been prepared during a time of unusual uncertainty and economic change; individuals interested in international economic law will seek scholarship such at this that recognizes the current international economic climate. This book should be of interest to a wide range of academics and student researchers, as well as policymakers and practitioners.

Susy Frankel is Professor at the Faculty of Law, Victoria University of Wellington and Director of the New Zealand Centre of International Economic Law.

Meredith Kolsky Lewis is Associate Professor and Director of the Canada–US Legal Studies Centre at the SUNY Buffalo Law School, Associate Professor at the Victoria University of Wellington Faculty of Law and Associate Director of the New Zealand Centre of International Economic Law.

Trade Agreements at the Crossroads

Edited by Susy Frankel and
Meredith Kolsky Lewis

 Routledge
Taylor & Francis Group

LONDON AND NEW YORK

First published 2014
by Routledge
2 Park Square, Milton Park, Abingdon, Oxfordshire OX14 4RN

and by Routledge
711 Third Avenue, New York, NY 10017

First issued in paperback 2014

Routledge is an imprint of the Taylor and Francis Group, an informa business

British Library Cataloguing in Publication Data
A catalogue record for this book is available from the British Library

Library of Congress Cataloging in Publication Data
Trade agreements at the crossroads / edited by Susy Frankel, Meredith Lewis.
  pages cm
  Includes bibliographical references and index.
  1. Commercial treaties. 2. International economic relations. 3. World Trade Organization. 4. Doha Development Agenda (2001–) 5. Global Financial Crisis, 2008–2009. I. Frankel, Susy. II. Lewis, Meredith Kolsky.
  HF1721.T687 2013
  382'.92 -dc23

                                                                    2013019798

ISBN 978-0-415-63525-7 (hbk)
ISBN 978-1-138-91804-7 (pbk)
ISBN 978-1-315-86772-4 (ebk)

Typeset in Times New Roman
by Wearset Ltd, Boldon, Tyne and Wear

Contents

Contributors

Ross Becroft is a principal of Gross & Becroft Lawyers in Melbourne, Australia. He is also a sessional academic at Melbourne Law School.

Peter Van den Bossche is Member of World Trade Organization Appellate Body, Professor of International Economic Law and Head of the Department of International and European Law at Maastricht University, the Netherlands.

Tracey Epps is Senior Trade Law Advisor, New Zealand Ministry of Foreign Affairs and Trade and part-time Senior Lecturer in the Faculty of Law, University of Otago.

Susy Frankel is a professor at the Faculty of Law, Victoria University of Wellington and Director of the New Zealand Centre of International Economic Law.

Kevin R. Gray is Counsel at the Trade Law Bureau, Government of Canada and Doctoral Candidate at the University of Ottawa, Faculty of Law.

Daniel Kalderimis is a partner at Chapman Tripp, Wellington, New Zealand.

Meredith Kolsky Lewis is Associate Professor and Director of the Canada–US Legal Studies Centre at the SUNY Buffalo Law School, Associate Professor at the Victoria University of Wellington Faculty of Law and Associate Director of the New Zealand Centre of International Economic Law.

Rafael Leal-Arcas is Senior Lecturer in Law at the Queen Mary University of London.

Sofya Matteotti is a research fellow at the World Trade Institute, Bern, Switzerland.

Olga Nartova is a research fellow at the World Trade Institute, Bern, Switzerland and Assistant Professor at DAH School of Law.

Luke Nottage is Professor of Comparative and International Business Law and Associate Dean (International) at University of Sydney Law School, Co-Director of the Australian Network for Japanese Law.

Iain Sandford is Counsel at Sidley Austin LLP, Geneva, Switzerland.

Xianchu Zhang is Professor of Law and Associate Dean, University of Hong Kong, Faculty of Law.

Introduction

The twenty-first century has thus far been marked by a global economic recession. Points of crisis can be isolated and aspects of recovery pinpointed; however, overall recession continues and many economies remain fragile. There is no shortage of theories and arguments as to why the recession has occurred. There has been, however, a shortage of agreed solutions as to how to bring recession to an end and spur economic growth. Multilateral or global initiatives to accomplish this goal have been thin on the ground. In particular, the World Trade Organization (WTO) Doha Round of trade negotiations remains moribund. At the same time, free trade agreements (FTAs) and bilateral investment treaties (BITs) have continued to proliferate, creating concerns over fragmentation and overlapping, potentially inconsistent, commitments. The combination of the global financial crisis, the lack of progress in the Doha Round, and the ever increasing number and variety of FTAs has created both a time of uncertainty and a heightened focus in international economic law scholarship on the implications of the issues creating this uncertainty. It is in this context that this book of essays is set. The issues discussed in this collection have been inspired by the current world economic and international trade and investment challenges, but the authors also focus in a forward-looking manner which will have enduring importance long after the current recession is behind us. To be sure, global recession and the stalling of multilateral negotiations tend to raise questions about the role of trade agreements – multilateral, plurilateral and bilateral – and what they might achieve in a climate of uncertainty characterised by a need to manage risk of many kinds, but such questions are also relevant in wealthier times. Regardless, the current economic crisis has sparked much scholarly interest and debate regarding these issues.

Since the formation of the WTO there has been a proliferation of non-multilateral trade agreements. All agree that this has created a changed situation. Some WTO members consider that they have had to turn to non-multilateral trade fora in order to make any meaningful progress. Others consider that the investment of resources in bilateral and plurilateral agreements ensures that the multilateral talks remain ineffective and cannot progress. In the face of these tensions certain theories arise about the future. One which draws on the history of previous multilateral trade rounds suggests that plurilateralism might carve a path back to the multilateral. Others suggest that may not be possible. Even if it is possible the problem may be that the multilateral round has to incorporate a set of norms that are reached outside of the multilateral process rather than negotiating those norms at the multilateral level where all voices can be heard. These complexities mean that assumptions about the value of trade agreements are being questioned not only by the anti-global or trade sceptics but even by those who might say that overall they favour trade liberalisation. Furthermore, participants in international agreements are concerned with emerging issues that have the potential to strengthen or weaken the global trading system, including matters of treaty interpretation, terms of new agreements, and effects of existing provisions.

This collection of essays adds to the international economic law literature through a consideration of a range of specific issues with the common backdrop of the current period of uncertainty and economic change. Trying times have inspired these authors to take new approaches to old problems; to identify and address emerging challenges; and to offer insights into the implications of various aspects of modern-day trade agreements. We present their explorations by organising the collection into three parts:

Part I: Trade agreements and dispute settlement
Part II: Trade agreements in the modern era: a focus on the Asia-Pacific
Part III: Evolving trade agreement dynamics: challenging established concepts

These three parts illustrate key areas in which, despite the troubled Doha Round, there is interesting and important activity. The first such area is dispute settlement, which continues to function, some suggest, as the mainstay of the WTO. The second part looks closely at some new actors in the multilateral system: China and Pacific Island countries. These new actors are vastly different in size and power, but share commonalities in challenges of how to integrate into the world trading system while retaining their cultural norms and domestic strengths. This global versus national identity tension is timeless, but how it plays out with new actors, when protectionist policies are popular even in nations more accustomed to global trading, lends a new perspective to the age-old tension. In Part III, the authors revisit and challenge what may have been considered settled concepts. The first two chapters in this part examine behind the border trade issues including how FTAs can and might be used to coordinate regulation in order to reduce protectionism. The third chapter looks at the challenges to MFN and how the International Law Commission may contribute to a coordinated interpretation. This part ends with an examination of how even the multilateral 'mainstay' of dispute settlement is reaching behind the border in order to, in some instances, gain traction for developing countries in particular.

Part I begins with a discussion of the role of dispute settlement when there are forums for disputes to be heard in multiple trade agreements. Peter Van den Bossche and Meredith Kolsky Lewis discuss the variety of dispute settlement mechanisms utilised in FTAs, some of which may be capable of resolving disputes that could also be brought before the WTO dispute settlement system. This chapter identifies a panorama of dispute settlement mechanisms currently existing under the WTO and under regional and bilateral free trade agreements, which range from non-existent to primarily diplomatic to highly rules-based. The availability of a choice of forum creates the potential for a clash between the dispute settlement procedures of the WTO and that of a bilateral or plurilateral trade agreement. The chapter discusses those potential clashes and the WTO jurisprudence that has touched on this subject. The authors identify possible ways for WTO panels to resolve potential situations involving overlapping jurisdiction and conclude with some predictions for the future co-existence of FTA and WTO dispute settlement.

In the second chapter of Part I, Iain Sandford discusses the potential for more creative approaches to dispute resolution in regional trade agreements. From the perspective of a practitioner, Sandford contends that because regional free trade agreements are not purely commercial but form part of a broader political relationship between countries, the dispute settlement framework should reflect that broader relationship. He argues that such an approach to FTA dispute settlement could complement WTO negotiations on improving dispute settlement rules. This he suggests is particularly true in the unique negotiating circumstances of the proposed enhanced Pacific Agreement on Closer Economic Relations (PACER Plus) where systems for resolving disputes that are perceived as legitimate by relevant stakeholders are likely to be more effective and accessible. In turn he suggests that this would make trade agreements more meaningful to those affected by them.

Next, Daniel Kalderimis explores the differences between WTO and BIT dispute resolution mechanisms and bodies. He notes that international investment protection is overwhelmingly regulated through an ad hoc system of over 2600 investment agreements contained in bilateral investment treaties (BITs) or the investment chapters of FTAs. He compares the ways in which these two dispute resolution systems operate and concludes there are more similarities than is often thought, even though the division between trade and investment is both very real and essentially arbitrary. He suggests that because of their commercial interconnectedness – one person's trade in services through cross-border commercial presence is another person's foreign direct investment – international trade and investment should not continue to operate on separate legal planes. Though, like all dispute settlement systems, the two systems follow a broadly comparable process, there are significant variations in procedure, evidence, strategy and technique. He concludes that there are more opportunities for better litigation inputs in the investment dispute system, but better outputs may come from the multifaceted approach of WTO dispute settlement.

Finally, concluding Part I, Ross Becroft examines the WTO's standard of review as a way of improving the way the WTO functions. He argues that a key issue for reform is development of a new approach towards standard of review for WTO panels to apply when they are adjudicating disputes. Becroft suggests this is important because the level of scrutiny or deference applied can affect substantive outcomes and, over time, affect the way the WTO Agreements are interpreted. The standard of review may also be viewed as an expression of the allocation of power between the WTO and its members. He contends that panels should adopt a standard of review that is based upon the division of jurisdictional competencies between the WTO and the membership provided for under the WTO Agreements. Where a member has retained particular competencies, then the standard of review that panels apply should be more deferential when scrutinising the measure in question. He argues that developing this type of new doctrine would not lead to a significant reinterpretation of the WTO Agreements and would satisfy a number of broader policy objectives, such as the enhancement of the legitimacy of the dispute settlement process.

In Part II, the Asia-Pacific region is under the spotlight. Xianchu Zhang commences the discussion with an analysis of market access as an institutional challenge for China. In the GATT/WTO negotiations market access has been a very sensitive issue, particularly for developing countries, because of concerns that the opening of markets will have negative impacts on domestic industries. Since the worldwide financial crisis, concerns over protectionism and market access in China seem to have deepened. In spite of this, China has largely honoured its WTO commitments to open its market through domestic legislative reform (most notably the Anti-Monopoly Law adopted in 2007). But some policies and practices in China have been highly controversial (such as the national champion policy for state-owned enterprises) and more disputes concerning market access are finding their way to the WTO. Against this backdrop this chapter critically examines the issues concerning market access in China with reference to WTO dispute settlement decisions, WTO trade policy review documents, and domestic enactments and practices, which are relevant not only to trade policy and WTO rules, but also to political ideology and developing Chinese infrastructure.

Rafael Leal-Arcas then looks at China and what he characterises as its 'mixed' approach to multilateral trade. Leal-Arcas contends that China assumes little responsibility for maintaining international order in global economic governance. He argues that China should hide less behind the status of a developing country and stand up to its own ambition to new leadership. Rather than playing a proactive role in the world trading system, China is attempting to establish itself as a gravity centre in Asia by concluding many low-quality, politically motivated FTAs in the region. If multilateralism continues to weaken, he suggests that China's policy towards regional trade agreements will have a major impact on the international trading system, the debate about regionalism and multilateralism, and the approach of the WTO towards FTAs.

In the final chapter of Part II, Luke Nottage examines product safety regulation in an FTA era. He identifies possibilities for deeper and broader economic integration in the Asia-Pacific that simultaneously incorporate regulatory safeguards and other governance mechanisms aimed at meeting the new expectations about sustainability and legitimacy characterising our brave new 'post-GFC' world. He notes these innovations may be built into FTAs or negotiated alongside them, but suggests they need to be addressed in a more comprehensive way. Asian (and indeed Australian) leaders and commentators have traditionally been reluctant to compare and examine developments in European integration, but Nottage shows how this attitude has diminished in regional proposals involving integration mechanisms. This chapter addresses free movement of consumer goods combined with 'fair' safety regulation, the WTO backdrop, the European approach, and certain trans-Tasman and Asia-Pacific developments. The chapter concludes that initiatives which successfully combine liberalisation with contemporary public interest concerns are essential to sustainable development in the Asia-Pacific region – and in turn, to reinvigorating the multilateral order.

Part III scrutinises behind the border regulation and ways in which there are attempts to coordinate aspects of regulations in order to improve trading relationships. Tracey Epps compares and contrasts different models and examples of regulatory integration in FTAs. Regulatory cooperation between countries has traditionally taken a variety of forms, in some cases encouraged and managed through formal governmental agreements, in some cases through international inter-governmental organisations, and in other instances through informal networks of regulators. Epps examines regulatory cooperation through a new generation of FTAs that have a broader focus than the traditional aim of liberalising trade through the reduction and elimination of barriers to trade in goods. This new generation of FTAs, she argues, recognises that international trade in goods and services cannot be viewed in isolation from many of the regulatory challenges that governments are facing. International trade liberalisation both relies on the regulatory environment, and also creates its own externalities that in turn call for regulatory responses. Epps recognises that in both cases, there is potential for cooperation between states to improve regulatory outcomes that will both further trade liberalisation and address the externalities associated with such trade. Further, there is a growing sense that FTAs provide a platform on which regulatory cooperation can be advanced in order to address broader social and economic issues. Epps accordingly explores and analyses the type of provisions in FTAs that enable regulatory cooperation and considers how they fit into the broader scheme of global governance.

Olga Nartova and Sofya Matteotti tackle a specific behind the border issue that is having an increasing impact on trade as it involves elements of protectionism, but often undertaken in the interests of environmental policy. They examine the thorny issues of implementing and monitoring process and production methods (PPMs) in an era where environmental problems are part of the centre stage. They examine the notion that trade measures can be subdivided into measures that are linked to products and measures that are linked to production, and that both groups of measures have a different legal status under the GATT. In view of the development of tools to fight climate change, there appears to be a rise in the instances of governments protecting domestic industry from competition in countries not applying the same environmental standards, in particular with respect to CO_2 emissions. One question that arises is how WTO members can track methods of production on products produced outside their territory, particularly if the carbon values are not detectable in the final commercial product. In this context, how can a country contest harmful emissions produced during the product's manufacture in another country? This chapter sketches out a legal framework addressing the management, administration and monitoring of production methods in international trade law.

In the penultimate chapter, Kevin Gray scrutinises the International Law Commission's (ILC) study of MFN clauses. This chapter argues that MFN is a worthwhile topic of study for the ILC because of the prolific jurisprudence in international economic legal disputes addressing the interpretation of MFN clauses. It also addresses the related question of the efficacy of the ILC as an international law-making body. Gray suggests an ILC study can shed a more generalist public international law perspective on some of the legal uncertainties surrounding MFN provisions and that there are advantages in studying the MFN principle removed from a particular dispute, as that may preempt further inconsistencies in legal interpretation and consequently serve as a useful reference for dispute settlement tribunals adjudicating issues of international economic law.

In the collection's final contribution, Susy Frankel analyses the way in which the developing world has turned the TRIPS Agreement on its head by using the remedy of cross-retaliation. Many have regarded the TRIPS Agreement as favouring the interests of developed countries over those of developing countries. Developing country potential non-compliance with the TRIPS Agreement is the main reason that the United States and EU negotiated in the Uruguay Round for the ability to cross-retaliate when a ruling of the DSB is not complied with. Thus, if a developing country infringed the TRIPS Agreement a developed country could retaliate under the GATT as retaliation under the TRIPS Agreement would likely have no effect. In practice, however, this has not occurred. Rather, developing countries which have won disputes against developed countries have been authorised, in three instances, to cross-retaliate against the developed countries under the TRIPS Agreement. This chapter assesses the risks and benefits that cross-retaliation may entail for intellectual property protection which, while being derived from international norms, is a system of requirements of behind the border regulation.

Part I

Trade agreements and dispute settlement

1 What to do when disagreement strikes?

The complexity of dispute settlement under trade agreements

Meredith Kolsky Lewis and Peter Van den Bossche[1]

Introduction

Since the end of the GATT era, there have been two major developments affecting the potential for resolving international trade disputes. The first, of course, was the establishment of the WTO and its Dispute Settlement Understanding (DSU).[2] The WTO dispute settlement system has been called 'the jewel in the crown' of the WTO. It has ushered in a number of innovations that most view as improvements over the dispute resolution procedures used in the GATT era. Briefly, these include: (1) instituting a reverse consensus rule, whereby all panel and Appellate Body reports placed on the DSB agenda are automatically adopted by the Members acting as the Dispute Settlement Body (DSB), unless every WTO member agrees that said report should not be adopted;[3] (2) the creation of a standing Appellate Body and the right to appeal panel decisions to said Body; and (3) a procedure by which a Member that has prevailed in WTO dispute settlement may (after the DSB has given authorisation by reverse consensus) suspend concessions against the unsuccessful party in the event that Member fails to comply with the relevant decision.

The second major development has been the exponential increase in the number of regional trade agreements[4] (RTAs), the majority of which contain their own processes for resolving disputes. While most RTAs address the issue of dispute settlement, there is great diversity in the types of dispute settlement procedures featured amongst RTAs.[5]

For many types of trade agreements[6] and many types of disputes, there is no potential for overlap with the WTO dispute settlement mechanism. Such instances would include disputes with non-WTO members; disputes arising under the terms of the trade agreement but not under the WTO covered agreements; and disputes for which the RTA provides no remedy but the WTO dispute settlement process does. The first section of this chapter will discuss the types of dispute settlement mechanisms countries are including in their RTAs, ranging from the diplomatic to the highly legalistic. The next section will then consider where along the continuum of RTA dispute settlement clauses lies the greatest potential for overlap with WTO dispute settlement. The chapter will then proceed to discuss, within the range of overlap, the issue of forum choice.

The availability of a choice of forum creates the potential for a clash between the dispute settlement procedures of the WTO and that of a bilateral or plurilateral trade agreement. This section identifies the potential clashes and discusses the WTO jurisprudence that has touched on this subject. The next section identifies possible ways for panels to resolve a situation involving overlapping jurisdiction. The chapter concludes with some closing remarks and predictions for the future co-existence of RTA and WTO dispute settlement.

RTA dispute settlement – a wide diversity of models

With the exponential increase in the numbers of RTAs in the past 15 years has come a vast variety of agreements. Like the animal kingdom, trade agreements come in a range of 'species'. RTAs vary from one another in a number of ways, including size, coverage, objectives, institutional inclusion and dispute settlement.[7]

Size

While 'RTA' may bring to mind a bilateral arrangement, this is but one species of trade agreement. To be sure, most RTAs are between two countries. However, there also exist agreements that link multiple partners. Historically, multi-party agreements have usually partnered neighbouring countries. Prominent examples include NAFTA, Mercosur, ASEAN and the European Union. More recently, however, there has been increased activity in negotiating plurilateral agreements amongst parties that are not all geographically contiguous. Examples include the Trans-Pacific Strategic Economic Partnership Agreement between Brunei, Chile, New Zealand and Singapore (also known as the P4); the Trans-Pacific Partnership currently under negotiation between the P4 countries above as well as Australia, Canada, Malaysia, Mexico, Peru, the United States and Vietnam;[8] the ASEAN + 1 agreements with China, India, Japan, Korea, Australia–New Zealand and the EU; and the Economic Partnership Agreements (EPAs) the EU has been negotiating with African, Caribbean and Pacific (ACP) countries.[9]

Coverage

The proliferation of RTAs has also come with significant variations in the coverage of these agreements. Many agreements exclude sensitive sectors such as agriculture, but others are more comprehensive. While in the past RTAs largely focused on goods, today many agreements include services, and – increasingly – chapters on investment. RTAs currently span a broad spectrum of coverage, ranging from very shallow agreements that many believe do not satisfy the GATT Article XXIV requirement that RTAs cover 'substantially all trade' between the parties, to agreements that strive for integration on issues falling outside the WTO's coverage, including 'behind the border' issues such as harmonising standards, and that include substantive labour and environment chapters.[10]

Objectives

Trade agreements also differ from one another in terms of the objectives of the participating countries. In some instances RTAs are entered into primarily to increase trade flows amongst the participating countries. However, other agreements are driven by motivations in addition to – or even instead of – economic considerations. Customs unions in particular tend to be pursued in order to achieve a high level of integration, which generally requires both economic and political cooperation. Non-economic objectives may include forming closer bonds with allies, facilitating development cooperation,[11] and even rewarding military or other forms of cooperation.[12]

Institutions

Plurilateral and bilateral trade agreements vary in the degree to which they maintain institutional structures. NAFTA, for example, has a Secretariat that administers certain of that agreement's dispute settlement provisions,[13] and each of Canada, Mexico and the United States maintains a section of the Secretariat, housed in the respective capital cities. The NAFTA Secretariat is funded by the three member governments. In contrast, many RTAs do not have any institutional existence outside the text of the treaties themselves.

Dispute settlement

The species of trade agreements also differ significantly in the ways in which they provide for dispute resolution. These differences – and the implications thereof for the WTO – are the focus of the remainder of this chapter.

Trade agreements generally provide for some form of dispute settlement, but not always.[14] When dispute settlement is provided for, the processes can range from diplomatic, power-based forms of resolution, to more judicial, rules-based procedures. The systems can be broadly characterised as falling into five different types, along this continuum.[15]

Diplomatic negotiations

The first type of dispute settlement occurs where the trade agreement merely provides for diplomatic negotiations – first between the parties themselves, and failing a resolution, then second to a joint committee with representatives of all the parties. This sort of dispute settlement falls at the extreme of the power-based, diplomatic end of the spectrum.

Diplomatic negotiations with external support

Another model is for there to be provision for the parties to seek assistance from impartial third parties in their diplomatic efforts to resolve their disputes. The

WTO Dispute Settlement Understanding's provisions for good offices, mediation and conciliation[16] are examples of mechanisms designed to help parties come to a negotiated resolution to their disputes.

Dispute settlement by ad hoc arbitrators

Trade agreements can also provide for dispute settlement by ad hoc arbitrators. Such arbitrators can be selected from a pre-existing roster of panelists, or be appointed pursuant to other processes. In some cases, jurisdiction of the arbitrator(s) will be subject to the consent of the respondent country. In other instances, jurisdiction can be made compulsory. The panel stage of WTO dispute settlement is an example of the latter circumstance.

Dispute settlement by a permanent tribunal

Moving closer to the rules-based, judicial end of the spectrum are dispute settlement mechanisms that utilise a permanent tribunal that will interpret the treaty and issue binding rulings. In such cases, jurisdiction tends to be compulsory. The WTO Appellate Body is an example of this type of dispute settlement.[17]

Dispute settlement by a permanent tribunal with standing for private parties

Lastly, at the furthest end of the spectrum would be a system that not only provides for a permanent tribunal to resolve disputes via compulsory jurisdiction and binding rulings, but also grants standing to private parties. The European Court of Justice would fit this description.[18]

General observations

Dispute settlement in trade agreements reflects a trade-off between two mutually exclusive objectives: ensuring that the other party meets its obligations, while also ensuring that there is sufficient policy space for a party to breach its own obligations when politically necessary. It is therefore not surprising that many trade agreements feature both diplomatic and rules-based provisions.[19] The majority of trade agreements reflect a preference, sometimes explicit, sometimes implicit, for the non-judicialised resolution of disputes. Thus, it is very common for agreements to start with a process for negotiating to resolve an amicable resolution. At the same time, many trade agreements further include (more) judicial, rules-based procedures to provide a mechanism for resolution when the diplomatic path is unsuccessful.

Notwithstanding the fact that most modern RTAs include some form of dispute settlement mechanism, in practice these mechanisms have only been used in a handful of agreements. Dispute settlement proceedings have been taken under the EC Treaty,[20] NAFTA, Mercosur and a few others. However, the dispute settlement provisions in most trade agreements have yet to be invoked.

Potential for overlapping jurisdiction between RTAs and WTO dispute settlement

With several hundred RTAs in force, it may seem likely, even inevitable, that there will be clashes of some sort between RTA dispute settlement and WTO dispute settlement. While there is some potential for overlap, not all agreements pose a potential conflict. For example, the following scenarios do not pose a risk of competing or conflicting with WTO dispute settlement procedures:

Non-judicial dispute settlement mechanisms

To the extent trade agreements fall on the diplomatic end of the continuum of dispute settlement mechanisms described above, there is not a problem of overlapping jurisdiction or other conflict with WTO dispute settlement. Examples would be RTAs that contain no dispute settlement mechanism or that provide solely for resolution via non-binding negotiations and diplomacy. If a dispute were to arise between Australia and New Zealand, for example, on a matter falling within the scope of the WTO covered agreements, such a dispute could be brought before a WTO dispute settlement panel.[21] There is no analogous proceeding under the Australia – New Zealand Closer Economic Relations Trade Agreement (CER), and therefore there is no potential for a jurisdictional overlap or clash.

Agreements with non-WTO members

Some regional trade agreements may include non-WTO members. If an issue were to arise under an RTA between a WTO member and a non-WTO member,[22] there will be no issue of potential conflict with WTO dispute settlement, even if the RTA provision is textually identical to a WTO provision and even if the RTA provides for rules-based, binding dispute settlement. Notwithstanding the use of WTO language by the parties, such a dispute could only be brought pursuant to the dispute settlement procedures provided for in the RTA, and could not be raised in WTO dispute settlement. The WTO Dispute Settlement Understanding (DSU) makes clear that WTO dispute settlement is only available to WTO members: 'The Members recognize that it [the dispute settlement system of the WTO] serves to preserve the rights and obligations of Members under the covered agreements....'[23] Accordingly, disputes with non-WTO members do not fall under the WTO Dispute Settlement Body's jurisdiction.[24]

Disputes arising solely under provisions of the RTA

While there is often a significant degree of overlap between the coverage of an RTA and the collective scope of the WTO agreements, it is also common for RTAs to include provisions that have no counterpart within the WTO. For example, recently formed RTAs often include an investment chapter. Such chapters go well beyond the scope of GATS obligations or obligations under the TRIMS Agreement, and indeed are more akin to a bilateral investment treaty that has been folded into an RTA. A dispute arising under such a chapter might well involve a provision which has no analogue in the WTO agreements. In such a case, the dispute could be brought pursuant to the dispute settlement procedures set forth in the RTA (or perhaps pursuant to any more specialised procedures provided for in the investment chapter itself), but it could not be taken to the WTO for resolution in that forum. Even if both RTA partners are WTO members, WTO dispute settlement would simply be unavailable in this example, for the DSU provides only for disputes '...arising under the covered agreements.'[25]

Choice of forum and jurisdictional overlap

We can see from the preceding section that when parties to an RTA have a dispute, it may not present any potential for overlap with WTO dispute settlement. In some instances the dispute can only be brought before the RTA dispute settlement mechanism, and in others the only option for a judicial-style resolution will be to bring the dispute to the WTO. Nonetheless, there are circumstances in which RTA parties will find themselves in a dispute that could be seen as a breach of the RTA, and thus taken to the RTA dispute settlement mechanism, but also could be viewed as a breach of a WTO obligation, and therefore resolved through the WTO's dispute settlement procedures.[26] This possibility raises a number of concerns.

First, the availability of a choice of forum may lead an economically stronger party to opt to avoid rules-based dispute settlement and instead elect the power-based option, (namely the RTA forum even if that is based on a rules-based procedure), which is likely to result in less favourable outcomes for the respondent and in turn raises concerns about justice and fairness.[27]

Second, the existence of multiple fora could lead to a prolongation of the dispute, with the complainant bringing its claim serially before different tribunals if it were not successful in the first instance, or to claims being brought concurrently, resulting in multiple actions proceeding in parallel to one another.

Third, the bringing of actions in different fora raises the possibility of rulings that are not consistent, or perhaps even conflicting.

And fourth, it would be more costly if subsequent – or even worse, parallel – proceedings were brought to resolve the same dispute. This is a particularly worrisome prospect for developing country respondents.[28]

How can such problems be avoided? Fortunately, States that participate in the WTO as well as RTAs are aware of the potential problems that could arise due to the availability of forum choice, and as a result many RTAs are drafted to include choice of forum provisions.

Choice of forum provisions

There are two main types of provisions relating to forum choice. The first are provisions that designate a specific forum for the resolution of disputes. Such a provision could specify that its forum is the exclusive forum for resolution of *all* disputes arising under the relevant agreement. Examples of this type of provision include the European Union, the WTO, the Andean Pact and COMESA. Alternatively, the forum selection provision could designate its own forum as the exclusive forum for resolving only certain types of disputes. An example of this is NAFTA, which provides that it is the exclusive forum for resolving SPS-type disputes between the parties.[29] Another possibility is for the choice of forum provision to specify that a different forum is the exclusive forum for resolving certain types of disputes. For example, under the EU–Chile FTA, a party raising an SPS dispute 'shall' have recourse to WTO dispute settlement unless both parties agree to a different forum.[30] Lastly, some RTAs allow for a change of forum by common agreement.

The second type of forum choice provision allows for the parties to elect, on a case-by-case basis, whether to bring their disputes to the agreement's own forum or to any other dispute settlement system that is available to resolve the dispute. This sort of 'free choice' provision is often combined with a proviso that, once having selected a particular forum, said forum will be the exclusive forum for the resolution of that dispute. In other words, 'double-dipping' is prohibited. If a complainant elects to bring its claim to the WTO and does not prevail, it is not permitted, under the terms of the RTA, to subsequently initiate a dispute covering the same rights and obligations, using the RTA's dispute settlement procedures.[31]

Why do parties choose one forum over another?

Given that parties sometimes have the option of initiating a dispute in the WTO or using their RTA dispute settlement procedures, what goes into the decision?[31] It has been argued that more powerful players are more likely to invoke RTA dispute settlement, where procedures may be less legalistic and more susceptible to influence.[33] The applicable law may also influence this decision.[34]

In practice, most RTA dispute settlement systems have not been invoked. NAFTA and Mercosur are notable exceptions to this general phenomenon. Thus, even in the cases where a conflict is possible, it thus far has rarely had the opportunity to rise to the level of an actual conflict because WTO members have overwhelmingly chosen to bring their disputes – even against RTA partners – under the WTO dispute settlement procedures rather than under any applicable RTA procedures. This may be due to the contrast in experience and legitimacy between the WTO, as an established institution, and a new and untested RTA. In addition, the WTO has built up a body of decisions that, although not formally binding on Members that were not a party to the dispute, do go some way towards ensuring predictability. Of course the WTO also provides an opportunity to appeal and experienced secretariat staff to assist.[35] Unlike (most) dispute settlement systems under RTAs, the WTO dispute settlement system also provides for a mechanism to enforce its rulings.

Furthermore, while RTA dispute mechanisms may be available alongside WTO procedures, the language of the WTO's Dispute Settlement Understanding (DSU) appears to be compulsory. Article 23.1 of the DSU provides:

When Members seek the redress of a violation of obligations or other nullification or impairment of benefits under the covered agreements or an impediment to the attainment of any objective of the covered agreements, they shall have recourse to, and abide by, the rules and procedures of this Understanding.[36]

In addition, the complaining WTO member need not prove or demonstrate any aspect of its allegations in order to avail itself of the WTO dispute settlement mechanism. This low threshold may additionally lead to complaints being brought before the WTO rather than elsewhere.[37]

Notwithstanding States' general preference for WTO dispute settlement, there have been instances where WTO dispute resolution panels and the Appellate Body have been confronted with the problem of overlapping jurisdiction. Below we discuss three cases that have implicated potential overlaps between the WTO's dispute settlement jurisdiction and that of an RTA.

Mexico – Taxes on Soft Drinks

In the *Mexico – Taxes on Soft Drinks* case,[38] Mexico invoked responsibilities under the North American Free Trade Agreement (NAFTA). Before discussing Mexico's argument and the Appellate Body's resolution of the issues, we will briefly explain the origins of the dispute so as to make clear why Mexico made reference to the NAFTA.

The genesis of this dispute can be traced to a disagreement between Mexico and the United States regarding the interpretation of a NAFTA commitment. Mexico believed that, pursuant to a side letter to the NAFTA, it would gain unlimited access to the US sugar market by 2001. The United States, however, relied upon a later side letter that limited the volume of sugar Mexico would be able to export until 2009 – which Mexico disputed ever having signed – and declined to grant Mexico the sugar access to which Mexico claimed it was entitled.[39] Mexico responded by filing a complaint against the United States pursuant to the dispute settlement provisions of the NAFTA. However, the United States refused to nominate a panelist to the arbitral tribunal, and as a result a panel was never formed and the dispute never heard.

Frustrated by the United States' actions, Mexico decided to impose new tax measures on sweeteners other than sugar used in the manufacture of carbonated beverages, *i.e.* soft drinks.[40] The primary non-sugar sweetener used in soft drinks is high fructose corn syrup (HFCS), which is manufactured almost exclusively by the United States and used in most US-manufactured soft drinks. In Mexico, the vast majority of domestically produced soft drinks were sweetened with sugar rather than HFCS. Thus the effect of Mexico's new measures was to impose a levy on the majority of US soft drink exports – a tax that largely did not apply to domestic soda manufacturers.

The United States responded by initiating a WTO dispute settlement proceeding, arguing that Mexico's tax measures violated its national treatment obligations. In particular, the United States alleged that Mexico had breached GATT Article III:2, first and second sentences, and Article III:4 by treating a like imported product (HFCS) less favourably than its domestic counterpart (sugar). In its submissions, Mexico made two sets of arguments that implicated the NAFTA and the potential interplay between that agreement and the WTO.

First, Mexico argued that the dispute was all part of the same sugar disagreement that had led Mexico to initiate its NAFTA dispute settlement proceeding, and that accordingly the panel should 'decline to exercise jurisdiction "in favour of an Arbitral Panel under Chapter Twenty of the North American Free Trade Agreement (NAFTA)." '[41] The panel did not accept Mexico's argument, stating that it did not have the discretion to decline to hear a dispute properly before it.[42] The Appellate Body affirmed the finding of the panel, noting that declining to exercise jurisdiction would run counter to various provisions of the DSU, including the obligations in Articles 3.2 and 19.2 not to 'add to or diminish the rights and obligations provided in the covered agreements.'[43]

Second, on the merits of the claim, Mexico raised a defence pursuant to GATT Article XX(d), arguing that its tax measures were 'necessary' to ensure compliance with 'laws or regulations which are not inconsistent with the provisions of this Agreement'.[44] In particular, Mexico argued that its measures were necessary in order to ensure the United States' compliance with its NAFTA obligations. Mexico thus invoked the United States' NAFTA obligations as a justification for its own alleged WTO violations. The panel found that the language 'to secure compliance' in Article XX(d) does not apply to measures taken by a Member in order to induce another Member to comply with obligations owed to it under a non-WTO treaty, and thus rejected Mexico's argument that 'the challenged tax measures are *designed* to secure compliance by the United States with laws or regulations.'[45] The Appellate Body agreed, finding that 'laws or regulations' under GATT Article XX(d) refer to the domestic legal regime of the member invoking the exception,[46] and 'do not include obligations of *another* WTO Member under an international agreement.'[47] The Appellate Body's legal conclusions meant it did not find it necessary to assess whether the United States had in fact breached its NAFTA obligations. However, the Appellate Body did note that Mexico's argument, if accepted, would have created an inappropriate overlap between the WTO and NAFTA:

> Mexico's interpretation would imply that, in order to resolve the case, WTO panels and the Appellate Body would have to assume that there is a violation of the relevant international agreement (such as the NAFTA) by the complaining party, or they would have to assess whether the relevant international agreement has been violated.... WTO panels and the Appellate Body would thus become adjudicators of non-WTO disputes.... [T]his is not the function of panels and the Appellate Body as intended by the DSU.[48]

What is perhaps most important about the *Mexico – Soft Drinks* case is the argument Mexico did *not* make, but which the Appellate Body nonetheless alluded to. As noted, Mexico did not argue that the panel did not have jurisdiction to hear the dispute; it instead asked the panel to decline to exercise that jurisdiction in favour of the NAFTA Chapter 20 panel. The Appellate Body, while finding no cause to decline jurisdiction in this particular case, stated that it was expressing 'no view as to whether there may be other circumstances in which legal impediments could exist that would preclude a panel from ruling on the merits of the claims that are before it.'[49] The Appellate Body went on to note arguments Mexico had not made but that could perhaps have made in this context. In particular, the Appellate Body noted that Mexico had acknowledged it was unaware of any legal basis that would permit it to raise, in WTO dispute settlement, the market access-related claims it had filed with the NAFTA Chapter 20 tribunal. In addition, the NAFTA panel had not yet been formed, and therefore could not be said to have already decided the dispute. Finally, the Appellate Body noted that 'Mexico has expressly stated that the so-called "exclusion clause" of Article 2005.6 of the NAFTA had not been "exercised."'[50] It explained, '[w]e do not express any view on whether a legal impediment to the exercise of a panel's jurisdiction would exist in the event that features such as those mentioned above were present.'[51] Thus the Appellate Body appears to have left open the possibility that the exercise of NAFTA Article 2005.6, or one of the other scenarios raised, could constitute a legal impediment that could lead a panel to decline to decide the merits of a dispute, even if it had jurisdiction to do so.

Brazil – Retreaded Tyres

The *Brazil – Retreaded Tyres* dispute involved a ban Brazil imposed on the importation of retreaded tyres. Brazil implemented its ban in an effort to reduce the number of waste tyres in the country; waste tyres were seen as leading to increased malarial breeding grounds and as an environmental hazard. Brazil's ban included an exception for tyres coming from other Mercosur countries. The European Communities challenged Brazil's ban; in particular taking issue with Brazil's decision to allow in imports from Mercosur but not from elsewhere.

Brazil defended its practice under GATT Article XX(b) and argued that it needed to allow an exception for tyres from Mercosur countries because a Mercosur tribunal had found Brazil's previous across-the-board ban to violate Mercosur. Brazil's position was thus that it needed to allow an exception for Mercosur tyres or it would be in violation of Mercosur.

The panel found that Brazil's ban fell within Article XX(b), and that the exception to the ban was not 'unjustifiable discrimination' (under the Article XX chapeau) because the volumes of waste tyres imported from Mercosur were too minor to undermine the health-related purpose of the ban itself.[52]

The Appellate Body disagreed with the reasoning of the panel, and stated that Brazil's actions violated the chapeau of GATT Article XX.[53] It accepted that Brazil might have good reasons for wanting to let in Mercosur tyres, and accepted that such imports were only in very small quantities. Nonetheless, even though the granting of the exception was arguably rational, this did not necessarily preclude it from being arbitrary or unjustifiable pursuant to the chapeau. The Appellate Body determined that Brazil's main motivation in granting the exception (complying with its obligations under Mercosur's Treaty of Montevideo as clarified by the Mercosur tribunal) was unrelated to the objective of the overall measure (protecting health) and as such was arbitrary or unjustifiable discrimination under the chapeau.[54]

It is interesting to note that while the Appellate Body's decision did result in finding Brazil's Mercosur-consistent actions to be WTO-inconsistent, it was not inevitable for Brazil to land in this legal dilemma. In its proceedings before the Mercosur tribunal, Brazil curiously did not argue that it was entitled to maintain its ban pursuant to Mercosur's GATT Article XX(b) analogue, Article 50(d) of the Treaty of Montevideo. Brazil could have done so, and the tribunal might have accepted that a complete ban was justified.[55]

Argentina – Poultry Anti-Dumping Duties

A third instance where a WTO dispute raised questions over the relationship between RTA dispute settlement and WTO dispute settlement was *Argentina – Poultry Anti-Dumping Duties*.[56] The case involved anti-dumping duties Argentina had imposed on imports of poultry from Brazil. Prior to initiating its WTO complaint, Brazil had challenged the same anti-dumping measure before a Mercosur *ad hoc* Arbitral Tribunal. Brazil was unsuccessful before the Mercosur tribunal, and subsequently decided to assert its challenge before a WTO dispute settlement panel.

Argentina argued that the panel should 'refrain from ruling' on Brazil's claim, or in the alternative, to be 'bound' by the result of the Mercosur proceeding.[57] Notably, Argentina did not attempt to argue that the matter was *res judicata*.[58] In support of its argument that the panel should refrain from ruling on Brazil's claim, Argentina invoked the doctrines of good faith and estoppel. The panel rejected these arguments. With respect to its alternative argument, Argentina asserted that the panel was 'bound' by the Mercosur ruling due to Article 31(3)(c) of the Vienna Convention,[59] and Article 3.2 of the DSU. VCLT Article 31(3)(c) requires taking into account, inter alia, 'any relevant rules of international law applicable in the relations between the parties' when interpreting a treaty. The panel noted that Article 31(3)(c) refers to interpreting a treaty, yet Argentina – instead of asking the panel to be mindful of the Mercosur ruling in *interpreting* the *Anti-Dumping Agreement* provisions at issue – had argued the panel must *apply* WTO rules (rather than interpret them) so as to be consistent with the Mercosur decision. The panel rejected this approach to Article 31(3)(c), and found no support for Argentina's approach in the text of Article 3.2 of the DSU. The panel noted that panels are not even bound by adopted WTO panel reports, and thus clearly were not bound by decisions of non-WTO tribunals.[60] As to whether the Mercosur decision would be relevant for interpretive purposes under VCLT Article 31(3)(c), this issue was not squarely put to the panel, but in dicta it questioned whether Mercosur law would even qualify as a relevant rule of international law 'between the parties'.[61]

The panel additionally referenced a provision of Mercosur law that had not yet come into force, which provided that if a party pursued dispute settlement under Mercosur or the WTO, it could not subsequently initiate another dispute in the other forum regarding the same subject matter.[62] The panel seemed to suggest in dicta that had that provision been in force, it could potentially be a reason for the panel to decline to exercise jurisdiction.[63]

Declining jurisdiction – many questions, few answers

What can be done about overlapping jurisdiction? There is no easy answer to this question. Generally speaking, one possibility is for tribunals to decline jurisdiction when multiple fora could be involved. This could be accomplished by the tribunal invoking the forum selection provision as a rationale for declining to exercise its jurisdiction. Such an action would be straightforward if the tribunal were invoking the forum choice provision within its own treaty. What is less clear, however, is whether a dispute settlement tribunal can decline jurisdiction on the basis of a forum selection provision in a *different* trade agreement. For example, can a WTO panel decline to exercise its jurisdiction on the basis of the exclusive forum selection provision in Mercosur's *Protocol of Olivos*?[64] In the *Argentina – Poultry Anti-Dumping Duties* case discussed above, Argentina could not invoke the *Protocol of Olivos* because it had not yet come into force. But what if it had been – should, or could, the panel have reached a different decision under those circumstances?[65] One answer would be to say that while Brazil might be in breach of Mercosur law by virtue of bringing consecutive disputes concerning the same matter in separate fora, this should not be the concern of a WTO panel, which should instead be encouraging the resolution of WTO-related disputes under the WTO dispute settlement system.[66] Alternatively, a panel could view Brazil's actions (had the *Protocol of Olivos* been in force) as a breach of the duty of good faith and decline to hear the case on that basis.[67]

A second possibility is for a dispute settlement tribunal to decline jurisdiction on the basis of something other than forum choice.

Res judicata

Res judicata, also known as claim preclusion, is the principle that once a dispute has been heard and a court or tribunal has given final judgment, the parties are thereafter barred from relitigating the same dispute in the same or in another forum. *Res judicata* is primarily a domestic law principle – would it be applicable in a situation of overlapping jurisdiction between the WTO and an RTA?[68] While in theory this might be possible, in practice it is quite unlikely. *Res judicata* will only be applicable where both actions concern the same parties; the same measure; and the same legal claim. It is the latter of these that would be the most challenging to demonstrate. Even if the language of an RTA provision is the same as language found within the WTO, a claim brought to the WTO is a claim for a violation of one or more provisions of the WTO covered agreements.

Whereas a claim brought to an RTA dispute settlement tribunal will be an allegation of a breach of one or more provisions of a different treaty – namely, the RTA. Lest this seem overly formalistic, it bears noting that even when multiple treaties invoke the same language, this does not mean that such provisions will, or should, be interpreted identically by their respective dispute settlement bodies. Article 31(1) of the VCLT requires that treaties must be interpreted in light of their object and purpose; object and purpose may differ from treaty to treaty.

Estoppel

In domestic litigation, estoppel is sometimes raised as an argument why the court should not hear a particular claim – often because the claimant has taken a contrary position in another proceeding. What would such an argument look like in the WTO context? It is an open question what would happen if an RTA had a single forum selection rule, but a party to the RTA nonetheless brought a WTO dispute after having availed itself of the RTA dispute settlement procedure.[69] This would, to be sure, be a breach of the terms of the RTA. But what would a WTO dispute settlement panel do under such a circumstance? One possibility would be, out of comity, to decline to exercise jurisdiction to hear the dispute – or to estop the claimant from proceeding. However, the panel might instead view its jurisdiction under the DSU as mandatory, and determine that it had no option but to hear the dispute, even though it had already been adjudicated pursuant to single forum selection procedures under the RTA.

Other potential arguments

Two other arguments claimants might assert are *lis alibi pendens*, and abuse of process. The first of these is Latin for 'dispute elsewhere pending' and is a doctrine that permits, on grounds of comity, a tribunal to decline to hear a matter when it is already being heard in a parallel proceeding. If successful, such an argument would only be applicable in the narrow situation of concurrent dispute settlement proceedings.

Abuse of process refers to the use of a judicial proceeding for an improper purpose. Even if this doctrine were recognised in theory by a WTO panel, it would be difficult to predict what type of situation would qualify as 'abuse' so as to invoke the doctrine successfully.

Conclusion

The proliferation of RTAs is showing no signs of abating. Indeed, with multilateral negotiations stagnant, we can expect to see the negotiation of even more such agreements. Although there is the potential for the dispute settlement mechanisms in RTAs to overlap with the WTO dispute settlement mechanism, this overlap will only be present with respect to a subset of RTAs, and with respect to a subset of the overall coverage of an RTA. Thus far, WTO panels and the

Appellate Body have been faced with relatively few cases implicating jurisdictional clashes. And these disputes can perhaps be characterised as 'near misses' in that there has generally been some reason (such as the *Protocol of Olivos* not yet being in effect) why a direct clash has not presented itself.

But what of the future? It may be that more RTAs will mean more WTO disputes raising issues overlapping with those already decided by an RTA dispute settlement mechanism. However, this is not necessarily the case. As noted above, WTO members have used the WTO dispute settlement mechanism actively, and there is no sign that this usage is abating with the increase in RTAs. The WTO dispute settlement system offers a number of advantages over RTA dispute settlement, including experience, legitimacy, appellate review, and a mechanism to enforce rulings. These advantages are unlikely to change. As such, we would expect that even though RTAs will continue to proliferate, the majority of disputes that could be brought before either RTA or WTO dispute settlement will be brought before the WTO only. However, it is also likely that as RTAs – particularly those with multiple parties – incorporate provisions that have no parallel in the WTO alongside those that mirror WTO provisions, disputes that arise may be brought to the RTA dispute settlement system as it may be the only place all of a party's claims can be heard. This may result in turn in RTA tribunals increasingly interpreting provisions with a WTO analogue, with the attendant possibility of inconsistent approaches being taken by such tribunals, both in comparison with each other, and with WTO panel and Appellate Body reports. It should additionally be expected that panels and the Appellate Body will at some point be faced with a 'head-on collision' and will need to address more squarely some of the questions that have as yet remained unanswered.

Notes

1 Meredith Kolsky Lewis is an Associate Professor and Director of the Canada–US Legal Studies Centre at the SUNY Buffalo Law School, Associate Professor at the Victoria University of Wellington Faculty of Law and Associate Director of the New Zealand Centre of International Economic Law. Prof. Dr. Peter L.H. Van den Bossche is a Member of the World Trade Organization Appellate Body and Professor of International Economic Law, Maastricht University.
2 Understanding on Rules and Procedures Governing the Settlement of Disputes, 15 April 1994, Marrakesh Agreement Establishing the World Trade Organization, Annex 2, 1869 U.N.T.S. 401; 33 I.L.M. 1226 (1994).
3 In the GATT era, the rule was the reverse; thus the losing party could (and sometimes did) block a decision from being adopted. Under the WTO system, however, unsurprisingly, all reports have been adopted because the prevailing party has never argued (much less with the agreement of all other Members) that a report in its favour should **not** be adopted.
4 We acknowledge the imperfection of the term 'regional trade agreements' as many such linkages connect countries that are not geographically near one another; however, we adopt this term (as opposed to 'free trade agreements' or 'preferential trade agreements') because it is the terminology used in the WTO agreements. In this chapter, 'RTAs' is used to refer both to regional trade agreements and customs unions.

5 As of this writing, 511 RTAs had been notified to the WTO (counting goods and services separately), with 319 of these in force. Online. Available at: www.wto.org/english/tratop_e/region_e/region_e.htm (accessed 23 November 2012). These figures do not capture the total number of RTAs in existence. Not all RTAs amongst WTO members have been notified, and there is no requirement for non-WTO members to report their agreements to the WTO.

6 For the purposes of this chapter, 'trade agreements' refers collectively to the WTO and to regional trade agreements.

7 McCall Smith 2000: 151.

8 Canada and Mexico were invited to join the negotiations in mid-2012 and commenced their participation in the fifteenth round of negotiations, to be held in Auckland, New Zealand in December 2012.

9 For information on these EPAs, see http://ec.europa.eu/trade/creating-opportunities/bilateral-relations/regions/africa-caribbean-pacific/.

10 The Trans-Pacific Partnership under negotiation is often referred to as a 'twenty-first century trade agreement', in part due to its inclusion of behind-the-border measures to reduce regulatory barriers to trade. See Lim *et al.* 2012; Barfield 2011, accessible at www.aei.org/article/economics/international-economy/the-trans-pacific-partnership/.

11 For example, the aforementioned EPAs between the European Union and its former colonies. See also Tracey Epps' chapter, 'Regulatory cooperation and Free Trade Agreements', in this volume.

12 For example, the Australia–United States FTA seems to have been motivated – on the United States side – by the wish to reward Australia for its support of the US's military actions in Iraq, as well as by the prospect of some economic gains. The United States–Bahrain FTA, however, would seem to have been driven largely by strategic political considerations.

13 The Secretariat administers disputes under NAFTA chapters 19 and 20. See generally www.nafta-sec-alena.org/ (accessed 2 August 2012).

14 The Australia – New Zealand Closer Economic Relations Trade Agreement, which dates back to 1983, makes no provision for dispute settlement. Online. Available at: www.dfat.gov.au/fta/anzcerta/index.html.

15 These categories are drawn from McCall Smith 2000. In some instances, more than one of these types features in the same agreement.

16 DSU Art. 5.

16 It is acknowledged that the Appellate Body itself does not issue binding rulings; its reports become binding only upon their adoption by the Dispute Settlement Body. Nonetheless, the provisions of the DSU – including the rule that reports are adopted unless there is consensus to the contrary – have the practical effect of giving Appellate Body decisions binding force.

18 See http://europa.eu/about-eu/institutions-bodies/court-justice/index_en.htm.

19 For a detailed discussion of this issue, see McCall Smith 2000: 134–43.

20 European Union, *Treaty Establishing the European Community (Consolidated Version as amended by the Treaty of Lisbon), Rome Treaty*, 25 March 1957.

21 Indeed, this occurred when New Zealand brought a dispute against Australia challenging the latter's ban on apples imported from New Zealand. See Appellate Body Report, *Australia – Measures Affecting the Importation of Apples from New Zealand*, WT/DS367/AB/R, adopted 17 December 2010.

22 For example, The Free Trade Agreement Between the Government of Ukraine and the Government of Kazakhstan (entry into force 19 October 1998). Ukraine is a WTO member while Kazakhstan is presently an observer, but not yet a member.

23 DSU Art. 3.2.

24 With the 2012 admission of Russia into the WTO, the remaining non-WTO members are generally of little trade significance.

25 See, for example, DSU Arts. 1.1, 2.1 and 3.2.

26 For an example of such overlaps, see Pauwelyn 2004.
27 Drahos 2005: 22 ('Bilateral dispute resolution will, more than multilateral dispute resolution, reinforce and promote structural inequality.').
28 Pauwelyn 2007. Online. Available at: www.acp-eu-trade.org/library/files/pauwelyn_ EN_100907_WTO_Legal-avenues-to-multilateralizing-regionalism.pdf (accessed 18 October 2012).
29 The North American Free Trade Agreement, Art. 2005(3) & (4).
30 European Union–Chile Free Trade Agreement, Article 189.4 (c).
31 Examples of such provisions can be found in NAFTA, ASEAN and the *Protocol of Olivos* applicable to Mercosur. Not all RTAs with free choice of forum provisions prohibit taking two bites at the apple. For example, under the CARIFORUM-EC Economic Partnership Agreement, if parties take a dispute to the EPA's dispute settlement mechanism, it would still be possible to later take substantially the same matter to WTO dispute settlement. Mercosur used to permit double-dipping under the *Protocol of Brasilia*, but this has since been repealed by the *Protocol of Olivos*. Online. Available at: www.sice.oas.org/trade/mrcsr/brasilia/pbrasilia_e.asp.
32 See Henckels 2008.
33 For example, Busch 2007.
34 Pauwelyn 2004: 252–5.
35 Davey 2006.
36 DSU Art. 23.1. See Kwak and Marceau 2006: 466–7.
37 Kwak and Marceau 2006: 467.
38 Appellate Body Report, *Mexico – Tax Measures on Soft Drinks and Other Beverages*, WT/DS308/AB/R, adopted 6 March 2006 [hereinafter 'Appellate Body Report, *Mexico – Taxes on Soft Drinks*']. For commentary on this dispute, see Davey and Sapir 2009; Alvarez-Jimenez 2006; Pauwelyn 2006.
39 For a discussion of sugar under the NAFTA, including Mexico's sugar quota and the competing side letters, see Hufbauer and Schott 2005: 312–27.
40 Mexico's measures comprised a 20 per cent tax on soft drinks and other beverages sweetened by substances other than sugar; a separate 20 per cent tax on services, such as brokerage and consignment, related to distributing such beverages; and bookkeeping requirements only applicable to those subject to the above taxes. See Panel Report, *Mexico – Tax Measures on Soft Drinks and Other Beverages*, WT/DS/308/R, adopted 7 October 2005, para. 2.2 [hereinafter 'Panel Report, *Mexico – Taxes on Soft Drinks*'].
41 Panel Report, *Mexico – Taxes on Soft Drinks*, para. 7.11; and Appellate Body Report, *Mexico – Taxes on Soft Drinks*, para. 40.
42 Panel Report, *Mexico – Taxes on Soft Drinks*, para. 7.18; and Appellate Body Report, *Mexico – Taxes on Soft Drinks*, para. 40.
43 Appellate Body Report, *Mexico – Taxes on Soft Drinks*, paras 48–53.
44 GATT Article XX(d). See Panel Report, *Mexico – Taxes on Soft Drinks*, para. 8.170.
45 Panel Report, *Mexico – Taxes on Soft Drinks*, para. 8.181.
46 Appellate Body Report, *Mexico – Taxes on Soft Drinks*, paras 68–9.
47 Appellate Body Report, *Mexico – Taxes on Soft Drinks*, para. 75.
48 Appellate Body Report, *Mexico – Taxes on Soft Drinks*, para. 78. For a critique of the Appellate Body's reasoning (although agreeing with the outcome), see Davey and Sapir 2009: 9–11.
49 Appellate Body Report, *Mexico – Taxes on Soft Drinks*, para. 54.
50 Appellate Body Report, *Mexico – Taxes on Soft Drinks*, para. 54. NAFTA Article 2005.6 is a 'fork in the road' provision which provides:

> Once dispute settlement procedures have been initiated under Article 2007 or dispute settlement proceedings have been initiated under the GATT, the forum selected shall be used to the exclusion of the other, unless a Party makes a request pursuant to paragraph 3 or 4.

Although Mexico did not argue that Article 2005.6 precluded WTO jurisdiction over the dispute, this argument was made by the Mexican sugar industry in an amicus brief. See discussion in Pauwelyn and Salles 2009: 77, 88–90 and nn.46–9.

51 Appellate Body Report, *Mexico – Taxes on Soft Drinks*, para. 54.

52 Panel Report, *Brazil – Measures Affecting Imports of Retreaded Tyres*, WT/DS332/R, paras. 7.288–7.289.

53 Appellate Body Report, *Brazil – Measures Affecting Imports of Retreaded Tyres*, WT/DS332/AB/R, adopted 17 December 2007, para. 232 [hereinafter 'Appellate Body Report, *Brazil – Retreaded Tyres*'].

54 Appellate Body Report, *Brazil – Retreaded Tyres*, para. 232.

55 The subsequent arbitral proceedings over compliance further brought into tension Brazil's obligations under Mercosur and the WTO. See Qin 2009. Online. Available at: www.asil.org/insights070905_update.cfm.

56 Panel Report, *Argentina – Definitive Anti-Dumping Duties on Poultry from Brazil*, WT/DS241/R, adopted 22 April 2003 [hereinafter 'Panel Report, *Argentina – Poultry Anti-Dumping Duties*']. The panel report was not appealed to the Appellate Body.

57 Panel Report, *Argentina – Poultry Anti-Dumping Duties*, para 7.17.

58 For a discussion of *res judicata*, see next section.

59 See Vienna Convention on the Law of Treaties, 23 May 1969, 1155 U.N.T.S. 331; 8 I.L.M. 679 (1969).

60 Panel Report, *Argentina – Poultry Anti-Dumping Duties*, para. 7.41.

61 The panel in the *EC–Biotech* dispute subsequently addressed this issue, concluding that the language 'the parties' refers to all parties to a treaty (in this case the WTO), rather than to just the parties to the particular dispute at hand. Panel Report, *European Communities – Measures Affecting the Approval and Marketing of Biotech Products*, WT/DS291/R, WT/DS292/R, WT/DS293/R, Add.1 to Add.9, and Corr.1, adopted 21 November 2006, para. 7.68. According to the panel's reasoning, all WTO members would need to be party to a separate treaty (in that case the Cartagena Protocol on Biosafety to the Convention on Biological Diversity (39 ILM 1027 (2000); UN Doc. UNEP/CBD/ExCOP/1/3 (2000)) in order for the terms of the separate treaty to looked to in dispute settlement as 'relevant rules of international law applicable in the relations between the parties'. The panel report was not appealed to the Appellate Body. For a critique of the panel's interpretation, see McGrady 2008: 589–618.

62 Protocol of Olivos for the Settlement of Disputes in Mercosur, signed 18 February 2002, in force from 10 February 2004 (2003) 42 ILM 2, at Art. 1.

63 Panel Report, *Argentina – Poultry Anti-Dumping Duties*, para 7.38. In the *Brazil – Retreaded Tyres* case discussed above, the Appellate Body noted this aspect of the Panel Report in *Argentina – Poultry Anti-Dumping Duties* in a footnote. See Appellate Body Report, *Brazil – Retreaded Tyres*.

64 See Protocol of Olivos.

65 This is a fascinating question, and one that may require resolving the thorny question raised in dicta in *Argentina – Poultry Anti-Dumping Duties* – what is the meaning of 'any relevant rules of international law applicable in the relations between the parties' in Article 31(3)(c) of the Vienna Convention on the Law of Treaties?

66 See Davey and Sapir 2009: 16. Davey and Sapir ascribe to this view, noting that allowing a provision such as the Protocol of Olivos to effectively act as a waiver of a party's right to WTO dispute settlement would deprive would-be third-parties of their rights to participate in WTO dispute settlement proceedings. They argue that WTO members should only be able to accomplish this result if approved by the WTO membership through obtaining a waiver.

67 Davey and Sapir 2009: 16.

68 For a discussion of this issue, see Pauwelyn and Salles 2009: 86.

69 This would have been the circumstance in the *Argentina – Poultry Anti-Dumping Duties* case discussed above, if the Protocol of Olivos had been in effect.

2 Expanding the trade litigator's toolkit

Developing tools to achieve effective and legitimate resolution of disputes under PACER Plus and other trade agreements

Iain Sandford[1]

Introduction: the problem of missing tools

Problems sometimes arise in any complex system with many moving parts. This is true of international trading relationships, just as it is true of any machine. But whereas a mechanic will draw on a full bag of tools to fix a broken machine, practitioners of international trade dispute resolution have only a few tools at their disposal to deal effectively with trade disputes. Some of these tools, such as the dispute settlement system of the World Trade Organization (WTO), are very powerful. However, under the broad WTO framework, there are limited opportunities to choose tools that are more specific than a dispute settlement panel to address the particular characteristics of each dispute. Thus, although the WTO dispute settlement framework is undoubtedly one of the great strengths of the multilateral trading system, it is not appropriate for every disagreement that arises in international commerce. Additional frameworks in Regional Trade Agreements (RTAs), including Free Trade Agreements (FTAs) and Economic Integration Agreements (EIAs), could be made to complement the WTO system and augment the trade litigator's toolkit.

This chapter considers an aspect of international trade institution building – namely the development of dispute settlement mechanisms. It focuses ultimately on issues and practices arising in Australasia and the South Pacific, although it draws on wider international experience with trade dispute resolution. It argues that RTAs currently under negotiation could complement WTO negotiations on improving the *Understanding on Rules and Procedures for Settlement of Disputes* (DSU) by providing a dynamic negotiating environment in which to innovate with respect to dispute settlement rules. This is particularly true in the unique negotiating circumstances of the proposed enhanced Pacific Agreement on Closer Economic Relations (PACER Plus). This negotiation between Australia, New Zealand and the 14 Pacific Islands Forum countries[2] provides an opportunity to create systems for resolving disputes that are at once perceived as legitimate by relevant stakeholders and are also effective at addressing disputes that, due to the characteristics of the region, may not be susceptible to effective resolution in other fora.

The chapter proceeds as follows. In the next section, the chapter describes the purpose of dispute settlement in trade agreements, suggesting that this purpose is to provide a framework for effective resolution of disagreements in a legitimate manner. The chapter then moves, in the third and fourth sections, to describe problems, gaps and issues arising out of the normal (or what this chapter refers to as the 'default') system of dispute settlement that is typically established under trade agreements. These include inherent limitations in the default system, a key problem affecting the perceived legitimacy of international trade dispute resolution systems – namely, a gap in transparency – and issues arising in the relationships between different trade agreements. The chapter then considers how these matters could be addressed in a positive manner in a particular trade agreement under negotiation in the Pacific region: PACER Plus. Accordingly, the fifth section outlines certain unique characteristics of the Pacific region that may require a special approach to disputes. The sixth section describes some ways in which innovative dispute resolution systems could be adopted in order to secure positive, effective and legitimate outcomes to a greater number of the problems that inevitably will arise in trade relations in the region over time. Finally, the seventh section concludes.

The purpose of dispute settlement systems: solving problems in an effective and legitimate manner

One purpose of a dispute settlement provision in a trade agreement is to provide a system for the *effective* resolution of disputes arising under the treaty. Effective resolution is in some ways an obvious purpose. But there are particular characteristics of international trade agreements that colour what can be considered to be effective in the context of international, *intergovernmental* trade relations.

Intergovernmental trade treaties are simultaneously instruments of governments' foreign policy as well as agreements about the conditions under which commercial actors will undertake cross-border trade relations. This dual character of trade agreements permeates not only the commitments and trade rules agreed to in such treaties, but also the institutional frameworks set up by the parties to manage their trading relations, including the systems for the resolution of disagreements.

The availability of an outlet for disputes is important both from the perspective of governmental interests (including as a matter of foreign policy) and also from that of commercial actors. From a governmental perspective, an outlet for disputes allows disagreements to be managed on a particular path, thereby allowing them to be taken off the day-to-day foreign policy agenda without overshadowing or otherwise souring the relationship between the parties. The commercial relevance of trade disputes means that from the perspective of private commercial actors, a commercially meaningful outcome will be desirable. Provided it is consistent with broader foreign policy objectives, governments generally want this as well. A commercially meaningful outcome to a trade dispute may include eventual withdrawal (or upholding) of an impugned trade measure, but it will usually also include timely resolution, compensation for losses, and certainty of outcome. Where trade regulation affects government policies in non-commercial areas, other stakeholders from civil society may also have an interest in the way a dispute under a trade agreement is resolved.

In addition to striving for effective resolution of disputes, dispute resolution frameworks that deal with disagreements under trade agreements also balance considerations of *legitimacy*. As Professor Weiler has argued (and like considerations of what is an *effective* resolution), considerations of legitimacy need to be considered from the perspective of the government stakeholders in the system (intergovernmental or 'internal' legitimacy) as well as from the perspective of non-governmental stakeholders ('external legitimacy').[3]

From the governmental perspective, the intergovernmental nature of trade agreements means that the treaty partners will generally want to ensure that the governments themselves (as opposed to private parties) address any disagreements. A classic illustration of this is the Australia New Zealand Closer Economic Relations Trade Agreement (CER) between Australia and New Zealand, which provides only for consultations in the event of disagreement between the parties; does not contemplate referral of any dispute to a neutral, third party process; and accords no standing to private interests.[4]

Where agreements do provide for dispute resolution by neutral, third party adjudicators, it is important that the system reflects procedural fairness and integrity so that its output is politically legitimate for the governmental parties, irrespective of the fact that a dispute will usually yield a result in which one side wins and the other loses. This may involve limitations on the power of the adjudicator. In the WTO system, for instance, although the consideration of disputes is delegated to panels and the Appellate Body, the membership of the WTO as a whole ultimately rules on disputes, through the process of adoption of panel and Appellate Body reports by the Dispute Settlement Body (DSB).

But private interest in trade agreement disputes means that non-governmental actors may sometimes also wish, themselves, to challenge measures that they perceive to be inconsistent with the agreed-to deal. In international practice, Bilateral Investment Treaties and similar agreements (such as the investment chapters of RTAs) frequently provide a right to investors to do this through the process of investor-state arbitration. And even where they have no legal standing to bring their own claims, non-governmental stakeholders desire at least to be able to observe what is going on in the dispute settlement process and to have some say in an appropriate form, such as through amicus curiae submissions.

Sometimes it is possible for private parties to avail themselves of the municipal law of the party whose measure causes the disagreement. Where it is available, determination of a dispute and enforcement of the outcome through domestic courts can be particularly effective for private parties, because domestic judicial decisions are legally binding and enforceable against a government in its own jurisdiction. An excellent example of this in the context of CER is the 'Project Blue Sky' litigation in which New Zealand broadcast media makers were able to invalidate an Australian media content standard that gave more favourable treatment to domestic content providers, contrary to the national treatment obligation under the CER Protocol on Trade in Services.[5] The ability to bring such a claim, however, depends on whether a claim under a treaty has some status in domestic law. Moreover, insofar as a domestic action could be relevant for the settling of a dispute between states (as opposed to a dispute between a private actor and a State), it would be unusual for a foreign sovereign to submit itself to the jurisdiction of another country's domestic courts to resolve a dispute that arises out of their relations at international law.

In addition, even for private parties in common law systems such as New Zealand's or Australia's, domestic litigation may not provide an effective outlet for several reasons. For one, the sovereign parliament may validly enact a law that cannot be interpreted consistently with an international treaty obligation. In such a case, the court must give effect to the domestic law. A second reason is that rights conferred on private parties by a treaty obligation simply may not be incorporated, as such, into the domestic law. Although, under common law conventions of statutory interpretation, a court may strive to interpret domestic law consistently with an unincorporated treaty obligation and give it meaning when applying domestic administrative law,[6] an international law standard that is not transformed into municipal law generally will not give rise to a right of action in the domestic courts. A third reason is that domestic courts will usually adopt a deferential standard of administrative review when looking at technical trade measures adopted by government agencies such as dumping or quarantine decisions.[7]

Resolution problems and gaps in the system of dispute settlement *within* trade agreements

The 'default' setting for RTA negotiations is to include in relation to disputes a chapter providing for the possibility of neutral third party adjudication, through a process that is similar to WTO dispute settlement. As such, the process has certain features, including that:

- there is a fairly legalistic process of litigation or arbitration involving considerations of due process and sound procedure;
- the process is limited to the States themselves, and generally does not involve private parties, except to the extent their interests are championed by a State; and
- the process is usually backed by a commitment to implement the decision, but with the possibility that a party may retaliate against a measure found not to be in conformity with the agreement by suspending benefits under the agreement owed to the other party.

Although this default system of dispute settlement has the advantage of being a known model for new agreements (which lends it a degree of legitimacy from the point of view of contracting States), it has important deficiencies. These take the form of generally high cost and political thresholds for disputes, *de jure* access barriers for non-state actors; apparent de facto barriers to access for classes of country, notably smaller developing countries;[8] and problems of enforceability where a non-complying State chooses not to implement a decision. They may also include problems of lack of transparency, gaps in the coverage of dispute settlement rules, or issues of overlapping jurisdiction.

The need to balance considerations of legitimacy – particularly intergovernmental legitimacy – with the need to achieve resolution of a dispute means that the standard 'default' state-to-state dispute resolution system in trade agreements sometimes fails to provide an effective outlet for disputes. In other work,[9] I have pointed to at least four 'resolution problems', which together mean that the default dispute settlement model in trade agreements fails to provide an appropriate outlet for many disputes.

These problems are:

- the *speed problem*, which describes the fact that dispute settlement under the default approach to trade dispute settlement usually takes a long time to yield a result;
- the *threshold problem*, reflecting the fact that state-to-state international trade dispute settlement is usually reserved for matters of high political importance or very substantial economic value;
- the *access problem*, which reflects the fact that certain stakeholders are either *de jure* denied standing to access the system (as in the case of private parties) or de facto make little use of it (as in the case of small developing countries); and, finally,
- the *enforcement problem*, reflecting the fact that remedies are prospective and do not compensate or prevent harm to affected interests, either through compensatory or injunctive relief.

In addition to issues with the ability of the default state-to-state dispute settlement model to deal effectively with some disputes, there are also issues affecting perceptions of the legitimacy of the system, particularly for non-governmental stakeholders. A crucial such matter is the issue of *transparency*.

Transparency has been commented on most frequently in relation to WTO dispute settlement. This, primarily, is a function of the fact that WTO dispute settlement has been used on numerous occasions, whereas RTA dispute settlement provisions have been invoked only rarely.

Before conclusion of the Uruguay Round, dispute settlement under the General Agreement on Tariffs and Trade 1947 (GATT) was difficult to access. A Contracting Party to the GATT 1947 that was not party to a panel proceeding could only access panel reports once they were circulated for consideration by the GATT Council. Public access was even more limited: in principle, reports became available to the public only if they were adopted by the GATT Council and subsequently published in the Basic Instruments and Selected Documents series – sometimes several years after the case was heard.

Transparency, both within the organisation and vis-à-vis external stakehold-ers, improved considerably with the adoption of the DSU. Article 10 of the DSU clarified and expanded third party rights of participation for WTO members (although there remained limitations). WTO dispute reports have, since the beginning, been derestricted and publicly available upon circulation to the WTO membership. The WTO has been active in placing material on its website, and panel and Appellate Body reports are usually available on that site shortly after paper copies are distributed to diplomatic missions in Geneva. All these innova-tions added considerably to the transparency and legitimacy of the system, as both an internal and external matter.

Early high-profile disputes highlighted additional issues of transparency. Examples include: *European Communities – Measures Affecting Beef and Beef Products (Hormones)*,[10] in which longstanding European bans on hormone-treated beef were found to be unlawful; *European Communities – Regime for the Importation, Sale and Distribution of Bananas*,[11] in which one group of develop-ing countries challenged the trade preferences given by European countries to another group of developing countries; *United States – Import Prohibition of Certain Shrimp and Shrimp Products* (the so-called *Shrimp-Turtle* case)[12] and *European Communities – Measures Affecting Asbestos and Asbestos-Containing Products*[13] (*EC – Asbestos*) cases, which challenged environmental and health protection measures by American and European governments.

As a result of these cases and others, a number of further innovations have arisen. Third party rights of participation for member governments have been expanded further, although there remain limits.[14] Amicus curiae briefs have been allowed from non-government actors in a number of cases, as well as from a WTO member in one case.[15] Hearings in a number of cases have been opened to the public.[16] The Secretariat's communication role has expanded.[17] Finally, panels and the Appellate Body have become very careful in documenting all important aspects of their proceedings in their public reports.[18]

Some WTO Members have remained sceptical about the appropriateness of opening up the dispute settlement process to influences outside of the WTO membership itself. For this reason, the Appellate Body's acceptance of amicus briefs has been strongly criticised. Indeed, its establishment in *EC – Asbestos* of a formal procedure for dealing with such briefs led to unprecedented and vocif-erous criticism by Members in the DSB.[19] Indeed, not all WTO Members agree that transparency is a problem in the dispute settlement system, which perhaps limits the likelihood of substantial evolution in the WTO system.

Negotiations on clarification and improvement of the DSU predate the start of the Doha Development Agenda (DDA) negotiations. Despite the mixed views of the WTO membership, several proposals have been made in that context to address internal and external transparency issues, such as:[20]

- open hearings;
- more timely access to submissions and better access to documents for third parties;

- webcast hearings;
- the opportunity for Members to observe proceedings, or to join proceedings at the Appellate stage;
- Publication of submissions, or the creation of a publicly accessible registry of dispute settlement filings.[21]

Whether these budding proposals will flower into amendments to the DSU is an open question that is now related to the broader fortunes of the DDA negotiations.[22]

Issues in the relationship *between* the WTO and RTA dispute settlement mechanisms

As the DDA negotiations have foundered, countries have increasingly turned to RTAs as an outlet for their trade liberalising ambitions. In the case of Australia and New Zealand, in addition to negotiations that have a special development dimension, such as PACER Plus, the countries are also pursuing ambitious negotiations with the United States and a wide group of Asia-Pacific economies in the Trans-Pacific Partnership, or 'TPP' negotiations.

These two negotiations have quite different scope and objectives, but each in its way highlights potential issues in the relationship between RTAs and the multilateral system. Indeed, these kinds of issues arise between most RTAs and the multilateral trading system of the WTO.

There is, in general, a dynamic relationship between regionalism and the WTO, due to a wide variety of connections arising out of overlapping membership and subject matter. Just as in the case of different market access frameworks, different institutional frameworks could in principle either complement or compete with one another. In particular:

- It is possible that the respective dispute settlement frameworks under the WTO and any RTA may establish overlapping jurisdictions for dispute settlement panels in relation to a trade dispute. They could therefore give rise to choice of forum issues or multiple proceedings dealing with the same dispute under different treaty frameworks.
- Similarly, having multiple agreements potentially relevant to a single dispute may make it possible for the different agreements to provide structures or systems for dispute resolution other than a dispute settlement panel, thereby giving an opportunity to pursue a different approach to the underlying problem.
- To the extent the agreements cover different things, the respective dispute settlement frameworks could provide an outlet for disputes that are not covered by the other, thereby allowing trade problems to be dealt with, when they might otherwise go unaddressed.

The first of these issues, overlapping jurisdictions, has been a significant focus in the literature in recent years, partly because it is seen as symptomatic of the broader problem of the fragmentation of international law, but also because so-called 'forum shopping' in private international litigation can be problematic where it leads to inefficient procedures or incompatible resolutions of the same dispute. A concern is that these same problems could manifest in the public international law context as well.

A prerequisite, of course, for the opportunity to choose between different trade dispute settlement frameworks is that different frameworks have to be applicable to the same dispute. As between RTAs and the WTO, this requires disputes to arise in connection with a common or equivalent rule or commitment. A typical example would be a national treatment violation, since RTAs frequently adopt a rule that incorporates by reference, or is otherwise similar to, Article III of the General Agreement on Tariffs and Trade 1994 (GATT 1994), providing for even-handed fiscal and regulatory treatment as between imported goods and domestically produced products.

Interestingly, issues of potentially overlapping jurisdiction appear to have arisen only rarely. The most celebrated example is the WTO dispute relating to *Mexico – Tax Measures on Soft Drinks and Other Beverages*[23] (*Mexico – Soft Drinks*). This case involved a claim by the United States that Mexican measures on soft drinks containing sweeteners other than sugar violated national treatment obligations under Article III:2 and III:4 of the GATT 1994. The record of the dispute indicates that the Mexican measures were adopted at least in part as a response to Mexico's inability to pursue its complaint about US measures affecting sugar imports through a dispute resolution process under the state-to-state procedures of Chapter 20 of the North American Free Trade Agreement (NAFTA), due to a failure by the United States to appoint panellists.

Although the dispute arose in complex circumstances where one party's apparently preferred dispute resolution option was not available to it in practice, and therefore presented no choice of forum issue as such, the Appellate Body left open the possibility that there may be circumstances when a WTO tribunal appropriately could decline jurisdiction in favour of a different, non-WTO, forum.[24] This suggests that WTO adjudicators are at least alive to the issues and potential problems of overlapping jurisdiction, in the rare circumstances where this may arise.

In addition to cases like *Mexico – Soft Drinks* where the dispute related, at least in part, to obligations that were common both to the NAFTA and the WTO, in many cases, there will simply not be equivalent rules. Given the rarity of cases in which the problem has arisen, it may be easy to overstate the significance of any problem of overlapping jurisdiction.

No choice of forum issue arises if a claim lies under only one dispute settlement framework. Claims may be brought under an RTA but not under the WTO dispute settlement system where they relate to so-called 'WTO-plus' rules or commitments – that is, rules or commitments that go beyond what has been agreed within the ambit of the WTO.

By their nature, RTAs will often provide for WTO-plus tariff or services *commitments*. With respect to tariffs, for example, the definitional principle for an

FTA is that tariffs should be reduced to zero on substantially all trade, whereas the GATT 1994 only requires WTO Members to apply tariffs below the level of tariff bindings set forth in each Member's schedule of commitments. In addition to WTO-plus market access commitments, frequently, RTA *rules* relating to intellectual property rights, competition and investment are also 'WTO-plus' in nature. In the case of the TPP, provisions addressing matters such as regulatory coherence, small and medium sized enterprises, trade and labour, and trade and environment appear likely to add WTO-plus rules as well.

In many countries' *domestic* law, it is axiomatic that a right must have a remedy.[25] To the extent that additional rights are conferred, there should be some additional outlet for disputes about compliance with them. Generally speaking, New Zealand and Australian treaty practice is thus to provide for such outlets for WTO-plus commitments in their RTAs through either the default state-to-state dispute settlement chapter, or through other dispute resolution provisions appropriate to the particular context.[26]

A further set of connections between the dispute settlement framework of RTAs and the WTO is the ability of regional negotiations to establish innovative frameworks to deal with disputes in different (and perhaps better) ways.

As noted earlier, there is a default state-to-state dispute settlement framework that is normally adopted in RTAs. Yet this default process has seldom been invoked as a tool to resolve actual trade disputes. An exception was early use of the Chapter 20 dispute settlement process under the NAFTA. This process has not, however, been used since 2001, giving rise to issues such as that described above in the *Mexico – Soft Drinks* case.[27]

In addition, however, RTAs sometimes create dispute settlement frameworks that solve particular problems in the negotiations and which provide a useful outlet for disputes. There are a number of examples,[28] of which it is useful to highlight two, by way of illustration.

First, Chapter 19 of the NAFTA (like Chapter 19 of the Canada–United States FTA (CUSFTA) that preceded it) establishes a 'binational' system of panels to replace the role of domestic courts in reviewing anti-dumping and countervailing duty (together 'AD/CVD') determinations.

Under Chapter 19, panels apply the domestic law and the domestic standard of administrative review of the importing country, but comprise qualified experts from both the importing and exporting country. Chapter 19 reportedly was an accommodation that bridged the desire by Canada's negotiators to have Canada exempted from US trade remedy laws and the desire of the United States not to do so.[29]

This is an example of the use of an innovative approach to dispute settlement frameworks to help the negotiators strike a deal. Further, unlike virtually every other dispute settlement framework established in FTAs, the Chapter 19 process has been frequently invoked.[30]

A second example is an innovative review process adopted under the Australia–United States FTA (AUSFTA) that deals with potential disputes at a much lower level of escalation than other dispute resolution systems in trade agreements.

Australia has a system of consumer pharmaceutical subsidies called the Pharmaceutical Benefits Scheme. Drugs are listed as qualifying for a subsidy on the recommendation of a body called the Pharmaceutical Benefits Advisory Committee (PBAC).

Under the AUSFTA, Australia undertook to institute a special non-binding independent review process to examine PBAC decisions declining to recommend the listing of new medicines.[31] Australia implemented this innovation on 1 January 2005, making the review process open to all pharmaceutical sponsors, not just those from the United States.[32] The process implemented by Australia involves a *de novo* 'second look'[33] at the written material that was available to PBAC, rather than a review of the recommendation by PBAC as such. The review is carried out by a reviewer and, in certain cases, a secondary reviewer appointed ad hoc for the task.[34]

Again, this alternative outlet for potential grievances by drug makers helped bridge a gap in the negotiations when Australia was unwilling to reform its system as desired by the United States. The new review system has been used on several occasions, without apparent controversy.[35]

In addition, RTAs can innovate in relation to systemic issues, such as transparency. For instance, they may provide for open dispute settlement hearings, or allow unsolicited amicus curiae briefs. Annex 15.B (Model Rules of Procedure for Arbitral Tribunals) of the P4 Trans-Pacific Strategic Economic Partnership Agreement between New Zealand, Singapore, Chile and Brunei Darussalam, for instance, contemplates hearings being opened to the public.[36] It also allows for arbitral panels to accept amicus curiae submissions, subject to certain procedures.[37]

Such innovative mechanisms in RTAs complement the alternative dispute resolution provisions of the WTO, which provide another potential outlet for innovative resolution of trade disputes. Article 5 of the DSU provides for 'good offices, mediation or conciliation' of disputes. Article 25 sets up a framework for expeditious 'arbitration'. Somewhat surprisingly, these provisions have each been rarely used, perhaps in part because of a concern that the outcome of using these mechanisms is less predictable than using the tried and tested consultations-panel-appeal process under Articles 4–19 of the DSU.[38]

All of these alternative approaches to resolving disputes can complement the standard system of dispute settlement under the WTO system. They can do so by providing an outlet for types of disputes that are not suitable for litigation through the normal WTO process, either because they involve private party interests and are therefore not amenable to the uniquely state-to-state system of the WTO, because they are relatively minor and would not trigger the level of trade or political interest that would lead a government to take them up in either in the WTO or under the state-to-state dispute chapter of an RTA, or for a variety of other reasons.

The challenge of trade dispute settlement in the Pacific

In the following section, this chapter applies considerations arising out of the matters surveyed above to the context of a particular trade agreement under negotiation; namely, PACER Plus. PACER Plus provides an excellent case study, because the traditional, default model of trade dispute resolution is particularly unsuited to the unique characteristics of the region. This section thus outlines some of the relevant characteristics of the region before the next section turns to identify a few areas in which consideration could be given to adopting alternative approaches to dispute resolution procedures.

The Pacific region is characterised by the prevalence of small island developing countries. The domestic economies of such countries are small, with an important reliance on remittances from expatriates abroad, overseas development assistance and exports for foreign exchange.[39] Industries in a number of countries are concentrated in a few areas, leading to a limited range of exports. Exports make an important contribution to these economies proportionate to other sectors, but, as absolute numbers, the volumes and values of exports tend to be tiny by comparison to those of Australia and New Zealand.

Commensurate with the size of these economies and their level of development, government resources are particularly constrained. Few governments in the Pacific can afford to devote substantial resources to trade policy; even less so to trade disputes.

Recognising the positive contribution that trade could play for such countries, Pacific Islands Forum leaders have agreed to engage in negotiations on a PACER Plus agreement. PACER Plus is conceived as a reciprocal FTA amongst all its 16 proposed members. It would thereby replace the existing one-way preferences for Pacific Islands Countries given by Australia and New Zealand, such as the South Pacific Regional Trade and Economic Cooperation Agreement (SPARTECA). It would supplement the Pacific Islands Countries Trade Agreement (PICTA) currently existing amongst the Pacific Islands Countries themselves. In pushing for this agreement, Australia has identified the negotiation of a PACER Plus agreement as an opportunity to promote a broad aid-for-trade programme in the Pacific,[40] although it clearly is conceived as involving trade liberalisation on the part of the Pacific Islands Countries as well.

How does dispute settlement fit in with this agenda? As in a commercial negotiation, no one starts from the proposition that disputes are going to be a big feature of the ongoing relationship between the parties. Indeed, negotiators will try to be clear and precise as to the details of the deal to be struck, and they will seek to negotiate an overall package that heads off likely disputes before they arise. But at the same time, in establishing a basis for an ongoing trade relationship, all the parties know that disagreements will come up. For that reason alone, it will be prudent to think about how effectively to create a safety valve for as yet unknown disputes. In addition, for a handful of issues that are impossible to resolve in the negotiations themselves, it could be that provision for an effective dispute resolution system could be part of a deal that gives each side a level of comfort with the commitments and concessions being made.

As to the interests of Pacific Islands Countries, the concentrated nature of their trade relationships and the political dynamics in the region weigh against Forum Islands Countries availing themselves of formal dispute settlement against Australia or New Zealand, even where a genuine and substantial concern exists. Such matters would threaten to damage a bilateral relationship with a key regional partner.[41] At the same time, effective dispute resolution is crucial to ensuring trade deals result in more trade and economic integration. Finding an appropriate means to deal with problems as they inevitably arise is therefore critical.

The characteristics of the Pacific Island Countries mean that a useful process of dispute settlement will tend to be relatively non-resource intensive, requiring minimal funding and minimal commitment of governmental human resources. Such a system also needs to be effective. Countries generally are reluctant to challenge trade partners' measures unless there is a strong case leading to confidence in the outcome.[42] The relative power imbalance between small economies (especially *very* small economies, such as many of those in the Pacific), on the one hand, and their larger regional trade partners, on the other, means that smaller countries will generally only use dispute resolution procedures where they can be confident of the outcome.

Dispute resolution in the context of international economic relations is not, of course, a one-way street. Exporters, importers or investors from Australia or New Zealand may well end up in disagreements with governments in the Pacific. In these cases, intervention by the Australian or New Zealand governments on behalf of an exporter, particularly through a full-scale state-to-state dispute settlement system, may be undesirable since it would likely to be perceived as bullying by a powerful regional neighbour, and may have an impact on the relationship that is out of proportion to the nature of the particular concern being addressed.

At the same time, exporters and investors on all sides will have legitimate interests in seeing any deal adhered to. And since disputes may often force a defending government to stick with a deal reached and ultimately adopt a policy that is better for economic development, resolution of disputes can have domestic governance benefits for the defending country as well. In this way, dispute resolution procedures can create incentives for governments to govern well by requiring higher standards of transparency and administrative fairness as well as adherence to the terms of agreements.

Options for PACER Plus

With the dynamics reviewed in the previous section in mind, it seems unlikely that using the default approach to trade dispute resolution in a PACER Plus agreement would prove to be an appropriate practical tool. If the standard state-to-state formal arbitral provisions were provided for in the agreement, such a framework would be unlikely to be used. The level of engagement required of governments and the likely complexity of the legal process involved will discourage any use by Pacific Islands Countries, and Australia and New Zealand are unlikely to have such strong concerns with trade measures in the Pacific that they would take the fairly aggressive step of forcing international trade litigation onto a Pacific Islands Country partner.

What then of a state-to-state mediation or arbitration process? A mediation process, modelled on – or perhaps even making use of – the 'good offices' provisions of the WTO Agreement may well be an appropriate tool in some circumstances, particularly for disputes amongst Pacific countries. Indeed, the existing PICTA agreement amongst the Pacific Islands Countries already contemplates a multi-phase dispute resolution process that involves bilateral consultation followed by mandatory mediation[43] before any recourse to arbitral dispute resolution. Although this process has not been used, PICTA provides an appropriately flexible template on which to build a dispute settlement process for a broader PACER Plus agreement.

The same may be true of use of WTO arbitration, for countries that are WTO Members.[44] Reference to such mechanisms has an advantage in the fact that they are already available at least for some disputes amongst some Pacific countries. There may be an opportunity to generalise this system amongst Pacific countries. Indeed, the main limitation on uptake of these procedures at present may well be a lack of appreciation that they are available. This could be addressed by adopting a regional framework for use of Article 25 (or similar) arbitration. At a minimum, this might include developing standard terms of reference and providing standard rules for a streamlined and expeditious arbitral procedure, which could operate in an effective and transparent manner.

The CUSFTA Chapter 19 experiment has not been replicated by the United States since NAFTA and controversy about the system still prevails more than 20 years after its inception.[45] It has proven a powerful process for aggrieved parties. Other trade partners have not shown enthusiasm for mimicking a process of bi-national review of administrative decisions in their own trade agreements.

In the context of a trade agreement in the Pacific region, there seems little need for a trade remedy-focused system of dispute resolution, given that anti-dumping and countervailing duty (AD/CVD) cases in Australia and New Zealand are seldom, if ever, directed at Pacific exports and that most Forum Islands Countries do not have AD/CVD laws. However, there are other aspects of administrative decision making, for example decisions in quarantine cases, where a special bi-national dispute or review system may give comfort to trade partners where decisions could otherwise be seen as sheltering domestic interests from foreign competition.

The key question with promoting a bi-national approach is whether all parties would have sufficient confidence in panellists from a trade partner reviewing expert decisions by domestic authorities. Given the asymmetry in trade policy capacity around the Pacific, were this question posed in a PACER Plus negotiation, the answer to this question from New Zealand or Australia could well be negative.

That said, a process involving a bi-national panel drawn from respected judges would not be inconceivable, where its mandate is to undertake an administrative review in place of a domestic tribunal or as an initial review subject to appeal.

Even though such a watered-down version of the Chapter 19 approach would retain complete domestic sovereignty over ultimate review decisions, it would at least give the exporting country a sense of participation in a review. For exporters, it would have the benefit of retaining access to domestic remedies and enforcement tools, but may also give comfort that the system is not inherently weighted against their interests.

Arguably, the best dispute resolution systems are ones that can satisfactorily address an issue before it manifests as a major disagreement. Approaches that can achieve that objective tend to be quite specific in their subject matter, keep the dispute as close to the actual interests affected as possible, and adopt a streamlined process. The PBAC review process referred to above, although non-binding, is a good illustration of a method for de-escalating problems and sending them off on their own course, without engaging the political levels of government, and thereby negatively affecting the relationship as a whole.

These kinds of processes, of course, use a unique format that does not necessarily translate into a useful tool for other categories of dispute. However, lessons can be drawn from these models for situations where there are tightly defined categories of problem that could benefit from a similarly streamlined process. Disputes as to the origin, tariff classification, or customs valuation of goods could be examples in a Pacific trade context. Because of the narrowly drawn issues in such matters, referral of a disagreement to an independent umpire for quick resolution is quite conceivable.[46] The process could be set up online, so as to give ready access to affected exporters offshore. Such a streamlined and low-expense model could also address the problem that trade values in the Pacific are frequently not of a magnitude that would justify domestic court action. The system would therefore promote resolution of problems. And through providing for regular, independent review of administrative decisions it could also promote better governance, because customs authorities around the Pacific could expect regularly to be the subject of independent scrutiny. Such scrutiny, particularly when coupled with appropriate transparency mechanisms, would promote the development of good governance based on the rule of law.

The same could be true for other formats, such as the creation of special 'independent review' mechanisms. The adoption of similar forms of independent review may be available for other kinds of trade cases where there may be a need to balance robust expert analysis with political discretion, for example, bio-security decisions.

Conclusion: expanding the toolkit to resolve disputes effectively and legitimately

There are few metaphors more frequently cited in trade circles than those that describe the relationship between RTAs and the WTO. One states that increasing regionalism leads to a 'spaghetti bowl' of overlapping but distinct commitments, which collectively add to the complexity of trade relations.[47] A second asks whether RTAs represent 'stepping stones' towards, or 'stumbling blocks' in the way of, freer trade through the WTO system.[48]

These metaphors are popular because they are apt in capturing two aspects of the fundamental tensions between regionalism and multilateralism in trade negotiations. Regionalism inherently derogates from the cornerstone WTO principle of non-discrimination in the form of most-favoured nation (MFN) treatment. The spaghetti bowl conjures up an untidy image, contrasting sharply with the order, predictability and stability of MFN. Similarly the stepping stones/stumbling blocks description raises the question whether RTAs do potentially more harm than good as a means towards liberalising trade on a global basis.

But in the twenty-first century, the relationship between RTAs and the WTO includes more dimensions than just discriminatory tariffs and tariff liberalisation. Indeed, as levels of protection through tariffs have decreased in importance, the significance of the WTO is as much about its institutional framework as it is about observance of these cornerstone principles. Yet the question of how RTA institutional frameworks relate to the WTO, its internal frameworks and systems, and evolution of the multilateral trading system as a whole has received less attention than other dimensions.

A 'toolkit' is a more apt analogy to describe useful institutional structures such as a dispute settlement system. It highlights that regionalism and multilateralism can be complementary in promoting a positive world economic order. Tools help to fix things when they have gone wrong, and, in fixing problems, it does not matter where the relevant tool comes from or how many tools remain in the toolkit unused. At present, the toolkit for those who would resolve disputes arising in a trading relationship is somewhat spare. There has been a lack of creativity in considering whether additional tools could be added in order to address the particular problems that arise in particular relationships.

The point of this chapter has been to suggest that dispute resolution provisions in trade agreements deserve creative attention, particularly in RTA negotiations. Different forms of dispute resolution are better suited to different types of dispute. Provided each process is considered legitimate by the relevant interests and does not undermine confidence in the overall relationship under the agreement, making available a greater range of options has the potential to allow problems to be managed in the most effective way.

As governments around the Pacific region continue to focus on PACER Plus negotiations, they would do well to apply creative attention to the provisions to be set out in that agreement to deal with the kinds of unique problems that inevitably will arise. Although there are a number of international precedents for creative dispute resolution clauses, the real lesson from the international experience is that it is sometimes useful to craft highly specific and bespoke mechanisms to deal with the unique problems that arise in a particular relationship. Promoting trade and development in the Pacific region turns up an array of unique problems. There is an opportunity, therefore, to innovate in identifying useful and positive responses.

Notes

1 BA, LLB, Victoria University of Wellington; LLM, University of Ottawa. Adjunct Professor of Law, University of Canberra, and Counsel, Sidley Austin LLP, Geneva. Contact: isandford@sidley.com. This paper draws on conference papers presented by the author at the New Zealand Centre of International Economic Law Conference in Wellington in October 2009 and at the 12th Georgetown University/British Institute of International and Comparative Law Conference on WTO Law in London in May 2012.

2 Cook Islands, Federated States of Micronesia, Fiji, Kiribati, Nauru, Niue, Palau, Papua New Guinea, Republic of Marshall Islands, Samoa, Solomon Islands, Tonga, Tuvalu, Vanuatu. In this chapter, this group of countries is referred to generally as the 'Pacific Islands Countries' or the 'Forum Islands Countries'.

3 See Weiler 2001.

4 The dispute resolution clause is set forth in Article 22.2 of the CER Agreement, which provides:

> The Member States shall, at the written request of either, promptly enter into consultations with a view to seeking an equitable and mutually satisfactory solution if the Member State which requested the consultations considers that:
> (a) an obligation under this Agreement has not been or is not being fulfilled;
> (b) a benefit conferred upon it by this Agreement is being denied;
> (c) the achievement of any objective of this Agreement is being or may be frustrated; or
> (d) a case of difficulty has arisen or may arise.

5 *Project Blue Sky Inc v Australian Broadcasting Authority* (1998) 194 CLR 355; (1998) 153 ALR 490; (1998) 72 ALJR 841; (1998) 8 Leg Rep 41; (1998) HCA 28.

6 See, for instance, in *Australia Minister for Immigration v Teoh* (1995) 183 CLR 273, [1995] HCA 20, (1995) 128 ALR 353 and in the case of New Zealand, *Tavita v Minister of Immigration*, [1994] 2 NZLR 257 (CA).

7 An example in the Australian context is revealed by an administrative law challenge to a decision by the Director of Quarantine. In a decision on appeal, the Full Court of the Federal Court of Australia allowed an appeal from the decision of Wilcox J in *Director of Animal and Plant Quarantine v Australian Pork Limited* [2005] FCA 671 that a decision had been *unreasonable* in the sense of *Associated Provincial Picture Houses Ltd. v Wednesbury Corporation* [1947] 1 KB 223. The full court rejected this finding, recalling that in line with the correct test under Australian law, the plaintiff

> had to show that the ultimate decision was not just unreasonable, but so unreasonable that no other similarly qualified decision-maker would have made it. That test necessarily allows for some degree of unreasonableness. Even if error in reasoning is disclosed, a conclusion of *Wednesbury* unreasonableness requires a major step further
> *Director of Animal and Plant Quarantine v Australian Pork Limited*
> [2005] FCAFC 206, at para. 63, per Heerey and Lander JJ

8 Some of the dynamics around the level of participation by developing countries in WTO dispute settlement are explored in a recent collection of case studies: Shaffer and Meléndez-Ortiz (eds) 2010.

9 Sandford and TanKiang 2011.

10 WT/DS26, WT/DS48. In the *EC – Hormones* dispute, which involved separate complaints by the United States and Canada, an issue arose in connection with the rights of one complainant in the separate panel proceedings involving the other. The Panel resolved to grant 'enhanced' third party rights in these cases, including a right to be present at the second substantive meeting of the Panel, in order to facilitate the

parallel proceedings. This approach was upheld by the Appellate Body: see Appellate Body Report, *EC Measures Concerning Meat and Meat Products (Hormones)*, WT/DS26/AB/R, WT/DS48/AB/R, adopted 13 February 1998, para. 154.

11 WT/DS27. In this case, a member's right to be represented by counsel of its choosing was initially contested by the EU. The Panel allowed such representation and this decision was affirmed on appeal: see Appellate Body Report, *European Communities – Regime for the Importation, Sale and Distribution of Bananas*, WT/DS27/AB/R, adopted 25 September 1997, paras 10 and 12.

12 WT/DS58. In this dispute, the United States attached an NGO submission to its submission. The Appellate Body affirmed that there was no impediment to the acceptability of briefs in this form in WTO proceedings. See Appellate Body Report, *United States – Import Prohibition of Certain Shrimp and Shrimp Products*, WT/DS58/AB/R, adopted 6 November 1998, para. 89 [hereinafter 'Appellate Body Report, *US – Shrimp*']. In so finding, the Appellate Body also highlighted the authority of the panel to seek information from 'any individual or body' pursuant to Article 13 of the DSU: Appellate Body Report, *US – Shrimp*, para. 104.

13 WT/DS135. In *EC – Asbestos*, the Appellate Body set up a special procedure for managing the receipt of an expected large number of amicus submissions. The controversy caused by this decision is discussed further below.

14 A good example of this was in the context of the 2005 arbitration of the EU's new tariff regime for bananas. The relevant provisions for arbitration did not provide for any third party rights, but the Arbitrator determined that it would allow participation by the African, Caribbean and Pacific group of countries in any event. See *European Communities – the ACP-EC Partnership Agreement – Recourse to Arbitration Pursuant to the Decision of 14 November 2001*, WT/L/616, 1 August 2005 at para. 10. Another example is the 2005 amendments made by the Appellate Body to its Working Procedures, in order to allow more flexible participation by interested WTO members. See WT/AB/WP/W/9.

15 Morocco submitted an amicus brief to the Appellate Body in Appellate Body Report, *European Communities – Trade Description of Sardines*, WT/DS231/AB/R, adopted 23 October 2002. At the DSB meeting adopting that report, Morocco explained that it had submitted an amicus brief because the DSU rules for third parties did not allow it to intervene in the proceedings at the appellate stage, having not done so before the panel.

16 The first example was *US – Hormones Suspension*, WT/DS320. A WTO news release on the open hearing is available online at: www.wto.org/english/news_e/news05_e/openpanel_12sep_e.htm.

17 This is evidenced by the wide array of material available on the WTO website. Examples of such work from the specialised teams assisting with the administration of disputes include the Appellate Body's Annual Reports and *Repertory of Reports and Awards*, or in the Legal Affairs Division's *One Page Case Summaries*, both available online at www.wto.org/english/tratop_e/dispu_e.htm#dsb.

18 The front part of Appellate Body reports, for example, now systematically addresses all procedural and related matters that arise in a proceeding. This detail is sometimes difficult to extract or understand in earlier reports.

19 See Minutes of Meeting, WT/DSB/M/102 & 103. There is evidence that the views expressed in the DSB have chastened panels and the Appellate Body in their approach to accepting such briefs. Panels now routinely decline to accept such submissions. The Appellate Body now deals with such briefs in its reports formulaically, without much indication of how, if at all, such briefs actually influence the process.

20 See in particular the proposals of the United States: TN/DS/W/86 (21 April 2006), TN/DS/W/79 (13 July 2005), TN/DS/W/46 (11 February 2003), and TN/DS/W/13 (22 August 2002). Other notable contributions have been made by Canada: TN/DS/W/41 (24 January 2003).

21 At present only a handful of WTO members appear systematically to make public their submissions in WTO proceedings, and even then, they are sometimes slow in putting them on the Internet. These members include New Zealand, Australia, the United States, the European Union and Canada.

22 There is, however, thoughtful support for these proposals. The Sutherland Report on the Future of the WTO (Sutherland *et al.* 2004) – a study for the former Director General Supachai Panitchpakti by eight leading international trade figures – made a number of relevant findings and recommendations, in particular that: 'the degree of confidentiality of the current dispute settlement proceedings can be seen as damaging to the WTO as an institution' (Recommendation 261); 'as a matter of course, the first level panel and Appellate Body hearings be open to the public' (Recommendation 262); Secretariat should undertake more technical assistance work in helping stakeholders understand the functioning of the system (Recommendation 264); and the nature and value of the system be sold to a wide public and political audience (Recommendation 265).

23 WT/DS308.

24 Appellate Body Report, *Mexico – Tax Measures on Soft Drinks and Other Beverages*, WT/DS308/AB/R, adopted 24 March 2006, para. 54.

25 As Elias CJ recently put it in the New Zealand context, '[t]hat rights are vindicated through remedy for breach is fundamental to the rule of law', *Attorney-General v Chapman* [2011] NZSC 110.

26 In some cases, the best remedy and mechanism for seeking it may not be the default dispute settlement provisions. This may be the case, for instance, where the treaty expressly provides particular rights to non-state actors. In this light, it is interesting that Australia announced in April 2011 a new policy such that it would generally no longer include investor-state dispute settlement frameworks in its Bilateral Investment Treaties and RTA investment chapters. See: Australian Government Department of Foreign Affairs and Trade (April 2011). To the extent that such new treaties purport to extend rights to investors that are not found elsewhere, this policy risks conferring rights with no effective disputes forum or remedy.

27 According to commentators, the lack of use of the NAFTA Chapter 20 process flows from the United States declining to appoint panellists since the *Cross-Border Trucking* dispute (*Cross-Border Trucking Services*, USA-MEX-98–2008–01, 6 February 2001). See Zamora 2011: 637; and Pauwelyn and Salles 2009: 77–8.

28 Several further alternative approaches to particular issues are outlined in Sandford and TanKiang 2011: 473*ff.*

29 Professor de Mestral recounts the history of the CUSFTA negotiations over AD/CVD:

> Faced with the refusal of the American negotiators to accept the principle of exclusion or alternatively of replacement of AD/CV laws with competition law, the Canadian delegation withdrew from the negotiations and only returned when it was agreed that a solution would be found. Negotiations on the future chapter 19 were rushed through in a final month, thus permitting the entry into force of CUSFTA on January 1, 1988.

See de Mestral 2006: 366.

30 The website of the NAFTA Secretariat provides an index to all relevant NAFTA dispute settlement reports. Online. Available at: www.nafta-sec-alena.org/en/DecisionsAndReports.aspx?x=312 (accessed 23 June 2012).

31 In connection with the conclusion of Chapter 2 (National Treatment and Market Access for Goods) of the AUSFTA (in particular Annex 2-C (Pharmaceuticals)), and as an integral part of the FTA, the parties reached an understanding such that: 'Australia shall provide an opportunity for independent review of PBAC determinations, where an application has not resulted in a PBAC recommendation to list', see clause 2,

Exchange of Letters Constituting an Understanding, 18 May 2004. Online. Available at: www.dfat.gov.au/fta/ausfta/final-text/letters/02_pbs.pdf (accessed 23 June 2012).

32 Information on the process is available online at www.independentreviewpbs.gov.au (accessed 23 June 2012).

33 See 'Instructions for Reviewers'. Online. Available at: www.independentreviewpbs. gov.au/internet/independentreviewpbs/publishing.nsf/Content/instructions-for-reviewers (accessed 23 June 2012).

34 Key parameters of the process are outlined in the 'Instructions for Reviewers'. Online. Available at: www.independentreviewpbs.gov.au/internet/independentreviewpbs/pub-lishing.nsf/Content/instructions-for-reviewers (accessed 23 June 2012).

35 The results of a recent example (an application by iNova Pharmaceuticals (Aust) Pty Ltd for review in relation to its product 'IMIQUIMOD, cream 50 mg per g (5%), 250 mg single use sachets, 12, Aldara®' are recorded in the public notes of PBAC out-comes for March 2009. Online. Available at: www.pbs.gov.au/info/industry/listing/elements/pbac-meetings/pbac-outcomes/2009–03/d_independent_review (accessed 23 June 2012).

36 Trans-Pacific Strategic Economic Partnership Agreement, Annex 15.B, para. 21.

37 Trans-Pacific Strategic Economic Partnership Agreement, Annex 15.B, paras 33–6.

38 For discussion of arbitration in relation to WTO disputes, see generally: Boisson De Chazournes 2005: 181; and Hughes 2004: 85. In relation to use of good offices under Article 5 of the DSU, see: Xuto 2005; and Sandford and TanKiang 2011: 474.

39 For discussion, see Browne and Lee 2006: 21.

40 See for example transcript Crean (18 August 2009).

41 Although the dynamic does not appear to have been the subject of study vis-à-vis the Pacific region, there is a body of literature analysing the reluctance of African coun-tries to challenge trade measures of trade and aid partners. Elements of this literature are well summarised in Sanson 2009: 1:

> Shaffer refers to the fear of political and economic pressure from the US and EC that makes developing countries abandon otherwise justified legal claims. [Author's reference: Shaffer 2003] These are not idle fears. For example in 1999 in the US, campaigners proposed cutting off funding to agencies that encouraged African countries to adopt intellectual property laws exceeding the basic TRIPS Agreement requirements. [Author's reference: Wilson 2004, available at www. peacecorpsconnect.org/wordpress/wp-content/uploads/2010/07/GTNMayJun04. pdf.] Kenya has not raised its issues over fish and flowers with the EU for fear of being locked out of the EU market. [Author's reference: Ochieng and Majanja 2006: 15]. As such, 'political considerations play a pivotal part in deciding whether or not to dispute'. [Author's reference: Ochieng and Majanja 2006].

42 This proposition is supported by the statistically high degree of success by complain-ants in trade dispute settlement proceedings. In the WTO, for example, there is an 88.96 per cent success rate (as calculated by worldtradelaw.net's Dispute Settlement Commentary Service (available online to subscribers at www.worldtradelaw.net/dsc/database/violationcount.asp (accessed 24 June 2012). The International Economic Law and Policy Blog at http://worldtradelaw.typepad.com/ielpblog/2007/04/a_puzzling_90_p.html provides an interesting, if informal, discussion of the reasons why, with one commentator (T. Broude) observing the similarity between the choice to make a complaint in the WTO with prosecution decisions by public prosecutors (who enjoy a similarly high success rate); and another (D. Palmeter) who stated

> Anecdotally, I believe there is a selection process going on in selecting the cases that are brought to the WTO. In my experience, governments need a high degree of confidence in success before bringing a case, well better than 50–50. There can be a high political cost for complaining and losing, not only in Geneva, but at home.

43 Article 22.3 of the PICTA provides for submission to arbitration only if mediation has failed.

44 Of the Pacific Islands Countries, only Papua New Guinea, Samoa, Tonga and Fiji are members as of 29 May 2012, although Vanuatu will become a member 30 days after it notifies domestic ratification of the accession package approved by the WTO General Council on 26 October 2011. Interestingly, non-membership of the WTO by some parties may not necessarily be an impediment to participation in WTO arbitral processes where key interests of a group of developing countries is affected: the WTO arbitrator in the *Bananas* arbitrations (see *European Communities – the ACP-EC Partnership Agreement – Recourse to Arbitration Pursuant to the Decision of 14 November 2001*, WT/L/616, 1 August 2005) did not take issue with the participation of ACP country Cape Verde in the arbitration, notwithstanding that it was not a WTO member at the time.

45 As illustrated by the constitutional challenge to Chapter 19 filed in the United States as a result of softwood lumber developments in 2001–2006 (see *Coalition for Fair Lumber Imports Executive Committee v United States* (Civil Action No. 05–1366 (D.C. Cir.)). The challenge was withdrawn as part of the 2006 softwood lumber resolution reached between the United States and Canada, the text of which is available online at www.ustr.gov/webfm_send/3254 (accessed 23 June 2012).

46 Such a system would need to have regard to other relevant international obligations, which include, for at least those of the countries negotiating PACER Plus that are WTO members, those set forth in Article 11 of the WTO Agreement on Customs Valuation or Article X of the GATT 1994.

47 The term 'spaghetti bowl' was first coined by Professor Bhagwati in 1995, see Bhagwati 1995. The description has since become a standard part of the trade lexicon, even referred to in speeches by the WTO Director General: see for example Lamy (31 October 2006).

48 The 'stepping stone' and 'stumbling blocks' expression appears in literature dating back at least as far as the 'spaghetti bowl' metaphor mentioned above. An example from the WTO Director General, prior to his current appointment, is Lamy 2002.

3 Exploring the differences between WTO and investment treaty dispute resolution

Daniel Kalderimis[1]

Introduction

A common topic at trade law conferences is the operation of the WTO Dispute Settlement Understanding (the DSU)[2] and, in particular, that forum's evolving dynamic between politics and adjudication.[3]

Less well explored is the relationship between WTO dispute settlement and investment treaty arbitration, the corresponding dispute resolution system for international investment. Although the WTO's reach technically extends beyond goods and services to investments,[4] international investment protection is overwhelmingly regulated through an ad hoc system of over 2600 investment agreements contained in bilateral investment treaties (BITs) or the investment chapters of regional free trade agreements (FTAs).[5]

In keeping with the theme of exploring how existing trade agreements should be implemented and future ones should be negotiated, I contend that there is something to be learned from comparing the way these two dispute resolution systems operate. Both have been in operation for roughly two decades,[6] in which time their internal procedures have come under increased pressure from external stakeholders. New international dispute resolution systems (such as for carbon credit disputes)[7] are likely to look to these existing, increasingly venerable, models for guidance. Moreover, many FTAs now typically include versions of *both* models. The NZ/China FTA is a good example: Chapter 16 provides for state-to-state trade dispute settlement; Chapter 11 provides for investor-to-state investment dispute settlement.[8] Both chapters provide for binding settlement by arbitration. At present, one might suppose that a Chapter 16 arbitration would resemble a WTO panel hearing and a Chapter 11 arbitration a BIT hearing. But should this be so; and will it remain so five or ten years from now?

In this chapter, I explore the systemic and cultural differences between the two models and offer some thoughts for the future. My starting point is that the division between trade and investment is both very real and essentially arbitrary. For all their commercial interconnectedness – one person's trade in services through cross-border commercial presence is another person's foreign direct investment – international trade and investment continue to operate on separate legal planes. There is no good economic or juridical reason for this. The reason belongs to history and politics.[9]

The different systems continue to reflect the different cultures of trade law negotiation (which gave rise to the WTO) and international commercial arbitration (on which investment treaty arbitrations have been modelled). Today, these differences can be described broadly as 'diplomatic/technocratic' and 'lawyerly/ corporate'. Though, like all dispute settlement systems, the two systems follow a broadly comparable process, there are significant variations in procedure, evidence, strategy and technique. In this chapter, I first discuss some examples and then consider some future implications.

The WTO approach to dispute settlement

The WTO is one of the world's most successful multilateral organisations, with 154 Member States.[10] It has become conventional to speak of the DSU as being the 'crown jewel' of the WTO system,[11] and of the DSU's operations as evidencing the 'legalisation' of the WTO.[12]

As with any process, however, the legalisation of the WTO is a relative concept – it all depends on where you have started and how far you have come. The GATT 1947 disputes process was effectively a diplomatic club, which Robert Hudec described as being 'wrapped in layers of diplomatic vagueness and indirection'.[13] It is fair to say that the WTO DSU, though now recognisably legal, remains strongly infused with diplomatic flavour. No doubt the creation of the Appellate Body, the adoption of the reverse consensus rule[14] and the drafting of dedicated dispute resolution procedures[15] has shifted the world trading system into a new juridical paradigm. And no doubt it has worked well. But, this is *in spite of* – though some might argue *because of* – rules of procedure which remain fairly basic.

Below, I concentrate on panel procedures and not on the Appellate Body process.

The nature of WTO dispute settlement is set out in DSU, Article 3.2, which recites that the dispute settlement system is 'a central element in providing security and predictability to the multilateral trading system'. In other words, a core objective of the system is to provide a stable and predictable interpretation of the covered agreements. This, as we shall see, is subtly different from the central objective of commercial arbitration, which is to produce a valid and enforceable award after giving both parties a full opportunity to be heard.

The ambassadorial tone of the WTO panel process can be gleaned from the rules on panel appointment set out in DSU, Article 8. The WTO Secretariat is required to maintain an 'indicative list' of appropriate panellists, which is updated every two years.[16] The individuals on the list are usually, though not always, trade diplomats. New Zealand's contributions to the list, which as at 21 May 2012 included Trade Minister Tim Groser, Crawford Falconer and David Walker, did not feature any legal academics or practising lawyers.[17]

Neither party has a unilateral right to appoint any of the three (or, exceptionally, five) panellists. Rather, it is the role of the WTO Secretariat to propose panel nominations to the parties – by convention, from the list – who shall 'not oppose nominations except for compelling reasons'.[18] If the parties cannot agree on the composition of the panel, either party may request the WTO's Director-General to appoint the panellists.

Panels sit in diplomatic meeting rooms at the WTO in Geneva. Although it has now been confirmed that parties may use private lawyers – a point which was debated in 1997 before the Appellate Body (see *EC-Bananas III*)[19] – party 'delegations' are often relatively large and include senior officials, both those based in Geneva and from the home country.

A panel's task is then described in Articles 6 through 16. I do not go through each provision, but merely summarise the highlights.

Article 7(1) establishes the default terms of reference of panels which, reflecting Article 3(2), are:

> ...[t]o examine, in the light of the relevant provisions in (name of the covered agreement(s) cited by the parties to the dispute), the matter referred to the DSB by (name of party) in document ... and to make such findings as will assist the DSB in making the recommendations or in giving the rulings provided for in that/those agreement(s).

Article 11 describes the function of panels, which is:

> ...to assist the DSB in discharging its responsibilities under this Understanding and the covered agreements. Accordingly, a panel should make an objective assessment of the matter before it, including an objective assessment of the facts of the case and the applicability of and conformity with the relevant covered agreements, and make such other findings as will assist the DSB in making the recommendations or in giving the rulings provided for in the covered agreements. Panels should consult regularly with the parties to the dispute and give them adequate opportunity to develop a mutually satisfactory solution.[20]

It is thus the Dispute Settlement Body (DSB) – a political entity rather than a judicial organ – which is empowered to establish panels, adopt panel reports and monitor compliance. A panel report is technically a recommendation to the DSB and not a decision. Some would say this is merely a matter of form. But there are indications that panels are careful not to overstep their role in the system. Although the Appellate Body has endorsed panels exercising judicial economy (meaning not addressing arguments which cannot affect the outcome of the dispute),[21] panels have in a number of cases applied an *arguendo* technique of tentatively rejecting a legal argument advanced by one of the parties and then considering at length the position which would obtain were that argument to be correct.[22] This approach of hedging one's bets reflects a somewhat diplomatic and conciliatory, rather than legal and doctrinal, approach to interpreting agreements.[23]

Article 12(1) provides that panels should, as a default, follow the Appendix 3 Working Procedures. These provide for a very basic order and format of the procedure leading to a two-part hearing, comprising a 'first substantive meeting' – at which the parties' primary cases are presented; and a 'second substantive meeting' – at which the parties' rebuttal cases are presented. The timing of panel reports is very tight: they are expected to be produced within nine months.[24] Although there is the power to extend the time, this timeframe focuses the approach of both the panel and the parties.[25]

This basic procedure is supplemented by specific panel powers:

a   Article 9, which provides the power to consolidate proceedings by combining claims brought by multiple claimants;
b   Article 10, which addresses the rights of third parties to make written submissions to and be heard by a panel. This is frequently used;
c   Article 13, which defines, extremely widely, the panels' right to seek information;
d   Article 14, which provides that panel deliberations shall be confidential; and
e   Article 15, which provides that the panel shall submit its draft report to the parties for an interim review.

These simple rules are the real power behind the 'crown jewels'. A panel hearing is where the facts are determined. While the Appellate Body has the power to uphold, modify or reverse panel findings on issues of law, and will complete the legal analysis of panels, it does not undertake a *de novo* review.[26] There is no right for the Appellate Body to remit cases for reconsideration by panels. In many ways, these guidelines for panel fact-finding are more interesting for what they do not say, than for what they do.

To begin with, there are no rules for the adducing of documentary or factual evidence. Instead, paragraph 4 of Appendix 3 provides 'the parties to the dispute shall transmit to the panel written submissions in which they present the facts of the case and their arguments'. To a litigator, this seems perilously close to conflating submissions and evidence. There is no general procedure for determining the authenticity of documents or the admissibility of evidence. Everything is a question of weight.[27]

Equally, there is no general procedure for disclosure between parties, and certainly not for the subpoena or deposition of a witness from the other party. Only one specific disclosure procedure exists in the whole suite of WTO Agreements, which is Annex V of the Subsidies Agreement, relating to subsidisation. It is possible for a party to seek information during pre-dispute consultations,[28] but there is no obligation on the responsive party to provide it. Although a panel has an Article 13 right to seek information from any party (indeed, any Member), there is no formal process for a party to present a document request through the panel.

Some other specific evidentiary tools do exist and are listed in Appendix 2 to the DSU. For instance, the Subsidies and Anti-Dumping Agreements contain provisions relating to investigations by parties of subsidisation and dumping;[29] and the SPS Agreement and TBT Agreements have special rules relating to expert evidence and require parties promptly to publish their SPS/TBT regulations and establish enquiry points to provide information.[30] The touchstone, however, is inquisitorial accuracy rather than adversarial due process. Not only are there no firm rules as to whether or how evidence should be obtained, adduced or admitted, but there are no rules for whether a witness or expert is competent or when it is appropriate for a panel to take judicial notice of a fact.[31] This flexibility has led to a variety of approaches to panel hearings. It appears that evidence can be given from the 'bar' as it were, as part of the submissions advanced by a party. It also appears, from the Appellate Body decision in *Thailand-Steel*, that a panel may base its findings on confidential evidence which is not disclosed to the other side.[32] Parties' cases are typically based on their own documents, which are provided with their brief. The main other source of information is publicly available government documents.[33] Fact witnesses do not generally appear, although affidavits and witness statements are beginning to be used.[34]

As one textbook has succinctly described the process: 'it is mainly just arguments and documentation provided by the parties, with questions from the panel'.[35] There is some possibility for the use of adverse inferences where a party has not complied with an information request from a panel.[36] However, panels lack the powers often associated with arbitral or other international tribunals to order provisional measures or injunctive relief.

A partial exception to the informal evidential process is the use of expert evidence. Parties cannot appoint their own expert witnesses, though they can have experts sit with them as members of their delegation. Appendix 4 to the DSU empowers a panel to appoint an expert review group, but, to my knowledge, no panel has yet done so.[37] Instead, panels have utilised their broad investigative powers under Article 13(2) to appoint individual experts. An expert will usually prepare his or her report in time for the second substantive hearing. The parties have no right to cross-examine the expert, who is there to assist the panel, but will often prepare questions for the panel to submit to the expert. It is possible, however, for the panel to permit direct questioning. Where cross-examination is allowed, it is fairly rudimentary and time-limited. Experts have been particularly widely used in SPS and TBT cases.[38] In some cases, panels have also relied upon expert evidence/submission from a party delegation.[39]

In short, and despite the increasing use of external legal counsel, WTO panels operate in a centralised, diplomatic, relatively speedy and inexpensive fashion. The WTO's rules of procedure and evidence are informal, but the end products – as will testify anyone who has ever read a panel report – are highly technical. And, of course, although this chapter does not touch upon it directly, the WTO system also has a permanent Appellate Body, which further systematises and centralises the process.

The BIT arbitration approach to dispute settlement

In contrast with the WTO DSU, and perhaps not unrelated to the dominant influence of lawyers in shaping and navigating the system, investment treaty arbitration operates in a decentralised, commercial, tactical, and often protracted and expensive fashion. The process is somewhat uneven, with no appeals (although there is the ICSID annulment system) and a prominent network of advocates and arbitrators who can appear interchangeably at different stages of the process.

To provide a little background, investment treaty arbitration arises, as its name suggests, out of a BIT or FTA investment chapter. Unlike the WTO system, and FTA chapters relating to goods and services, it is customary for investment rights to be directly enforceable by an investor against a host state using international arbitration. This is facilitated by a clause in the investment treaty or chapter by which both states' parties agree to arbitrate any qualifying dispute. That standing offer of arbitration is converted into an arbitration agreement by the investor filing a request for arbitration with the relevant institution.

As stated above, there is no WTO multilateral equivalent for international investment protection. Instead, the system is a patchwork of over 2600 BITs and investment chapters, all separately providing for binding arbitration of disputes. Most investment treaties/chapters offer aggrieved investors two or more options of different forms of arbitration through which they can pursue their claims. One common form is arbitration under the Convention on the Settlement of Investment Disputes between States and Nationals of Other States 1966 (ICSID Convention), which has 148 Member States[40] and its own dedicated Arbitration Rules.[41] Another common form is arbitration under the UNCITRAL Rules of Arbitration. These, for instance, are the two options provided to investors in Article 153 of the NZ/China FTA.

The two systems work slightly differently. When an investor files a request for arbitration under the ICSID Convention, the arbitration is administered by the ICSID Secretariat, which can assist with appointing arbitrators and providing facilities at its Washington DC headquarters. Where an arbitration is commenced under the UNCITRAL Rules, the system is entirely ad hoc. There is no secretariat (which can sometimes make appointing a tribunal somewhat tricky) and no oversight, save through national court powers and procedures. The procedure is determined and overseen by the tribunal.

Most investment treaties/chapters anticipate three-person tribunals. Both the ICSID and the UNCITRAL Rules permit each side to appoint one arbitrator, with the presiding arbitrator appointed by agreement of the parties (in the case of the ICSID Convention, with a default procedure in the absence of agreement)[42] or by agreement of the two party-appointed arbitrators (in the case of the UNCITRAL Rules, with a default procedure in the absence of agreement).[43] There is no limitation – apart from fundamental impartiality and independence rules – as to who can sit as an UNCITRAL arbitrator. The ICSID Convention additionally requires that, unless the parties agree otherwise, they may not appoint a national of either party.[44] ICSID keeps a default list of panellists,[45] but there is no requirement for parties to select from it. The arbitrators on the list are, almost without exception, lawyers. For instance, New Zealand's panellists – Sir Kenneth Keith KBE, David Williams QC, Campbell McLachlan QC and Sir Ian Barker QC – are all eminent jurists and, save for Professor McLachlan QC, present or former judges.[46]

ICSID awards may be annulled using a very restrictive procedure specified in Article 52 of the ICSID Convention. As at the end of 2011, 38 annulment applications had been filed, of which only 11 had been successful in whole or in part.[47] There is no standing Annulment Body. Instead, ad hoc annulment tribunals are appointed by ICSID.

UNCITRAL awards may be challenged or appealed on questions of law, according to the arbitration legislation of the place the arbitration is held. For instance, the default rule in New Zealand is that an arbitration award may be challenged for serious procedural defects, but not appealed on questions of law.[48]

So much for the overall framework: what about the procedure?

The ICSID Arbitration Rules provide that the tribunal must hold its first session within 60 days or such other period as the parties may agree. This first procedural meeting sets the timetable for the first stage of the dispute, which is typically a jurisdictional challenge. This is one respect in which investment disputes procedurally differ from WTO disputes. Whereas a WTO panel automatically has jurisdiction to hear complaints by Members about alleged breaches of covered agreements,[49] investment arbitral tribunals are only entitled to hear disputes falling within the scope of the standing arbitration clause: that is, disputes brought by a qualifying investor of the home country with respect to a covered investment, in accordance with the provisions of the relevant investment treaty. Where the dispute is also an ICSID arbitration, the additional jurisdictional requirements in Article 25 of the ICSID Convention must also be satisfied.[50]

Although one might think that these sorts of jurisdictional questions would be relatively straightforward, they have in fact occasioned great debate. Three examples might suffice. In *Soufraki*,[51] an arbitral tribunal ruled, and an annulment review upheld, that the claimant was not an Italian national for the purposes of the relevant BIT and the ICSID Convention, despite him holding an Italian passport and the Italian government certifying his Italian nationality in the arbitration. Second, in recent years there has been great debate over whether the concept of investment imports a requirement to contribute to the development of the host economy, with different views continuing to be taken.[52] Third, and as an example only of the various procedural roadblocks which may arise from the relevant treaty language, in 2009 a sole arbitrator enforced a 'fork-in-the-road' provision, pursuant to which the investor is deprived of recourse to investor-state arbitration because it had previously chosen to pursue the same claims before the host state's national courts.[53]

This jurisdictional/merits bifurcation means that most investment treaty cases take well over two years from the filing of a request for arbitration to an award on the merits.

The process is more formal than a WTO panel hearing. This may not be obvious from perusing the ICSID Arbitration Rules (see Rules 29–38) and the UNCITRAL Arbitration Rules (see Articles 17–32). Both, like the DSU, provide:

1 for the filing of written pleadings and evidence, followed by an oral hearing;
2 a power for the tribunal to order a party to produce documents (ICSID Arbitration Rules, Rule 34(2)(a); UNCITRAL Arbitration Rules, Article 27(3)); and
3 that there are no formal evidential rules of admissibility or weight (ICSID Arbitration Rules, Rule 34(1); UNCITRAL Arbitration Rules, Article 27(4)).

Both, however, also contemplate that the oral hearing will be genuinely evidentiary. The ICSID Arbitration Rules thus provide expressly for the examination of fact and expert witnesses by the parties (Rule 35) and the UNCITRAL Arbitration Rules allow for the live hearing of witnesses and for the use of witness statements (Articles 28 and 27(2)). Transcripts of these hearings, often produced in real time, are routine. Further, relatively standardised international arbitration procedures have now emerged, which are helpfully summarised in the *International Bar Association Rules for the Taking of Evidence in Commercial Arbitrations*. These are typically incorporated by reference into a tribunal's first procedural order, either as a controlling procedure or as a referent. Even if they are not, they are habitually referred to. The compromise reached in these rules between civil and common law court procedure has become the default approach to evidential issues in international arbitrations, including investment arbitrations.

Thus, investment arbitrations typically involve a form of disclosure, based upon requests for documents and responses to those requests which, in the case of a dispute, go to the tribunal for determination. Documents can also be provided to accompany written pleadings. Fact evidence, in the form of written witness statements, is typically exchanged well in advance of an evidential hearing, as are rebuttal witness statements. Parties typically appoint their own expert witnesses. Though tribunals are empowered to appoint their own expert, it is relatively uncommon that they do so. All witnesses will then usually be cross-examined. Experts are sometimes 'hot-tubbed' or 'conferenced', in which case, they will be present on the stand at the same time, and be able to field and discuss questions together. Sometimes they are also asked to file a joint report noting areas of agreement and disagreement.

Arbitral tribunals have powers to award injunctions (in some jurisdictions, *ex parte*) and a range of remedies, including damages, which a WTO panel cannot order. It is also possible to obtain injunctions from domestic courts in support of an arbitral agreement or arbitral order.[54]

International arbitration standard practice is really a diluted form of adversarial litigation procedure, with the fundamental objective, as stated in Article 17(1) of the UNCITRAL Arbitration Rules:

[s]ubject to these Rules, the arbitral tribunal may conduct the arbitration in such manner as it considers appropriate, provided that the parties are treated

with equality and that at any stage of the proceedings *each party is given a full opportunity of presenting its case* [emphasis added].

This is, in fact, the fundamental objective of *any* arbitral tribunal, whatever the governing procedural rules. Whereas an UNCITRAL tribunal must produce an award which will be enforceable in a domestic court according to the standards prescribed in the New York Convention,[55] an ICSID tribunal must produce an award which will withstand annulment by an ad hoc committee under Article 52(1) of the ICSID Convention. The essence of both Article V of the New York Convention and Article 52(1) of the ICSID Convention is procedural fairness. Provided the parties have been accorded a proper opportunity to be heard, and the tribunal has been properly constituted, remained within its jurisdiction and provided sufficient reasons, its award is very likely to stand.

Two systems developing in parallel

Despite their diverse traditions, the WTO and investment treaty systems have faced remarkably similar issues over recent years, such as whether and how to receive amicus curiae briefs, whether to permit open access to hearings, how to safeguard 'judicial' standards and address conflicts of interest, whether to recognise a doctrine of precedent and how to reconcile trade/investment disciplines with non-economic values. Although not identical, they are dealing with these issues in comparable ways.

Amicus briefs

The *amicus* debate has proved a lightning rod for both systems. In the WTO system, this issue was raised controversially in the *US – Shrimp* dispute (where the Appellate Body ruled that, pursuant to Article 13 of the DSU, panels had the right to accept amicus briefs)[56] and brought to a head in 2000 in *EC – Asbestos* (in which the Appellate Body promulgated procedures pursuant to Rule 16(1) of the Working Procedures for Appellate Review for the submission of amicus briefs).[57] Even though the Appellate Body rejected every one of the 18 amicus briefs filed in that case, many WTO Members considered formal procedures a step too far and delivered a rebuke to the Appellate Body.[58] This controversy has been described as 'a typical example of the ethos of diplomats ... coming into head-on collision with the rule of lawyers'.[59] The result of this collision appears to have been that the vast majority of amicus briefs are rejected by WTO panels and the Appellate Body; and, if accepted, are not given much, or any, weight.[60]

In the early 2000s, amicus briefs were accepted by two NAFTA[61] arbitral tribunals constituted under the UNCITRAL Rules, using general case management powers: *Methanex v United States*[62] and *UPS v Canada*.[63] On a similar basis, amicus briefs were accepted by tribunals in two ICSID disputes against Argentina in 2005 and 2006.[64] The situation has since been clarified for NAFTA and ICSID arbitrations. The NAFTA Free Trade Commission in 2004 issued guidelines for the acceptance of amicus briefs,[65] which were applied in *Glamis Gold v United States*.[66] The ICSID Arbitration Rules were amended in 2006 expressly to permit the filing of amicus briefs[67] and these new rules were recently applied in *Biwater Gauff v Tanzania*.[68] Proposals were made, but not ultimately accepted, to amend the UNCITRAL Rules expressly to permit and regulate the filing of such briefs in investment treaty cases.[69]

Transparency

A separate, but related, issue is access to hearings by non-parties. Athough the DSU is silent as to whether hearings should be open or closed, in practice they have not been open to the public.[70] WTO disputing parties are increasingly, though certainly not universally, opting for public hearings. For instance, the public were admitted by agreement to a 2007 hearing in *EC-Bananas III* and to the *Australia v NZ Apples* hearings in September 2008 and June/July 2009. The *US – Country of Origin Labelling* hearings in December 2010 were open and, most recently, the *Canada – Renewable Energy* hearing was split into an open hearing (March 2012) and a closed one (May 2012). While Canada, the United States, the European Communities and Japan have favoured openness, other powerful members oppose it, such as Brazil, China, Mexico and India. As part of the DSU review, the United States is seeking to open all panel and Appellate Body hearings to the public.[71]

Article 28(3) of the UNCITRAL Arbitration Rules also provides that hearings shall be closed. In contrast, the US and Canada's non-binding position is that all NAFTA arbitrations should be public.[72] This has been the agreed position for most, if not all, NAFTA hearings since 2003, including those held under the UNCITRAL Arbitration Rules.[73] Historically, ICSID arbitrations were also closed; thus a tribunal presiding over a dispute against Bolivia in 2003, and a tribunal presiding over a dispute against Argentina in 2005, each declined access to NGO attendance.[74] The ICSID Arbitration Rules now expressly permit a non-party to apply for leave to attend hearings.[75] The US Model BIT provides both for open hearings (Clause 29(2)) and the filing of amicus briefs (Clause 28(3)).

There is a growing trend for even greater transparency, with both WTO reports and arbitration awards now routinely published and available online, often together with voluntary publication of a party's pleadings.[76]

Regulating conflicts of interest

The WTO has generated Rules of Conduct, which apply to panels, the Appellate Body and expert witnesses, setting standards of independence and impartiality.[77] The governing principle of these Rules provides that each person covered by them 'shall be independent and impartial, shall avoid direct or indirect conflicts of interest and shall respect the confidentiality of proceedings'.[78] A similar, though perhaps more controversial, attempt was made for international arbitration by the IBA, which produced *Guidelines for Conflicts of Interest in*

International Arbitration.[79] These detailed, but non-binding, Guidelines divided potential conflicts into Green, Amber and Red lists. Some have felt that their precision has been less, rather than more, helpful and they have not set a de facto standard, as have the IBA's Rules of Evidence. While investment treaty case law is now replete with adversarial challenges to arbitral independence (with the result that detailed case law is being produced),[80] the WTO conflict of interest rules have been rarely applied and tested. This is perhaps an example of how the cultures of the investment treaty arbitration and WTO dispute settlement systems differ.

Incorporating non-trade or investment values

Moving from the procedural to the substantive, both systems have grappled with how to balance enforcing the obligations central to the trading/investment system with non-trade and investment values. The Appellate Body, in a range of well-known cases from *US - Shrimp*[81] to *US – Gambling*,[82] has an established jurisprudence for applying the general exception provisions in GATT Article XX and GATS Article XIV. This permits members to determine their own domestic policy objectives, and then accords a margin of appreciation to the measures taken to achieve those objectives, with a sliding scale of deference reflecting the relative importance of the interest or values at stake.[83] This has injected flexibility into the WTO and made it easier to link the WTO with non-trade values.

Investment treaty tribunals, generally lacking general exception provisions to apply, have taken one of three options: applied the substantive investment protection without any form of balancing; found some way to read down the substantive protection, often by reference to customary international law; or sought to utilise non-precluded measures clauses found in some older BITS, typically involving the US.[84] All of these approaches have been seen in the *US/Argentina* cases, which remain the richest – and most controversial – source of investment treaty case law to date.

Applying precedents

While neither the WTO nor the investment treaty system observes a formal doctrine of precedent,[85] there is now extensive reference in both systems to prior decisions. A de facto doctrine of precedent – or at least close consideration of the *corpus* of case law – is now emerging. This is happening in a more coordinated fashion in the WTO, due to the role and authority of the Appellate Body. Thus in *US – Stainless Steel (Mexico)* the Appellate Body said that ensuring 'security and predictability' in line with art 3.2 of the DSU implied that 'absent cogent reasons, an adjudicatory body will resolve the same legal question in the same way in a subsequent case'.[86]

Some – though by no means all – investment treaty tribunals are making increasingly bold statements in this regard. To give one example, in 2009 the NAFTA *Glamis Gold* arbitral opined:[87]

The reality is that Chapter 11 of the NAFTA contains a significant public system of private investment protection. The ultimate integrity of the protections given to the many individual investments made under Chapter 11 is ensured by reference to a multitude of arbitral panels occupied by persons who are only occasionally reappointed. The ultimate integrity of the Chapter 11 system as a whole requires a modicum of awareness of each of these tribunals for each other and the system as a whole.

Enforcement of decisions and awards

Finally, both the WTO and investment treaty arbitration have faced enforcement difficulties. In the WTO, the focus is on ensuring compliance. The only binding remedy for non-compliance is the right of the winning party to suspend concessions. This can be a difficult remedy. First, it is protectionist – rather perversely responding to a trade-limiting measure by authorising another. Second, not all parties have appropriate or effective trade-limiting measures at their disposal. This has raised the spectre of cross-retaliation under a different agreement, often TRIPS. Applications to cross-retaliate were made and approved by Ecuador in *EC – Bananas III*[88] and Antigua in *US – Gambling*,[89] but not implemented; and Brazil gained approval in *US-Cotton* but has not implemented the measures.[90] The United States opened up a new spectre of cross-retaliation in the *EC – Aircraft* dispute,[91] in which it applied to cross-retaliate against breaches of the SCM agreement by suspending GATS concessions.[92] However, the Article 22.6 arbitration was suspended in January 2012 on the parties' request.

In investment treaty arbitration, where the typical remedy is money damages, the problem is evidenced by the *US/Argentina* cases.[93] The ICSID system, like the WTO system, relies in practice upon voluntary compliance. Argentina's response to investors seeking to enforce awards has been to invite them to do so by applying to have them registered in an Argentina court. This is not realistic, but has left claimants with little effective recourse. We are starting to see two responses. First, Bolivia (in 2007) and Ecuador (in 2009) formally denounced their adherence to the ICSID Convention,[94] hoping to avoid in their cases the pressure which a steady stream of awards has built up against, for instance, Argentina.[95] Second, claimants are attempting more audacious forms of enforcement, such as seeking worldwide freezing orders from courts in New York or London,[96] or awaiting opportunities to execute awards over offshore commercial assets of host states.[97]

If anything shows both the similarity and the differences between WTO and investment treaty dispute resolution it is the approach to enforcement. Both systems are working generally, though not very well for the hard cases. The response in the WTO is tortuous diplomacy – enforcement, sequencing and the question of compensation are all on the agenda for the DSU review, which has now run for more than 10 years. The response for investment treaty arbitration is strategic worldwide litigation, which runs the risk of killing (or perhaps maiming) the golden goose.

Where to from here?

Over the medium term, further convergence between the two systems is inevitable. Trade and investment are discrete – and often very closely related – points along a commercial continuum. Many of the key concepts, such as national treatment and fair and equitable treatment, underpin both systems.

Even now, cross-fertilisation is happening. For instance, there have been several cases where the same dispute has triggered both WTO and arbitration procedures. For instance, the *US/Canada Softwood Lumber* dispute – which involved US duties imposed on Canadian lumber the US claimed was illegitimately subsidised – played out in front of NAFTA and the WTO for several years before the parties reached a 2006 settlement agreement[98] which provided for disputes to be determined by LCIA arbitration.[99] Three proceedings have now been commenced alleging breaches of this settlement agreement, with the most recent heard in February and March 2012.[100] In 2001, Mexico responded to what it considered to be the US's failure to accord Mexico an agreed NAFTA sugar quota by imposing taxes on the imports of US soft drinks. The US successfully challenged these taxes in the WTO.[101] In addition, a private investor took preliminary steps to launch investment treaty arbitration against Mexico for an alleged breach of NAFTA's investment chapter.[102] Similarly, in a dispute between Brazil and Argentina relating to the latter's anti-dumping duties on the former's chicken imports, Argentina unsuccessfully argued that the WTO panel should decline to rule because Brazil had previously and unsuccessfully challenged the duties through a Mercosur ad hoc arbitral tribunal.[103]

More recently the plain packaging tobacco disputes are being pursued through parallel proceedings, with Phillip Morris filing a request for ICSID arbitration against both Uruguay (under the Switzerland–Uruguay BIT)[104] and Australia (under the Hong Kong–Australia BIT);[105] and Ukraine[106] and Honduras[107] requesting consultations (a preliminary step to commence the WTO dispute settlement process) with Australia alleging potential breaches of the TRIPS or TBT agreements.

Even where specific disputes do not overlap, the investment treaty system has frequently borrowed from the jurisprudence of its more mature sibling.[108] Several figures in the trade law world, such as Dr Federico Ortino, are also figures in the investment world. I expect we will see more of these kinds of overlaps and synergies in the future.

Nonetheless, the two systems have some important formal procedural differences, of which the three most marked are *the standing issue* (only states may access the WTO system, whereas investment treaty arbitration is investor-state); *the remedies available* (the only binding WTO remedy is an authorisation to suspend concessions or impose trade remedies, whereas investment treaty arbitration involves money damages);[109] and *the appellate system* (the WTO has a standing Appellate Body and investment treaty arbitration does not).

Underlying these stark differences are a host of different assumptions which can be seen most clearly in the different ways in which cases are presented and evidence is obtained and adduced. In the WTO, evidence is obtained and adduced through an inquisitorial procedure with more than a trace of a diplomatic meeting about it. In investment treaty arbitration, it is obtained and adduced according to adversarial rules which would not be out of place in a domestic courtroom.

This is an interesting comparison for two reasons. First, because we are still in the early days of the 'noodle bowl' of free trade agreements, which often contain both WTO facsimiles in their goods and services chapters and BIT facsimiles in their investment chapters. The next generation of IEL lawyers are being trained to understand both trade and investment issues. It may not be long before officials negotiating new FTAs or amendments to existing FTAs sit down and ask themselves whether two entirely different disputes procedures are required within the same instrument, or whether one or the other seems to work best. If direct enforcement is more effective, why not allow exporters the right to take cases directly and be awarded damages? If investment arbitration has legitimacy problems, why not require permanent checks and balances, such as state-party vetting, espousal or centralised appeals?

In other words, we may be witnessing a battle akin to 'Beta vs VHS'. I hope not, however, because neither system is flawless. Indeed, they have diametric strengths and weaknesses.

The WTO DSU has been more assiduous in deciding trade disputes which engage other policy interests. But its informal process is unlikely to cope as complaints become increasingly fact-intensive. The greater the complexity, the more important the rigour of the fact-finding process. Principles of adversarial procedural fairness, such as equality of arms and a right to test the opponent's case, are likely to further infiltrate the WTO process. Information from private companies is also likely to become essential to the just resolution of (particularly trade remedies) disputes.[110] There is nothing wrong with inquisitorial procedures per se, but they only work effectively when controlled by experienced judges with strong investigative powers who are not afraid to use them. That does not describe a WTO panel.

Investment treaty arbitration, while more robust as a litigation process, is significantly less advanced in how it addresses stakeholder concerns. It is now a common critique that the commercial genesis of investment arbitration has partially obscured the public or administrative aspects of the process.[111]

Is the net result likely to be a messy third way – that WTO and investment treaty procedures may over time combine into a *mélange* of both?

I think two things can be said for sure. First, litigation craft will be increasingly important in the future. The amateur approach of the WTO is giving way to a professional era of dispute resolution. Many parties are now represented by private law firms and this trend will continue.[112] Some diplomatic culture will, no doubt, always remain. But a default form of document disclosure and cross-examination would seem to be on the horizon. I do not think the ongoing review of the DSU will come as far as I am suggesting. But I would not bank on this being the last revision we see.

Second, transparency and legitimacy will become increasingly important. I doubt the pressure for the investment treaty process to include a right of appeal or a better annulment procedure is going to dissipate. The flaws in the growing system have been exposed by, and heavily critiqued following, the early *US/Argentina* cases.[113] In time I also expect that investment treaty lawyers (or their clients) are likely to self-regulate so as to sit less interchangeably as counsel, party-appointed experts, arbitrators and annulment panellists.

In making these predictions an important question is whether the WTO's more primitive procedures are necessarily connected with its greater legitimacy – implying that if we change the former, we will lose the latter. I do not think so. The WTO's legitimacy seems to me to derive from better balanced agreements and greater oversight from the Appellate Body, as well as from the DSB and the General Council; rather than from informal panel procedures.

I hope I am right because I suspect the trend towards greater legalisation is all one way. Regionalisation, fragmentation and the breakdown of states as gate-keepers of international law make investment treaty arbitration likely to be the more enduring model. In the near term, further trade concessions are likely to be obtained through regional FTAs rather than the WTO. Investment treaty arbitration's direct access by private investors has led to a sustained upswing in new cases. Although less mature, it is growing faster. The 'privatisation of globalisation' will exacerbate this trend.

A final question is how trade and investment disputes will be framed, or conceptualised, as both systems mature. This is more a question for academics than practitioners. Will they be seen as primarily commercial – and borrow mostly from the world of arbitration; or as requiring a knowledge of and sensitivity to politics and diplomacy – and thus reflect the legacy of the GATT? The answer remains to be seen.

To conclude, I say only this. Both systems are being increasingly, and properly, understood as forms of global administrative law. This implies due process, and likely a more legalistic process. But it also implies greater sensitivity to stakeholders and appearance. As a litigator, I would rather conduct a BIT dispute, as investment treaty arbitration offers greater procedural support for parties to build their own case and attack their opponent's case. In short, its *inputs* are arguably better. As a stakeholder of both systems, however, I believe the WTO system is presently striking a better balance of competing policy rights and sensitivity to other values and interests. In short, its *outputs* are arguably better. The *mélange* idea may yet have something going for it.

Notes

1 Daniel Kalderimis is a Partner at Chapman Tripp, Wellington, New Zealand.
2 More formally, the Understanding on Rules and Procedures Governing the Settlement of Disputes, which appears as Annex 2 to the Final Act of the Uruguay Round.
3 A topic given renewed emphasis by the review of the DSU in parallel with – though not formally as part of – the Doha single undertaking negotiations. See Prost 2005: 202; and Mercurio 2004: 796–7.

4 See, for example, the Agreement on Trade-Related Investment Measures and the General Agreement on Trade in Services, which extends to the supply of services through cross-border commercial presence; see Article I(2)(c)).

5 See UNCTAD (2008–9).

6 Although BITs have been around for over 50 years (the first BIT was concluded between the Federal Republic of Germany and Pakistan in 1959: see Lowenfeld 2008: 554–5), the modern 'regime' of investment treaty arbitration truly began only during the 1990s as disputes steadily increased. Similarly, although the General Agreement on Trade and Tariffs dates back to 1947, the WTO commenced with the conclusion of the Uruguay Round in 1994.

7 See Zeller 2009; Ratliff (unpublished); and Vranes 2009a.

8 New Zealand – China Free Trade Agreement, signed 7 April 2008, entered into force 1 October 2008. Online. Available at: www.chinafta.govt.nz/ (accessed 21 May 2012).

9 This includes the history and politics of the OECD's failed 1998 Multilateral Agreement on Investment and the fate of the so-called 'Singapore issues', including investment, at the 2003 WTO Fifth Ministerial Conference in Cancún.

10 See the WTO website. Online. Available at: www.wto.org/english/thewto_e/whatis_e/tif_e/org6_e.htm (accessed 21 May 2012).

11 See, for example, Ehlermann 2002: 639; and Prost 2005: 190.

12 See Busch *et al.* (2009): 1 (describing the DSU as 'one of the most legalistic institutions on the international stage'); and Evans and de Tarso Pereira 2005: 251. See generally Jackson *et al.* 2002: 146–57.

13 Hudec 1999: 10.

14 See DSU Art. 16(4).

15 The procedures of GATT panels were previously codified to some extent during the Tokyo Round in an annex to the 'Understanding on Notification, Consultation, Dispute Settlement and Surveillance of 28 November 1979' entitled 'Agreed Description of the Customary Practice of the GATT in the Field of Dispute Settlement'.

16 See *Indicative List of Governmental and Non-Governmental Panelists*, WT/DSB/33, 6 March 2003.

17 See *Indicative List of Governmental and Non-Governmental Panelists – Revision*, WT/DSB/44/Rev.17, 3 November 2011 (accessed 21 May 2012).

18 See DSU Art. 8(6).

19 Appellate Body Report, *European Communities – Regime for the Importation, Sale and Distribution of Bananas*, WT/DS27/AB/R, adopted 25 September 1997. See generally Mitchell 2005: 154.

20 The standard of review is different for trade remedy disputes, where a panel effectively acts as an appellate entity from the decision of a state investigating authority. See Andersen 2005: 184.

21 Appellate Body Report, *United States – Measure Affecting Imports of Woven Wool Shirts and Blouses from India*, WT/DS33/AB/R, adopted 23 May 1997, and Corr.1, p. 18.

22 See, for example, the panel decision in Panel Report, *Mexico – Definitive Countervailing Measures on Olive Oil from the European Communities*, WT/DS341/R, adopted 21 October 2008. Interestingly, the Appellate Body is *not* entitled to exercise judicial economy but must address each legal issue raised in an appellate proceeding regardless of whether it is necessary to resolve the dispute: DSU Art. 17(12).

23 The same observation has been made, for instance, by Benitah on the International Economic Law and Policy Blog managed by www.worldtradelaw.net (30 July 2008).

24 See DSU Art. 20.

25 This recently happened, for instance, in the NZ/Australia dispute under the SPS

Agreement (*Australia – Measures Affecting the Importation of Apples from New Zealand*, WT/DS367), in which the second substantive hearing was held in July 2009 and the panel's decision was not released until 9 August 2010.

26 See DSU Arts. 17(6) and (13).
27 See Appellate Body Report, *European Communities – Anti-Dumping Duties on Imports of Cotton-Type Bed Linen from India*, WT/DS141/AB/R, adopted 12 March 2001, para. 6.34. An exception to this approach is Annex II to the Anti-Dumping Agreement which contains a 'best information' rule for making decisions about whether goods are being exported for less than their normal price: see Art. 17(6).
28 See DSU Art. 4; and Andersen 2005: 188.
29 See SCM Agreement Art. 12 and Annex VI; and Anti-Dumping Agreement Art. 6(7) and Annex I.
30 See SPS Agreement Art. 11(2) and Annex B; and TBT Agreement Arts. 10 and 14(2) to 14(4).
31 See Andersen 2005: 189.
32 The Appellate Body in this case held that the panel was entitled to base its findings under the Anti-Dumping Agreement on confidential evidence which was available to the Thai investigating authority but not to Poland or any of its representatives. Appellate Body Report, *Thailand – Anti-Dumping Duties on Angles, Shapes and Sections of Iron or Non-Alloy Steel and H-Beams from Poland*, WT/DS122/AB/R, adopted 5 April 2001, paras 107–12 [hereinafter 'Appellate Body Report, *Thailand – H-Beams*']. See also Matsushita, Schoenbaum and Mavroidis 2006: 130.
33 See Andersen 2005: 185.
34 See Andersen 2005: 185.
35 Lester and Mercurio 2008: 219.
36 See, for example, Appellate Body Report, *Canada – Measures Affecting the Export of Civilian Aircraft*, WT/DS70/AB/R, adopted 20 August 1999, para. 203.
37 See Cossy 2005: 209.
38 As to SPS cases, see SPS Agreement Art. 11(2) which mandates the use of experts.
39 See, for example, Panel Report, *Japan – Measures Affecting Agricultural Products*, WT/DS76/R, adopted 19 March 1999, as modified by Appellate Body Report WT/DS76/AB/R.
40 See the ICSID website. Online. Available at: http://icsid.worldbank.org/ICSID/Front Servlet?requestType=CasesRH&actionVal=ShowHome&pageName=MemberStates_ Home (accessed 21 May 2012). Note that there are 158 signatories, but 10 signatory States have not ratified the Convention.
41 See ICSID Convention Art. 6(1)(c).
42 See ICSID Convention Arts. 37–40 and Arbitration Rules, Rule 2.
43 See UNCITRAL Rules Arts. 8–10.
44 See ICSID Convention Art. 39 and Arbitration Rules, Rule 1(3).
45 Termed the Panel of Conciliators and Arbitrators: see ICSID Convention, Section 4.
46 See http://icsid.worldbank.org/ICSID/FrontServlet?requestType=ICSIDDataRH&ac tionVal=SearchPanel (accessed 21 May 2012).
47 ICSID, *The ICSID Caseload – Statistics (Issue 2012–1)*, 15.
48 See Arbitration Act 1996, s 6 and Schedules 1 (art 34) and 2 (cl 5).
49 See DSU Art. 1(1).
50 Pursuant to Article 25, ICSID's jurisdiction extends to: (1) any legal dispute; (2) arising directly out of an investment; (3) between a Contracting State; (4) a national of another Contracting State; and (5) which the parties to the dispute consent in writing to submit to ICSID.
51 *Soufraki v UAE* 2004; *Soufraki v UAE* 2007.
52 See *Salini Costruttori SpA & Anor v Morocco* 2001; *Phoenix Action Ltd v Czech Republic* 2009; and *Malaysian Historical Salvors v Malaysia* 2009.

53 *Pantechniki S.A. Contractors & Engineers v Albania* 2009, applying both a fork-in-the-road provision in the relevant BIT and Article 26 of the ICSID Convention.

54 But see ICSID Arbitration Rule 39(6), which requires the parties' consent to obtaining injunctions from domestic courts in support of ICSID arbitrations.

55 Its full title is the Convention on the Recognition and Enforcement of Foreign Arbitral Awards 1958, with 146 States parties as of May 2012. See: www.uncitral. org/uncitral/en/uncitral_texts/arbitration/NYConvention_status.html (accessed 21 May 2012).

56 Appellate Body Report, *United States – Import Prohibition of Certain Shrimp and Shrimp Products*, WT/DS58/AB/R, adopted 6 November 1998 [hereinafter 'Appellate Body Report, *US – Shrimp*'].

57 Appellate Body Report, *European Communities – Measures Affecting Asbestos and Asbestos-Containing Products*, WT/DS135/AB/R, adopted 5 April 2001 [hereinafter 'Appellate Body Report, *EC – Asbestos*'].

58 See *Minutes of the General Council Meeting of 22 November 2000*, WT/GC/M/60, 23 January 2001.

59 Kuijper 2009: 124.

60 See, for example, Lester and Mercurio 2008: 200; and Durling and Hardin 2005: 224–5.

61 The North American Free Trade Agreement between Canada, the United States and Mexico, which came into force on 1 January 1994.

62 *Methanex v United States* 2001.

63 *United Parcel Service v Canada* 2001.

64 See *Aguas Argentinas, SA, Suez and Vivendi Universal v Argentina* 2005 and *Aguas Provinciales de Santa Fe v Argentina* 2006: *Order in Response to a Petition for Participation as Amicus Curiae*.

65 Statement of the Free Trade Commission on non-disputing party participation (7 October 2004).

66 *Glamis Gold v United States* 2005.

67 See ICSID Arbitration Rule 37(2).

68 *Biwater Gauff (Tanzania) Ltd v Tanzania* 2007.

69 See the submissions from a prominent NGO to this effect (December 2007). Online. Available at: www.iisd.org/pdf/2008/investment_revising_uncitral_arbitration_dec. pdf (accessed 21 May 2012), and an unofficial report prepared by Paulsson and Petrochilos (2006): 133. The revised 2010 UNCITRAL Arbitration Rules do not, however, make explicit the power of UNCITRAL Tribunals to accept amicus briefs, but rely upon the general power of such Tribunals to conduct the proceedings (see art 17(1)).

70 See Yanovich and Zdouc 2009: 363; see generally DSU, Articles 4(6) and 14(1), relating to the confidentiality of consultations and panel deliberations.

71 See Evans and de Tarso Pereira 2005: 262.

72 See Foreign Affairs and International Trade Canada (7 October 2003). This is not, however, Mexico's default position.

73 Thus the *Methanex* and *UPS* hearings were held in public (see *Methanex v United States* and *United Parcel Service v Canada*). For a recent example, see the May 2009 hearing in *Merrill Ring v Canada*: ICSID (2009).

74 See *Aguas Argentinas, SA, Suez and Vivendi Universal* 2005; and *Aguas del Tunari v Boliva* 2003.

75 See Arbitration Rule 32(2).

76 Under WTO rules, the default position is that pleadings are confidential: DSU, Article 18(2). See generally Appellate Body Report, *Thailand – H-Beams*, para. 68 (addressing the unauthorised distribution of pleadings to a third party).

77 See *Rules of Conduct for the Understanding on Rules and Procedures Governing the Settlement of Disputes, as adopted by the DSB on 3 December 1996*, WT/DBS/

RC/1 (11 December 1996); adopted by Article 8 of the *Working Procedures for Appellate Review*, WT/AB/WP/5 (4 January 2005).
78 Rule II(1).
79 These Guidelines were approved by the Council of the International Bar Association on 22 May 2004.
80 Two recent examples include *ConocoPhillips Company v Venezuela* 2012; and *Urbaser SA and Consorcio de Aguas Bilbao Bizkaia, Bilbao Biskaia Ur Partzuergoa v The Argentine Republic* 2010.
81 Appellate Body Report, *US – Shrimp*.
82 Appellate Body Report, *United States – Measures Affecting the Cross-Border Supply of Gambling and Betting Services*, WT/DS285/AB/R, adopted 20 April 2005, paras 306–7. See also Appellate Body Report, *EC – Asbestos*, paras 171–4.
83 Kalderimis 2011: 142–3.
84 Kalderimis 2011: 144–51.
85 See, for example, Lester and Mercurio 2008: 204–5, with respect to the WTO; and Commission 2007, with respect to investment treaty arbitration.
86 Appellate Body Report, *United States – Final Anti-Dumping Measures on Stainless Steel from Mexico*, WT/DS344/AB/R, adopted 20 May 2008, para. 160.
87 *Glamis Gold v United States* 2009: para. 5.
88 Decision by the Arbitrators, *European Communities – Regime for the Importation, Sale and Distribution of Bananas – Recourse to Arbitration by the European Communities under Article 22.6 of the DSU*, WT/DS27/ARB/ECU, 24 March 2000.
89 Decision by the Arbitrator, *United States – Measures Affecting the Cross-Border Supply of Gambling and Betting Services – Recourse to Arbitration by the United States under Article 22.6 of the DSU*, WT/DS285/ARB, 21 December 2007.
90 Decision by the Arbitrator, *United States – Subsidies on Upland Cotton – Recourse to Arbitration by the United States under Article 22.6 of the DSU and Article 4.11 of the SCM Agreement*, WT/DS267/ARB/1, 31 August 2009.
91 *European Communities and Certain Member States – Measures Affecting Trade in Large Civil Aircraft – Recourse to Article 7.9 of the SCM Agreement and Article 22.2 of the DSU by the United States*, WT/DS316/18, 12 December 2011 [hereinafter '*EC – Aircraft*, WT/DS316/18'].
92 *EC – Aircraft*, WT/DS316/18, US request for authorisation from the DSB to take Countermeasures, 12 December 2012.
93 See Kalderimis 2011: 146–51.
94 ICSID (16 May 2007); ICSID (9 July 2009); ICSID (26 January 2012); see also Vincentelli 2010.
95 In order for a party to leave the ICSID Convention they must denounce it: art 71. There is a six month delay before the denunciation is effective. However, any rights or obligations under ICSID that arose before the denunciation notice is effective are still able to be enforced through the ICSID system: art 72.
96 See for example: *ETI Euro Telecom International NV v Republic of Bolivia* [2008] EWHC 1689 (Comm) where Bolivia successfully resisted a freezing order application in aid of an ICSID arbitration.
97 This is a difficult technique due to sovereign immunity considerations (as reflected in art 54(1) of the ICSID Convention). See the recent provisional Hong Kong Court of Final Appeal decision confirming that a doctrine of absolute immunity applies in Hong Kong: *Democratic Republic of the Congo v FG Hemisphere Associates LLC* [2011] 4 HKC 151 (HKCFA). Outside the ICSID context, one investor has captured headlines with his failed attempts to enforce an arbitration award against Russian assets abroad, including fighter jets and Impressionist art: Blomfield (17 November 2005).
98 Extended in January 2012 until October 2015.
99 For the final WTO Appellate Body decisions, see Appellate Body Report, *United*

States – Final Countervailing Duty Determination with Respect to Certain Softwood Lumber from Canada, WT/DS257/AB/R, adopted 17 February 2004; and Appellate Body Report, *United States – Final Dumping Determination on Softwood Lumber from Canada – Recourse to Article 21.5 of the DSU by Canada*, WT/DS264/AB/RW, adopted 1 September 2006.

100 The arbitral pleadings and awards are available at: www.dfait-maeci.gc.ca/controls-controles/softwood-bois_oeuvre/other-autres/agreement-accord.aspx (accessed 22 May 2012).

101 See Appellate Body Report, *Mexico – Tax Measures on Soft Drinks and Other Beverages*, WT/DS308/AB/R, adopted 24 March 2006. See generally Van Damme 2009: 311–3.

102 See *Food & Drink Weekly* (27 October 2003).

103 See Panel Report, *Argentina – Definitive Anti-Dumping Duties on Poultry from Brazil*, WT/DS241/R, adopted 19 May 2003; and the award (*'laudo arbitral'*) of the ad hoc arbitral tribunal dated 21 May 2001.

104 See http://icsid.worldbank.org/ICSID/FrontServlet (accessed 22 May 2012).

105 The relevant documentation is available on the DFAT website. Online. Available at: www.dfat.gov.au/foi/disclosure-log.html (accessed 22 May 2012).

106 On 13 March 2012, see www.wto.org/english/tratop_e/dispu_e/cases_e/ds434_e.htm (accessed 22 May 2012).

107 On 4 April 2012, see www.wto.org/english/tratop_e/dispu_e/cases_e/ds435_e.htm (accessed 22 May 2012).

108 To give one example, see *Continental Casualty Company v The Argentine Republic* 2008.

109 Mercosur is the Common Market of the South Cone, established by the Treaty of Asuncion dated 26 March 1991. Although DSU revision proposals to include compensation for breach would remove or reduce this distinction. See Mercurio 2004: 847.

110 See Prost 2005: 202–3.

111 See, for example, Van Harten 2006; Kingsbury and Schill 2009; Burke-White and von Staden 2010.

112 See Sacerdoti 2005: 125.

113 See especially *CMS Gas Transmission Company v The Argentine Republic* 2005 and *CMS Gas Transmission Company v The Argentine Republic* 2007.

4 The WTO standard of review

A means to strengthen the trading system

Ross Becroft[1]

Introduction

In these times of global economic uncertainty, there may be a temptation for countries to reduce their commitment to international institutions such as the WTO. However, it is vital that efforts continue to be made to enhance the functioning of the WTO and, in particular, that of the dispute settlement system, upon which countries rely more than ever in the absence of an outcome to the Doha Round of negotiations.

An important issue that is in need of improvement concerns the standard of review that WTO panels apply when they are adjudicating disputes. The standard of review refers to the method by which panels review member measures. Superficially, it does not seem like an issue which ought to demand the attention of the international trading community. It is, nonetheless, important because the level of scrutiny or deference applied can affect substantive outcomes, and over time, affect the way the WTO Agreements are interpreted. The standard of review may, in a wider sense, be viewed as an expression of the allocation of power between the WTO and its members.[2] The current standard, the 'objective assessment' test adopted by the Appellate Body in *EC – Hormones*,[3] does not provide an adequate theoretical basis for a standard of review. The present standard has developed in a confusing and inconsistent manner, and it has frequently led to a highly intensive standard being applied.

In this chapter I contend that panels should adopt a standard of review that is based upon the division of jurisdictional competencies between the WTO and the membership provided for under the WTO Agreements. The term 'jurisdictional competencies' refers to the responsibilities that the WTO and members must each carry out in connection with specific obligations and disciplines.[4] Where a member has retained particular competencies, then the standard of review that panels apply should be more deferential when scrutinizing the measure in question.

Developing this type of new doctrine would not lead to a significant reinterpretation of the WTO Agreements. The doctrine would be clearly rooted in the text of the WTO Agreements, and it would satisfy a number of important broader policy objectives, such as the enhancement of the legitimacy of the dispute settlement process.

This approach would generate a standard of review that could vary depending upon the nature of obligations under particular WTO Agreements. Therefore, certain obligations under, for example, the GATT and the trade remedies agreements would be reviewed with differing degrees of deference. It may also affect the way SPS disputes are reviewed, and in this regard, the chapter will refer to some of the arguments put forward in the case of *Australia – Apples*.[5] In addition, this new approach would not represent a significant departure from that taken in decisions such as *US – Continued Suspension*, where the Appellate Body adopted a more deferential approach.[6]

The nature and purpose of a standard of review in WTO dispute settlement

The expression 'standard of review' refers to the manner in which an adjudicative body reviews a party's compliance with a form of regulation or the correctness of prior decisions made in the same matter. It therefore conceptualizes in legal form the scope or extent of the review task performed. A number of different words and phrases are used to describe the same process. These include the expressions 'intensity of review' and 'intrusiveness of review', both of which frequently appear in the literature. The key concept to bear in mind is the relative comprehensiveness of the review exercise. Therefore, if a reviewer limits the process of review, it may be said that the reviewer applies a degree of deference or restraint in relation to the conduct or decision being reviewed. In everyday language, it may be said that the reviewer exercises some 'leeway' or grants some 'room to move' to the original decision maker. It is also sometimes referred to as the 'margin of appreciation' that a reviewer exercises towards the decision or conduct being reviewed. In short, it may be envisaged as a spectrum depicting the relative intrusiveness or deference exercised by the reviewer in relation to the subject under review.

The most intrusive type of standard of review is frequently referred to as de novo review, and highly deferential approaches generally consist solely of procedural (but not substantive) oversight. If standards are viewed as being along a spectrum then the test of reasonableness, such as is often adopted by domestic courts, would be somewhere in the middle.

In the WTO context, the standard of review refers to the way in which panels review measures to determine compliance with the terms of the WTO Agreements. The application of a particular standard of review is not generally significant if a panel is simply reviewing whether domestic regulation complies with WTO obligations because a panel is usually the adjudicator of first instance. The issue becomes more complicated where a panel is reviewing a measure of a member that is based upon an earlier adjudicative or investigative process. If a panel applies an extremely deferential standard of review, then there is unlikely to be a consistent interpretive approach to various WTO obligations. By contrast, if an extremely intrusive approach is taken by panels, then arguably panels would be overreaching and potentially undermining the ability of members to determine their own policies in key areas. The challenge is to formulate a standard that provides sufficient oversight of member measures in order for the WTO to achieve compliance and its broader objectives, but without undermining the legitimacy of the WTO as an institution.

Standards of review have both constitutional and administrative law dimensions.[7] From a constitutional point of view, they help to shape the allocation of responsibility both within an institution, and between the institution and its constituency.[8] Further, standards of review are also about the institution ensuring that there is sufficient oversight of the decisions under review.[9] These purposes are also applicable for the WTO. Whilst the constitutional architecture is different from a domestic legal system, these issues are still relevant. Arguably, the standard of review in WTO dispute settlement is more relevant than in the case of many other international dispute settlement systems, because the decisions that are under review are often matters that have already been investigated, decided upon or litigated within the member states. Without a properly formulated standard of review, there may be the perception that the WTO is 'second guessing' the policy decisions of members in sensitive areas of policy such as trade remedies, quarantine, health and the environment.

In many legal systems it is common for separate standards of review to be applied in relation to questions of fact and legal questions. The standard of review of facts is frequently more deferential in character than the legal standard and is more likely to generate controversy (along with the correct characterization of a question as being legal or factual or of a mixed nature). In the case of the WTO the same standard has been applied to date in relation to facts and law.[10]

There is no express standard of review set out in the Dispute Settlement Understanding (DSU) or the other covered agreements, with the exception of Article 17.6 of the Anti-Dumping Agreement, which does purportedly prescribe a more deferential standard for anti-dumping disputes. This was included as part of the Uruguay Round of negotiations at the request of the United States.[11] To date, there have been concerns about the efficacy of this unique standard.[12] Separately to this, a general standard of review has evolved from various panel and Appellate Body decisions.

The current WTO standard of review and its limitations

In the decision of *EC – Hormones* the Appellate Body identified Article 11 of the DSU as encapsulating the standard of review that panels must apply. The Appellate Body set out the wording of this Article with the following emphasis:

> The function of panels is to assist the DSB in discharging its responsibilities under this Understanding and the covered agreements. Accordingly, a panel should make an <u>objective assessment of the matter before it,</u> including <u>an objective assessment of the facts</u> of the case and the <u>applicability of and conformity with the relevant covered agreements,</u> and make other such

findings as will assist the DSB in making the recommendations or in giving the rulings provided in the covered agreements. Panels should consult regularly with parties to the dispute and give them adequate opportunity to develop a mutually satisfactory solution (underlining added).[13]

In describing the practical meaning of Article 11 as a standard of review, the Appellate Body in *EC – Hormones* stated:

> The duty to make an objective assessment of the facts is, among other things, an obligation to consider the evidence presented to a panel and to make factual findings on the basis of that evidence. The deliberate disregard of, or refusal to consider, the evidence submitted to a panel is incompatible with a panel's duty to make an objective assessment of the facts.[14]

The above passage makes it clear that it is the duty of panels to assess evidence in a substantive sense, and therefore, objective assessment involves more than merely procedural oversight. Objective assessment also appears to be quite different from de novo review, which has been excluded as a possible standard in various decisions.[15] Objective assessment has also been designated as the standard of review of both facts and law.[16]

This objective assessment test has remained as the WTO standard of review for all disciplines outside anti-dumping ever since *EC – Hormones*. However, as I will discuss later in this chapter, its meaning has changed over time based on the way it has been interpreted and applied in a number of decisions.

There are several difficulties with the current standard of review. Fundamentally, the wording of Article 11 is more about panels having regard to principles of due process, and its interpretation in *EC – Hormones* also incorporates the requirement for panels to review matters fairly and in good faith.[17] However, this does not assist panels in defining how intensively they should review factual and legal issues. In other words, the concept of objective assessment does not instruct panels as to whether they should apply a standard that is closer to de novo review or total deference.[18] Without such guidance, there is the potential for panels to apply too much or too little scrutiny and to be generally unclear about their review task.

In a number of decisions following *EC – Hormones* the Appellate Body and panels have seen fit to make statements to clarify the standard of review and, in doing so, the standard has been varied, both in the way it is formally expressed and in the way it is applied. It is arguable that this is due, in part, to the objective assessment test being inadequate. This situation is not ideal because the standard of review test remains unclear, and it has sometimes been applied inconsistently, and in a way that diverges from the present formal test.

In this regard, the Appellate Body has stated on several occasions that the standard of review will vary depending upon the substantive obligations being reviewed. The Appellate Body has confirmed this approach in decisions such as *US – Lamb*,[19] *US – Cotton Yarn*[20] and *US – Countervailing Duty Investigation on*

DRAMS.[21] For example, in *US – Countervailing Duty Investigation on DRAMS*, the Appellate Body stated that:

> [Article 11] .. must be considered in the light of the obligations of the particular covered agreement at issue in order to derive the more specific contours of the appropriate standard of review.[22]

This type of standard should lead to a different standard of review being applied under particular WTO Agreements. In matters where there has been a prior national-level process, such as in trade remedy matters, this approach should result in a more deferential standard being applied. However, in many cases the standard actually applied is no more deferential than would otherwise apply.[23] Indeed, in various cases, the Appellate Body has reversed certain findings of panels on the basis that the standard applied was too deferential. Arguably, this has pushed the standard that is actually required to be applied more in the direction of de novo review.

For example, in *US – Softwood Lumber VI (Article 21.5 – Canada)*, which dealt with compliance in respect of threatened injury determinations under the Subsidies and Countervailing Measures and Anti-Dumping Agreements, the Appellate Body found that the panel had not applied the correct standard of review in reviewing a decision of the United States International Trade Commission in that it 'failed to engage in the type of critical and searching analysis called for by Article 11 of the DSU'.[24] The Appellate Body was quite critical of the panel's acceptance that the USITC's explanation of the measures provided reasoned support for its conclusion.[25] The Appellate Body suggested that a panel must determine whether the domestic authority's conclusions are reasoned and adequate and that this is should involve the following kinds of steps:

> The panel should test whether the reasoning of the authority is coherent and internally consistent.

> The panel must undertake an in-depth examination of whether the explanations given disclose how the investigating authority treated the facts and evidence in the record and whether there was positive evidence before it to support the inferences made and conclusions reached by it.

> The panel must examine whether the explanations provided demonstrate that the investigating authority took proper account of the complexities of the data before it, and that it explained why it rejected or discounted alternative explanations and interpretations of the record evidence.

> A panel must be open to the possibility that the explanations given by the authority are not reasoned or adequate in the light of other plausible alternative explanations.

... and must take care not to assume itself the role of initial trier of facts, nor to be passive by 'simply *accept[ing]* the conclusions of the competent authorities'.[26]

The above extract demonstrates the present requirement for panels to conduct an extensive review of the issues, but without somehow engaging in de novo review. In *US – Softwood Lumber VI (Article 21.5 – Canada)*, the result was that the Appellate Body overturned some of the panel's findings concerning injury to the local producers, but it could not complete the analysis, which left parts of the dispute unresolved.[27]

A similar outcome occurred in the *US – Countervailing Duty Investigation on DRAMS* case[28] and the *US – Continued Zeroing* case.[29] In both of these decisions, the Appellate Body overturned certain panel findings on the basis that panels had failed to evaluate evidence in its totality in order to draw conclusions about whether the measures were justified. In *US – Continued Zeroing* the Appellate Body noted that compliance with Article 11, means that a panel must:

evaluate evidence in its totality, by which we mean the duty to weigh collectively all of the evidence and in relation to one another, even if no piece of evidence is by itself determinative of an asserted fact or claim.[30]

In that case, the European Communities successfully argued that the panel did not engage in any cumulative appreciation of the evidence in failing to consider the dumping margin calculations to corroborate the fact that the zeroing methodology was used.[31] Once again, a highly intensive form of review was required to be exercised by the panel. The finding that a panel has failed to appreciate evidence as a whole and has been selective in its assessment of evidence has been a common basis for non-compliance with DSU Article 11 but reasoning errors have also led to such findings.[32]

A survey of the difficulties with the current standard of review would be incomplete without mention of the anti-dumping standard as prescribed in Article 17.6 of the Anti-Dumping Agreement. Article 17.6(i) deals with the standard of review of facts and Article 17.6(ii) concerns the standard of review of law. Under Article 17.6(i), panels must not overturn findings of a domestic authority so long as the establishment of the facts was proper and the evaluation was unbiased and objective.[33] Arguably, Article 17.6(i) has not been applied in a manner which has led to any discernible deference in favour of domestic authorities.[34] In other words, there may be no major difference in practice between the anti-dumping standard and the objective assessment test that applies to other WTO Agreements. The Appellate Body, in *US – Hot Rolled Steel*, has suggested that Article 17.6(i) and Article 11 of the DSU both require panels to actively and thoroughly assess the facts of the case.[35]

Article 17.6(ii) provides that panels shall interpret the Anti-Dumping Agreement in accordance with customary rules of interpretation of public international law. Further, where panels find that a provision of the Anti-Dumping Agreement admits more than one permissible interpretation, panels must find a measure to be in conformity with the Anti-Dumping Agreement if it rests on one of those permissible interpretations. One difficulty with Article 17.6(ii) is that Articles 31 and 32 of the Vienna Convention on the Law of Treaties (VCLT), requiring treaty provisions to be read in good faith according to their ordinary meaning and context, is likely to lead to only one correct interpretation of a treaty provision. Nonetheless, the Appellate Body in *US – Hot-Rolled Steel* and *US – Continued Zeroing* has suggested that the VCLT may in fact give scope for multiple interpretations.[36] This is despite the fact that to date no multiple interpretations have been found in applying Article 17.6(ii). Therefore, it is unlikely that Article 17.6(ii) has produced any more deference towards WTO members in their legal interpretations of the Anti-Dumping Agreement than would otherwise apply in cases dealing with other WTO Agreements.

Accordingly, despite the apparent similarities in the way the general and anti-dumping standards are applied in practice, there is the ongoing issue that a discrete standard exists for anti-dumping disputes, which is ostensibly quite different from the standard that is applied in respect of other WTO Agreements. This is particularly anomalous in relation to similar trade remedies, such as countervailing duty and safeguard measures for which the general standard of review applies.

Developing a standard of review based on jurisdictional competencies

Problems with the current standard of review suggest the need for a new approach to this issue. A new model for a standard of review should be developed that would better assist panels to understand their review task and which would be conceptually cogent.

One such proposal is to develop a new doctrine that is based upon the division of responsibilities between members and WTO panels to carry out particular obligations related to the review of measures. I refer to this division of responsibilities as the 'jurisdictional competencies' that apply to the WTO and each member. This expression was discussed by the Appellate Body in *EC – Hormones* in the context of the Sanitary and Phytosanitary Measures Agreement where it was noted that:

> The standard of review applicable in proceedings under the *SPS Agreement*, of course must reflect the balance established in that Agreement between the jurisdictional competencies conceded by the Members to the WTO and the jurisdictional competencies retained by the Members for themselves. To adopt a standard of review not clearly rooted in the text of the *SPS Agreement* itself, may well amount to changing that finely drawn balance; and neither a panel nor the Appellate Body is authorized to do that.[37]

Whilst the above quotation may arguably be more about making sure panels do not interpret provisions in a manner that deviates too far from the text of the

WTO Agreements, it does make the important point that the standard of review should *itself* take into account the relative jurisdictional competencies of the WTO and the membership as reflected in the text of the Agreements.

If the standard of review were indeed based on this principle, then where a WTO Agreement does not provide for members to retain any jurisdictional competencies, then a general standard of review should apply that is highly intensive in nature. This general standard would require panels to examine all available and sufficient evidence and carry out a comprehensive review of measures to determine whether the measure complies. Such a test may be applied to disputes under the GATT where a panel would often be the adjudicator of first instance. By way of example, in *Chile – Alcoholic Beverages*, the panel reviewed the question of whether laws which applied different rates of taxation to Chilean Pisco and other alcoholic beverages was inconsistent with GATT Article III:2.[38] In this case, the panel correctly applied a highly intensive standard of review in examining whether the Chilean product was a like product compared with similar beverages. Accordingly, the panel did not grant any deference to the respondent member's previous examination of the issues.

Where, by contrast, an Agreement does provide for the retaining of jurisdictional competencies by members, the general standard would be modified to take into account these competencies. In other words, there would be less oversight of domestic measures by panels. This would potentially generate a specific standard of review for disputes arising under different WTO Agreements. Panels would therefore apply more or less deference depending upon the type of dispute. This new test is likely to result in a significant degree of deference in trade remedy cases, and a lesser degree of deference in SPS cases. Under these WTO Agreements members retain jurisdictional competencies in relation to certain obligations. For example, under Article 5.1 of the SPS Agreement, measures are required to be based on a risk assessment, with scientific and economic factors that members are to take into account listed in that Article. Therefore, panels would review whether members have carried out a risk assessment pursuant to Article 5.1, rather than panels to, in effect, conduct a new risk assessment. As stated above, cases dealing principally with GATT provisions would involve close scrutiny and no deference to members. This test would only apply to the standard of review of facts and not the standard of review of law, which would remain highly intensive principally to ensure consistency in the interpretation of the WTO Agreements.

This outcome can be represented in approximate terms as being along a spectrum, as set out below in Figure 4.1:

Figure 4.1 Spectrum of panel deference for selected WTO agreements.

The type of criteria that panels would look for in applying a modified standard of review would include whether the relevant WTO obligations contemplate any prior review and decision making by a domestic authority. In some instances this will be formally required by an Agreement, and in other instances it will be implied by the nature of the obligations in the relevant discipline. An important consideration is to consider to what extent the panel is operating as a second tier of review.

This new test does not involve drawing a 'black letter' distinction between measures that can and cannot be substantively reviewed by panels. The proposal would in practice be more graduated in mediating the intensity with which panels review disputes. It is still important for panels to, at the very least, ensure that any domestic investigation and review processes have been undertaken in a rigorous manner.[39] Whilst jurisdictional competencies might set the contours of a new standard, panels should still review the quality of decision making within that framework. This would include considering the relative formality of domestic processes together with the quality of analysis and reasoning undertaken, and also calling upon expert evidence when required to verify the issues.

Applying a variable standard of review would not be overly complicated because similar obligations and processes would be reviewed in a like manner. For example, a similar standard would be applied across the trade remedy agreements given they contemplate formal domestic review processes and there are similar concepts such as injury to local producers. In this regard, a panel's treatment of safeguard measures would be very similar to its treatment of anti-dumping and countervailing measures because of the requirement in each case for competent authorities of WTO members to thoroughly investigate the factual basis for imposing measures and the similar procedures followed by those authorities during those investigations. Further, safeguard, anti-dumping and countervailing investigations each require competent authorities to establish that a domestic industry has suffered economic injury and that there is a causal connection between the sanctioned conduct: that is, the increase in imports or dumped or subsidized imports and any injury suffered.

This new approach has several major advantages. First, it would create a new theoretical grounding for the standard that is clearer and more capable of consistent application compared with the objective assessment test. Second, it would guard against the standard of review becoming too intensive in nature, which the cases discussed in the previous section reveal is an ongoing risk. Third, it would not be difficult to adopt given that there are already precedents whereby a variable standard has been referred to based upon the obligations at issue.[40] Fourth, it would allow for greater clarification of the anti-dumping standard of review and generate a theoretical basis to justify a standard that is relatively consistent in respect of other trade remedy disputes.[41]

This new standard of review would also maintain an approach to treaty interpretation that is closely based on the treaty text. However, that aside, from a broader policy perspective it would promote the legitimacy of the WTO dispute settlement process amongst the membership. If, for instance, a standard were adopted that provided no deference to members in respect of any measures, and which had no connection with the governing agreements, this might lead to a diminution of confidence in the system as a whole.

The Appellate Body decision in *US – Continued Suspension* provides a good example of how the standard of review has already evolved in some disciplines, and how this could fit in with a new flexible standard.[42] This case dealt with the issue of whether a European directive, which banned imports of meat products from hormone-treated cows, was based upon a scientifically justified risk assessment as required by Article 5.1 of the SPS Agreement.[43] The Appellate Body found that the panel had not applied the correct standard of review because the panel sought to determine whether the risk assessment relied upon by the European Communities was based on the correct scientific evidence, instead of determining whether the risk assessment is supported by coherent reasoning and reputable scientific evidence.[44] Therefore, the panel had applied a standard of review that was not sufficiently deferential. The Appellate Body noted:

> [Instead] the Panel seems to have conducted a survey of the advice presented by the scientific experts and based its decisions on whether the majority of the experts, or the opinion that was most thoroughly reasoned or specific to the question at issue, agreed with the conclusion drawn in the European Communities' risk assessment. This approach is not consistent with the applicable standard of review under the *SPS Agreement*.[45]

Article 5.1 of the SPS Agreement is an example of where a specific and more deferential standard ought to apply. This article clearly contemplates a national-level process of carrying out a risk assessment, which is obviously an important check on the ability of members to unilaterally implement SPS measures. As to how much deference should apply, there is of course still the need for panels to test the claims and evidence at issue. Panels should be thorough in their review because there is only very broad guidance in the text of the SPS Agreement as to what constitutes a valid risk assessment and what is meant by sufficient scientific evidence.[46] It is difficult to determine whether the standard of review applied by the Appellate Body in *US – Continued Suspension* comprises the same degree of deference as would eventuate under the variable standard advocated in this chapter.

The approach taken in *US – Continued Suspension* was more recently accepted by the panel in *Australia – Apples*.[47] This dispute concerned the very rigorous screening procedures that Australia put in place in response to its concerns about the spread of diseases such as fire blight. New Zealand argued that the measures contravened Article 5.1 because *inter alia* they were not based on a proper risk assessment and there was insufficient scientific evidence to justify the measures.

In *Australia – Apples*, Australia took the issue further in arguing strongly for a more deferential and agreement-specific standard of review.[48] Australia contended that the standard of review should be informed by the particular WTO Agreement and obligation at issue.[49] Further, Australia argued that the standard of review must maintain the balance between trade liberalization goals and domestic regulatory rights.[50] These arguments were not accepted by the panel and there was no formal recognition of a more deferential standard of review, but such arguments may nonetheless have influenced the intensity of the panel's analysis of the issues.[51] Australia unsuccessfully appealed these findings, with the Appellate Body reaffirming the approach taken in *US – Continued Suspension*.[52]

It would appear from the findings in *US – Continued Suspension* and *Australia – Apples* that the Appellate Body has signalled the development of a modestly more deferential standard of review, at least in the case of disputes concerning Article 5.1 of the SPS Agreement. Through these decisions, the Appellate Body has strongly emphasized that panels should not second guess national governments in respect of health and safety measures that have a reputable scientific basis. It nonetheless remains unclear whether these cases represent a more permanent shift in the approach of the Appellate Body. In particular, it is not absolutely clear whether the Appellate Body would apply a similar approach in disputes concerning other WTO Agreements, but the inference from subsequent trade remedy cases is that this more deferential approach may be confined to disputes under the SPS Agreement.[53] This is not particularly desirable in that this situation is anomalous and, as outlined above, there is more of a case for deference in relation to the trade remedy agreements, where there have been significant domestic investigatory processes already undertaken in connection with measures. There is certainly the potential for WTO tribunals to further develop the standard of review but WTO tribunals have to date exercised a degree of caution and conservatism on this issue.

Conclusion and consequences

It is widely acknowledged that the dispute settlement system is the WTO's key institutional asset, and the most prominent achievement of the Uruguay Round. It is important for the WTO to build upon this success. The proposed reframing of the standard of review is an example of a subtle but nonetheless important reform. Adopting a standard that more formally recognizes the relationship between the decision-making processes at the national and supranational levels would provide a firmer foundation for the fundamental question of how intrusive the WTO should be in domestic affairs. This approach could enhance legitimacy and would be more workable than the current standard. It would also show the progressive nature of panel and Appellate Body interpretations of the WTO texts, but without reshaping the meaning of the WTO Agreements and the key objectives of those Agreements. It is not suggested that the standard of review is or should be *the* mechanism to mediate WTO-Member tensions. There does, however, need to be more certainty about this issue so that Members and panels better appreciate the nature of the review process and a more consistent body of case law can evolve within this theoretical framework. In the absence of such reform and were the current 'drift' to continue, major users of the system may persist in raising this issue in appeals before the Appellate Body.[54]

The development of a new standard of review doctrine has the potential to improve both legitimacy and certainty of the dispute settlement system, and strengthen the WTO as an institution. It is important that WTO tribunals continue to develop interpretations that build upon the Uruguay Round reforms, particularly in the absence of the completion of the Doha Round.

Notes

1 Principal, Gross & Becroft Lawyers, Sessional Academic Melbourne Law School. This topic is dealt with in further detail in the author's book, *The Standard of Review in WTO Dispute Settlement: Critique and Development*, Cheltenham, UK and Northampton, MA, USA: Edward Elgar Publishing, 2012. The author practices law in the international trade, customs and commercial fields and has a PhD from the University of Melbourne.
2 Oesch 2003a: 23, in which the author states: 'In substance, standards of review express a deliberate allocation of power to decide upon factual and legal issues.'
3 Appellate Body Report, *EC – Hormones*, WT/DS26/AB/R, WT/DS48/AB/R, adopted 13 February 1998 [hereinafter 'Appellate Body Report, *EC – Hormones*'].
3 Appellate Body Report, *EC – Hormones*, para. 115, where this expression is used in a WTO dispute settlement context.
5 Panel Report, *Australia – Measures Affecting the Importation of Apples from New Zealand*, WT/DS367/R, adopted 17 December 2010, as modified by Appellate Body Report WT/DS367/AB/R [hereinafter 'Panel Report, *Australia – Apples*'].
6 Appellate Body Report, *United States – Continued Suspension of Obligations in the EC – Hormones Dispute*, WT/DS321/AB/R, adopted 14 November 2008 [hereinafter 'Appellate Body Report, *US – Continued Suspension*'].
7 Oesch 2003b: 636.
8 Oesch 2003b: 636.
9 Oesch 2003b: 636.
10 Appellate Body Report, *EC – Hormones*. There have been very few statements by the Appellate Body reconfirming this approach. In Appellate Body Report, *Argentina – Safeguard Measures on Imports of Footwear*, WT/DS121/AB/R, adopted 12 January 2000, para. 122 the Appellate Body stated that

> In addition to 'an objective assessment of the facts', we note too, that part of the 'objective assessment of the matter' required of the panel by Article 11 of the DSU is an assessment of the 'applicability of and conformity with the relevant covered agreements'. Consequently, we must also examine whether the Panel correctly interpreted and applied the substantive provisions of Articles 2 and 4 of the *Agreement on Safeguards*.

11 Horlick and Clarke 1997: 298.
12 Durling 2003; Greenwald 2003; Hamilton 2003; Tarullo 2002; Horlick and Clarke 1997.
13 Appellate Body Report, *EC – Hormones*.
14 Appellate Body Report, *EC – Hormones*, para. 133.
15 Appellate Body Report, *EC – Hormones*, para. 117.
16 Appellate Body Report, *EC – Hormones*, para. 118.
17 Appellate Body Report, *EC – Hormones*, para. 133.

18 See Desmedt 1998: 697. Desmedt notes:

> Clearly the 'objective assessment' principle is not all that helpful in ascertaining towards which extreme (*de novo* or total deference) the Appellate Body would lean. The notion of objectivity rather assumes an alternative to the EC's proposals for the development of an appropriate standard of review. The question is if the Appellate Body will further develop the confines of this review through the principle of objectivity rather than vacillating between total deference and *de novo* review.

19 Appellate Body Report, *United States – Safeguard Measures on Imports of Fresh, Chilled or Frozen Lamb Meat from New Zealand and Australia*, WT/DS177/AB/R, WT/DS178/AB/R, adopted 16 May 2001, para. 105.

20 Appellate Body Report, *United States – Transitional Safeguard Measure on Combed Cotton Yarn from Pakistan*, WT/DS192/AB/R, adopted 5 November 2001, paras 75–8.

21 Appellate Body Report, *United States – Countervailing Duty Investigation on Dynamic Random Access Memory Semiconductors (DRAMS) from Korea*, WT/DS296/AB/R, adopted 20 July 2005, para. 184 [hereinafter 'Appellate Body Report, *US – Countervailing Duty Investigation on DRAMS*'].

22 Appellate Body Report, *US – Countervailing Duty Investigation on DRAMS*, para. 184.

23 Some exceptions to this proposition are discussed later in this chapter.

24 Appellate Body Report, *United States – Investigation of the International Trade Commission in Softwood Lumber from Canada* – Recourse to Article 21.5 of the DSU by Canada, WT/DS277/AB/RW, adopted 9 May 2006, para. 113 [hereinafter 'Appellate Body Report, *US – Softwood Lumber VI (Article 21.5 – Canada)*'].

25 Appellate Body Report, *US – Softwood Lumber VI (Article 21.5 – Canada)*, para. 124.

26 Appellate Body Report, *US – Softwood Lumber VI (Article 21.5 – Canada)*, para. 93.

27 Appellate Body Report, *US – Softwood Lumber VI (Article 21.5 – Canada)*, paras 157–61.

28 Appellate Body Report, *US – Countervailing Duty Investigation on DRAMS*, paras 144–58 and 188.

29 Appellate Body Report, *United States – Continued Existence and Application of Zeroing Methodology*, WT/DS350/AB/R, adopted 19 February 2009 [hereinafter 'Appellate Body Report, *US – Continued Zeroing*'].

30 Appellate Body Report, *US – Continued Zeroing*, para. 336.

31 Appellate Body Report, *US – Continued Zeroing*, para. 337.

32 Regarding reasoning errors, see for example, Appellate Body Report, *United States – Definitive Safeguard Measures on Imports of Wheat Gluten from the European Communities*, WT/DS166/AB/R, adopted 19 January 2001, paras 161–3.

33 The Appellate Body has stated that the function of Article 17.6(i) is to 'prevent a panel from "second guessing" a determination of a national authority'. See Appellate Body Report, *Thailand – Anti-Dumping Duties on Angles, Shapes and Sections of Iron or Non-Alloy Steel and H-Beams from Poland*, WT/DS122/AB/R, adopted 5 April 2001, para. 116.

34 The same comment may be made in respect of the way the legal standard of review under Article 17.6(ii), which is also intended to be deferential, has been applied.

35 See Appellate Body Report, *United States – Anti-Dumping Measures on Certain Hot-Rolled Steel Products from Japan*, WT/DS184/AB/R, adopted 23 August 2001, para. 55 [hereinafter 'Appellate Body Report, *US – Hot-Rolled Steel*'].

36 Appellate Body Report, *US – Hot-Rolled Steel*, para. 61; Appellate Body Report, *US – Continued Zeroing*, paras 259–317.

37 Appellate Body Report, *EC – Hormones*, para. 115. This issue was raised by the Appellate Body in rejecting an argument by the European Communities that a new 'deferential reasonableness' standard of review should be applied in 'all highly complex factual situations'. The Appellate Body was rejecting the imposition of a new standard of review that imported new adjudicatory concepts, such as one based on reasonableness and was maintaining a textual approach to this issue.

38 Panel Report, *Chile – Taxes on Alcoholic Beverages*, WT/DS87/R, WT/DS110/R, adopted 12 January 2000, as modified by Appellate Body Report WT/DS87/AB/R, WT/DS110/AB/R, paras 7.16–88.

39 This is necessary to also counter the suggestion that there may be a bias towards local producers in, for example, domestic trade remedy investigations.

40 For a discussion of how the standard of review has been applied to date under various WTO Agreements see Ehlermann and Lockhart: 2004: 491.

41 See, for example, Ministerial Declaration on Dispute Settlement Pursuant to the Agreement on Implementation of Article VI of the General Agreement on Tariffs and Trade 1994 or Part V of the Agreement on Subsidies and Countervailing Measures, which recognizes 'the need for consistent resolution of disputes arising from anti-dumping and countervailing duty measures'.

42 Appellate Body Report, *US – Continued Suspension*.

43 Article 5.1 of the SPS Agreement stipulates that members shall ensure that their sanitary or phytosanitary measures are based on an assessment, as appropriate to the circumstances, of the risks to human, animal or plant life or health, taking into account risk assessment techniques developed by the relevant international organiza-tions. This case has been going for more than 10 years. In 1998 the AB upheld the US complaint on the EC ban on the importation of hormone-treated beef violated the SPS Agreement. A key finding was that the ban was not 'based upon' a risk assessment. In 1999 the DSB authorized the US to impose retaliatory measures.

44 Appellate Body Report, *US – Continued Suspension*, para. 590.

45 Appellate Body Report, *US – Continued Suspension*, para. 598.

46 Article 2.2 of the SPS Agreement provides:

> Members shall ensure that any sanitary or phytosanitary measure is applied only to the extent necessary to protect human, animal or plant life or health, is based on scientific principles and is not maintained without sufficient scientific evid-ence, except as provided for in paragraph 7 of Article 5.

47 Panel Report, *Australia – Apples*, para. 7.226, where the panel referring to *US – Con-tinued Suspension* unequivocally stated: 'The Panel finds no reason to articulate a standard of review that departs from such guidance.'

48 *Australia – Measures Affecting the Importation of Apples from New Zealand (DS376) – First Written Submissions of Australia*, Geneva 18 July 2008, paras 175–89 [herein-after '*Australia – Apples, First Written Submissions of Australia*'].

49 *Australia – Apples, First Written Submissions of Australia*, paras 175–9.

50 *Australia – Apples, First Written Submissions of Australia*, paras 180–3.

51 *Australia–Apples*, WT/DS367/R, adopted 17 December 2010 at paras 7.216–29.

52 Appellate Body Report, *Australia – Measures Affecting the Importation of Apples from New Zealand*, WT/DS367/AB/R, adopted 17 December 2010, para. 222. For the grounds of appeal relied upon by Australia see: *Australia – Measures Affecting the Importation of Apples from New Zealand, Notification of an Appeal by Australia*, WT/DS367/13, 3 September 2010. Australia claimed *inter alia* that the panel erred in its interpretation and application of what constitutes a proper risk assessment under Articles 5.1 and 5.2 of the SPS Agreement. New Zealand also appealed certain find-ings. See *Australia – Measures Affecting the Importation of Apples from New Zealand, Notification of an Other Appeal by New Zealand*, WT/DS367/14, 15 September 2010.

53 See, for example, *United States – Definitive Anti-Dumping and Countervailing Duties on Certain Products from China*, WT/DS379/AB/R, adopted 25 March 2011, paras 491–527; Panel Report, *United States – Measures Affecting Imports of Certain Passenger Vehicle and Light Truck Tyres from China*, WT/DS399/R, adopted 5 October 2011, upheld by Appellate Body Report WT/DS399/AB/R, paras 7.15–21; Appellate Body Report, *United States – Measures Affecting Imports of Certain Passenger Vehicle and Light Truck Tyres from China*, WT/DS399/AB/R, adopted 5 October 2011, paras 122–5 and 257.

54 For example, Appellate Body Report, *Chile – Price Band System and Safeguard Measures Relating to Certain Agricultural Products*, WT/DS207/AB/R, adopted 23 October 2002, paras 227–41, the Appellate Body rejected claims by Chile that the panel's analysis of its price band system (which amounted to unlawful variable tariffs on certain agricultural products) was inconsistent with DSU Article 11. In this case, like many, the Appellant alleged that the panel refused to consider evidence, performed only a cursory review and committed 'factual errors' in its analysis. This use of Article 11 as a 'catch all' criticism of panel findings, may to some extent result from ambiguities in the standard of review.

Part II

Trade agreements in the modern era

A focus on the Asia-Pacific

5   Market access

An institutional challenge to China

Xianchu Zhang[1]

Market access is a general term to cover a number of measures a country may take to restrict imports or investment, which include both tariff and non-tariff barriers on trade of goods and restrictive regulations on investments and imported services. In the GATT/WTO negotiations market access has been a very sensitive issue, particularly for developing countries due to their deep concerns that the opening of markets will lead to loss of revenue and negative impacts on domestic industries.[2] In its course of integration into the world economy, China has faced challenges resulting from its further market opening as not only the second largest economy and the largest developing country, but also a socialist Party-State regime. To a considerable extent, such unique status gives rise more to institutional challenges than to economic implications in China's market development and transition to rule of law governance. This chapter highlights China's progress and ongoing concerns in this regard.

China's implementation of its WTO commitments

As an initial matter, China's serious commitments to transforming its economic system and its impressive achievements thus far should be recognized. China's accession to the WTO has indeed changed the country greatly. By the end of the first five years of China's WTO membership in 2006, significant reforms, including elimination of all licensing requirements for imported goods and lowering agricultural tariffs even below the rates of the EU and Japan, had made China one of the developing countries with the lowest trade barriers. China's ratio of imports to GDP – an important criterion to measure an economy's openness – had moved from 5 percent in 1978 to 30 percent.[3] China overtook Germany in 2009 to become the world's largest exporter[4] and in 2010 surpassed Japan to become the world's second largest economy.[5] The most recent report of the World Bank predicted China will become the world's largest economy before 2030.[6]

China's WTO membership has also led to legal infrastructural reform. In its Protocol on Accession to the WTO, the Chinese Government promised

> to apply and administer in a uniform, impartial and reasonable manner all its laws, regulations, rules and other measures of the central government as

well as local regulations, rules and other measures issued or applied at the sub-national level pertaining to or affecting trade in goods, services, trade-related aspects of intellectual property rights or the control of foreign exchange.[7]

In order to bring the Chinese legal system in line with the WTO regime, between 1999 and 2005, approximately 2000 national laws and administrative regulations as well as local enactments were amended or abolished.[8] The *Foreign Trade Law* and three foreign investment enterprises laws[9] were all overhauled. Moreover, China's WTO commitments to open more business sectors have led to the development of a new market landscape, including increases in trade in both goods and services.[10]

The implementation of China's WTO commitments has been further mapped out in the Provisions on Guiding Foreign Investment Direction of 1995 as amended in 2002 (Guiding Provisions) and the Guiding Industrial Catalogue of Foreign Investment, which has been amended five times since its first promulgation in 1995 (Guiding Catalogue). The *Guiding Provisions* have formed the policy basis for the government to examine and approve foreign investment projects by classifying them into one of four categories: encouraged, permitted, restricted or prohibited.[11] Foreign investment projects in the encouraged areas enjoy certain preferential treatment, such as broader operational flexibility or tax breaks.[12]

The *Guiding Catalogue* sets out in detail the permissible forms and owner-ship structures for foreign investment projects in various industrial sectors according to the four-category classification of the *Guiding Provisions*. It has been amended several times to reflect changes in market conditions and the gov-ernment's policy preferences in further opening its market according to the Protocol Schedule. The latest version of the catalogue was promulgated on 24 December 2011 and became effective on 30 January 2012.

The 2011 *Guiding Catalogue* not only honors China's promises under its WTO Accession Protocol, but also reflect the government's latest endeavor to upgrade its economic structure. For instance, more new and high technology investments are included in the encouraged areas, such as specialized equipment manufacturing, key components of new-energy automobiles, touch system and functional and environmentally friendly clothes. Venture capital, vocational skills training, and services related to research, development and commercial consultation have been listed as encouraged sectors for the first time. Some industries have been liberalized from restricted or prohibited categories to become permitted sectors, such as production of carbonated beverages, construc-tion and operation of medical institutes and establishment of foreign leasing companies.[13] These changes represent new market access opportunities beyond China's WTO commitments.

As such, all market access commitments have been met according to the accession schedule; some sectors were even opened ahead of schedule. These developments have indicated that China has charted the course of its further reform pursuant to the disciplines of the WTO regime.[14] According to Pascal Lamy, the WTO Director-General, China's implementation of its WTO commitments has, in many areas, set a good example for the world.[15] In July 2010, the Chinese Government declared that all the promises and commitments that China made in 2001 for its WTO accession had been fully honored.[16] This announcement seemed to be accepted by Mr Lamy in his response to a question about recent complaints by foreign companies about China's discriminating practice in certain business deals, although he qualified his endorsement with the key word "overall."[17]

Market access trade disputes with China

Notwithstanding China's efforts, its progress apparently has not fully met the expectations of other WTO members. The first Trade Policy Review of China in 2008 identified certain non-tariff barriers as having replaced some former tariffs and noted that most service sectors were still subject to a high degree of state control.[18] The 2010 Trade Policy Review of China continued to call upon the Chinese Government to reduce regulatory and other barriers and to further liberalize its trade and investment regimes to foster competition and achieve a more efficient allocation of resources in the economy.[19]

In fact, some trade disputes with the United States arose immediately after China's accession to the WTO. In 2002, China tried to restrict the import of transgenic soybeans from the United States with some administrative circulars on the grounds of safety of agricultural products. The suspension of imports, nonetheless, was postponed twice after the high level intervention of the American Government. The Chinese Government finally approved the imports in 2004 with the use of accompanying safety certificates.[20] Since then the import of transgenic soybeans from the United States into China seems to have normalized.

In March 2004, the United States filed its first complaint against China at the WTO alleging that the preferential tax treatment provided by the Chinese Government to domestic integrated circuit producers violated China's national treatment obligations under Article III of the GATT. Although both domestic and foreign manufactures were eligible for the tax rebate, the measure did appear to discriminate against imported semiconductors to be used in the domestic market. Soon after, the EU, Japan, Mexico and Taiwan also asked to join the consultations. The dispute was resolved a few days before it went to the WTO panel with China's agreement to eliminate the rebate for any new semiconductor producers and to phase out the practice by April 2005.[21]

In March 2006, the EU and the US requested consultations with China regarding China's imposition of a 25 percent surcharge on imported automobile parts used in manufacturing motor vehicles in China, which was equivalent to the average tariff rate applicable to complete motor vehicles. Later, a WTO panel found China's measure was inconsistent with Article III of the GATT and other relevant provisions. China appealed the panel's decision. The Appellate

Body upheld the panel's findings in December 2008 and recommended that China bring its measures into conformity with its obligations under the Agreement.[22] In 2009, the Chinese Government decided to eliminate the surcharge.[23]

China also signed a memorandum of understanding with the United States, in November 2007, to terminate by 1 January 2008 a range of subsidies measures (including tax credits and other incentives, designed to encourage exports) which were alleged to have violated both the WTO agreements and China's Protocol of Accession.[24]

In June 2008, Canada and the United States requested consultations with China regarding Chinese measures prohibiting foreign financial information suppliers from directly soliciting subscribers for their services in China, and instead to provide their services only through a designated official agent. They claimed that such measures were inconsistent with the provisions on market access and national treatment of the General Agreement on Trade in Services (the "GATS"). The dispute was resolved with the promulgation of a new decree by the Chinese authorities to allow foreign institutions to provide financial information services directly to their subscribers in China subject to government approval.[25]

More recently the WTO Appellate Body handed down another final decision in the dispute between the United States and China over China's domestic measures, *inter alia*, to reserve trading rights with respect to imported films, audiovisual entertainment products, sound recordings and publications to state-designated or -owned enterprises. The Appellate Body, upholding the panel's conclusions, found such measures, and in particular the *Guiding Catalogue* of 2007 prohibiting foreign investment entities from engaging in distribution services, were violating national treatment and market access commitments under the GATS. China was requested to bring its measures in question into conformity with China's WTO accession obligations.[26] The state authorities of China adopted new *Measures for Administration of Import of Audio and Video Recordings* on 6 April 2011, which separate import distribution as a commercial right from the administrative control over import examination and supervision. As a result, business entities including foreign investment firms may engage in import and distribution of audio and video products as long as they comply with the registration and permission procedures.

Ongoing concerns with market access in China

Since the worldwide financial crisis, concerns over protectionism and market access in China seem to have deepened. In the domestic market, local governments have adopted various mandates to buy locally.[27] Moreover, the State Commission of National Development and Reform (SCNDR), the state authority in charge of economic planning, has ordered local governments to favor domestic firms in their implementation of the national stimulus.[28] In the same period, the vigorous promotion of indigenous innovation policy at both national and local levels, as part of national development, has further fueled the controversy over foreign firms' market access to China.[29] For example, in the indigenous innovation catalogue adopted by the Shanghai Government comprising 258 products, only two were from enterprises comprising Chinese manufacturers partnered with foreign investors.[30]

As a result, market access has remained a serious concern among China's major trading partners in recent years. For example, the American Chamber of Commerce in its White Paper 2009 on the State of American Business in China (White Paper), and its Market Access report on China of 2011, highlighted the less transparent and predictable regulatory environment facing American companies in China as compared with previous years. With respect to market access, two government procurement policies have been particularly identified as protective measures: technology transfer as a mandatory condition for government approval for investment and sales in support of large-scale projects, and the requirement for a majority of the equipment used for public projects to be domestically designed and built.[31] In the 'Market access' report of 2011, licensing and accreditation, capital requirements, limitation on foreign ownership and intellectual property protection are identified as major institutional barriers to market entry in China.[32]

The European Union Chamber of Commerce in China, in its European Business in China Position Paper 2010/2011 (EU Position Paper), which was based on a survey of some 1400 EU enterprises in China, has echoed the concerns of the American Chamber. According to the document, barriers to access to China's market were most serious among all BRICS[33] countries, as measured by the Product Market Regulation (PMR), a comprehensive and internationally comparable set of indicators.[34] The previous Position Paper also found that trade barriers in China, particularly industrial policy interventions and restrictions on foreign investment, such as establishment costs in capital requirements, licensing, forced joint ventures and co-ownership caps, have been on the rise for the last three years. These barriers have cost EU businesses €21 billion in lost trade opportunities annually, which is the equivalent to one-fourth of current EU exports to China and renders China less appealing as an investment destination for EU firms. As such, most survey respondents identified promotion of fair competition and breaking up existing monopolies as the most urgent steps needed to improve market conditions in China in the coming years.[35]

Against this backdrop, market access has increasingly become an urgent agenda item at the top levels of the Chinese Government. In recent years, senior leaders have repeatedly assured foreign governments and investors that China would continue to unswervingly commit to a fair and open market economy.[36] Indeed, President Hu Jintao agreed to eliminate discriminatory indigenous innovation criteria for foreign suppliers on his visit to the US in 2011.[37] However, this promise is subject to a number of uncertainties given that the government has made clear that China is unlikely to join the WTO Agreement on Government Procurement in the near future, notwithstanding China's promise to participate in the agreement "as soon as possible" when it acceded to the WTO in 2001 and that it began its official negotiations to join the GPA in 2007.[38]

From foreign investors' perspective the above complaints may be well grounded. But from China's perspective, certain concerns with its own development strategy and immature market conditions may have to be taken into account. As the largest developing country in the world, in addition to its WTO commitments, China has been facing serious domestic challenges in many aspects, such as: unbalanced regional development; huge unemployment and social stability pressures; further domestic economic system reforms; modernization of its institutional infrastructures; lack of a competition culture; and inexperience in dealing with market/financial risks. From the very beginning of its economic reform and market opening, China has maintained a gradual approach to ensure stable progress in the domestic transitions and in its integration into the global market.[39] Moreover, some of the demands from developed country firms go beyond the market access commitments stipulated in China's Accession Protocol. Even in the EU Position Paper, what was sought to improve access to the Chinese market was called "WTO-plus reform."[40] Indeed, the Chinese Government has made some offers on such "WTO-plus" concessions in recent years; opening its mandatory third party liability automobile insurance market to foreign insurers[41] and allowing foreign banks to issue credit cards in China are the latest examples.[42] Thus, although the proposals made in these reports may be in China's long-term development interests, it will still be up to the Chinese Government to decide the best strategy and timetable for implementing further reforms according to domestic conditions.

That said, some of China's rules, measures and policies concerning trade and investment are indeed controversial and may not be consistent with its WTO obligations or with WTO rules. In addition to the aforementioned disputes over market access decided by WTO panels and the Appellate Body, some other incidents have also been noted for their Chinese socialist market economy characteristics, such as the government's rejection of the proposed acquisition of majority shares of Xuzhou Construction Machinery Group Co. (known as "Xugong") for US$375 million by Carlyle in 2005[43] and the decision of the Ministry of Commerce (MOFCOM) to apply the Antimonopoly Law of China for the first time to reject the proposed acquisition of Huiyuan, the largest juice maker in China, by Coca-Cola through a wholly owned subsidiary for HK$17.9 billion.[44] Since this incident, state authorities have seemed to relax their enforcement approach. For example, in 2011 out of 194 M&A applications, all were approved by MOFCOM (four approved with conditions) except for five withdrawals.[45]

Despite the increasing international attention in market access to China, more controversial industrial policies have emerged recently. For example, the Guiding Opinions Concerning Promotion of Movie Industry Development promulgated on 21 January 2010 provide that theaters shall use no less than two-thirds of their screen time to show domestically produced movies.[46] In the auto industry, promulgation of the new development plan has been delayed since 2009 due to controversies over the draft indigenous innovation policy's mandatory requirement of majority Chinese control over the production of core automobile components, including batteries, electronic machinery and control systems, even in Sino-foreign joint ventures.[47] Some new policies and practices, such as the deletion of auto manufacturing from the encouraged investment areas list in the 2011 Guiding Catalogue, elimination of foreign auto brands from the government procurement catalogue, tightened market restrictions and alleged forced technology transfers[48] are other examples worrying foreign investors.

Characteristics of the Chinese socialist market economy

The brief review above well illustrates China's market opening after its WTO accession as a challenging process with inconsistent policies and practices. As the 2009 White Paper pointed out, with respect to market access and national treatment, there has been a continuing conflict between China's desire to develop its world-class enterprises and its stated commitment to an open and competitive market.[49] This observation touches on the inherent contradiction of the so-called socialist market economy in China, also known as the Chinese characteristics of the market economy.

At a very basic level, the current Constitution of China guarantees the state will safeguard public ownership and sectors as the basis and leading force of the national economy,[50] although the private sector has also been recognized as an "important part" of the socialist market economy under the administration, guidance, assistance and supervision of the state.[51]

According to the Decision on Certain Issues Concerning Improvement of the Socialist Market Economy promulgated by the Central Committee of the Communist Party of China (CPC) dated 14 October 2003, the primacy of public ownership had to be maintained, but could be realized through different means. As such, although the Decision called for vigorously developing a private economy by eliminating institutional barriers and enabling market access, Section 1 (4) explicitly identified shareholding control as a means to enhance public ownership in the market and state monopolies in key sectors of the national economy. This is the ideological basis underlying the restrictive industrial policy and measures that have been developed.

Moreover, the dual track legislation governing business organizations within the current legal system has been maintained thus far, with one line of legislation made according to the political classification of the ownership (such as different laws and regulations governing state-owned enterprises, foreign investment enterprises, enterprises under collective ownership and private firms, respectively). The other more based on the different forms of liability (such as the Company Law, the Partnership Enterprises Law and the Sole Proprietorship Enterprise Law). With the legislative reforms in recent years, the legal environment for business operation in China has been improved a great deal. However, in the transitional period from the planned economy to a market economy, the current legal framework still suffers from a rigid political ideology to a large extent and fails to provide a level playing field in the market.[52] Due to the inherent conflict between socialism and capitalism, under state-driven marketization, the government has been suspicious of non-state institutions not under its control for their potential threat to the political regime and therefore tends to suppress such institutions.[53] Even after more than 30 years of reform, the CPC's ultimate goal still centers more on maintaining power than on promoting market equality and competition.[54]

Such political ideology has guided economic development with a national champion strategy to enable China to better compete in a further opened and globalized market, purauant to which huge state-owned or controlled companies have been created with the government's full support and monopolies in the domestic market. By 2007, through government arranged reorganizations the number of huge companies directly under control of the Central Government had dropped from 196 to 151, but their contribution to the national economy reached 44 percent of the China's GDP. Apparently, the Government has used the reform to reposition the entire state sector. According to a Government plan, the concentration of the state sector will be further enhanced by reducing the number of centrally controlled enterprises to 80–100 and establishing 30–50 internationally competitive, super-sized companies.[55] The worldwide financial crisis has apparently delayed the implementation of the plan. By May 2012 the Central Government had only been able to trim the number of such enterprises down to 117.[56]

A report of the China Enterprise Confederation and China Enterprises Director Association released in September 2009 further showed that the business revenue of China's top 500 companies, of which 349 are state-owned or controlled, accounted for 83.5 percent of national GDP and their earning capacity had exceeded that of their United States counterparts for the first time, although they still lagged behind the world-leading enterprises in resource allocation, market innovation and international presence.[57] In fact, most of the impressive earning capacity of these giant enterprises should apparently be credited more to their domestic monopolies than to their real market competitiveness. Among the 500, only 220 are involved in overseas business and 86 percent of these firms had less than 30 percent of an international market exposure.[58]

The implementation of such a national champion strategy will inevitably affect foreign firms' market access opportunities in China. In the course of nationwide debate over Carlyle's proposed acquisition of Xugong, the Central Government promulgated the Guiding Opinions to Promote Adjustment of State Assets and Reorganization of State-owned Enterprises on 18 December 2006. The circular made it clear that the state would maintain "absolute control" in seven business sectors, including military industry, power, oil and coal supply, telecommunications, civil aviation and other means of transportation. In other sectors, such as equipment manufacturing, autos, electronic information, construction, iron and steel production, nonferrous metal, chemical industries, exploration and design, and science and technology, the state should keep "relatively strong control."

The Antimonopoly Law of 2007

China's first Antimonopoly Law, which was adopted in 2007 and became effective on 1 August 2008, is considered crucial to deepening reform in China and to promoting its becoming more market-driven.[59] Most of the rules against monopolistic conduct in the market indeed look similar to those in developed countries. However, Article 4 of the Law explicitly stipulates that the Government shall only formulate and implement competition rules suitable for China's socialist market economy. Article 7 allows the government to protect the undertakings of state-monopolized businesses due to their strategic importance to the national economic lifelines and to national security. Moreover, Article 12 merely subjects the governance of the Law to "undertakings" of legal persons, other organizations or natural individuals engaging in commodities and services trade. The narrow scope of Article 12 seems to indicate the Government's unwillingness to directly subject state entities and the monopolized businesses under its control to the jurisdiction of the Law.[60]

Chapter 5 of the Law includes some separate rules dealing with administrative monopolies, such as abuse of administrative powers, forced purchases, regional blockades, discriminatory standards, forced restrictions on competition, and eliminating or restricting competition by enactments in violation of national laws and regulations. Some legislative branch actors, nonetheless, take the view that given the current political and market conditions in China one can hardly expect the Law to fundamentally solve the problem of administrative monopolies and unequal competition, although as the relevant legislation in this regard it has to include some rules against such market conduct in general terms.[61] A careful reading will further reveal that Article 33 of the Law merely subjects administrative monopolies trading in goods to its jurisdiction, leaving untouched all the government monopolistic schemes involving services trade.

As such, some experts have observed that:

> The monopolistic interests of SOEs have always been sophistically preserved by the various government departments using commercial and national reasons. In turn, this creates poor services and uncompetitive rates for consumers. A futile regulation like Chapter 5 (of the Antimonopoly Law) would only be nominal and symbolic at the best.[62]

For foreign investors, the aggressive expansion of foreign trade and investment in China has given rise to the sensitive question of how the antimonopoly rules would be applied to them. Although the business environment in China is still quite different from other jurisdictions, mergers and acquisitions (M&As) have been a very dynamic means of attracting foreign investment since the 1990s. The wave of foreign M&As in China has gained momentum from the accelerated marketization, the further market opening and the improvement of legal conditions under China's WTO obligations and commitments. In fact, M&As in China reached an all-time high in 2008 with deals worth US$159.6 billion recorded – 44 percent more than in 2007. Inbound M&As posted a 34.2

percent increase as compared with 2007, making China a global investment haven despite the global financial meltdown.[63]

As a matter of fact, aggressive foreign investment has even divided the state authorities in their positions towards further market opening. In May 2004, the State Administration of Industry and Commerce (SAIC), the state agency responsible for business registrations and market supervision, published an investigatory report entitled "Multinationals' Activities to Restrict Competition in China and the Counter-Measures." According to the report, some multinationals had obtained their dominant market position in China with monopolistic tendencies in several business sectors. Large multinationals such as Eastman Kodak, Microsoft and Tetra Pak were named in the SAIC's investigation and in its accusation list. Some other unnamed transnational companies were also found to have built up their dominant positions in China through their technological, capital and managerial advantages. According to the report, the multinationals' aggressive expansion constituted a threat to the security of the national economy.[64]

The Ministry of Commerce (MOFCOM), however, apparently disagreed with this radical position. In a research paper, the Research Institute of the MOFCOM argued that foreign investments made an important contribution to China's economic development. They had neither threatened the economic safety of China, nor controlled the technology market or any sensitive business sector.[65] Mr Shang Ming, the Head of the Treaty and Law Department and the Director of the Antimonopoly Office of MOFCOM, then further pointed out that the Antimonopoly Law should be equally applied to both domestic and foreign enterprises. The antimonopoly enactment should aim at promoting and safeguarding fair competition of all kinds of enterprises on the market against monopolistic activities.[66]

The divergence seemed to escalate and led to some further twists when the Antimonopoly Law drafting entered into the final stages. In early 2006, Mr Li Deshui, the then Director General of the National Bureau of Statistics, warned in an interview that foreign "malicious M&As" in China would threaten economic security and national sovereignty and called for action to curb such a trend.[67] On the contrary, Mr Hu Jingyan, Director of the Foreign Investment Department of MOFCOM, then continued to openly refute the proposition against the expansion of foreign businesses in China. According to him, there were neither emerging foreign monopolies in any region or business sector, nor any foreign control of economic lifelines in China.[68]

This internal debate among different state authorities inevitably led to uncertainties and inconsistency in practice. Over the strong opposition of experts and scholars, the Antimonopoly Law fails to establish a unified system and assigns enforcement powers to MOFCOM, the SAIC and the SCNDR. According to Professor Wang Xiaoye of the China Social Science Academy, a leading authority in China, "No country in the world appoints so many administrative departments to enforce the law and to protect market competition. Without a unified and authoritative law enforcement organ, it will be difficult to effectively enforce the Antimonopoly Law."[69]

As such, it is not clear at present to what extent the three-way split of enforcement authority can create a fair and effective legal regime to deal with both domestic administrative and foreign monopolies on the market. However, as a positive development, MOFCOM recently further amended a controversial 2006 regulation issued jointly by six state authorities regarding foreign M&As.[70] The revision seems to indicate that MOFCOM has exclusive jurisdiction over foreign M&As in the new enforcement structure. More importantly, the new Provisions completely delete some special notifications rules exclusively applicable to foreign M&As and subject them instead to the newly promulgated Concentration Provisions of the State Council, which are equally applicable to all types of enterprises. On the other hand, the 2009 Provisions still retain a separate set of rules governing foreign M&As where inadequately defined terms such as "public interests," "the social and economic order" and "loss of state assets" continue to be sticky issues for foreign investors.[71]

Thus, multinationals, although praising the Government's continuing effort to improve the legislative framework by promulgating a series of implementing rules,[72] do not hide their worries about the potential market barriers created in enforcement of the Antimonopoly Law and uncertainties over the procedures.[73] In this regard, the promulgation of the Rules on the Implementation of the National Security Review Mechanisms, by MOFCOM in August 2011, has particularly worried foreign investors in their M&A activities as a potential future barrier, due to their broad and ambiguous scope of application.[74]

Domestic private sector market access problems

The deep concern over market access in China has another crucial aspect, namely maintaining a level playing field for the domestic private sector. Although the leadership of the CPC seems to be taking an elitist position by incorporating private economic forces into the socialist system, further development of the Chinese private economy still faces serious barriers. Thus far, ideological resistance and institutional obstacles have continued to deny equal entitlement of market access to the domestic private economy; in certain areas biased practices against private enterprises by state-controlled monopolies have even increased in recent years. A phenomenon known as "state sectors advance and private sectors retreat" has attracted both domestic and international attention.[75]

Even before the worldwide financial crisis, the pace of private sector development in China had slowed. For instance, a decrease in private enterprise registrations since 2007 has been recorded in at least seven provinces, including Beijing and Shanghai. During the financial crisis RMB4.8 billion "rescue credit" was issued under government policies in 2009; however, less than 5 percent of the credit was provided to small and mid-sized enterprises (which make up 99 percent of all enterprises in China). Soon after, the China Social Science Academy published a more detailed report which warned that 40 percent of small and mid-sized enterprises had closed down and another 40 percent were badly struggling to survive.[76]

According to a recent survey, despite some encouraging policies, difficult situations facing the private economy have not changed significantly. Among 80-some industries surveyed, the state sector is entitled to access to 72; foreign investments are permitted to enter into 62, whereas the domestic private economy is allowed access to only 41.[77]

Moreover, unlike foreign investors, domestic private economic actors are neither treated with special policies and guarantees under China's WTO commitments, nor entitled to effective legal remedies through meaningful legal proceedings against the government. For example, to the government's surprise, the first lawsuits filed under the Antimonopoly Law were not disputes between competing enterprises, but were all brought by small private enterprises against government administrations. Within 18 days after the Antimonopoly Law became effective, the State Administration of Products Quality Inspection was named a defendant in three cases for abusing its administrative power to block market access by way of monopolized and compulsory licensing, certifying and fee charging. It was further reported that a department head of the Administration committed suicide in the period after the allegations triggered criminal investigations of the violations and dealings with the fee profits. The People's Court refused to accept the lawsuits on statute of limitations grounds.[78] Later, some private firms tried to sue two giant state-controlled oil companies, Sinopec and China National Petroleum, for their alleged monopolistic conduct resulting in the closure of 663 private oil dealers and 45,000 gas stations, although as many as 14 instructions on equal treatment had been issued by the leaders of the State Council on this matter.[79]

As such, under the "national champion" policy, the state sector has accomplished its dynamic development in the past decade at the cost of opportunities for the private economy. A 2011 statistic that proves the case is that the cumulative revenues of the top ten private companies in China were still RMB846.2 billion shy of that of Sinopec, a company under the direct control of the Central Government, alone.[80] Recently, the World Bank recommended in its *China 2030* report that the Chinese Government complete its transition towards a market economy with further opening-up and state sector reform.[81] However, such modest advice was met with strong political resistance. The Beijing press conference of Robert Zoellick, World Bank President, was even disrupted upon the launch of the Bank's report,with protestors decrying the recommendations as being a poison violating socialist principles.[82]

Moreover, the Supreme People's Court has recently made it clear that in implementing the Antimonopoly Law against administrative monopolies, the People's Court will now only accept legal actions against "concrete administrative decisions" affecting the specific parties concerned, leaving controversies on discriminatory policies and measures untouched. As such, a government monopoly policy can neither be challenged, nor be made subject to other legal enforcement schemes.[83] Against this background, Professor Yasheng Huang of MIT convincingly argues:

to a large extent the fact that the private sector was still able to grow in an enormously difficult environment after the Tiananmen crackdown is a tribute to the agility and acumen of Chinese entrepreneurs, not to the wisdom of the policy of the Chinese Government.[84]

Concluding remarks

As China has increasingly integrated into international markets and the WTO system, issues concerning market access have become much more challenging. Although China has implemented well what was stipulated in its WTO Accession Protocol in the transitional period, non-discrimination as the fundamental WTO principle will continue to test the Government's commitments to a market economy. Indeed, given its size, its early stage of market development, and the complex conditions China faces as the largest developing country, the gradual approach has proven wise and should be stuck to. However, upon graduating from the transitional period, China has seen more trade disputes with its trading partners and has been subject to more external pressures, including the rulings of the WTO dispute settlement body. In this context, as reflected above, China has taken a positive and responsible approach to ceasing or changing its measures found to be inconsistent with WTO rules in a timely manner after bilateral settlements were reached or decisions rendered. This should also be considered evidence of China's serious commitment to reform consistent with the WTO principles and rules.

However, China cannot just be satisfied with what has been achieved. Since competitive edges in the globalized market may only be created through further market opening and reforms, these steps are needed more for China's interests for its future development than the interests of foreign traders and investors.

Based on the above it is clear that market access in China is a daunting challenge that not only concerns foreign traders and investors as well as other WTO members, but also the domestic private economy. China's WTO membership has been widely considered to be a new external impetus for domestic reform. But thus far ideological resistance has rendered further reform a long, difficult and unpredictable process.[85]

In this context, market access has also carried significant political sensitivities and implications in China. Given the inherent contradiction of the socialist market economy, further market access will inevitably demand, and lead to, less government control, more business autonomy and further competition with the dominant public ownership. As such, market development may play a catalytic role for further reform of the political and governance regime. To a large extent the real obstacles to an effective implementation of China's WTO commitments and obligations are the problem of its "internal barriers" derived from political authoritarianism.[86] The real fear of the government is the historical proof that a free market, once genuinely established, may not tolerate an authoritarian regime.

Notes

1 Professor, Faculty of Law, The University of Hong Kong. The author would like to express his gratitude to the Research Grant Committee of the University of Hong Kong and Mrs Li Ka Shing Fund of the University of Hong Kong for their kind support to this research project. This chapter is an updated and expanded version of my presentation at the conference "Trade Agreements: Where Do We Go from Here?" at Victoria University of Wellington, New Zealand on 22 October 2009.
2 Zoellick (5 December 2002).
3 Lamy (6 September 2006).
4 Atkins (9 February 2010).
5 Whipp (16 August 2010).
6 The World Bank 2012.
7 The Protocol on the Accession of the People's Republic of China, 11 November 2001, art. 2 (A)(2).
8 *Trade Policy Review Report by the People's Republic of China*, WT/TPR/G/161, 17 March 2006, at 316.
9 They include the Law of Sino-Foreign Equity Joint Ventures, the Law of Sino-Foreign Contractual Joint Ventures and the Law of Wholly Foreign Owned Enterprises.
10 For the details of China's market access commitments, see Annex 8 and 9 of the Protocol on the Accession of the People's Republic of China, dated 11 November 2001.
11 Arts. 3 and 4 of the Guiding Provisions.
12 Arts. 9 and 11.
13 An English translation of the Guiding Catalogue of 2011 is available at www.lawin-fochina.com/display.aspx?lib=law&id=9125 (accessed 12 February 2012).
14 Ya Qin 2007: 720–41.
15 Lamy (6 September 2006).
16 See China Daily (20 July 2010).
17 Roman (25 July 2010).
18 *Trade Policy Review: Report by the Secretariat – China* (Revision), WT/TPR/S/199/Rev.1, 12 August 2008.
19 WTO (2010).
20 Brandt and Rawski 2008: 654.
21 The dispute was recorded in the WTO Dispute Settlement as DS309. For a detailed discussion of the dispute, see Hufbauer, Wong and Sheth 2006: 55–61.
22 Panel Report, *China – Measures Affecting Imports of Automobile Parts*, WT/DS339/R/WT/DS340/R/WT/DS342/R/and Add.1 and Add.2, adopted 12 January 2009, upheld (WT/DS339/R) and as modified (WT/DS340/R/WT/DS342/R) by Appellate Body Reports WT/DS339/AB/R/WT/DS340/AB/R/WT/DS342/AB/R.
23 See *Caijing* Magazine (Financial Magazine) (29 August 2009).
24 HKTDC (6 December 2007).
25 *China – Financial Information Services*, DS/378, withdrawn on 20 June 2008. The new decree was entitled Provisions on Administration of Provision of Financial Information Services in China by Foreign Institutions of 30 April 2009 with the effective date on 1 June 2009. An English translation of the Provisions is available at www.bjreview.com.cn/document/txt/2009-07/20/content_208369.htm (accessed 31 May 2012).
26 Appellate Body Report, *China – Measures Affecting Trading Rights and Distribution Services for Certain Publications and Audiovisual Entertainment Products*, WT/DS363/AB/R, adopted 19 January 2010.
27 Hornby (18 February 2009).
28 See the *Sydney Morning Herald* (1 July 2009).

29 For a brief discussion of the policy and disputes at issue, see Zhang 2011b: 223–8.
30 McGregor 2011: 19.
31 AmCham-China 2009: 12–20.
32 AmCham-China (29 April 2011).
33 BRICS refers to Brazil, Russia, India, China and South Africa.
34 European Union Chamber of Commerce in China, *European Business in China Position Paper 2010–2011*, Executive Summary.
35 European Union Chamber of Commerce in China, *European Business in China Position Paper 2009/2010*, 2 September 2009, Section One.
36 See Ministry of Foreign Affairs of the People's Republic of China (29 April 2010); Talley (11 May 2011).
37 White House Office of the Press Secretary (19 January 2011).
38 Qingfen (21 March 2012).
39 Chen 2009.
40 European Union Chamber of Commerce in China, *European Business in China Position Paper 2010–2011*, Section one, point 5.1 (market access).
41 Ni (20 February 2012).
42 See South China Morning Post (7 February 2012).
43 Asia Money (1 September 2008).
44 The MOFCOM decision with the series number [2009] 22 was published at http://fldj.mofcom.gov.cn/aarticle/ztxx/200903/20090306108494.html (accessed 30 May 2012).
45 Xu (3 February 2012).
46 The Guiding Opinions are available at www.fdi.gov.cn/pub/FDI/zcfg/law_ch_info.jsp?docid=117418 (accessed 30 May 2012).
47 See Automotive World (22 February 2010); and Wang (2005).
48 See Shirouze (27 February 2012); Shirouze (28 February 2012); and Ensinger (7 September 2011).
49 AmCham-China 2009: 20–1.
50 Arts. 6 and 7 of the Constitution of China of 1982 as amended in 2004.
51 In the original provision of the Constitution of 1982, the non-public sector was only stipulated as a supplement to the public economy. Its status was upgraded by constitutional amendments in 1999 and 2004.
52 Zhang 2011a: 142–62.
53 Clarke 2007b: 560.
54 Link and Kurlantzick 2009: 13.
55 Yi and Baoping 2009: 45; *Jinghua Shibao* (*Beijing Times*) (5 March 2008); and the Speech of Mr Li Rongrong, the then Director of State-Owned Assets Supervision and Administration Commission (SASAC) on 16 December 2008, at www.gov.cn/ztzl/2008-12/16/content_1179606.htm (accessed 30 May 2012).
56 *Zhongguo Jingji Shibao* (*China Economic Times*) (17 May 2012).
57 China Daily (7 September 2009).
58 People's Daily (8 September 2009).
59 See Cao Kangtai (the Director of the Legislative Office of the State Council), The Explanatory notes to submit the draft Antimonopoly Law to the National People's Congress of PRC, on 25 June 2006, *Zhonghua Renmin Gongheguo Renmin Daibiao Dahui Changwu Weiyuanhui Gongbao* (Bulletin of the Standing Committee of the National People's Congress of PRC), No. 6 (2007), at 523–4.
60 By comparison, under India's Competition Act of 2002, any department of the government which is or has been engaged in any business activity, investment or other undertaking is subject to the uniform governance of the Act. See s. 2 (h) of the Act.
61 Economic Law Division of the Legislative Committee under the Standing Committee of the National People's Congress ed. 2007: 37.
62 Li and Young 2008: 186–202.
63 See China Daily (6 January 2009).

64 The report was printed at *GONGSHANG Xingzheng GUANLI* (Journal of State Administration of Industry and Commerce) 2004: 43.
65 Lin Hua of the Research Institute of the MOFCOM 2005: 32–5.
66 Interview with Shang Ming, the Director of the Antimonopoly Office of MOFCOM, *Zhongguo Wang* (China Net) (23 December 2004).
67 Dickie (8 March 2006).
68 See *Xinhua* News Agency (16 September 2006). Online. Available at: http://big5.xinhuanet.com/gate/big5/news.xinhuanet.com/classad/2006-09/16/content_5098110.htm (accessed 30 May 2012).
69 Quoted from China Daily (15 November 2006).
70 The 2009 Provisions were issued on 22 June 2009, at www.fdi.gov.cn/pub/FDI_EN/Laws/law_en_info.jsp?docid=108906 (accessed 30 May 2012).
71 Art. 3 of the 2009 Provisions stipulates that foreign investors shall not cause over concentration, restrict or eliminate competition, disturb the social and economic order or public social interests, or result in loss of the state assets.
72 Since the adoption of the Antimonopoly Law a series of more detailed implementing provisions have been issued by different state authorities, including Anti-Price Monopoly Regulations and Anti-Price Monopoly Administration Enforcement Procedural Regulations by the National Development and Reform Commission, Regulations on Prohibiting Monopoly Agreements and Regulations on Curbing Abuse of Administrative Power to Eliminate or Restrict Competition by the State Administration of Industry and Commerce; and Measures for Undertaking Concentration Notification, Measure for Undertaking Concentration Examination, and Provisions on M&As of Domestic Enterprises by Foreign Investors by the Ministry of Commerce.
73 AmCham-China 2009: 26–36; also see Li 2009: 179–86; and Neumann and Zhang 2006: 21–9. Recently, at least three senior officials of the MOFCOM and the SAIC in charge of foreign acquisition approval were arrested for the conspired corruption. See Financial Magazine (28 October 2008).
74 European Commission 2012: 9; and Bradsher (28 August 2007).
75 Wheatley (2 March 2010); Mines (29 August 2010); Anderlini and Dyer (25 November 2009).
76 See *Zhongguo Pinglun* (China Review) (12 June 2009). Juan Jose Daboub, Managing Director of the World Bank also voiced a warning about the serious deceleration of the private economy in China's recovery from the worldwide financial crisis. Daboub (10 June 2009): 2.
77 See *Guiji Caijing Shibao* (*International Business Times*) (29 November 2011). Online. Available at: www.ibtimes.com.cn/articles/20111129/020921_all.htm (accessed 30 May 2012).
78 See *Xin Jingbao* (*The Beijing News*) (27 August 2008); and the report of the progress of the cases by the Chinacourt (14 August 2008).
79 See *Jinghua Shibao* (*Beijing Times*) (12 October 2008); and *Bandao Wang* (Peninsula Website) (30 June 2009).
80 See *Xinhua* News Agency (27 August 2011).
81 The World Bank 2012.
82 See China Daily (28 February 2012).
83 The statement of the Supreme People's Court was published on 3 November 2008, at http://news.xinhuanet.com/legal/2008-11/03/content_10299026.htm (accessed 30 May 2012).
84 Huang 2008a.
85 Huang 2008b.
86 Potter 2001; Wu 2007: 750–71.

6 China's regionalism

Working towards a regional comprehensive economic partnership?

Rafael Leal-Arcas[1]

Introduction

This chapter argues that China's attitude towards multilateral trade is unclear. Moreover, China assumes little responsibility for maintaining international order in global economic governance. This chapter argues that China should hide less behind the status of a developing country and stand up to its own ambition to new leadership. China, for example, seems to go against "traditional" powers (mainly the United States), and tends to focus on South–South regionalism.[2]

The results of the July 2008 World Trade Organization (WTO) mini-ministerial conference, composed of a trade G-7,[3] are evidence of this. At the mini-ministerial, WTO members' attempt to salvage a deal in the Doha Round broke down. Import-sensitive China and India were pitted against the United States' demands for predictable market access for farm products.[4]

In addition, for most of the Cold War period, China "was not prepared to play entirely by the rules."[5] By the 1990s, however, China had fully accepted the identity of statehood and the rights and duties implied by sovereignty.[6] It accepted these pluralist rules at a time when the rules of the game were changing.

The dynamics of this changing order were driven by economic liberalization and values, including universal human rights. In 2005, the then United States Deputy Secretary of State, Robert Zoellick, gave a speech entitled "Whither China: From Membership to Responsibility,"[7] which focused on the rise of China's international influence and the management of a Sino-United States great power relationship. Zoellick expressed anxiety about China's remarkable economic growth and growing influence as well as uncertainties about how China would use its power. He said "[M]any countries hope China will pursue a peaceful rise, but none will bet their future on it."[8]

Many documents and speeches related to United States foreign policy reinforce the idea of China as an international stakeholder. For example, the 2006 United States National Security Strategy reaffirmed China's international status as a global player and urged that "[China] must act as a responsible stakeholder that fulfills its obligations and works with the United States and others to advance the international system that has enabled its success."[9] This chapter argues that it is necessary to pave the way for responsible multilateralism[10] for the common goal[11] of establishing peace, security, and prosperity in the twenty-first century.[12]

The chapter is divided into four parts. After the introduction, the first part deals with the criteria to be a global economic superpower, and concludes that China is one of the three global economic superpowers today (the US and the European Union [EU] being the other two; the EU remains the world's biggest economy[13]). The next part examines China's attitude towards multilateral trade and China's preference for regionalism. This leads to an analysis of China's position within the WTO. The final part presents some concluding remarks.

A new global economic superpower

The establishment of the People's Republic of China took place in 1949. Since then, not only has China undergone an extraordinary transformation domestically, but it has rapidly become one of the pre-eminent States in regional and global politics.[14]

The economic rise of China over the past three decades has been extra-ordinary. China today is the largest exporter in the world and the largest lender to the United States. Talk of a G-2 composed of the United States and China reflects this shift and indicates that China is now regarded as a near equal power to the United States. As part of its growing influence, China has recently been actively engaging in economic diplomacy through a wide range of means, including its entry into the WTO in December 2001, bilateral trade agreements, foreign aid and investment projects in Africa, cooperation on international financial regulation and climate change.[15] This has placed China at the center of most major international policy discussions.

Compared to other major world economies, Chinese leaders seem to see a tri-umphant future because Europe and Japan – suffering from the deepest post-war recession – are barely worth considering as rivals, and the US – one of the three global economic superpowers – has passed its peak.[16] Predictions are that by 2019 China will have overtaken the United States to become the country with the largest economy in the world,[17] suggesting an end to the United States' long reign as the driving force in the global economy.

The definition of a global economic superpower is key to understanding China's rise. According to Bergsten, for a country to be considered a global economic superpower, it must meet three criteria: (1) it must be large enough to significantly affect the world economy;[18] (2) it must be sufficiently dynamic to contribute meaningfully to global economic growth;[19] and (3) it must be open enough to trade and capital flows to have a major impact on other countries.[20] China meets these criteria.[21]

As Bergsten has said, China poses a major challenge to the world economy by virtue of being a new global economic superpower.[22] It is a historically unique global economic superpower in three ways. First, it is still a poor country with a Gross Domestic Product (GDP) per capita of around US$6,000, compared to US$50,000 in the case of the United States and US$35,000 in the case of the

EU.[23] Second, China is not a democracy in the Western conception of the term. And third, it is not yet a market economy.[24]

This third point, however, is debatable. Article 15 of China's WTO Accession Agreement allows WTO Members, on a bilateral basis, to give China market-economy status in anti-dumping cases. For example, countries including Australia, New Zealand,[25] Argentina, Brazil, and several Asian countries treat China as a market economy in anti-dumping cases, whereas the EU and the United States treat China as a non-market economy.[26] China's economy since the late 1970s has changed from a centrally planned system that was largely closed to international trade, to a more market-oriented economy that has a rapidly growing private sector.[27] Reforms started in the late 1970s with the phasing out of collectivized agriculture and expanded to include the gradual liberalization of prices, fiscal decentralization, increased autonomy for state enterprises, the foundation of a diversified banking system, the development of stock markets, the rapid growth of the non-state sector, and the opening to foreign trade and investment.[28] China has generally implemented reforms in a gradualist or piecemeal fashion. In recent years, China has re-invigorated its support for leading state-owned enterprises in sectors it considers important to economic security. This is done with the purpose of fostering globally competitive national champions.[29]

Despite being a historically unique global economic superpower, China's rapidly growing economic,[30] political, and cultural[31] engagement and influence[32] is both undeniable and remarkable,[33] even though China's rise in global power is not yet at the level of the United States during the twentieth century or Great Britain during the nineteenth century.[34] China's economy is 70 times greater than when leader of the Chinese Communist Party, Deng Xiaoping, ditched hard-line communist policies in favor of free-market reforms in 1978. After overtaking the United Kingdom and France in 2005, China became the third nation to complete a spacewalk, hosted the Olympic Games, and surpassed Japan as the biggest buyer of United States Treasuries.[35] As of May 2011, China had accumulated a reserve of US$1.159 trillion in United States Treasuries, accounting for slightly more than 25 percent of the total issuance.[36] This accumulation is a necessary part of China's export-led growth strategy as it allows the renminbi to be kept undervalued. Nonetheless, China's rise has come sooner than expected.

According to Zoellick and Lin, China and the United States must cooperate and become the engine for the G-20. "Without a strong G-2, the G-20 will disappoint."[37] Therefore, UK foreign secretary David Miliband has argued that China is the twenty-first century's indispensable power with a decisive say on the future of the global economy, climate change, and world trade.

According to Pierrre Defraigne, China's rise since 1978 has been made possible by several dysfunctions of global economic governance: (1) the collapse of the Bretton Woods system on August 15, 1971 with the decoupling of dollars and gold,[38] floating exchange rates,[39] and the quick liberalization of capital flows in just a decade had created the right conditions for capital to move to China; (2) China's decision to adopt market capitalism under a new brand, i.e., a socialist market economy, epitomized by China's accession to the World Trade

Organization (WTO); and (3) the building up of massive structural external imbalances between the United States and Asia. These imbalances forced a massive over-indebtedness among the average and poor American households, which led to a structural trade deficit for the United States and a trade surplus for China.[40]

Regarding the first point, Michael Dooley *et al.* argue that the structure of the Bretton Woods system is still de facto in place.[41] It is based on the relationship between a center country (or group of countries) and a periphery. In the 1950s, the US was the center region. This was characterized by an uncontrolled capital and goods market.[42] Japan and Europe were the periphery, and were characterized by undervalued currencies, control of capital flows and trade, reserve accumulation, and using the center region as a financial intermediary.[43] Foreign direct investment shifted from the United States to the periphery as long-term investment.[44] The collapse of Bretton Woods was due in part to a change in European strategy: a shift to free goods and financial markets, leading to a regime of floating exchange rates.[45]

The fall of the Bretton Woods system has also created the right conditions for China to develop economically, since China started to switch to a periphery strategy. Progressively since the 1990s, Asian countries have constituted themselves as a new periphery, adopting undervalued currencies, sizeable foreign exchange rate intervention, and export-led growth.[46] China's and some of the Asian countries' strategy has been to manage their dollar exchange rates by accumulating reserves in US dollars.[47] The outcomes are that the United States is driving a large current account deficit to compensate for its trade deficit, the US dollar is kept artificially overvalued, and Asian currencies are kept undervalued.[48]

China's attitude towards multilateral trade

China was one of the original contracting parties to the 1947 General Agreement on Tariffs and Trade (GATT). It ceased to be a member in the aftermath of the 1949 Chinese Revolution and establishment of an alternative seat of government by the Nationalist Party in Taiwan. Following more than 15 years of negotiations, China once again became a member of the world trading system, joining the WTO as its 143rd member in December 2001.[49]

China's most recent trade expansion started in 1978, when the country initiated reforms and opening-up policies. For the past decade, its position as a strong player in international trade has been remarkable.[50] Structural reforms in China, including trade liberalization, have resulted in annual real GDP growth rates in excess of 10 percent over the past few years, rising per capita income, and poverty reduction. Nevertheless, Defraigne argues that, because China's export sector has been severely hit by the world recession that began in 2008, it must change its growth model in three ways: (1) from export-driven to domestic demand-driven growth; (2) towards more egalitarian growth; and (3) towards more sustainable growth.[51]

In 2008, China was the world's third largest trader,[52] compared to having been the 11th largest trade power in 1998 and the 32nd in 1978.[53] In 2010, China passed Germany as the world's second largest exporter of good and services.[54] Yet, in Bergsten's view, China has been playing at best a passive role and at worst a disruptive role with respect to the global trading system. China's current account surplus in 2010 was around 5.2 percent of its GDP,[55] its annual global surpluses were around US$306 billion (by far the largest in the world),[56] and it has the largest store of foreign currency, which exceeded US$1.8 trillion by mid-2008.[57] These figures place serious pressures on the global trading system.[58] Broadly speaking, as China uses an export-led growth strategy, the size of its exports substantially exceeds the size of its imports, pushing down other countries' trade balances. The artificially undervalued renminbi reduces the possibility of self-regulation of the economic system. It leads China's trade partners towards current account deficits and makes their currencies higher than they would normally be.

Although recently less so, why has China been so passive at the WTO's multilateral trade negotiations? Does China only want to take the benefits of the world trading system, but no obligations? It is pertinent to remember that, in the early 1990s, Deng Xiaoping brought forward his views on how China should approach international affairs: "Observe calmly; secure our position; cope with affairs calmly; hide our capacities and bide our time; be good at maintaining a low profile; and never claim leadership." However, given China's size in the world economy, it can no longer afford to follow Deng Xiaoping's suggestion of assuming a passive because, even if China is passive role in world affairs because, it has a de facto impact on world affairs.

China's preference for regionalism

In general, Chinese leaders and strategists have preferred the predictability and manipulability of bilateral relationships to the inherent messiness and complexity of multilateralism.[59] Multilateralism and regionalism/bilateralism are not mutually exclusive.[60] As a matter of fact, several countries in different regions of the world work intensively on regional treaties aimed at integrating regional markets and free trade. The EU is one example. Even though European countries have worked for more than 50 years towards European integration in several areas, such as market integration, European countries – with the European Community on the sideline with wide influence in the GATT and now the EU as a Member of the WTO – have also worked to improve the multilateral system.[61] That said, the EU is an extreme example of regionalism.[62] It is interesting to note that European economic and political integration does not prevent European countries from pursuing multilateralism.[63] Similarly, even if China's preference is regionalism, multilateralism also presents certain benefits that cannot be reached at a regional level.[64]

Not all the WTO Agreements seem to fit China's needs. Rather than playing a proactive role in progressing a more economically meaningful and demanding multilateral liberalization agreement at the WTO, China's focus is to establish itself as a gravity center in Asia[65] by concluding many politically motivated and arguably low-quality bilateral free trade agreements (FTAs)[66] in the region.[67]

For example, China's free trade agreement with the Association of Southeast Asian Nations (ASEAN),[68] the biggest FTA in the world by population coverage, covers only a small share of China's trade with ASEAN so as to diminish ASEAN's fears of being swamped by China.[69] Moreover, an example of China's strategy to shape a new regional structure is the economic and political cooperation between China and ASEAN. China–ASEAN cooperation has brought a new type of intra-Asian regional cooperation with China, which reflects China's commitment to good-neighbor diplomacy. In November 2001, China and ASEAN began negotiations to set up a free trade area. In 2002, a framework agreement for the planned free trade area was signed. The new Asian regionalism stimulated by the China–ASEAN free trade agreement would dominate the future economic landscape of Asia. However, doubts remain as to whether the deal will have real teeth given that there is no rigorous mechanism for settling disputes.[70] This China–ASEAN FTA took effect for China and six ASEAN countries (Brunei, Indonesia, Malaysia, the Philippines, Singapore, and Thailand) in January 2010, thereby eliminating barriers to investment and tariffs to trade on 90 percent of products, and will expand to the remaining four ASEAN countries (Cambodia, Laos, Myanmar, and Vietnam) by 2015.[71] A key motivating factor behind these efforts is water transport along the Upper Lancang/Mekong River covering China, Laos, Myanmar, Thailand, and Vietnam; as well as rail and road links between Yunnan Province of China and Chiang Rai in Thailand.[72]

On the other hand, limited progress has taken place with countries seeking economically meaningful free trade agreements with China, the exception being New Zealand with which China has a high-quality FTA.[73] One would argue that China's trade policy strategy is the creation of a powerful Asian trading bloc, given China's strong position in Asia[74] and how difficult it is to move forward multilaterally.[75]

If multilateral trade continues to weaken, and given that there are already many common Asian values in the region, the likelihood of a Comprehensive Economic Partnership (RCEP)[76] of a like-minded group of countries[77] led by China acting as the *prima donna* or *prima inter pares*[78] within the next decade is very high. This would be part of China's strategy of promoting regional identity.[79] Should this crystallize, one could envisage a tripolar global trade regime with a new Asian pole to counteract the already existing power centers in the EU and the United States.[80] Moreover, it would most likely mean further deterioration of the multilateral trading system.[81] From a broader perspective, China's grand strategy is arguably about multipolarity,[82] the acquisition of more power on the world stage, the protection of Chinese national interests, and independence within interdependence.

Another example of China's interest in Asian regionalism is the fact that China signed a bilateral FTA with Singapore in October 2008, investment agreements with the Philippines, harmonized food safety standards with Thailand (to facilitate agricultural trade), and many agreements with the other Mekong Delta countries (Cambodia, Laos, Myanmar, Thailand, and Vietnam).[83] Politics around the various agreements between China and ASEAN (whether as a bloc or its

Member States individually) are delicate as ASEAN Member States want to avoid China's domination, but at the same time build their economies by inter-acting with China.[84]

Beyond trade, China's interests in leading a powerful Asian bloc are also apparent in finance. With the goal of the creation of an East Asian version of the International Monetary Fund (IMF),[85] China is browbeating trading partners into using the renminbi as opposed to US dollars, and floating ideas about creating a new international reserve currency,[86] even though many analysts argue that there is no immediate alternative to the dollar as the vehicle for international trade. China wants to promote the global use of its own currency. If more world trade will be denominated in renminbi, China's contribution to the new IMF-like East Asian reserve fund may mean that a crisis-prone country in the region will borrow partly in renminbi.[87]

China's economic rise is driving East Asian regional integration. Without a doubt, the progress of East Asian regional integration depends very much on the pace of China's economic advancement in the region. Major economic powers in Asia have reacted to China's successful advance: Japan's comprehensive economic partnership initiative with ASEAN in January 2002 is an example of a prompt response to China's FTA initiative with ASEAN mentioned above. Similarly, India is accelerating its pace of negotiating FTAs with various ASEAN countries. As it stands, these agreements between India and ASEAN countries cover only trade in goods, but they will be extended to trade in services, investment, and other areas of economic cooperation.[88] China is trying to make use of its strategic location to extend its influence in economic development for broader market access in Southeast Asia.[89] Certainly, China's most important trading partners are East Asia and Southeast Asia.

China's position at the WTO

One wonders the extent to which China is serious about multilateralism,[90] given China's minimal involvement in it.[91] China is a strong economic power with increasingly sophisticated production in the coastal regions. Since joining the WTO in December 2001, China has enjoyed significant economic growth.[92] The rigorous economic regulation requirements needed to join the WTO have worked as a catalyst for Chinese political and economic reform.[93] For the last 30 years, no other country has benefited more from globalization than China. Hundreds of millions of Chinese have come out of poverty to become middle class.[94]

Yet, China insists on keeping the status of a developing country[95] within the WTO, despite its size both economically (as of 2010, the second largest economy in the world, compared to the 11th in 1998) and demographically (the most populated country in the world). That said, China's claim of developing country status is solely a political decision, not a legal one. There are no definitions of a developing or developed country in the WTO framework. Only least-developed countries are defined with reference to the definition provided within the United Nations framework.

Being a developing or least-developed country at the WTO may be an advantage since, according to the various WTO Agreements, it can result in special and differential treatment granted from other WTO Members. However, even though the various WTO Agreements grant special treatment to developing and least-developed countries, such rules are not always applicable in the WTO dispute settlement system. In a few cases, Panels have refused to impose obligations on developed countries if the rule of special treatment is not precise or if it is undefined.[96]

Throughout most of the Doha Round of negotiations, China declared that it should have no liberalization obligations and even came up with a new category of membership ("recently acceded members")[97] to justify its relatively passive role during multilateral trade negotiations. At the Cancún WTO Ministerial Conference, China made the point that it had already undertaken heavy commitments by way of tariff cuts and so it would be improper to expect newly acceded members to take on further commitments without giving them the benefit of special and differential treatment provisions as had been made clear in the joint proposal on agriculture by the G-20.[98] However, though a developing country, China has risen so much recently in economic terms that it no longer needs financial aid from the EU through the generalized system of preferences.[99]

Let us compare for instance China with other BRIC countries[100] (i.e. Brazil and India),[101] with whom China is more or less on a par economically.[102] It is acknowledged that there are areas where China differs significantly from Brazil or India – for instance politically, in terms of legal culture, philosophically, and socially. There are, therefore, limitations to the comparison.[103] When comparing China with India and Brazil, we see that China has played a rather passive role both in WTO dispute settlement and the Doha Round of multilateral negotiations.[104]

In fact, in the first years after China's accession to the WTO,[105] China's inclination was to handle trade disputes through negotiation rather than WTO adjudication.[106] When threatened with WTO litigation, China opted to compromise to avoid formal WTO complaints.[107] This preference for diplomatic settlement of trade disputes appears to be more frequent among East Asian WTO Members, illustrating partly a cultural trend. Also, none of the WTO cases involving China was brought by or against an East Asian country. A plausible explanation is that, in its early years as a WTO Member, China avoided being part of the WTO's adjudicative dispute settlement process because of a lack of WTO legal expertise.[108] This point can be illustrated by the fact that during the period 2002–8, China was mainly acting as a third party in WTO disputes, thus benefiting from an inside view of the WTO legal system.[109]

Since 2006, China's interactions with the world trading system have shown a marked shift from an initial focus on amending domestic legislation in order to comply with WTO rules and disciplines, to a more confrontational stance. For instance, up until March 2013, China had brought 11 cases before the WTO as complainant.[110] It remains a small number given the fact that China has been involved in 30 WTO disputes as a respondent.[111] Nevertheless, China has adopted a more active stance towards the WTO dispute settlement system, in particular by using the WTO's adjudicative mechanism more frequently. Since 2008, China has been involved in 11 panel settlements.[112] Half of these disputes concern anti-dumping measures, and most of them are related to China's export policy.[113] Thus, China seems to be more actively involved in protecting its export-led strategy rather than other issues covered by the WTO.[114]

On the multilateral trade negotiations front, for the Doha negotiations to succeed, greater leadership from China is necessary. In fact, no global solution will be possible without China. Other emerging economies similar in size and economic weight to China, particularly Brazil and India, are playing important roles multilaterally. For example, in the agricultural G-20 (not to be confused with the G-20[115] of finance ministers and central bank governors established in 1999), both Brazil and India seem to act as leaders.[116]

Why has China been so passive at the WTO? Arguably, because China is a rather young WTO Member; it still needs to improve its skills and competences on WTO matters. However, this argument is unconvincing as Chinese diplomats are very skilled and capable.[117] Culturally, it tends to avoid disputes as going to court is not an honorable thing to do[118] and because China has much influence from Confucius (which means that China has more than a 2,000-year-old tradition of settling disputes by using mediation instead of using courts as is the case in the Western world).[119] Understanding Chinese culture can be important to an overall understanding of China's role in both the politics of the Doha Round negotiations and more generally in the development of international trade law. China also tends to avoid the WTO dispute settlement system for fear of retaliation,[120] and it has a rather inefficient bureaucracy.[121] Whatever the reason that China initially took a backseat at the WTO and did not make much use of the WTO dispute settlement system, one should acknowledge that since China entered the WTO in December 2001, in nearly every trade dispute where China was not a complainant or respondent, it has intervened as a third party. From this point of view, China is contributing to the development of WTO law.

Conclusion

Undoubtedly, the world needs to adjust to China's re-emergence, but China should also provide more, globally. As analyzed earlier, China behaves like a small country with little systemic effect and responsibility to maintain international order. Therefore, China's attitude towards multilateral trade is unclear and China assumes little responsibility to maintain international order in global economic governance.

China is expected to assume multilateral responsibility commensurate with the benefits it derives from the world trading system. Why? Because with greater political power and a greater voice comes greater responsibility. Compared with India or Brazil, with whom China is on a par economically and in terms of new leading and emerging economic powers, China's role in the world trading system is rather passive both at the WTO's dispute settlement system as well as in the Doha Round of multilateral trade negotiations. China, therefore, appears to lack an internationalist view towards multilateral trade affairs, being more focused on its internal development and concluding many low-quality, politically motivated regional FTAs.

China should therefore play a more prominent multilateral role, not only at the WTO, but also at the IMF and the World Bank as well as in international economic governance. For example, at the IMF – where China is pushing for a greater say for itself and other developing countries – the voting power of each member is calculated on the basis of its donations. According to the IMF, as of March 2013 China's share of votes at the IMF was 3.81 percent of the total because it only contributes 4 percent of the total funding.[122] The United States contributes 17.69 percent of the funding, whereas the EU contributes over 31 percent of the total funding. In this sense, major actors such as the European Commission expect China to donate more money to the IMF and to assume a responsibility commensurate with the benefits it derives from the world trading system.[123]

Notes

1 Senior Lecturer in Law, Queen Mary University of London. This chapter is a revised and updated version of an article previously published as *On China's Economic Rise: Multilateral versus Regional Attitudes in Trade Agreements and the PCA with the EU* in volume 27 of the Chinese (Taiwan) Yearbook of International Law and Affairs. It is republished here with permission.
2 That said, according to the United Nations Conference on Trade and Development, as global indicators continue to reveal the breadth of the 2008 financial crisis, developing countries in general may soften the impact on their economies by increasing cooperation with other nations of the South. See Bridges Weekly Trade News Digest (12 February 2009).
3 This trade G-7 should not be confused with the finance G-7 representing the most industrialized nations in the world. The trade G-7 has replaced the so-called "Quadrilateral Trade Ministers' Meeting" and is composed of the Quad plus China, India, and Brazil. Its purpose is to see how key trade and investment matters can be moved forward.
4 For further details, see Leal-Arcas 2008a: 301–21.
5 Foot 2001: 24.
5 Gong 1991: 3–16.
7 Zoellick (21 September 2005).
8 Zoellick (21 September 2005): 3–4.
9 The White House (2006).
10 On Chinese responsibility in international relations, see Zhang and Austin 2001.
11 Bruno Simma proposes other goals, in addition to peace and security: solidarity between states at different levels of development; environmental health; and the protection of human rights. These are explained in more detail in Simma 1994: 236–43. See also de Wet 2006: 54–7 (describing the emergence of the international community as a process by which international and regional organizations as well as individuals were brought under the reach of international law that had formerly been reserved to states).
12 See remarks by Christensen (3 August 2006), US-China Economic and Security Review Commission.
13 CIA "The World Factbook, country comparison: GDP." Online. Available at: www.cia.gov/library/publications/the-world-factbook/rankorder/2001rank.html.

14 For an analysis of China's transformation, see Brandt and Rawski 2008; Eichengreen *et al.* 2008; *Foreign Affairs* (January/February 2008): 1–66; Oi *et al.* 2009 (presenting an accurate view of China's current reforms in privatization and markets, governance, questions of health care, environmental degradation, and social inequality).

15 On climate change, see Leal-Arcas 2011a: 25–56; Leal-Arcas 2011b; Leal-Arcas 2001: 282–94.

16 *The Economist* (21 March 2009): 13.

17 *The Economist* (16 December 2010).

18 In 2008, the International Monetary Fund ranked China as the third wealthiest nation in the world in absolute terms. See IMF (October 2009), showing a nominal GDP list of countries. According to the CIA, China's economy is already the second in the world as a country, only behind the US: see https://www.cia.gov/library/publications/the-world-factbook/rankorder/2001rank.html?countryName=China&countryCode=ch&regionCode=eas&rank=3#ch.

19 According to the International Monetary Fund, China has been growing economically in a very impressive and fast manner in the last years. See IMF (28 October 2009); see also Aziz (December 2006). Moreover, while the world is in crisis, China continues to grow economically at a pace of 6 percent to 8 percent annually.

20 See, for example, China's recent investment in Africa and the Middle East. Predictions are that by 2015, China will take over from the EU and the US regarding Middle East energy markets.

21 See Bergsten 2008: 9.

22 Bergsten 2008: 10.

23 See CIA, "The World Factbook: China." Online. Available at: www.cia.gov/library/publications/the-world-factbook/geos/ch.html#Econ.

24 Under WTO law, there is no definition of market economy. One valid definition, however, is "an economy in which the price mechanism determines what is produced and traded, though too often price signals are distorted by subsidies, industry policy and other types of government intervention." See Goode 2007: 274. For an analysis of what features of a legal structure suited to a market economy are missing in the case of China, see Clarke (2007a): 1–24.

25 China is recognised as a market economy in the New Zealand-China Free Trade Agreement. See New Zealand Ministry of Foreign Affairs and Trade (2008).

26 For an overview of anti-dumping and the non-market economy treatment of China by the EU and the US, see Snyder 2001: 369–434.

27 See CIA "The World Factbook: China." Online. Available at: www.cia.gov/library/publications/the-world-factbook/geos/ch.html.

28 CIA "The World Factbook: China." Online. Available at: www.cia.gov/library/publications/the-world-factbook/geos/ch.html.

29 CIA "The World Factbook: China." Online. Available at: www.cia.gov/library/publications/the-world-factbook/geos/ch.html.

30 Early economic analyses of China's rapid integration in the world economy are, for example, The World Bank (September 1997).

31 See for example the World Expo 2010 in Shanghai.

32 According to a study conducted in late 2007 by the Bertelsmann Foundation of Germany among residents in Brazil, UK, China, France, Germany, India, Japan, Russia, and the US, 50 percent of people who participated in a public opinion poll viewed China as a world power today, and 57 percent said it would be a superpower by 2020.

33 A clear example of China's engagement and influence in today's world is the 2008 Beijing Olympic Games.

34 Bergsten *et al.* 2008: 209.

35 Piboontanasawat and Hamlin (14 January 2009).

36 US Department of the Treasury (15 August 2011).
37 Zoellick and Lin (6 March 2009).
38 On August 15, 1971, after US gold stocks were approaching the symbolic level of $10 billion, compared to $13 billion in 1967 and $25 billion in 1949, the US government decided to take action. In a dramatic Sunday night broadcast, President Nixon announced that the US would no longer convert foreign-held dollars into gold or other reserve assets, "except in amounts and conditions determined to be in the interests of monetary stability and in the best interests of the United States." See Nixon (15 August 1971). Public Papers of the Presidents: Richard Nixon 1971, 263. For a broadcast of President Nixon's address, see "Nixon Ends Bretton Woods International Monetary System 1971." Online. Available at: www.youtube.com/watch?v=iRzr1QU6K1o.
39 A floating exchange rate is the "movement of a foreign currency exchange rate in response to changes in the market forces of supply and demand." Currencies strengthen or weaken based on a nation's reserves of hard currency and gold, its international trade balance, its rate of inflation and interest rates, and the general strength of its economy. See Downes and Goodman 1998: 215.
40 Defraigne (2009): 23.
41 Dooley *et al.* (September 2003).
42 Dooley *et al.* (September 2003).
43 Dooley *et al.* (September 2003).
44 Dooley *et al.* (September 2003).
45 Dooley *et al.* (September 2003).
46 Dooley *et al.* (September 2003).
47 Dooley *et al.* (September 2003).
48 Dooley *et al.* (September 2003). For further details on the consequences of the 2008 financial crisis on the Bretton Woods system and why the US did not collapse following the crisis, see Dooley *et al.* (February 2009).
49 For further information on China at the WTO, see www.wto.org/english/thewto_e/countries_e/China_e.htm.
50 Zhao (1 June 2007): 2.
51 See Defraigne (2009): 24.
52 See generally WTO (21 and 23 May 2008).
53 Embassy of the People's Republic of China in Switzerland (3 October 1999).
54 World Bank Database, available at http://databank.worldbank.org/ddp/home.do?Step=1&id=4.
55 http://bit.ly/pY7X94.
56 http://bit.ly/pY7X94.
57 IMF (April 2011).
58 See Bergsten 2008: 14.
59 Zhao and Webster 2011: 324 (which explores the main features of China's FTAs, finding that China has adopted a flexible FTA strategy that attends closely to its unique social and economic prerogatives at this time, and also matches well with partner expectations).
60 Leal-Arcas 2011c: 597–629.
61 For an overview of the EC in the world trading system, see generally Leal-Arcas 2008b; Leal-Arcas 2008c: 157–82.
62 Leal-Arcas 2012.
63 Leal-Arcas 2010a: 463–514.
64 Leal-Arcas 2010b: 259–73.
65 In fact, few regional initiatives are undertaken by other countries without first considering what China thinks or how China might react.
66 See GATT Article XXIV for a definition of a free trade agreement.
67 On this point, see the views by Bergsten 2008: Ch. 1.

68 ASEAN is composed of 10 members. The six founding countries are Brunei, Indonesia, Malaysia, the Philippines, Singapore, and Thailand. The remaining members are Vietnam, Laos, Cambodia, and Myanmar. The aims and purposes of the Association are to accelerate economic growth, social progress and cultural development, and to promote regional peace and stability.

69 See generally Leal-Arcas 2011d: 93–120.

70 The development of infrastructure within China has been a key focus for the Chinese government in its economic development initiatives. See KPMG (September 2009).

71 Bilaterals.org (April 2009).

72 Asian Development Bank (26 June 2005).

73 China's free trade agreement with New Zealand, signed in early 2008, is an exception to the argument that China concludes many low-quality, politically motivated bilateral FTAs in the region. This exception seems to be due to the fact that New Zealand is the first WTO Member to approve China's WTO accession and the first to grant it market-economy status.

74 Bergsten *et al.* 2008: 16.

75 For an analysis of China's FTAs, see Wang 2011: 493–516.

76 The RCEP is composed of all 10 ASEAN countries and six other countries: Australia, China, India, Japan, New Zealand, and South Korea. For further details on the RCEP, see http://csis.org/publication/asean-and-partners-launch-regional-comprehensive-economic-partnership.

77 Here I am referring to China, Japan, South Korea, and Vietnam.

78 On East and South Asian regionalism, see Wang 2006: 269–305; Kawai and Wignaraja (August 2009).

79 Bergsten 2008: 16.

80 Buckley *et al.* 2011.

81 According to Francis Snyder, China's policy towards regional trade agreements will have a major impact on the international trading system, the debate about regionalism and multilateralism, and the policy of the WTO concerning RTAs. See Snyder 2009: 1–57.

82 On multipolarity in the world trading system, see Narlikar and Wickers 2009.

83 For further details, see Leal-Arcas 2010c: Ch. 6.

84 Bilaterals.org (April 2009).

85 The International Monetary Fund's original role was to help nations with short-term cash crunches relating to trade financing and to manage the gold-standard currency valuation system. In recent decades, the IMF has morphed into providing long-term loans to developing countries on the condition that these countries recognize their laws and economies to prioritize servicing debt, for instance, by cutting government budgets, such as education and health spending, liberalizing trade and investment policies and providing new intellectual property and investor protections. One after another, countries which followed the IMF policy formula – and who were touted as poster children of success – have collapsed economically and socially, such as the case of Argentina in 2001. See Wallach (2005).

86 On monetary affairs, it is interesting to note the proposal by Zhou Xiaochuan, governor of China's central bank, who has suggested creating a "super-sovereign reserve currency" to replace the dollar over the long run. For an analysis of this proposal, see Bergsten (8 April 2009). See also China Briefing (24 March 2009).

87 Mallaby (26 May 2009).

88 ICTSD (June 2009).

89 Fu-kuo (13 May 2008).

90 According to China's own accounting, it has joined more than 130 intergovernmental international organizations and committed to 267 multilateral treaties. See State Council Information Office White Paper (22 December 2005).

91 Recent FTAs signed by China include those with ASEAN countries, Hong Kong,

Macao, Pakistan, as well as the Gulf countries. See *Trade Policy Review – Report by the People's Republic of China*, WT/TPR/G/161, 17 March 2006 at paras 77–82.

92 Sutherland 2008: 125–36.

93 For an analysis of the argument that China's economic growth will rely on its successful integration into the global economy, see Yueh (May 2003).

94 *The Economist* (21 March 2009): 13.

95 In fact, China continues to use its self-proclaimed status as the "world's largest developing nation." On this note, see Mitchell (May 2007).

96 See WTO cases interpreting Article 15, first sentence of the Anti-Dumping Agreement: Panel Report, *United States – Anti-Dumping and Countervailing Measures on Steel Plate from India*, WT/DS206/R and Corr.1, adopted 29 July 2002, para. 7.110; and Panel Report, *European Communities – Anti-Dumping Duties on Malleable Cast Iron Tube or Pipe Fittings from Brazil*, WT/DS219/R, adopted 18 August 2003, as modified by Appellate Body Report WT/DS219/AB/R, para. 7.68. None of these findings were appealed to the WTO Appellate Body.

97 See Government of India, Ministry of Commerce and Industry (11 September 2003). In addition to China, the other countries under the category of "newly acceded members" were: Albania, Armenia, Bulgaria, Croatia, Ecuador, Former Yugoslav Republic of Macedonia, Jordan, Kyrgyzstan, Moldova, Mongolia, Oman, Panama, Saudi Arabia, and Chinese Taipei.

98 The Group of 20, or G-20, is a group of developing countries focused on tearing down industrialized countries' barriers to agricultural trade. The group includes 23 countries.

99 The idea of granting developing countries preferential tariff rates in the markets of industrialized countries was originally presented by Raul Prebisch, the first Secretary-General of UNCTAD, at the first UNCTAD conference in 1964. The Generalized System of Preferences was adopted at UNCTAD II in New Delhi in 1968. Under the standard GSP, preferential access to the EU market is provided to 176 developing countries and territories in the form of reduced tariffs on around 6,400 goods when entering the EU market, with no expectation of reciprocal treatment.

100 BRIC is a term used in economics to refer to Brazil, Russia, India, and China. General thinking is that the term was first prominently used in a prediction by Jim O'Neill, former chief global economist at Goldman Sachs. Goldman Sachs has argued that the economic potential of Brazil, Russia, India, and China is such that they may become among the four most dominant economies by the year 2050. This will certainly affect the four European Union (EU) Member States which are members of the G-7. These countries encompass over 25 percent of the world's land coverage and 40 percent of the world's population. The BRIC countries have taken steps to increase their political cooperation, mainly as a way of influencing the United States' position on major trade accords, or, through the implicit threat of political cooperation, as a way of extracting political concessions from the United States, such as proposed nuclear cooperation with India. For further detail on the BRICs, see Goldman Sachs (2007). For a thorough analysis of the trade relations between the EU and the BRICs unilaterally, bilaterally, and multilaterally, see Leal-Arcas 2009: 345–416.

101 Russia joined the WTO in August 2012.

102 I am referring here to Brazil and India, the public lobbyists on behalf of the emerging markets, which are much more proactive multilaterally than China. For a comparison between China and India in the WTO, see Qin 2008.

103 One way to compare developing countries of the WTO is by looking at the various WTO Agreements and comment on whether those agreements are sufficiently suited to take into account the degree of development in the specific countries. For example, in the draft proposal for a "new" plurilateral Government Procurement Agreement – to which China is not yet a Party, but in which it has observer status –

individual examinations of the needs of the developing country would need to be made. See the revision of the Agreement on Government Procurement, GPA/W/297 of 11 December 2006, Art. IV.

104 When asked by the US to issue a joint statement in support of the DDA in 2006, China refused. See *BNA WTO Reporter* (19 April 2006).

105 For an analysis on China's reasons to join the world trading system in 2001 in the face of the reputedly onerous accession commitments it was required to fulfill, see He and Sappideen 2009: 847–71.

106 Quite the opposite to China's approach, it is interesting to note that Robert Hudec encouraged the judicialization of trade disputes. See Hudec 1992; see also Jackson, Davey and Sykes 2008; Trubek 2008: 3–4; Schneider 2006: 119–24 (arguing that certain international disputes are increasingly judicialized).

107 See, for example, BNA WTO Reporter (25 May 2004).

108 Thomas (2011): 21.

109 Thomas (2011): 8.

110 Online. Available at: www.wto.org/english/tratop_e/dispu_e/dispu_by_country_e.htm.

111 Online. Available at: www.wto.org/english/tratop_e/dispu_e/dispu_by_country_e.htm.

112 Online. Available at: www.wto.org/english/tratop_e/dispu_e/dispu_by_country_e.htm.

113 Online. Available at: www.wto.org/english/tratop_e/dispu_e/dispu_by_country_e.htm.

114 Thomas (2011): 7.

115 This so-called G-20 is composed of the finance ministers and central bank governors of 19 countries: Argentina, Australia, Brazil, Canada, China, France, Germany, India, Indonesia, Italy, Japan, Mexico, Russia, Saudi Arabia, South Africa, South Korea, Turkey, the United Kingdom, and the United States. The European Union is also a member, represented by its rotating presidency and the European Central Bank. To ensure that global economic fora and institutions work together, the Managing Director of the International Monetary Fund (IMF) and the President of the World Bank, plus the chairs of the International Monetary and Financial Committee and Development Committee of the IMF and World Bank also participate in G-20 meetings on an ex-officio basis. For further information, see www.g20.org/about_ what_is_g20.aspx.

> The G-20 thus brings together important industrial and emerging-market countries from all regions of the world. Together, member countries represent around 90 per cent of global gross national product, 80 per cent of world trade [including intra-EU trade] as well as two-thirds of the world's population. The G-20's economic weight and broad membership gives it a high degree of legitimacy and influence over the management of the global economy and financial system.

116 This new phenomenon of India and Brazil playing hardball at the WTO is clearly explained by Fareed Zakaria in Zakaria 2008: 37.

117 See Runnalls *et al.* 2002.

118 On this point, see Gao 2005: 315–51.

119 See, for example, Zakaria 2008: 109–14, explaining the correlation between the Chinese legal system and Confucianism. Also, Farah 2008: 193–226.

120 Information gathered from Xiaotong (4 April 2009).

121 This attitude, however, is slowly changing to a more aggressive and proactive role of China in the WTO. See Gao 2007: 34.

122 For a list of IMF members' voting power, see IMF, "IMF Members' quotas and voting power, and IMF Board of Governors." Online. Available at: www.imf.org/ external/np/sec/memdir/members.htm#3.

123 European Commission (2006): 14.

7 Asia-Pacific regional architecture and consumer product safety regulation beyond Free Trade Agreements

Luke Nottage[1]

Introduction: beyond FTAs

More and more countries are concluding and negotiating Free Trade Agreements (FTAs), including throughout the Asia-Pacific region.[2] This was not such a problem when the world economy was growing, but it and the multilateral World Trade Organization (WTO) regime are now in crisis. Inefficient 'trade diversion' is likely even if bilateral FTA partners begin to connect up under regional FTAs, as under the recent ASEAN–Australian–NZ Free Trade Agreement (AANZFTA). This is because greater liberalisation already achieved between bilateral FTA partners tends to be preserved under such regional agreements. And burgeoning FTAs diminish the incentives for national governments to press for a new multilateral system.

Nonetheless, a 'crisis Round' to try to revive the multilateral system seems unlikely. The persuasiveness of conventional economic models, and market forces as the best way to maximise socio-economic growth, are under broader threat in the wake of the Global Financial Crisis (GFC).[3]

We now need a fundamental reassessment of the roles and potential of FTAs, compared to other arrangements, in advancing sustainable socio-economic integration among states.

One possible response is the 'back to the future' agenda proposed by Australia's Productivity Commission (PC) in its December 2010 Research Report and largely adopted by the April 2011 'Gillard Government Trade Policy Statement'.[4]

Concerned about trade diversion, domestic interest group lobbying and other inefficiencies purportedly resulting from the negotiation of bilateral and regional FTAs, this approach urges much greater emphasis on multilateral or even unilateral liberalisation initiatives. It is also sceptical about attempts to build into FTAs greater protections for labour standards or environmental protection, preferring that these be addressed by governments through separate mechanisms. But this approach can be criticised as unrealistic both by free trade advocates, given the persistent blockage in the WTO Doha Round,[5] and by those harbouring grave doubts about laissez-faire approaches to economic affairs, particularly in the wake of the GFC.

A second approach involves blowing cold on FTAs as well, but also the entire free trade regime epitomised by the existing WTO system. On this view, trade agreements should not incorporate protections for workers, the environment, consumers or indigenous people because those protections instead should prevail over the economic rights promoted by trade agreements. In other words, the discourse and values of human rights simply cannot be reconciled with – and should not be subjected to – the discourse and values of economics and free trade.[6]

By contrast, this chapter proposes a plausible 'third way' forward. A starting point is to accept that many FTAs may indeed be sub-optimal from a narrow economic perspective, but to view that as a price to pay to secure some further expansion in 'free trade'. Yet the next step is to consider the incorporation of more protections and safeguards into future trade agreements, or other measures to promote elements of 'fair trade' in parallel with FTAs, as involving a different trade-off. That is, even if this risks further diminishing economic gains from free trade, such innovations can help enhance the acceptability and legitimacy of FTAs or other instruments for economic integration, particularly in a post-GFC era characterised by growing concern to effect simultaneous improvements in transnational governance mechanisms.[7]

Indeed, many economists might well agree that if politicians, government officials and a wider array of stakeholders are increasingly investing so much time and resources into negotiating various FTAs anyway, the additional marginal costs involved in agreeing on some further matters – not hitherto found within or alongside conventional FTAs – may be quite minimal. Those costs anyway could be outweighed by marginal benefits, in the form of reductions in a variety of transaction costs currently incurred in managing risks in cross-border trade and investment. In any event, sound public policy can incorporate many values other than those reflected in economic cost-benefit analysis, such as participation rights or maintaining the coherence and overall integrity of a regulatory system. Such considerations provide another justification for expanding the scope of FTAs in novel ways, or for enhancing governance mechanisms alongside them.

In striving to balance free and fair trade nowadays, a rough analogy would be the ways in which the European Union (EU) has evolved so it is not just an economic community. Despite – or perhaps because of – the steady expansion of EU membership, it has addressed 'fair trade' concerns about regulatory safeguards, democratic legitimacy and accountability, alongside its original core objectives of 'free movement' of people, capital, goods and services.[8] The EU has achieved this over many decades, often by trial-and-error and in a variety of ways, ranging from core or additional treaties, diverse European law harmonisation measures, through to 'soft law' initiatives.

This analogy is starting to seem more plausible for the Asia-Pacific region, for three main reasons. First, although this region does remain very diverse in terms of social and legal or political systems, economic integration has burgeoned since the 1980s.[9] This will intensify even further as pan-Asian production networks have been forced to turn away from European and US markets, harder hit by the GFC than major Asian economies. The 'diversity gap' is narrowing significantly as the EU itself expands and becomes more diverse, at least when compared to the more developed democracies of East Asia, Australia and New Zealand. The EU has had to develop various mechanisms to preserve degrees of national sovereignty and to acknowledge the interests of sub-groups within Europe. Political, economic and ideological divergence does remain higher in East Asia compared to even the expanded EU, but convergence has been growing in parallel with longer-standing economic 'regionalisation'. Even large differences can also be addressed through careful institutional design of representation in common institutions, for example, and it can also be argued that such initiatives would feed back into further convergence in Asia – as seems to have occurred in Europe.[10]

Second, the GFC has intensified debate about the pros and cons of more limited political 'regionalism' in Asia compared to other parts of the world. The then Prime Ministers of Australia and Japan called, respectively, for a new 'Asia Pacific Community' (in 2008) or 'East Asian Community' (2009) that would go beyond existing regional architecture. Former Japanese Prime Minister (PM) Hatoyama was also more forthright about the potential for at least some institutional innovation based on the EU experience.[11] Former Australian PM Kevin Rudd, when subsequently serving as Australia's Foreign Minister, argued that his own proposals continue to find resonance among regional leaders. He pointed to the strengthening of the 'G-20' forum for (mostly macro-) economic policy coordination, with its strong representation from Asia-Pacific states compared to the earlier 'G-7' forum. Rudd also welcomed the US and Russia becoming members of the East Asia Summit. Nonetheless, the roles of these forums and other regional institutions or arrangements remain a major topic of discussion.[12]

Third, throughout the region following the GFC, considerable distrust has re-emerged about leaving socio-economic ordering to outright market fundamentalism. Former PM Rudd consistently protested about the excesses of market fundamentalism, although for example this did not seem to directly influence the reforms to consumer protection legislation enacted in Australia over 2009–10 – aspects of which are also likely to be followed in New Zealand. Such views underpinned his electoral victory in 2007, but also former PM Hatoyama's victory in Japan in 2008. The latter's administration and its successor intensified measures to promote consumer rights and product safety regulation, while continuing to actively promote both the WTO system and bilateral or regional FTAs.[13]

More generally, the former EU Commissioner and now WTO Director-General, Pascal Lamy, has long pointed out that both East Asia and the EU share an appreciation not only of diversity, but also the need to balance free markets with other social and political values.[14] This approach is most obvious and expressly stated within the foundational documents and actual practices of ASEAN, the 'Association of South East Asian Nations' established in 1967 and formalised by a Charter in 2003. It is reflected, for example, in the 'regionalized governance' approach of the ASEAN Comprehensive Investment Agreement signed in 2009.[15] Alongside a commitment to establish an 'ASEAN Economic Community' by 2015 involving liberalisation of capital, goods and services, and (skilled) labour – albeit at differential rates for member states – ASEAN has also established a human rights mechanism to promote its 'political' and 'socio-economic' community aspects pursuant to the Charter.[16] With ASEAN as one catalyst, a similar hybrid or multi-track approach to enhancing regional integration may well emerge in North-East Asia as well, with over four times the economic scope of South-East Asia but traditionally a greater 'organization gap' in terms of formal inter-state treaties. China itself has combined economic liberalisation with distinctly socialist socio-political ideology, while developing increasingly strong and varied 'transgovernmentalist' links alongside burgeoning economic relations with Korea and Japan.[17]

This chapter therefore outlines some possibilities for deeper and broader economic integration in the Asia-Pacific that simultaneously incorporate regulatory safeguards and other governance mechanisms aimed at meeting the new expectations about sustainability and legitimacy characterising our brave new 'post-GFC' world. These innovations may be built into FTAs or negotiated alongside them, but this needs to be done in a more concerted and comprehensive manner. The EU can provide important pointers even though it cannot offer a precise 'model', and despite the fact that Europe is itself facing another round of serious economic and governance problems.[18] Asian (and indeed Australian) leaders and commentators have traditionally been reluctant to compare and examine developments in European integration; but this attitude has been diminishing in recent years, as illustrated by the ASEAN initiatives and proposals for an Asia-Pacific or East Asian Community.[19]

Particularly suggestive are integration mechanisms that involve greater 'inter-governmentalism', rather than the 'supranationalism' associated with the EU currently, as the former permits more scope to preserve the national sovereignty interests long emphasised in the Asian region.[20] In the trans-Tasman context discussed further below, free movement in goods, services and capital has been promoted by FTAs, but additional economic integration between Australia and New Zealand has been achieved through mutual recognition regimes and arrangements for the free movement of people that rely on an even softer inter-governmentalist mechanism – parallel legislation in both countries. These and other aspects of this bilateral relationship may well come to influence other Asia-Pacific states, by illustrating alternative pathways towards more sustainable economic integration that could seem less threatening to 'Euro-sceptics' in this region.

The first section of this chapter explains existing and potential options for promoting 'free but fair' movements of capital, people and services in the Asia-Pacific region, including a focus on recent relations between Australia and New Zealand. The next section addresses free movement of consumer goods combined with 'fair' safety regulation: the WTO backdrop, the European approach, and certain trans-Tasman and Asia-Pacific developments. The final section concludes that such initiatives to marry liberalisation with contemporary public interest concerns are essential to sustainable development in the Asia-Pacific region – and hence, potentially, to reinvigorating the multilateral international economic order.

Free but fair movement of capital, people and services

Measures to facilitate free movement of capital and people per se, as opposed to services more generally, are not covered extensively by the WTO regime itself. However, all these matters are increasingly being folded into FTAs or can emerge alongside or out of them, although states need to respond to growing citizen concern that diverse public interests be reflected in these treaty regimes.

Investment treaties

Bilateral Investment Treaties (BITs), for example, are already increasingly being transformed into investment chapters within FTAs. On a preferential basis, going beyond commitments that may be more widely available under the WTO's General Agreement on Trade in Services (GATS), these investment chapters often introduce substantive liberalisations. Investment chapters also fold in substantive protections (such as the host state's obligations to extend 'fair and equitable treatment' and not to expropriate without adequate compensation), traditionally derived instead from separate BITs. In addition, investment chapters (and BITs) increasingly provide for consent by the host state to direct arbitration claims by foreign investors, instead of them having to ask their home states to attempt a 'diplomatic protection' claim against the host state for interfering with the foreign investment.[21]

The growth of investor-state arbitration protections in Asia-Pacific treaties creates some actual and potential backlashes. For example, one logical consequence of greater constraint on host state discretion once the foreign investment has been allowed in, due to the higher risk of being subjected to claims directly by foreign investors, is that host states will scrutinise more carefully the investment in the first place. Treaties often preserve, for example, broad discretion for rejecting foreign investments (prior to entry or establishment) on 'national interest' grounds. The risk then is that the home state will 'retaliate' after its investors are rebuffed, to send a message that it disapproves of such exercise of host state discretion. It might rebuff potential investors from the other state by invoking the same type of reserved discretion (direct 'tit-for-tat'). Alternatively, it might find some other means to 'punish' the other state.[22]

One way to avoid such escalation would be to elaborate criteria for the 'national interest' regarding bound Foreign Direct Investment (FDI), and to entrench them through FTAs. Yet states traditionally guard their discretion jealously in this respect, partly for domestic political reasons.[23] Particularly in the aftermath of the GFC, pressures have re-emerged to fend off foreign investors.[24] Yet for most countries the overall long-term trajectory is likely to remain competition to attract FDI, albeit in more healthy and balanced forms. A compromise may be restrictions on 'national interest' discretion extended on a bilateral basis, to preserve broader long-term relations. And regional FTAs containing such clearer criteria may allow those member states not party to a bilateral dispute to intervene at least informally, defusing tensions to preserve overall mutual benefits.[25]

A second backlash is evident in growing concerns about investor-state arbitration provisions themselves, particularly among South American countries but also in Africa, and even now in Australia.[26] Again, a new generation of investment treaties will probably need to recalibrate the balance between foreign investors and host states, to reflect contemporary trends and conceptions concerning the public interests involved. One way to achieve this is through provisions negotiated in each treaty, as in the 2008 Australia–Chile FTA.[27] But another option is for arbitral institutions (in the relevant countries but also potentially further afield, for example, the International Chamber of Commerce) to elaborate more balanced Investment Arbitration Rules, and then get states to include them in treaties as at least one more option for foreign investors to invoke when claiming against the host state. At a micro-level, one major attraction would be the expectation of fewer disputes when the foreign investor seeks execution of the arbitral award. At the macro-level, such Investment Arbitration Rules would offer quite harmonised sets of up-to-date provisions tailored to the needs and expectations of a broader range of stakeholders.[28]

Beyond the FTA or BIT itself, through side agreements it may also be possible to address specific contemporary concerns, such as restrictions on arguably legitimate environmental protection measures imposed by host states that might impact on foreign investors and hence generate arbitration claims. Similar side agreements might also be developed to enhance consumer protection and public health measures.

Already, the North American Commission for Environmental Cooperation (NACEC), established alongside the North American Free Trade Agreement (NAFTA) among Canada, Mexico and the US, points the way to resolving such tensions in the field of environmental protection. Admittedly, the NACEC does not protect domestic environmental laws from all challenges under NAFTA and its investment chapter. However, it includes mechanisms encouraging effective enforcement of domestic laws, at a time when nations remain reluctant to allow international institutions to scrutinise such regimes. As one analysis concludes:[29]

> The NACEC establishes the first regional environmental organisation in North America and gives it interesting, innovative mandates; it addresses environmental issues related to economic integration in more detail than any other agreement outside the European Union; and it provides new opportunities for direct public participation in its implementation. In all of these respects, the NAAEC offers lessons for other countries seeking to address shared environmental problems against a backlog of increasing economic integration – which is to say, all countries.

The NACEC has already been used as a model for bilateral agreements between Canada and Chile and between Jordan and the US, as well as a regional agreement among the US and Central American states.

Regrettably, however, Australasia so far has lacked even this sort of first step towards a new institutionalised solution for balancing foreign investment with evolving environmental concerns. A Commission was not included in the Australia–US FTA concluded in 2004, for example. The need may have been less because both countries enforce their respective environmental laws reasonably well, compared to developing countries, and because trans-border pollution issues are minimal simply due to geography. But some features of the NACEC, such as resources to initiate reviews and monitoring or NGO participation rights,[30] could have been usefully institutionalised even in this bilateral relationship.

A much softer regional framework was created through an Environment Cooperation Agreement (ECA) concluded in conjunction with the Trans-Pacific Strategic Economic Partnership Agreement (P4 FTA, signed in 2005 by New Zealand, Singapore, Brunei and Chile), although this FTA does not yet include an investment chapter. The side agreement was included consistently with the 'Framework for Integrating Environment Issues into Free Trade Agreements' announced by the New Zealand government in 2001.[31] Australia will come under pressure to commit to such a side agreement now that it has joined the TPPA negotiations – together with the P4 countries and the United States, Malaysia, Peru and Vietnam, as well as now Japan, Mexico and Canada.[32] That renegotiation allows scope for further regional institutionalisation of environmental protection policy, along the lines of the NACEC.

In the context of the AANZFTA and Australia's relationship with ASEAN, two Parliamentary Committees in Australia recommended in June 2009 that the government pursue environmental protection objectives within its FTAs.[33] The Productivity Commission's report to the Australian Treasurer on future policy directions regarding FTAs recommended 'a cautious approach to referencing core labour standards' in trade (and investment) agreements, adopting reasoning that suggested that the Commission was also reluctant to see environmental protections built into future FTAs.[34] Yet the April 2011 Gillard Government Trade Policy Statement agreed with the Commission's Recommendation 4(a) to the extent 'consistent with [the] approach articulated in the Statement'. The latter noted that it was continuing FTA negotiations involving Korea, Malaysia and the TPPA 'where the inclusion of labour and environment provisions is under active consideration'. This suggests that the present Australian government is open to their inclusion provided they do not 'constitute disguised protectionism'.[35]

Unfortunately, the impetus and opportunity for Australia to incorporate even softer mechanisms for inter-governmental cooperation in setting or reviewing environmental and public health protection measures is diminished by its recent policy shift regarding investor-state arbitration. The Productivity Commission had recommended that future FTAs not include such provisions if they would afford foreign investors greater rights than local investors. This left some scope to tailor and cap provisions so they could still be included in FTAs with developing countries that provided only low levels of protection to Australian investors, and one reading of the Trade Policy Statement also seemed to allow for this policy.[36] But recent indications are that the Gillard Government, subjected in June 2011 to its first-ever claim under an investment treaty (brought by the Hong Kong subsidiary of a global tobacco company), wished to exclude investor-state arbitration in all future treaties.[37]

A more balanced approach could have included, in future treaties, express exclusions for genuine public health measures adopted by the host state and/or mechanisms for joint standard-setting, along the lines of NACEC in the field of environmental protection. It may still emerge given the strong push by countries like the US to include investor-state arbitration provisions in the TPPA, or if a new Government reverts to Australia's longstanding policy of including such provisions at least in treaties with developing countries.

Movement of people

As for free movement of people in the Asia-Pacific region, developments have been much slower and more uneven compared to free movement of capital or trade in goods and services. In particular, Australia and New Zealand have been pioneers in many respects:[38]

> There is a long history of arrangements, collectively known as the Trans-Tasman Travel Arrangement (TTTA), which allow New Zealand citizens to enter, reside and work in Australia, and Australian permanent residents to receive reciprocal access to New Zealand. These arrangements have been supplemented by the Social Security Agreement, the Reciprocal Health Agreement and the Child Support Agreement.

More recently, for example, Australia and Japan have also concluded a Social Security Agreement (in 2007).

Experience in other regions shows how important such arrangements are to promote cross-border mobility, even where FTAs or other agreements exist aimed at liberalising labour market access. Even within the EU, for example, labour mobility has remained comparatively low, despite treaty-based freedom of movement including rights of residence. But the EU has been promoting various policies to improve the situation particularly since the mid-1990s. Part of the problem has been with portability of social security, health benefits and supplementary pensions. Another impediment has been recognition of qualifications. Only a few occupations (architects and various health care professionals) gain automatic recognition; workers in others have to apply to the host country to assess the equivalence of their qualifications. Interestingly, the Trans-Tasman Mutual Recognition Arrangement (TTMRA) is *more* ambitious, declaring mechanisms for all occupations to be equivalent so as to 'sort out the problems after the event'.[39]

By contrast, like GATS, conventional FTAs themselves generally commit to very limited liberalisation regarding foreigners being able to provide services in the other jurisdiction(s). There are even fewer binding commitments to promote deeper integration through recognition of qualifications. Out of 25 East Asian FTAs signed by January 2007, for example, mutual recognition was only given within ASEAN (engineers and nurses, subject to minimum qualification requirements), under the Korea-Singapore FTA (engineers qualified from 20 Korean universities or two Singaporean universities), and the Singapore–US FTA (for graduates of four US law schools, if Singaporean citizens or permanent residents). Under China's agreements with Hong Kong and Macau, the latter's permanent residents can sit the mainland's qualifying exams for law and health care.[40]

As well as such exceptional provisions in certain cross-border arrangements in Asia, some limited immigration-related measures have already been included in the 2005 Japan-Philippines Economic Partnership Agreement (JPEPA). They aim especially to facilitate access by Filipino nurses and caregivers to Japan's burgeoning aged-care sector. Nurses will need six months' Japanese language training, for example, and have three years to pass a government exam during employment. Article 103 requires adherence to listed 'internationally recognised labor rights', which even seems to commit Japan to adhere to two core conventions (Nos 29 and 111) of the International Labour Organization (ILO) that the country (unlike the Philippines) has not yet ratified.[41]

Initiatives like those found in JPEPA point the way for other states to build in labour law or human rights protections that may go beyond international (ILO or UN) obligations, which even developed countries may be unwilling to assume on a multilateral basis. The JPEPA provisions were apparently included at the insistence of the Philippines, an interesting development given that instead it often has been the developed country partners to FTAs which press for labour protections. For example, NAFTA ushered in another side agreement on labour protections, primarily at the insistence of trade unions in the US (and Canada) concerned primarily about production capacity relocating to Mexico and enjoying low-cost advantages due to reduced labour standards there.[42] If other regional FTAs liberalise labour mobility, as well as movement of capital, goods and services, pressure for labour protections may well emerge from both developing and developed country partners, albeit for different reasons. US union representatives are already pressing their government to include in the TPPA a stronger labour agreement than the P4's 'Memorandum of Understanding on Labour Cooperation'.[43]

Services (and judicial cooperation)

Free movement in services accelerated worldwide from 1995, after GATS took effect within the WTO framework. It has expanded through subsequent multilateral negotiations, notably through agreements on financial services and on telecommunications, and more recently through FTAs. Many FTAs, including those in East Asia, adopt a GATS-style hybrid positive list approach in which commitments are made by parties expressly identifying market access undertakings for specific service sectors. This is subject to any restrictions on access (for example, national treatment) and distinguishing between cross-border trade in services (mode 1, for example, e-commerce), consumption abroad (mode 2, for example, tourism), commercial presence (mode 3) and movement of natural persons (mode 4). Others adopt the 'negative list' approach, allowing free trade in all service sectors unless expressly limited. This model in effect covers the GATS equivalent of modes 1, 2 and 4, with mode 3 instead usually covered (and indeed amplified) by a horizontal investment chapter applicable to both goods and services.[44]

In such negative list FTAs, trade in financial services often remains more restricted, for example by carving out those services completely or reverting to some form of positive list approach.[45] Investment chapters usually now include investor-state arbitration provisions (as outlined above). However, these sometimes restrict this option regarding financial services.[46] The possibility of building such flexibility into FTAs in sensitive sectors, especially after the GFC disaster, should offer some hope for those concerned about extending financial market deregulation through future agreements like the expanded TPPA presently under negotiation.[47] Admittedly, however, considerable deregulation remains entrenched through many existing FTAs, which in turn draw on the GATS regime – arguably ripe for reassessment in the wake of the GFC.[48]

GATS and FTAs usually provide more limited commitments pertaining to mode 4 type movement of natural persons involved in supplying services. In any case, labour mobility appears to depend largely on other specific arrangements regarding for example social security protection and recognition of occupational qualifications. In the latter respect, the TTMRA goes much further than any other development found within or alongside FTAs in the Asia-Pacific. The arrangement is often overlooked, yet it seems particularly timely to revisit the TTMRA because one express understanding was that it was 'intended that this Arrangement will contribute to the development of the Asia Pacific region by providing a possible model of cooperation with other economies, including those in the South Pacific and APEC'.[49] In sum:[50]

> The [TTMRA], which came into effect on 1 May 1998, is a non-treaty arrangement between the Commonwealth, State and Territory Governments of Australia and the Government of New Zealand. It is a cornerstone of a single economic market and a powerful driver of regulatory coordination and integration. Further, the Arrangement is a key instrument in developing an integrated trans-Tasman economy and a seamless market place as envisioned by the Australia and New Zealand Closer Economic Relations Trade Agreement (CER) signed in 1983.

The TTMRA is implemented in New Zealand through the trans-Tasman Mutual Recognition Act 1997 (the Act), which is overarching legislation. This means that all laws are subject to it unless specifically excluded or exempted. In particular, the TTMRA has implications for the sale of goods and the registration of occupations.

Because this – like the TTTA described above – is not a treaty, each country enacts parallel legislation. There are also elaborate provisions regarding permanent and temporary exemptions, and referrals to a Ministerial Council for determination if a dispute arises after a country implements measures to protect public health, safety or the environment.[51]

Those with a sense of European history will remember, as explained further in the next section,[52] that the EU has developed mutual recognition principles ('negative harmonisation') but also continues joint attempts to minimise disputes about public health exceptions and the like ('positive harmonisation' by specifying minimum standards). Admittedly, that protracted process has been underpinned by treaties, supra-national law-making bodies (especially the European Commission or EC), and a permanent supra-national dispute resolution body (the European Court of Justice or ECJ). But the incipient softer model from the trans-Tasman context seems to be bearing fruit and should appeal to other Australasian economies.[53]

Implications for free trade in goods are discussed in the next section, but one example regarding trade in services in which the TTMRA has already made a major difference, comes from the mutual recognition of lawyers' qualifications.[54] Since 2006 the TTMRA has also formalised mutual recognition for the issuance of securities and other financial products.[55] Because that is partly designed to promote investment, and inspired by developments in the EU, some have called for trans-Tasman mutual recognition of imputation credits in order to eliminate double taxation of dividends.[56] In 2003, Australia's Productivity Commission confirmed many other gains from mutual recognition.[57] It is therefore surprising that neither Australia nor New Zealand has explored incorporating some variant of the comprehensive TTMRA into its FTAs with new partner countries, or at least through parallel legislation as in the trans-Tasman context.

Nor has either Australia or New Zealand yet offered to other countries an equivalent to the Trans-Tasman Court Proceedings and Regulatory Enforcement Agreement (TTCPREA) signed in 2008. One important feature is that a court in one country is treated like a court in the other regarding civil proceedings, significantly expanding chances of enforcing judgments. For example, a New Zealand company can commence litigation in a local court and enforce its judgment in Australia even if the Australian defendant did not consent to the New Zealand court's jurisdiction or have a sufficient commercial presence in New Zealand. However, it can still resist enforcement on the basis that the judgment is contrary to Australian public policy. The TTCPREA also preserves the right for the Australian defendant to object that the New Zealand court is *forum non conveniens* (i.e. Australia is the more appropriate forum).[58]

The model is similar to the legislation providing for enforcement of judgments within Australia, just as the TTMRA draws on the mutual recognition regime within Australia enacted in 1992. But the TTCPREA was also inspired by the 'Brussels I Regulation' of 2001 (superseding the Brussels Convention of 1968), which had also dramatically improved enforcement of judgments within the EU. Yet no efforts have ever been made public by the Australian government, for example, to extend similar treatment to other FTA partners.[59] A prime candidate in Australasia would be Singapore, which shares an English law heritage.[60] In the Asia-Pacific more generally, the US is another possibility, especially as the Australian and US governments gave 'trust in each other's highly developed legal system' as one ostensible reason for not including investor-state arbitration provisions in their 2004 FTA.[61] But then why not also extend a judgments enforcement regime like the trans-Tasman one to Australia and Japan, within or alongside the FTA they are now negotiating? After all, both these countries have also now built up considerable trust between their judiciaries.[62] They might even propose an 'opt-in' plurilateral mutual recognition regime within the expanded. Nations like the US and Singapore, and other states with shared legal traditions (such as Malaysia), might be tempted eventually to opt-in.

At the least, Asia-Pacific countries should consider developing a network of treaties covering other aspects of cross-border judicial cooperation, focusing on actual and potential FTA partners. Australia already has bilateral treaties with Thailand (1998) and Korea (2000). But these seem to have arisen quite serendipitously,[63] before Australia embarked on an active FTA programme, and government officials do not seem to have realised that judicial cooperation treaties fit quite naturally with contemporary FTAs. If both could be negotiated in tandem, greater attention to judicial cooperation treaties could also help countries gain a better appreciation of each others' traditions in judicial administration and civil procedure. Such harmonising measures would also complement mutual recognition of lawyers' qualifications, already implemented in the trans-Tasman context.[64]

Over the long term, such efforts to establish closer relations among the courts and legal professions in the Asia-Pacific region, even in a core group of countries, should make it easier to establish at least some elements of a supranational judicial system. Again, this does not need to be in the style of a full-blown European Court of Justice. An initial step could be a 'preliminary reference' procedure allowing national courts to seek non-binding opinions interpreting harmonised law, especially parallel legislation or law derived from a common source (like UN 'model laws'), from a panel of eminent jurists appointed by respective states. This would represent a softer approach than the EU's reference system, which in addition often gives 'direct effect' to EU law by allowing affected firms and individuals to claim violations in national courts. Yet economists have recently illustrated how other institutions with advisory powers, for example within APEC, have registered significant successes in influencing market integration policy outcomes.[65]

Free movement of consumer goods, but with better safety regulation

The WTO backdrop

The WTO system contains important Agreements on Technical Barriers to Trade (TBT) and Sanitary and Phytosanitary Measures (SPS), underpinned by a Dispute Settlement Understanding (DSU) institutionalising claims among member states. This has a significant harmonising effect, although the WTO does not impose a generic 'negative harmonisation' agenda like that in the EU based on the 1979 *Cassis de Dijon* decision by the European Court of Justice (ECJ) (discussed below). The TBT and SPS Agreements similarly envisage a system whereby states can set regulations impeding trade only if justified by identifiable safety hazards, under the watchful eye of a supranational judiciary and the DSU. They expressly give considerable weight to standards from specified international bodies. By contrast, the more venerable General Agreement on Tariffs and Trade (GATT, art. XX) provides no such overt guidance in promoting harmonisation.

The WTO system continues to generate debate regarding the ways it deals with scientific controversy, and more generally in balancing commercial and public interests. One option is to formally amend the system to advance more politically acceptable but still trade-enhancing 'positive harmonisation' mechanisms, where member states or the WTO itself specifically agree on joint minimum standards.[66] A more realistic shorter-term alternative is to allow greater scope for democratic values to feed into the current 'negative harmonisation' regime.[67] This may be easier to achieve nowadays in an era of proliferating bilateral or regional FTAs, especially in Agreements involving the EU or its states on one side. It may also be possible with countries like Japan that have already experimented with novel forms of public–private governance, albeit within their borders rather than supranationally.[68] So far, however, such FTAs have focused on going beyond the WTO primarily in more market-opening ways. Even procedurally, they have not innovated by institutionalising novel dispute resolution processes or collaboration in standard-setting bodies among the nations involved.

The European approach

The EU suggests a way forward since, from small beginnings in 1957, the EU's primary agenda has also been economic liberalisation among its members. However, the mandate has slowly broadened, now encompassing a strong emphasis on consumer protection, and tensions have always been evident with more statist traditions particularly within certain continental European nations.

The EU's liberalisation agenda has also, in fact, combined two different models.[69] A decentralised model of 'negative harmonisation', centred on national governments and the ECJ, has relied mainly on the principle of non-discrimination on the ground of nationality. A major development was the ECJ's judgment in *Cassis de Dijon*.[70] It held that goods produced to the standards set in a home (exporting) state will be presumed equivalent to goods produced to standards imposed – even without openly differentiating between home and foreign goods – by a host (importing) state, and therefore allowed entry. The exception was where the host state could justify its standards under a mandatory requirement (such as consumer protection) and the proportionality principle. This leaves states freedom to regulate, subject to non-discrimination, but free movement creates 'competitive federalism' or 'regulatory competition' between states. It is hoped that the outcome will be a 'race to the top', leading to an optimal regulatory framework.

The EC soon realised that this approach reduced the need for its Directives (whose norms states must incorporate into their domestic law, albeit with choice as to form and methods) aimed at the harmonisation or 'approximation' of states' standards or laws 'as directly affect' the establishment or functioning of an integrated market. Harmonisation initiatives could be restricted to areas where states legitimately invoked mandatory requirements or derogations from fundamental freedoms of movement. Such 'positive harmonisation', involving a centralised model (imposing convergent standards) premised largely on market failure (practical limits to free movement, and responsiveness of state regulators anyway) and the fear of a 'race to the bottom', thus started to become a less prominent approach to economic integration.

In 1985, the EC proclaimed a new deregulatory era. But it did not abandon product safety to free trade combined with the possibility of divergent national interpretations of mandatory limits. Instead, the EC finally obtained enactment of the 1985 Product Liability Directive.[71] It also announced a 'New Approach' to standard-setting.[72] Rather than proposing detailed (design) standards for legislative approval, which still at that time had to be unanimous, it brought in a faster harmonisation process allowing more scope for market forces. The legislature would enact broad 'essential safety requirements'. The preferred means to achieve these requirements would be elaborated by standard-setting organisations.[73]

This drew on a longer-standing tradition of the EC in effect delegating more technical matters to expert committees, especially, for example, in the field of food regulation, in a system of 'comitology' or committee-centred governance.[74] However, the New Approach seemed to envisage more input from industry interests, especially in national standardisation bodies, albeit with more financial and other support offered to consumers represented in an increasingly influential body, the European Committee for Standardization (CEN). Market forces were further engaged by providing that compliance with the technical standards provided a presumption of conformity with the essential safety requirements. Specifically, for many products but subject to 'safeguards' if goods were found to be unsafe, suppliers could then affix the 'CE' mark needed to trade goods across the EU, instead of having to go through tests to prove compliance with the essential requirements.

New Approach Directives began to proliferate for many types of goods. Yet, because they were usually quite diverse 'maximal harmonisation' measures (pre-empting stricter safety requirements being set by national member states), pressure emerged to enact a Directive setting basic requirements for consumer goods not covered, or not fully covered, by New Approach Directives. The original General Product Safety Directive (GPSD) of 1992, itself following the basic structure of New Approach Directives, was the result. It included a general safety provision (GSP) requiring suppliers to provide only safe consumer goods.

From the late 1990s, safety failures and governance issues created momentum for further reform. Strengthening the product liability regime was seen as insufficient. Instead, the GPSD was given more teeth in 2001.[75] The revised Directive clarified the powers of national regulators (delegated for enforcement) to order mandatory recalls of unsafe goods within the distribution chain, as well as those in the hands of consumers. Requirements to disclose information about product accidents became stricter, and improvements were made to the system for sharing cross-border the data on emergent risks – the so-called RAPEX system described further below. Regulators also had to be guided by the precautionary principle. This much-debated principle has evolved from earlier US law, and especially environmental regulation in the EU and worldwide, into a central 'constitutional' element for the EU more broadly pursuant to the 1992 Maastricht Treaty.[76]

Some have called for a European Product Safety Agency,[77] concentrating on risk assessment recommendations like the new European Food Safety Authority. The latter works alongside the EU's Food Regulation (EC/178/2002), itself an outcome of Europe's BSE disaster and broader concerns about food safety. Amended in 2005 to strengthen traceability requirements, the Regulation also imposes risk disclosure obligations on suppliers and creates an information-sharing system (RASFF) similar to RAPEX for general consumer goods.[78] But some have urged closer assimilation of both regimes including the introduction of a CE-Mark system, allowing foods to be presumed safe rather than the opposite as under the current Regulation.[79]

Asia-Pacific developments

Already we can see analogies emerging particularly in the trans-Tasman context, as mutual recognition rules have grown, although so far there has been less formal joint standard-setting by Australian and New Zealand bodies. The broader CER agenda generated the TTMRA, although (as noted above) the latter is not a treaty, and it was not pushed along – nor is it now enforced – by a supranational court like the ECJ. The TTMRA does apply mutual recognition principles to allow free movement of goods, except for:[80]

1   Exclusions: for legislation related to customs controls and tariffs, intellectual property, taxation and specific international obligations related to the sale of goods.
2   Permanent exemptions: currently applied to laws relating to (a) weapons, fireworks, film and other classifications, pornography and gaming machines (all these also exempted from the MRA within Australia); as well as

(b) quarantine and endangered species; (c) ozone protection, agricultural and veterinary chemicals, and certain risk-categorised foods (scheduled for the next five-yearly Review).

3   Special exemptions (for up to 12 months, but open to roll-overs) combined with cooperation programmes (to try to align relevant standards in both countries to extend mutual recognition): applied to (a) therapeutic goods, hazardous substances, radio communications standards, road vehicles and gas appliances, but no longer (b) most consumer product safety standards.

4   Temporary exemptions (for up to 12 months, 'substantially for the purpose of protecting the health and safety of persons or preventing, minimising or regulating environmental pollution').

Indeed, New Zealand has already gone one step further than envisaged under the TTRMA regime. Its 'permanent exemption' for mutual recognition of film (and computer game) classifications has been sidestepped by New Zealand *unilaterally* deciding to recognise non-restricted or non-banned classifications (G, PG or M) given in Australia (and indeed, if the item is not classified there, from the United Kingdom).[81]

By contrast, New Zealand seems reluctant to cede much sovereignty in relation to intellectual property, a major 'exclusion' under the TTMRA. As early as 1999, David Goddard and the New Zealand Institute for Economic Research suggested that a joint Patent Registry would be more efficient than greater exchange of information.[82] But other New Zealanders remain more sceptical.[83]

Successive cooperation programmes regarding 'special exemptions' have remained unsuccessful in establishing an 'Australia New Zealand Therapeutic Products Authority' (ANZTPA). Health ministers first proposed harmonisation in 1991, the governments began exploring the possibility of a joint agency in 2001, and an agreement was reached in 2003. They concluded considerable preparatory work in 2005 and 2006, but New Zealand announced on 16 July 2007 that it would not proceed with the necessary legislation.[84] Despite the attraction of leveraging off the much larger and well-resourced drugs regulator in Australia, major sticking points for New Zealand proved to be its more liberal standards regarding the advertising of prescription drugs directly to consumers, as well as the regulation of complementary or traditional medicines. It is worth remembering, however, that it is only since 2004 that the EU has made it compulsory to use its centralised EMEA for licensing of certain drugs (for example, using recombinant biotech processes, or for AIDS or cancer) rather than using national regulators and then seeking mutual recognition within EU member states.[85]

The ANZTPA means going beyond not only the EMEA but also an existing trans-Tasman standard-setting agency for foodstuffs,[86] now known as Food Standards Australia New Zealand (FSANZ). The latter develops standards for composition, labelling and contaminants for foodstuffs produced or imported for sale in Australia and New Zealand. It evolved out of Australian legislation and a small national body in 1991, and then the bilateral Agreement Concerning a

Joint Food Standards System concluded in 1995 (and amended in 2002). However, FSANZ sets bi-national standards (through a Food Standards Code) primarily regarding labelling and composition of foods, only dealing with specified chemical and microbiological standards and pre-market assessments of novel foods (such as genetically modified or irradiated foods). There remains national development and implementation of food regulations for food safety, primary production and maximum residue levels for agricultural and veterinary chemicals. Each country also separately regulates the import and export of food, manages food emergencies, and implements the Code.[87]

Outside these areas of 'vertical' or product-specific product safety regulation, Australia and New Zealand have not yet superimposed joint frameworks on the mutual recognition regime to the same extent as the EU's New Approach Directives. Nor have the countries collaborated as closely in promoting a transnational standard-setting body like CEN.[88] Both New Zealand and Australia retain their own peak standard-setting bodies, and indeed the Australian counterpart attracted considerable critical scrutiny during a Productivity Commission review in 2006. A particular concern is the limited scope for consumer input into standard-setting compared, for example, with the EU.[89]

Australia and New Zealand also do not have an equivalent to the 'horizontal' GPSD, incorporating a GSP, and an EU-like CE mark system generally. Yet there already exists, for example, an Agreement on Mutual Recognition in Relation to Conformity Assessment between New Zealand and the European Community (EU/NZ MRA), in effect from 1999, which allows New Zealand exporters to Europe to apply CE marks.[90] New Zealand, Australia and Singapore also participate in all three aspects of an APEC scheme to promote mutual recognition of conformity assessment for regulated electrical equipment. However, all other APEC members so far participate only in the 'information exchange' aspect.[91]

Bilaterally, for example, the 2008 China–New Zealand FTA includes Annex 14 on 'Cooperation in the Field of Conformity Assessment in Relation to Electrical and Electronic Equipment and Components'. This requires China Compulsory Certification (CCC) results to be recognised by New Zealand, for example, and allows for New Zealand certification bodies to receive accreditation. More generally, New Zealand officials have long believed that 'standards and TBT issues must be addressed in FTAs' and that 'consultation between the relevant regulatory authorities in the partner countries is very important in resolving problems in this area'.[92]

Although not extending to an equivalent of the GPSD and concomitant improvements in joint standard-setting activities, Australia's Productivity Commission recommended some specific reforms in 2006 and then again in 2008 as part of a broader reform of consumer law nationwide. These reforms were approved in principle by the Ministerial Council for Consumer Affairs (MCCA), which includes consumer affairs ministers from the federal and state governments as well as New Zealand, as well as by the Council of Australian Governments (CoAG). Accordingly, from 2009 the Australian Treasury (the federal government agency responsible for consumer policy) began working on revisiting federal legislation relating to product safety, which state governments would then re-enact or 'apply' nationwide. This was eventually achieved by enacting the 'Australian Consumer Law' (Schedule 2 of the Australian Competition and Consumer Act 2010, Cth) in two main stages, in turn adopted by all Australian states and territories.[93]

The New Zealand government is not bound by the CoAG agreement. Nonetheless, given New Zealand's agreement in principle at the MCCA level and earlier history of revising consumer law in the light of Australian legislative reforms, we can expect the country largely to follow whatever legislative amendments emerge from Australia. However, it seems unlikely that New Zealand will give up to Australian regulators its current powers under the Fair Trading Act to impose bans or set safety standards for general consumer goods. Such standards would therefore remain subject to the TTMRA, meaning that in principle goods produced to Australian mandatory standards would have to be allowed into New Zealand. However, as mentioned above, the TTMRA allows a state like New Zealand temporarily to impose different standards to protect human health. The other state can then refer this situation to a Ministerial Council to try to resolve the dispute and generate a joint standard, pursuant to art. 4.2.2 of the Agreement.

By contrast, the EU minimises such disputes through its Directives, which also bring in European as well as national standard-setting bodies (such as CEN), and ultimately lets the ECJ rule on any remaining issues. Australia and New Zealand could now consider adopting more European law elements to their trans-Tasman regime, such as supranational standard-setting bodies (with greater funding and participation rights for consumers), a variant of the CE mark system, and a GSP (including the precautionary principle). A supranational court is not essential, but it has efficiency advantages and could well eventually emerge out of the mutual trust in the judiciaries of the two countries, evident from the recent TTCPREA. Meanwhile, aspects of the present Trans-Tasman compromise could indeed become an inspiration for other FTA partners in the Asia-Pacific region.

A second major set of product safety innovations for Australia and New Zealand, as well as the region more generally, also derives inspiration from recent developments particularly in Europe. As mentioned above, the GSPD regime was revised in 2001 to strengthen the system for suppliers to disclose serious product safety risks to regulators and therefore the general public. Japan added such requirements to its product safety legislation in 2006, regarding specified risks (currently, carbon monoxide leaks or fires caused by product failures) and accidents (requiring hospital treatment). China added similar regulations in 2007, Canada did so in 2011, and the US has had similar requirements since 1990 – albeit with less need or separate impact, given its uniquely high levels of highly publicised product liability litigation.[94]

The Australian Consumer Law eventually followed the Productivity Commission's recommendations in 2006, repeated in 2008, for mandatory reporting requirements. (However, suppliers only need to disclose actual serious accidents or deaths caused by their consumer products, not risks thereof even in the event of a 'near-miss'). If New Zealand decides also to amend its Fair Trading Act accordingly, the two countries should set up a central clearing-house for receiving notifications from suppliers. The institution would then analyse them (considering, for example, the need to ban unsafe goods more widely or to mandate new safety standards). It could then disseminate information quickly and appropriately to the public, although the Australian Consumer Law imposes comparatively strict confidentiality obligations on regulators receiving accident information via suppliers' mandatory reports.[95]

The EU's 'RAPEX' system provides a model that appears to be working well, according to a report reviewing implementation of the revised GSPD more generally.[96] Indeed, the EC has already signed information-sharing agreements with the US Consumer Product Safety Commission (in 2005) and the Chinese Administration for Quality Supervision (in 2006). The 2008 Japan–EU Summit also agreed to explore similar information-sharing. Dangerous product notifications to RAPEX have risen significantly every year since the revised Directive came into effect from 2004, with about half resulting from mandatory action taken by national regulators. In 2008, these were twice the notifications to US regulators for comparable product categories. Consistently, around half of all notifications deal with Chinese products. As of 10 March 2009, 3338 reports were on the RAPEX–CHINA collaborative database; Chinese regulators had investigated 669 and action had been taken in China in 352.[97]

Surely there is scope to share data on risks or at least accidents on both bilateral and regional bases within the Asia-Pacific region. So far all we have is some faltering steps via APEC regarding food safety particularly since 2007, and an AusAID-funded capacity-building exercise from November 2008 regarding general consumer product safety.[98] But information cannot flow properly unless and until all major economies in the region begin to share information on product-related accidents and risks obtained from suppliers themselves.

Indeed, recall already how in 2008 Fonterra (formerly the New Zealand Dairy Board) voluntarily disclosed to the New Zealand government its growing concerns about melamine-tainted milk products produced by its joint venture with Sanlu in China. The government's voluntary disclosure then to the Chinese government led the latter to chase up the local government, and resulted in the belated resolution of what indeed turned out to be a major health risk.[99] But to minimise similar problems in the future, one way forward would be to:

a   require New Zealand manufacturers (and, indeed, parent companies) to disclose serious actual or likely injuries from products (including those of subsidiaries) – both in NZ and in FTA partners – to its home government; and
b   require the New Zealand government to disclose serious problems to a partner like China under an FTA.

The simpler alternative is for each country, as in Canada's Product Safety Act 2011, to require all manufacturers to disclose actual or likely serious injuries, *wherever they occur*, which the home government would then make publicly available.[100] This could be fed into a new central clearing-house, which might indeed then be linked up with the EU (and therefore called for example, 'RAPEX-ASIA-PACIFIC').

We can expect more and more countries to enact accident or risk disclosure requirements. This will occur partly for practical reasons, not just because these countries like to imitate others or protect consumer interests to the same extent. After all, exporters to Canada or Australia (for example, from New Zealand) are likely soon to find importers there insisting on contract terms requiring exporters to notify them of serious product-related accidents in their home countries. This will occur so that the Canadian or Australian importers can comply with the new legislative requirement to notify regulators there about serious accidents that occur overseas, as well as domestically. Exporters therefore should become more willing also to disclose such information to their own regulators, because their compliance costs will come down – they will increasingly be collecting and monitoring this information anyway, for their contracting partners abroad. Indeed, exporters may then join with consumer groups to press for national legislation imposing disclosure obligations on all manufacturers – not just exporters – in order to level the playing field domestically.

Conclusions

We are likely to witness more and more 'add-ons' to obligations traditionally found within the WTO and FTA agreements. However, varying constellations of interest groups domestically as well as internationally may generate some such innovations more quickly or pervasively, as with product safety risk information dissemination or joint standard-setting activities.

A more technical complication is that some of these innovations may be built in within FTAs themselves, such as investment chapters or even mutual recognition arrangements like the TTMRA. This may give rise to drafting difficulties or delay FTA negotiations, but this chapter has already shown how governments are already starting to address such issues, even within the Asia-Pacific region.

Other innovations may continue to be set out separately from FTAs, as with a judgments enforcement mechanism and regulatory cooperation treaty like the TTCPREA. However, especially as governments and others increasingly devote so many resources to negotiating FTAs themselves, we should already be thinking about taking those opportunities to negotiate additional measures to facilitate free movement in goods, services, capital and people. For example, justice ministry officials from each country are likely to be on negotiating teams anyway; while their colleagues are talking about economic issues like tariff level reductions, they could take time out to negotiate a judgments enforcement mechanism. Or tax officials on the teams, during their own 'down time', might negotiate new treaties to avoid double taxation or to promote portability of social security entitlements (as outlined above). This would have the additional advantage of highlighting innovative mechanisms for preventing and resolving disputes touching on traditional sovereignty concerns (such as taxation), which might be extended to other types of disputes (such as those between investors and host states[101]).

Even if broader agreements are not negotiated in parallel in quite this way, FTA negotiators and policy-makers still need to think more holistically. Drawing from comparative regional integration studies by political scientists and others,[102] they should anticipate that a 'classic' FTA nowadays is likely to be or become only one core treaty, to be fitted into a larger framework in a more transparent way. At present, even in the trans-Tasman context, we face an increasingly complex set of arrangements that is difficult to perceive in a comprehensive fashion. Ironically, the picture risks becoming even more complicated since Australia and New Zealand agreed in 2004 to develop a long-term vision for a seamless trans-Tasman business environment: a Single Economic Market (SEM). Reportedly:[103]

> SEM is not about prescribing a particular set of institutional arrangements to govern trans-Tasman markets. Rather, it is about identifying innovative actions that could reduce discrimination and costs arising from different, conflicting or duplicate regulatory requirements. The aim is to ensure that trans-Tasman markets for goods, services, labour and capital operate effectively and support economic growth in both countries. The SEM also provides an opportunity to work cooperatively to influence international trends and potentially work together to address external challenges facing our two economies.

Achievements recorded for 2005–6 include a Treaty on Mutual Recognition of Securities Offerings, a Review of the trans-Tasman MoU for Business Law Harmonisation (including a new five-year Agenda),[104] and establishment of a trans-Tasman Council for Banking Supervision. But these and many other developments towards an SEM are often very disparate and not readily apparent, especially as a whole or for those outside the highest levels of government. This creates additional challenges as both Australia and New Zealand venture into regional arrangements like AANZFTA and the TPPA.[105] Further, developing cooperation in what still appears to be quite an ad hoc fashion makes the Trans-Tasman model difficult to perceive, and hence to adopt for other countries in the Asia-Pacific region that are presently negotiating their own FTAs.

Accordingly, just as we have now 'Model BITs' and (de facto, for large economies like the US) some 'Model FTAs', perhaps we should be developing a true 'Model Economic Partnership Agreement' that goes well beyond what Japan is currently including in its own 'EPAs' nowadays.[106] This would make it easier to realise that even the Asia-Pacific region is beginning to institutionalise several elements not so dissimilar to some basic building blocks of the EU. Such an initiative would also highlight where we still differ, so we can have more fruitful discussions about possible justifications for such variation. This more ambitious 'post-FTA' agenda makes it more likely that we will identify – and indeed acclaim – areas where our partnerships do or can achieve a more sustainable balance of both economic efficiency and democratic legitimacy, particularly in the Asia-Pacific.

Notes

1 This is an edited and updated version of a paper originally presented at the NZ Centre of International Economic Law conference, 'Trade Agreements: Where Do We Go From Here?', 22–23 October 2009, Wellington. A longer version, containing extensive further references and some additional coverage, is available at http://ssrn.com/abstract=1509810. I thank especially Ichiro Araki, Shiro Armstrong and Philomena Murray.
2 Kawai and Wignaraja 2009.
3 Quiggin 2010.
4 Productivity Commission 2010; and Australian Government Department of Foreign Affairs and Trade (April 2011).
5 See, for example, the dissenting opinions of Associate Commissioner Andrew Stoler (Productivity Commission 2010, Appendix A).
6 Kelsey 2010.
7 Kinley 2009; Spence 2011: 245.
8 Hix 2010.
9 Bath and Nottage 2011.
10 Hix 2010.
11 Murray 2010.
12 Flitton (24 July 2011). See also generally Dent 2010.
13 Nottage 2010.
14 Murray 2004: 44.
15 Zhong 2011.
16 Saul 2011.
17 Calder and Yee 2010.
18 Murray 2010.
19 Nakamura 2009.
20 Baldwin 2011.
21 Nottage and Weeramantry 2012.
22 That remains one possible interpretation of China's detention of Stern Hu, an Australian citizen, after Chinese investors failed in bids for Rio Tinto and OZ Minerals earlier in 2009. Compare generally Bath 2011.
23 Pokarier 2008.
24 See, for example, UNCTAD (2009). New Zealand's amendment in 2008 to its FDI legislation added extra criteria for 'public interest'. See Kalderimis 2009 and, more generally on how to assess 'national interest', *Tiroa E and Te Hape B Trusts v Chief Executive of Land Information* [2012] NZHC 147.
25 Some guidance may emerge from a joint APEC-UNCTAD 'Study of the Core Elements in Existing RTAs/FTAs and Bilateral Trade Agreements' underway in 2009 by the APEC Investment Experts' Group: APEC 'Investment Experts' Group'. Online. Available at: http://apec.org/Groups/Committee-on-Trade-and-Investment/Investment-Experts-Group.aspx. However, most treaties retain broad provisions which, furthermore, apply mostly to the post-establishment phase. Similarly, at a multilateral level, the OECD Council's Recommendation on 'Guidelines for Recipient Country Investment Policies Relating to National Security' (adopted on 25 May 2009) deal very broadly with non-discrimination, transparency, regulatory proportionality, and accountability or oversight possibilities. See OECD (2009).
26 Nottage 2011.
27 Burch and Nottage 2011.
28 Nottage and Miles 2009.
29 Markell and Knox 2003: 13.
30 Connelly 2005.

31 See NZ MFAT 'New Zealand and the World Trade Organisation'. Online. Available at: www.mfat.govt.nz/Trade-and-Economic-Relations/NZ-and-the-WTO/Trade-Issues/0-environment-framework.php. See also, in the NZ-China FTA, the inclusion (apparently, at the final stages of negotiation) of loose commitments on sustainable development: see the Preamble, available via NZ MFAT 'New Zealand China free trade agreement'. Online. Available at: http://chinafta.govt.nz/1-The-agreement/2-Text-of-the-agreement/index.php.

32 Elms and Lim 2012.

33 See Brightling and Feldman 2009 (contrasting the EU and the US). But they go on to review the quite limited types of provisions found in all US FTAs (without examining, however, the NAFTA side agreement creating the NACEC) and suggest that separate multilateral environmental agreements remain the best way forward.

34 Productivity Commission (December 2010): Ch. 14.3.

35 Australian Government DFAT (April 2011).

36 Nottage 2011.

37 Nottage 2013.

38 See NZ MFAT 'Australia New Zealand closer economic relations'. Online. Available at: www.mfat.govt.nz/Trade-and-Economic-Relations/2-Trade-Relationships-and-Agreements/Australia/0-trade-agreement.php.

39 Shah and Long 2009: 2948.

40 Fink and Molinuevo 2008: 304–5.

41 Formacion 2008.

42 Compa 2001.

43 Wallach and Tucker 2010; Elms and Lim 2012.

44 Fink and Molinuevo 2008: 269–72.

45 Fink and Molinuevo 2008: 272–6.

46 Fink and Molinuevo 2008: 301–3.

47 Kelsey 2010.

48 Delimatsis and Sauvé 2010.

49 Recital E, at Ministry of Economic Development 'Full text of the TTMRA', Online. Available at: www.med.govt.nz/business/trade-tariffs/trade-environment/economic-relationship-with-australia/trans-tasman-mutual-recognition-arrangement/full-text-of-the-ttmra.

50 Reproduced from Ministry of Economic Development 'Trans-Tasman mutual recognition arrangement'. Online. Available at: www.med.govt.nz/business/trade-tariffs/trade-environment/economic-relationship-with-australia/trans-tasman-mutual-recognition-arrangement.

51 For more details, including the Australian counterpart legislation, see the *Users' Guide* (2006) at Department of Innovation, Industry, Science and Research (2006), and in the next section.

52 Nottage 2007a.

53 Kirby 2010: 18–20 (discussing the longer version of this chapter).

54 Walker 2004.

55 Bryony *et al.* 2008 (suggested: McCormack *et al.* 2008).

56 Muck 2009.

57 Australian Government Productivity Commission 'Review of Mutual Recognition'. Online. Available at: www.pc.gov.au/projects/study/mutual-recognition.

58 By contrast, the 2005 Hague Convention on Choice of Court Agreements does not include *forum non conveniens*, but it is premised on the parties having consented to a court's jurisdiction. See generally Mortensen 2009: 222, describing the trans-Tasman treaty as 'arguably the world's most liberal scheme for the transnational enforcement of judgments'.

59 Compare, for example, art. 14.6 of the AUSFTA:

> The Parties shall work together to examine the scope for establishing greater bilateral recognition of foreign judgments of their respective judicial authorities obtained for the benefit of consumers, investors, or customers who have suffered economic harm as a result of being deceived, defrauded, or misled…

This consultation requirement, found in Chapter 14 on 'Competition-related Matters', rounds out provisions aimed more specifically at facilitating enforcement of judgments obtained by each other's competition regulators.

60 In September 2010, the Supreme Court of New South Wales concluded a Memorandum of Understanding allowing it to consider referring a question governed by Singaporean law to the Supreme Court of Singapore, to be determined there as expeditiously as possible, and vice versa. See Brereton (2011).

61 Nottage and Miles 2009: 32.

62 Spigelman 2006.

63 Spigelman 2007.

64 See above. In addition, following commitments by the Australia and New Zealand governments to bring the Judgments Treaty into effect as soon as possible, ADR institutions in both countries have signed a mutual collaboration agreement: see AMINZ 'Trans-Tasman Mediation Agreement Signed'. Online. Available at: www.aminz.org.nz/Story?Action=View&Story_id=1186.

65 See, for example, Dee and McNaughton 2010. Compare, for example, Haggard 2011, urging consideration of modalities for introducing private standing to claim violations of FTA commitments.

66 Reich 2004.

67 Joerges 2009.

68 Nottage 2005.

69 Nottage 2007a.

70 (Case 120/78 [1979] ECR 649).

71 Nottage 2004: Ch 2.

72 Egan 2001. Baldwin 2011: 15–6, 32–4 also emphasises how the ECJ case law promoting mutual recognition led to a broader shift towards cooperation in adopting shared standards, epitomised by the Single European Act 1986 incorporating qualified voting by member states.

73 Howells 2000.

74 Joerges and Vos 1999.

75 Fairgrieve and Howells 2006.

76 Vogel 2003.

77 Hodges 2005.

78 Alemanno 2009.

79 Brack 2009.

80 See Trans-Tasman Mutual Recognition Act 1997, respectively Schedules 1, 2 and 3; and Council of Australia Government www.coag.gov.au regarding Temporary Exemptions (s. 46(3) of the Australian legislation).

81 See, for example, Regulations 4 and 12 of the Films, Videos, and Publications Classification Regulations 1994 (NZ). Online. Available at: www.legislation.govt.nz/regulation/public/1994/0189/latest/DLM194134.html.

82 Cited in Walker 2004: 89.

83 Frankel and Richardson 2011.

84 von Tigerstrom 2007: 302–5.

85 Miller 2006: 121–8.

86 von Tigerstrom 2007: 308–9.

87 In New Zealand, these activities are conducted by the New Zealand Food Safety Authority, recently established largely out of the Ministry of Agriculture. For a brief

explanation of its relationship to FSANZ, see New Zealand Food Safety Authority 'Food standard Australia New Zealand (FSANZ)'. Online. Available at: www.food-safety.govt.nz/policy-law/food-regulation/australia-nz-cooperation/FSANZ/. In Australia, however, several of the country-specific activities (e.g. regulating primary production hygiene) are also carried out by FSANZ.

88 More broadly, however, see NZ MFAT 'Australia'. Online. Available at: www.mfat. govt.nz/Foreign-Relations/Australia/1-Trade-and-Economic-links/index.php.

89 Nottage 2007b.

90 See Ministry of Economic Development 'European Union and New Zealand mutual recognition arrangement'. Online. Available at: www.med.govt.nz/business/trade-tariffs/trade-environment/trade-agreements-and-partnerships/european-union-and-new-zealand-mutual-recognition-arrangement and the text at Delegation of the European Union to New Zealand www.delaus.ec.europa.eu/newzealand/EU_NZ_relations/agreements_mra.htm.

91 The last two aspects include mutual recognition of (a) test reports and (b) certification. See Ministry of Economic Development 'APEC mutual recognition arrangement for Electric and Electronic Equipment'. Online. Available at: www.med.govt. nz/business/trade-tariffs/trade-environment/trade-agreements-and-partnerships/apec-mutual-recognition-arrangement-for-electric-and-electronic-equipment.

92 Scollay and Trewin 2006: 24.

93 Nottage 2009.

94 Harland and Nottage 2009.

95 Nottage 2011.

96 See Commission of the European Communities (2009).

97 Freeman 2009.

98 See Food Standards Australia New Zealand 'APEC food safety cooperation forum'. Online. Available at: www.foodstandards.gov.au/scienceandeducation/apec2011/; APEC 'Ensuring product safety for consumers: APEC capacity-building workshop'. Online. Available at: www.apec.org/~/media~/media/Files/Events/2008/08_scsc_PrdtSafetyConsWkshp_GI.ashx.

99 Nottage 2010.

100 Nottage 2011.

101 Burch and Nottage 2011; Burch *et al.* 2012.

102 Murray 2010.

103 NZ MFAT 'Australia: CER and SEM'. Online. Available at: http://mfat.govt.nz/Foreign-Relations/Australia/0-CER-SEM.php.

104 For background on the 1988 and 2000 MoUs, which include consumer law as an area for (loose) cooperation, see Walker 2004.

105 Elms and Lim 2012.

106 Compare generally Heydon and Woolcock 2009: 187–95.

Part III

Evolving trade agreement dynamics

Challenging established concepts

8 Regulatory cooperation and Free Trade Agreements

Tracey Epps[1]

Introduction

Governments around the world face challenging regulatory agendas. On the one hand, there is in many states a desire to reduce unnecessary, inefficient, or burdensome regulation. On the other hand, the need for regulation continues unabated in both economic and non-economic areas and governments must make decisions that satisfy competing interests. As Sunstein notes, a twenty-first-century regulatory system must promote economic growth, innovation, and job creation while also protecting public health and welfare.[2] Even where governments succeed in keeping regulation at an optimal level, a modern regulatory agenda will nevertheless occupy a vast amount of resources, both financial and human.

The expertise required to design and implement regulations in a modern economy is enormous and growing. In many areas, complexity seems to be increasing as new scientific and technological developments make possible activities that were unheard of a generation ago. Developments in fields such as genetic engineering, nanotechnology, communication technologies, and computing present unimagined opportunities, but also risks. Globalisation also creates regulatory challenges, creating new and complex problems for domestic regulation and requiring cooperation across national boundaries. Businesses are more engaged than ever in an international environment, with many operating as part of global supply chains that bring their own regulatory challenges. Environmental threats cross boundaries and in the most extreme cases – such as climate change – threaten the entire planet and cannot be dealt with by one country alone. Health risks also cross boundaries as international trade brings not only greater variety of goods, but also provides a vector for the spread of pests and diseases, while the international movement of people creates opportunities for the spread of unwanted diseases. Freedom of movement of people and liberalised international trade not only gives consumers a greater choice of goods and services, but creates opportunities for the spread of crimes such as money laundering, and drug and people trafficking.

It is little surprise then that governments continue to seek out ways in which to better address the regulatory challenges they face. One avenue for doing so is through cooperation with regulators in other countries. Where problems transcend national boundaries, the need for cooperation is obvious. Climate change is a case in point. One country's reduction in carbon emissions may have little effect on the global problem if other countries continue to increase their emissions without paying heed to the risks and consequences associated with such behaviour. Even where problems are domestically focused, cooperation by domestic agencies with their counterparts in other countries can be beneficial by bringing to bear the expertise and experience of others who have had to deal with similar problems. Cooperation can also assist in preventing problems from arising in the future, such as where countries cooperate in order to regulate and manage the spread of diseases across a particular region.

Regulatory cooperation between countries has traditionally taken a variety of forms, in some cases encouraged and managed through formal governmental agreements, in some cases through international inter-governmental organisations, and in other cases through informal networks of regulators. This chapter examines a relatively new and different forum for regulatory cooperation, namely, free trade agreements (FTAs). There has been a proliferation of FTAs over the past 15 years. In addition to liberalising trade through the reduction and elimination of trade barriers that goods face when they cross the border of another country, such as tariffs, import quotas, and restrictions, FTAs have also placed emphasis on reducing what are known as 'behind-the-border' barriers to trade – domestic regulations such as health regulations that make it difficult for goods to enter foreign markets, and those that prevent the entry of or make it difficult for foreign services suppliers to provide their services in and/or operate in foreign markets. Now, a new generation of FTAs recognises that international trade in goods and services cannot be viewed in isolation from many of the regulatory challenges that governments are facing. International trade liberalisation both relies on the regulatory environment, and also creates its own externalities that in turn call for regulatory responses. In both cases, there is potential for cooperation between states to improve regulatory outcomes that will both facilitate trade liberalisation, and address the externalities associated with such trade. Further, FTAs provide a platform on which regulatory cooperation can be advanced in order to address broader social and economic issues.

The purpose of this chapter is to explore and describe the type of provisions in FTAs that enable regulatory cooperation and consider how they fit into the broader scheme of global governance. The first section examines the why and how of regulatory cooperation. It begins by discussing the case for regulatory cooperation between states and then looks at how such regulatory cooperation actually takes place. This includes examining the concept of informal governance networks, their characteristics and advantages, and criticisms of these networks. This discussion will lay the groundwork for drawing some conclusions about regulatory cooperation provisions in FTAs. The second section introduces the concept of FTAs, examining the changing nature of such agreements, and exploring why they might provide for regulatory cooperation alongside liberalisation of barriers at and behind the border. The third section highlights some examples of provisions found in a growing number of FTAs that encourage and promote regulatory cooperation. The final section seeks to fit regulatory coopera- tion provisions of FTAs into a broader global governance framework as described in the first section.

Regulatory challenges and cooperation

The OECD has broadly described 'regulatory cooperation' as

> the range of institutional and procedural frameworks within which national governments, sub-national governments, and the wider public can work together to build more integrated systems for rule making and implementa- tion, subject to the constrains of democratic values such as accountability, openness, and sovereignty.[3]

Regulatory cooperation thus defined has a long history.[4] As the OECD's defini- tion suggests, cooperation occurs at different levels of government and involves a variety of actors and subject matters. It takes place both through formal inter- national processes between governments (as well as through private organisa- tions) and through more informal networks between government departments or regulatory agencies. As discussed in the next section, regulatory cooperation may take many different forms, from highly ambitious programmes to achieve standardisation and harmonisation of regulations, to simpler and less ambitious forms of cooperation such as information-sharing between agencies from differ- ent countries.

Cooperation by countries in the regulatory sphere is motivated by several factors. These include first a desire to advance shared norms and achieve common goals. Common goals will often arise from situations that one country acting alone cannot adequately address through regulation or otherwise. Some- times this will be the case where activities in one country have an impact beyond that country's borders. For example, because the activities of financial institu- tions in one country have the potential to affect the operation of financial markets and to impact upon financial stability in other countries, countries have engaged in international efforts to coordinate regulation.[5]

A second factor that motivates regulatory cooperation is the increasingly complex and challenging nature of many subjects of regulation. Particularly notable are the fields of health and safety, and the environment, where unique regulatory challenges arise due to new and emerging technologies that pose new and uncertain risks. Mandel highlights biotechnology,[6] nanotechnology,[7] and synthetic biology[8] as technologies that are anticipated to revolutionise fields as diverse as health care, agriculture, and energy, but that also present unknown and potentially serious risks. In these areas, there is a large degree of scientific uncertainty, which leads to problems in formulating regulatory responses, and to divergent approaches being taken in different countries. Divergences between regulatory approaches can cause significant disruptions to trade when products in one country are denied entry into another on the basis of different standards or regulations.[9] Mandel suggests that such uncertainty presents an opportunity to bring together diverse stakeholders to 'produce a collaborative governance product rather than a resource-draining adversarial battle'.[10]

The motivation for regulatory cooperation then is fairly clear. What of the benefits? Marchant *et al.* identify a number of potential benefits of international coordination in regulating nanotechnology.[11] These are worth setting out as – while developed with nanotechnology in mind – these kinds of benefits have a broader application and are relevant in other areas of regulation. Marchant *et al.* speak in terms of international 'coordination', a term which has slightly different connotations than 'cooperation'. Coordination can be seen as one of the most important outcomes of cooperation – it will not come about by itself; regulatory cooperation is required. Therefore, the benefits of coordination can also be seen as benefits of cooperation.

Marchant *et al.* first note the trade benefits: to the extent that regulatory divergences can be avoided, disruptions to trade in nanotechnology products would be avoided. Second, they highlight the efficiencies that could be created for researchers, manufacturers, and distributors of nanotechnology products in international commerce. These efficiencies could include reduced costs and legal risks for collaboration between scientists and engineers on research and development, as well as facilitation of market access for companies that produce and distribute nanotechnology products. As well, for companies whose production of nanotechnology products takes place across several countries, coordination of environmental and safety and health requirements has the potential to help the global supply chain flow more smoothly. Third, Marchant *et al.* suggest that developing similar or equivalent levels of environmental and health and safety protection for workers and consumers in different countries could help to avoid a regulatory 'race to the bottom' whereby some countries seek to encourage nanotechnology investments (and potentially protect their own industries) by relaxing their regulatory protections. Fourth, they suggest that coordination would also assist in producing economies of scale benefits for regulators and provide opportunities for learning from the experiences of others, rather than leaving it to each individual jurisdiction to independently evaluate the risks of nanotechnology products and decide on appropriate regulatory responses.[12] Finally, they argue that, through agreement on substantive principles, coordination can help to 'steer' national regulators towards superior forms of regulation.

Such benefits are not only applicable in the case of new technologies. Regulatory divergence across all kinds of product standards and regulations can inhibit trade, thus suggesting there are benefits to be had wherever coordination can minimise those divergences, while still allowing countries to pursue regulatory agendas that meet their domestic policy objectives. Global supply chains for all kinds of products will benefit from coordinated regulation in areas such as customs procedures, health and safety regulations, and technical product requirements.[13] Avoidance of a regulatory 'race to the bottom' will have benefits in all areas of the economy where regulation is deemed beneficial. Marchant *et al.*'s final point about steering national regulators towards superior forms of regulation is a particularly important one with wider relevance. Regulatory cooperation is enormously important in enabling countries to respond effectively to myriad regulatory issues and challenges that they face. Many countries suffer from a lack of expertise and resources with regard to their regulatory programmes. Only very few countries have strong expertise across the wide range of complex regulatory issues confronting them.[14] In particular, emerging technologies tend to exacerbate existing problems with regulatory agency staffing, funding, lack of scientific expertise, and coordination. Mandel notes, for example, that in the US, the Environmental Protection Agency (EPA), the Food and Drug Administration (FDA), the United States Department of Agriculture (USDA), and the Office of Safety and Health Administration (OSHA) have all been identified as under-staffed, underfunded, and lacking personnel properly trained to handle pertinent emerging technologies. Similar concerns have been reported with respect to European regulatory agencies.[15] Where there is a lack of expertise and resources, there is a risk that the quality of regulation will suffer. Hence regulatory cooperation has significant benefits to offer in enabling regulators to work together towards better quality regulation.

While there is strong motivation for countries to cooperate across a range of regulatory agendas, there are also obstacles. Shaffer and Pollack discuss a particularly important obstacle, namely, conflicts among states with different interests in how the costs and benefits of cooperation ought to be distributed.[16] They compare regulatory cooperation to the classic Prisoner's Dilemma in international relations. In the latter, two participants have a shared interest in reaching a particular outcome. The key obstacle to achieving that outcome by cooperating is the recognition that the other participant may cheat on their agreement, which would lead to an undesirable outcome for the non-cheating participant. The different outcome scenarios are such that both parties rationally choose to cheat, even though so doing leads to a worse outcome than would be achieved by cooperating.[17] In regulatory cooperation, however, states do not simply choose between cooperating or not cooperating; they also choose specific terms of cooperation.[18] The terms of cooperation states obtain (for example, the standards to be chosen where the states are working towards standardisation of quality levels for a particular product) will in most cases produce winners (who secure cooperation on terms closer to their preferences) and losers (forced to cooperate on terms favourable to others). As to what terms of cooperation are obtained, Krasner suggests that state power plays a key role.[19] State power may be employed to determine who is party to the negotiations in the first instance; to dictate the rules of the game, including the possibility of a single state moving first and imposing a de facto standard on others; and to employ issue-linkages (including through the application of threats and promises in related issue-areas) to induce states to accept their preferred standards.[20]

As noted above, regulatory cooperation exists at different levels. Traditionally, regulatory cooperation between countries tended to be at the level of national governments and consisted of law-like and formal mechanisms.

Marchant uses the term 'old governance' to describe such approaches, namely, those that are state-centric, that concentrate regulatory authority in legislative and regulatory bodies (domestic legislatures and agencies; international organisations and treaty bodies); and that rely on top-down legal mandates (statutes and regulations; treaties).[21] This concept of regulatory cooperation is contrasted with so-called 'new governance' where regulatory authority is decentralised across a range of public, private, and public-private actors and institutions.[22] The concept of 'new governance' is said to have led to the rise of so-called 'transgovernmental' institutions in which national regulators, legislators, prosecutors, and even judges – rather than central states as such – collaborate in the regulatory sphere.[23]

Slaughter refers to 'transgovernmental networks' where the state remains central, but state power is deployed in new ways through flexible, informal networks composed of sub-state actors, working outside centralised state control. Slaughter categorises networks as including government networks within international organisations, those within the framework of an executive agreement, and those that are 'spontaneous'.[24] Transgovernmental networks act as forums for discussion, helping regulators to define common problems and raise awareness of them, share experiences in dealing with those problems, and exchange views on appropriate regulatory responses. This may include collection and dissemination of research or statistical and other technical information to assist regulators in dealing with problems that have been identified. Processes of information exchange can occur in the context of an orientation towards regulatory harmonisation where regulators build 'shared normative expectations' and create consensus around common regulatory standards.[25] Transgovernmental networks can also act as conduits for the provision of technical assistance and capacity-building, and can facilitate cooperation between regulators with respect to the enforcement of national laws.

As Marchant *et al.* note, these mechanisms entail a modified, more nuanced role for government.[26] Further to this, Zaring suggests that the interests and perspectives of the agencies engaged in international regulatory cooperation can usefully be understood separately from the interests of the states of which they are a part.[27] Officials will meet as representatives of their agencies rather than their actual nations.[28] The full implications of this are not clear, but one possible benefit is depoliticisation of issues as the focus of agencies is likely to be primarily on technical subject matter (rather than political relationships), and there is the possibility for technical experts to lead the cooperation agenda based on the interests of their agencies. Reliance on agency-level officials also leads to a certain degree of informality. Indeed, the type of transgovernmental mechanism described by Slaughter, and discussed by Marchant *et al.* and Zaring, is associated with informality.

Regulatory networks may be considered to be informal where they are established in the absence of a constitutive treaty setting out the obligations of the participants, or an organisation with a permanent body that has the task of implementing the obligations set forth in the treaty. Rather, informal networks so described typically do not impose any binding legal obligations on the participants (whether states or state agencies) and there are no enforcement mechanisms.[29] Another sense in which some networks are said to be informal is where they are described as being not particularly ambitious projects (for example, aiming at sharing experiences and information rather than at harmonisation or norm creation).[30]

Informal networks also tend to use soft law as opposed to hard law. The term 'hard law' is used in international law to include a regime that relies on the authority and power of the state, including in particular for enforcement.[31] Abbott and Snidal describe it as referring to 'legally binding obligations that are precise (or can be made precise through adjudication or the issuance of detailed regulations) and that delegate authority for interpreting and implementing the law'.[32] In comparison, the term 'soft law' is used to refer to law that is not 'hard'. Abbott and Snidal describe soft law as beginning where legal arrangements are weakened along 'one or more of the dimensions of obligation, precision and delegation'.[33] According to this definition, an agreement or obligation will be soft if, for example, it is precisely worded yet not formally binding, but likewise if it is formally binding, but with content so vague that there is almost complete discretion in its implementation. There is significant debate in international law about the benefits or otherwise of soft law; however, Zaring suggests that where regulatory cooperation enjoys widespread adherence then it does not matter whether it is binding or not, so long as it is followed.[34]

So-called new governance approaches to regulatory cooperation have a number of perceived benefits. An oft-cited advantage of these kinds of informal networks is that they are nimble and flexible, with the capacity to respond quickly to needs or problems as they arise, as opposed to the much slower traditional treaty process.[35] Marchant *et al.* suggest that informal arrangements can more easily be proactive and anticipatory. They also stimulate experimentation with different policy options which has the potential to lead to improved regulation.[36] Marchant *et al.* find another advantage in the capacity of these approaches to encourage the participation of a wide range of stakeholders in the design and implementation of regulation. They find that this allows regulators to draw on the expertise and other capacities of private actors, reduces fiscal demands on the state, and helps build political support and buy-in.[37] Participation in informal networks may lead to effective informal enforcement for norms that are developed within the network. Even where networks are labelled 'informal', there often tends to be some form of enforcement, whether based on interpersonal bonds, individual socialisation, or preferences for reciprocity.[38]

Despite the advantages of informal transgovernmental networks, there are also criticisms of these 'new governance' approaches to regulatory coordination. The overarching criticism is that the networks lack accountability.[39] The term accountability refers to the concept of responsiveness of the government to the public, something which can be assured through a variety of mechanisms, both substantive (such as principles and limits defining the mandate of regulators) and procedural (requiring a particular mode of decision making and giving the public an opportunity to respond to or reject decisions made).[40] Philip Alston has suggested that the growth of informal networks implies the marginalisation of governments and their replacement by special interest groups. He argues that it

> suggests a definitive move away from arenas of relative transparency into the back rooms … and the bypassing of the national political arenas to which the United States and other proponents of the importance of healthy democratic institutions attach so much importance.[41]

Slaughter suggests that the accountability critique contains three broad claims. First, that these networks are invisible and there is a lack of access for groups affected by decisions and policies resulting from their deliberations and activities. Slaughter finds this to be a process objection, because it denies those affected by decisions the opportunity to participate in the process. She references a term coined by Perez, 'technocratic elitism', which refers to government by bureaucrats without popular input. The concern is that this way of operating threatens to replace democracy with technocracy.[42] In this regard, Svetiev suggests that even where repeated interactions between officials is not enough for strong, self-enforcement of shared norms, various officials may still come to share certain beliefs, values, and underlying assumptions or even ways of approaching problems to make them more manageable for analysis. He suggests that these can influence the decisions and policy outcomes or even the substantive law. He considers this to be problematic because there is little or no domestic accountability.[43]

The second strand of the accountability critique, as noted by Slaughter, is the charge that bad decisions are being made, being those that are likely to be narrowly focused, less deliberative, less responsive to the full range of affected constituencies, and less creative.[44] Also, Lang and Scott have suggested that the quality of regulation may suffer where it appeals to the 'false universalities of particular forms of rational knowledge'.[45]

The third strand of the accountability critique as noted by Slaughter is that governmental networks lack legitimacy. Slaughter suggests that this critique arises out of the very process established by informal networks – they 'cannot be captured or controlled in the ways that typically structure formal legitimacy in a democratic polity'.[46] The legitimacy critique can arguably be overcome, however. Marchant *et al.* suggest that public agencies should 'initiate private and collaborative regulatory schemes when they can improve outcomes, "orchestrate" and support the resulting regulatory network, and stand ready to intervene with mandatory regulation where necessary'.[47]

In the final section, I consider how regulatory cooperation provisions in FTAs fit into the model of governance described above. I suggest that these provisions lay the groundwork for the establishment of regulatory networks and that as they develop they have the potential to become another layer of transgovernmental networks. I also return to the critiques highlighted here, along with the benefits of informal networks. In the next section, I turn to consider FTAs and consider

why provisions, requiring the trading partners to engage in regulatory cooperation, are becoming a standard feature of so many agreements.

FTAs and regulatory cooperation

As noted in the introduction, the negotiation of bilateral and regional FTAs has
exploded over the last decade, particularly so as the Doha Round of multilateral
negotiations has foundered and governments have sought opportunities for
deeper trade liberalisation with like-minded trading partners. When the General
Agreement on Trade and Tariffs (GATT) was negotiated in the 1940s, trade liberalisation focused on the reduction of quantitative barriers to trade that goods
faced at the border in the form of tariffs and import quotas. From the 1990s, the
emphasis on so-called 'behind-the-border' barriers increased, such barriers
involving domestic regulations that impede the ability of goods and services to
enter and compete in foreign markets. This emphasis is particularly seen in bilateral and regional FTAs where countries look to deepen trade liberalisation and
economic integration. FTAs often include so-called 'WTO-plus' obligations in
areas that are the subject of WTO rules (such as sanitary and phytosanitary
measures and technical barriers to trade). Countries will agree to affirm their
WTO obligations in these areas, and also agree to additional obligations such as
stricter transparency requirements and regulatory cooperation provisions. They
often also seek to work together to develop rules that implicate areas of domestic
regulatory policy that, while they may have been the subject of international regulatory cooperation, have been too difficult to successfully address through the
multilateral trade agenda due to their centrality to government regulatory decision making, such as increased protection for intellectual property.

In addition to deeper liberalisation and WTO-plus commitments, countries
are also increasingly contemplating regulatory cooperation in their FTAs. To this
end, many FTAs provide an institutional framework for a wide variety of cooperative regulatory activities between the governments and agencies of partner
countries. They do so by including provisions that either require or encourage
the trading partners to work together on various regulatory matters. In most
cases, provisions regarding cooperation will envisage that activities be undertaken at the departmental or agency level rather than at the central political level.

To some extent, the rationale for promoting regulatory cooperation through
FTAs coincides with the rationales proposed in the previous section for regulatory cooperation as a general proposition. The predominant rationale for inclusion of provisions relating to regulatory cooperation appears to be to facilitate
trade, a benefit noted by Marchant *et al.* in the nanotechnology context. Regulatory cooperation enables countries to take actions to prevent problems from
arising in the trading relationship, to address problems that do arise, and, more
generally, to enhance the trading relationship. The importance attached to regulatory cooperation as a tool for trade facilitation is reflected in various FTAs that
give regulatory cooperation prominence as one of the overall objectives of the
agreement. A typical formulation is that found in the *US–Chile FTA*,[48] which

includes among its objectives to 'establish a framework for further bilateral, regional, and multilateral cooperation to expand and enhance the benefits of this Agreement'.[49] This kind of objectives provision makes it clear that cooperation is seen as something that can help the Parties to attain the benefits of trade liberalisation.

A similar approach is taken in the *EC – Chile EPA/FTA*[50] where the Parties 're-affirm the importance of economic, financial and technical cooperation, as a means of contributing towards implementing the objectives and principles derived from' the Agreement.[51] In the field of technical regulations, the Agreement recognises that 'cooperation on standards, technical regulations and conformity assessment is a key objective in order to avoid and reduce technical barriers to trade and to ensure the satisfactory functioning of trade liberalisation.'[52]

A second rationale for regulatory cooperation provisions is to enhance and promote cooperation between countries with a view to obtaining the benefits available from greater international coordination across a range of regulatory issues, as discussed in the previous section. FTAs can be used to push a regulatory cooperation agenda that might otherwise not gain momentum. Domestic agencies may treat FTAs as an opportunity to promote their own areas of interest. For example, an agency interested in promoting a particular environmental agenda might conclude that it is helpful to include obligations regarding environmental regulatory cooperation in an FTA. This might assist them in obtaining greater funding resources from their central government as money is allocated for implementation of the FTA. This rationale for regulatory cooperation provisions is particularly important due to the regulatory challenges faced by governments both individually and collectively, as discussed above. The value in regulatory cooperation to address some of these issues supports Nottage's suggestion that we are likely to witness more and more add-ons to obligations traditionally found within FTAs.[53]

A third rationale for the inclusion of regulatory cooperation provisions in FTAs is to promote development. International trade is widely considered as an important input into a country's economic and human development.[54] FTAs that involve a developing country partner often include provisions that provide for regulatory cooperation designed to further development. In some cases, the cooperation might be aimed at technical assistance and capacity-building-type activities to bolster a country's ability to meet its trade-related obligations (for example, capacity-building that will help a country to design and implement legislation for the protection and enforcement of intellectual property rights) and to increase its trade flows. In other cases, cooperation provisions might be aimed at promoting development in a more generic sense less directly related to trade.

A possible fourth rationale for including regulatory cooperation provisions in FTAs might be to avoid any risk of a perceived regulatory 'race to the bottom' whereby countries lower their regulatory standards in order to ensure the competitiveness of their industries. The 'race to the bottom' argument is that countries will reduce their regulatory standards, such as environmental or labour protections, in order to protect the competitiveness of their industries.[55] Again, the benefits of regulatory cooperation in avoiding a regulatory race to the bottom were noted by Marchant *et al.* in the nanotechnology area, but such perceived benefits also extend to other areas where regulation pushes up the cost of production. The 'race to the bottom' objective dovetails with concerns of groups who are demandeurs of including strong environmental and social components in FTAs.[56] A related objective of regulatory cooperation might be to help address the (perceived or real) negative externalities of trade; for example, it has been suggested that international trade liberalisation has negative consequences for the environment. The simple act of shipping or flying goods around the globe can contribute to increased carbon emissions, for example.[57] However, potential negative externalities such as this may be able to be addressed in part through regulatory cooperation to ensure that desired environmental standards are maintained.

Regulatory cooperation provisions

Regulatory cooperation (whether initiated informally or through a treaty – FTAs or otherwise) involves a 'toolbox' of practices that can be used depending on the situation. Some of the more common practices incorporated in FTAs include:

- *Information sharing*: this involves countries sharing information and institutional experience through means such as seminars and joint visits.
- *Work sharing*: this covers joint activities between agencies such as data sharing or research collaboration.
- *Mutual recognition agreements*: these involve trading partners agreeing to recognise each other's standards as equivalent to each other.
- *Harmonisation*: this involves a situation where countries establish common rules or standards such as food safety standards.

The first two practices noted (information and work sharing) have 'soft' law characteristics, while the third and fourth (mutual recognition agreements and harmonisation) are harder obligations. In general, many FTAs have hard law characteristics in that their commitments are legally binding and backed up by dispute settlement systems. However, when it comes to making provision for regulatory cooperation, they may use a combination of hard and soft law. Provisions concerning regulatory cooperation may be mandatory, requiring that 'the Parties take a certain action or refrain from acting in a certain manner (e.g. 'the Parties shall cooperate...'). Such obligations may be subject to dispute settlement systems that follow the example of the World Trade Organization (WTO) where independent third party panels are established to hear complaints and issue findings as to whether or not one party has breached relevant commitments. The WTO model enables panels to authorise the winning party to suspend concessions if the responding party fails to bring their measures into compliance. However, FTAs also incorporate soft law through obligations that simply require

Parties to use their 'best endeavours' to ensure that certain actions are taken (e.g. 'the Parties shall endeavour to ensure that policies and practices are…' or 'the Parties shall consider cooperating with respect to…'). While such obligations may be subject to dispute settlement provisions in FTAs, it will be difficult to prove that a country has failed to use its 'best endeavours' as the term 'best' is a vague one without a clear benchmark for what kind of steps a country must take. In some cases, these kind of obligations will not be subject to dispute settlement at all and, therefore, will be legally unenforceable.

In this section, I discuss a range of provisions in different FTAs that provide for regulatory cooperation. These provisions are provided by way of illustrative example and have been selected in order to demonstrate the range of both the topic areas that are the subject of regulatory cooperation, as well as the various tools of cooperation contemplated.

Health and safety

Health and safety is an important area for regulatory cooperation in FTAs. This stems in large part from the fact that differences in health and safety regulations can be hugely disruptive to trade. Differences in perceptions of and approaches to risk mean that countries can end up with differing health and safety regulations that hinder trade, even where protection of domestic industry is not intended. The case of trade in biotechnology products is illustrative. It has been reported, for example, that after the EU amended its regulations in 2004 to impose labelling and traceability requirements for genetically modified food and feed, the American Soybean Association experienced a significant drop in exports of 70 per cent between 1998 and 2012.[58] Considering these kinds of situations, it is not surprising that trade facilitation is a primary driver for many regulatory cooperation provisions within FTAs.

Measures providing for regulatory cooperation concerning health and safety are typically found in either the sanitary and phytosanitary (SPS) or technical barriers to trade (TBT) chapters of FTAs. The obligations in SPS chapters usually build on those in the WTO's Agreement on the Application of Sanitary and Phytosanitary Measures (SPS Agreement) which deals with risks arising from additives, contaminants, toxins, and disease-causing organisms, and explicitly recognises the right of countries to enact trade-restrictive measures to protect against these threats. The obligations in TBT chapters similarly build upon those in the WTO's Agreement on Technical Barriers to Trade (TBT Agreement) which recognises the right of countries to protect health, while also disciplining countries' implementation of technical regulations and voluntary standards.

In the *Canada–Costa Rica FTA*,[59] a provision in the SPS chapter states that the Parties recognise the 'benefits from a bilateral program of technical and institutional cooperation', and to this end establishes a Committee to 'provide a regular forum for consultations and cooperation to, *inter alia*, enhance effectiveness of the Parties' regulations with a view to improving food safety and SPS conditions'.[60] This Committee is authorised to consider the design, implementation, and review of technical and institutional cooperation programs; the development of operational guidelines to facilitate implementation of, *inter alia*, mutual recognition and equivalence agreements, and product control, inspection and approval procedures; the promotion of enhanced transparency of SPS measures; the identification and resolution of SPS-related problems; the recognition of pest- or disease-free areas; and the promotion of bilateral consultation on SPS issues under discussion in multilateral and international fora.[61] These various activities all have the potential to facilitate trade.

Mutual recognition and equivalence allow importation of products to take place despite different regulations among countries. They enable trading partners to accept importation of products in cases where the other country's SPS measures are equivalent to one's own or are sufficient to achieve the importing country's desired outcomes in terms of health protection. Transparency measures also facilitate trade by making it easier for an exporting business to ascertain exactly with what measures they are required to comply. Identification and resolution of SPS-related problems may be seen as a proactive form of dispute settlement. If countries are able to talk about problems before they result in the imposition of a trade barrier, it is less likely that an actual trade dispute will arise. Recognising pest-free areas also facilitates trade because even if a pest is present in one region of a country, recognition that other areas are pest-free will allow trade to continue from those areas and, thus, trade disruption can be minimised. Finally, promotion of bilateral consultation on SPS issues, under discussion in multilateral and international fora, allows like-minded trading partners to develop common positions and promote those more broadly. This can enhance the opportunity for cooperation and trade facilitation outside the immediate partnership.

The *Chile–Mexico FTA*[62] provides that

> through mutual cooperation, the Parties shall facilitate trade in agricultural, fish and forest products that present no sanitary or phytosanitary risks and undertake to prevent the introduction or spread of pests or diseases and to improve plant and animal health and food safety.[63]

Provision is made for establishment of a Committee on Sanitary and Phytosanitary Measures, whose mandated functions include 'promoting cooperation and exchanges of technical staff, including cooperation in the development, application and observation of sanitary or phytosanitary measures'.[64] Subcommittees are also established to deal with, among other things, animal health, plant health, food safety, fisheries, and agricultural chemicals.[65] These subcommittees have the authority to prepare terms of reference for activities in their respective spheres of competence and to report the results to the Committee, and to establish specific agreements on matters of interest involving greater technical and operational detail, for presentation to the Committee.[66] The function of the Committee, which promotes cooperation and exchanges of technical staff, is potentially valuable because these kinds of activities can lead to shared understandings and common positions on issues that might otherwise impede trade. They also allow the learning and experience of one country that has faced a particular problem to be shared with its trading partner, before the same or similar problem arises there, thus increasing the possibility of that partner taking a similar regulatory approach to the first country.

In the *US–Chile FTA*, the Committee on Sanitary and Phytosanitary Matters provides a forum for, *inter alia*, consulting on issues, positions, and agendas for meetings of the WTO SPS Committee, as well as the various *Codex* committees and other international fora on food safety and human, animal, and plant health.[67] This kind of cooperation can be valuable in promoting common positions in those wider fora, and increase the potential for agreement there. Even if this goal is not achievable, the development of shared positions, or at least discussion of positions, can be valuable in promoting understanding between the bilateral partners.

A different (and much broader) type of cooperation in the health and safety sphere is envisaged in the *East African Community Free Trade Agreement*.[68] At a broad level, the Parties undertake to 'co-operate in health, cultural and sports and social welfare activities within the Community'. The list of specific matters on which the Parties agree to undertake cooperative activities is extremely wide ranging and includes:[69]

- taking joint action towards the prevention and control of communicable and non-communicable diseases;
- promoting the management of health delivery systems and better planning mechanisms to enhance efficiency of health care services;
- harmonising national health policies and regulations and promoting the exchange of information on health issues in order to achieve quality health;
- cooperating in promoting research and the development of traditional, alternate or herbal medicines;
- cooperating in the development of specialised health training, health research, reproductive health, the pharmaceutical products, and preventive medicine; and
- promoting the development of good nutritional standards and the popularisation of indigenous foods.

These matters are related more closely to development in a broader sense than to the immediate trade-related aspects of development. For example, cooperating in the development of specialised health training, health research, and reproductive health is a matter of public health that is essentially unrelated to trade. While improved health standards are likely to aid in boosting economic development and the capacity to trade, this is nevertheless a matter of human development that does not have a close and immediate impact on trade flows in the traditional sense of trade liberalisation. However, the *East African Community Free Trade Agreement* includes broader objectives than some other FTAs, and refers specifically to raising the standard of living of African peoples. This recognises that while trade may be a contributor to development, it is not sufficient in and of itself. Rather, there are many other critical aspects of development that must be addressed. Further, the Parties to this Agreement have a common interest in these development objectives. Such commonality is not present in the US FTAs discussed above.

Technical barriers to trade

Regulatory cooperation in matters of technical barriers to trade tends to be largely focused on trade facilitation. As with health and safety measures, differing technical regulations can be extremely disruptive to trade and as such there are significant trade liberalisation gains to be made by reducing those differences. Cooperation between countries' agencies is one of the most effective ways of doing so. The *New Zealand–China FTA*[70] includes in its TBT chapter the objective of promoting regulatory cooperation to manage risks to health, safety, and the environment.[71] It explicitly recognises the 'important relationship between good regulatory practices and trade facilitation', and further to this, states that the Parties agree to 'seek to cooperate in the areas of standards, technical regulations, and conformity assessment'.[72] This obligation is to be implemented by establishing work programmes on information exchange and cooperation.[73] The Agreement also requires work programmes to exchange information on matters including regulatory systems, incidental analysis, hazard alerts, product bans and recalls, and domestic practices and programmes for product surveillance activities.[74] It also requires the Parties to cooperate on good regulatory practice, and the development and implementation of risk management principles including product monitoring, safety, compliance, and enforcement practices.[75] Programmes under the Trans-Tasman Mutual Recognition Arrangement are also good examples of successful regulatory cooperation in the area of technical barriers to trade. Relevant programmes include those described briefly above – the Trans-Tasman Equipment Energy Efficiency Programme, the Gas Technical Regulators Committee, and the Electrical Regulatory Authorities Council cooperation programmes.

Labour and environment

Regulatory cooperation provisions are commonly found in the labour and environment areas, although they do not generally have as strong a trade facilitative function as those in the health and safety and technical areas. Rather, it would seem that such provisions seek to obtain the benefits that cooperation can bring in the environmental area. In addition, the fourth rationale discussed in the previous section plays an important role, namely, the desire to ensure the competitiveness of domestic industries and to address the potential negative externalities of trade. As noted, civil society also has a strong interest in provisions that promote labour and environmental interests.

One FTA employing mandatory provisions for regulatory cooperation on environmental matters is the *Japan–Mexico FTA*.[76] Article 147 says that the

'Parties shall cooperate in the field of the environment'. The choice of which cooperative activity, however, is discretionary. Article 147 provides that cooperative activities may include: exchange of information on policies, laws, and other measures related to the preservation and improvement of the environment; promotion of capacity and institutional building to foster activities related to the Clean Development Mechanism under the Kyoto Protocol; encouragement of trade and dissemination of environmentally sound goods and services; encouraging the exchange of information for identification of investment opportunities; and promotion and development of business alliances in the environmental field. It provides that implementing arrangements may be made between the governments of the two countries to set out the details and procedures of cooperative activities.

There are a number of possible reasons for these provisions. The identification of investment opportunities and promotion and development of business alliances are likely to contribute to trade the goal of trade facilitation (albeit in a rather narrow sense as the focus is on trade and investment in the environmental area, such as in the area of environmental services). Encouraging trade and dissemination of environmentally sound goods is trade facilitative but would also ensure the maintenance of high regulatory standards as the more trade in these types of goods, the higher environmental standards that would ensue as a consequence. The possibility of working together to foster activities related to the Clean Development Mechanism has a development-related goal. The Mechanism allows developed countries to earn and trade emissions credits through projects implemented in developing countries, which they can use towards meeting their commitments under the Kyoto Protocol. The provision for exchange of information on preservation and improvement of the environment may be related to the development goal, as well as a desire to avoid a regulatory race to the bottom.[77] It also has potential to advance the environmental regulatory agendas of the Parties more generally.

The introduction of the concept of Implementing Arrangements allows agencies of the Parties to work together to enter into more detailed arrangements than would be practical or desirable under the main body of the FTA itself. This kind of provision is a soft law instrument that does not commit the Parties to binding obligations. It is, therefore, a potentially powerful tool in the sense that agencies are given flexibility to make detailed arrangements to pursue the desired ends.

In the *US–Chile FTA*, the Parties agree to undertake cooperative environmental activities, including through specific cooperative projects that are identified and set out in the Annex to the Agreement, and by negotiating a *US–Chile Environmental Cooperation Agreement* to establish priorities for further cooperative environmental activities.[78] The specific cooperative projects include reducing mining pollution in Chile, reducing methyl bromide emissions, improving agricultural practices in Chile, building capacity to protect wildlife in Chile and the Latin American region and working together to improve the environmental quality of fuels. The FTA states that the Cooperation Agreement would include all kinds of cooperative work, from exchanging professionals, technicians, specialists, organising joint conferences, seminars, having collaborative projects and demonstrations, facilitating linkages among representatives from academia, industry, government, and other activities. A number of the projects noted here are quite specific to Chile, which is identified as the Party required to improve its environmental practices. This may perhaps reflect the second rationale for regulatory cooperation – a desire of one trading partner (in this case the US) to ensure that its industries maintain a competitive advantage, or at least, do not face a disadvantage vis-à-vis other partners due to differing environmental regulations, as well as demands from domestic stakeholders. Finally, a development rationale may also play a role, with the number of projects being undertaken with respect to the Chilean environment suggestive of the view that there is room for development with respect to environmental issues in Chile.

Another model of an FTA with regulatory cooperation provisions in the environmental area is the *New Zealand–China FTA* which contains an Environmental Cooperation Agreement between the Ministries of the Environment of the Parties which agree to undertake cooperative activities including environmental management, environmental remediation, nature conservation, and technologies for environmental benefit. It provides for a variety of forms of cooperation, including exchange of experience and information, exchange of visits, joint seminars and workshops, and anything else upon which the Parties agree.

On the labour side, the *US–Chile FTA* recognises that 'bilateral cooperation on labor matters will provide enhanced opportunities for the Parties to improve labor standards, and to further advance their common commitments, including the ILO Declaration on Fundamental Principles and Rights at Work and its Follow-up (1998)'.[79] In order to advance such cooperation, the Agreement establishes a Labour Cooperation Mechanism, the work of which is carried out by the Parties' respective labour ministries. The Labour Cooperation Mechanism is authorised to 'undertake cooperative activities on any labour matter it considers appropriate', including on fundamental rights and their effective application; labour relations; working conditions; issues related to small and medium enterprises; social protections; and technical issues and information exchange. Activities may be carried out by the Parties through 'any form they deem appropriate'.

Social matters

Some FTAs – particularly those signed by the European Union – make provision for a much broader range of cooperation in social areas beyond environment and labour. In the *EC–Egypt FTA*,[80] for example, the Parties are required to conduct regular dialogue on social matters, including

> all issues related to (a) migrant communities' living and working conditions; (b) migration; (c) illegal migration; and (d) actions to encourage equal treatment between Egyptian and Community nationals, mutual knowledge of cultures and civilisations, the furthering of tolerance and the removal of discrimination.

The Agreement also provides that with a view to consolidating cooperation between the Parties in the social field, projects and programmes shall be carried out in any area of interest to them, with priority given to reducing migratory pressures, promoting the role of women in economic and social development, and bolstering and developing Egyptian family planning and mother and child protection programmes; improving the social protection system; improving the health care system; improving living conditions in poor areas; and implementing and financing exchange and leisure programmes for mixed groups of Egyptian and European young people residing in the Member States. Another area of social cooperation is with respect to the fight against drugs (e.g. encouraging a joint approach to reducing demand). These types of provisions present a very different scenario from the type of trade facilitative provisions discussed above, or those that seek to address the perceived negative effects of trade (such as diminished competitiveness) and reflect the EU's approach to FTAs – that international trade and investment should be used as a tool to achieve global sustainable development, and that the EU should be working with its trading partners to improve environmental and social standards.[81]

Economic and commercial matters

Regulatory cooperation provisions appear to be most common in the areas discussed above, that is, health and safety related areas, and social areas such as environment and labour. However, they also appear in more explicitly commercial contexts. For example, the *New Zealand–China FTA* has a chapter dedicated to 'cooperation' which includes an Article focused on economic cooperation. It lists the aims of economic cooperation under the chapter as being to build on existing agreements or arrangements already in place for trade and economic cooperation and to advance and strengthen trade and economic relations between the Parties. In relation to small and medium enterprises, it provides for cooperation to build on existing agreements or arrangements, to promote a favourable trading environment for the development of such enterprises, and to build their capacity to trade effectively under the Agreement. These types of provisions appear to be strongly grounded in the rationale that regulatory cooperation is supportive of trade facilitation.

The *EC–Chile FTA* requires the Parties to 'establish close cooperation' aimed at 'stimulating productive synergies, creating new opportunities for trade and investment and promoting competitiveness and innovation'.[82] It also provides for quite specific forms of economic cooperation, including to 'promote and consolidate the Parties' efforts towards a sustainable agriculture and agricultural and rural development', with cooperation to focus on capacity-building, infrastructure, and technology transfer. While this includes cooperation directed at sanitary, phytosanitary, environmental, and food quality matters, it also includes diversification and restructuring of agricultural sectors, and measures aimed at supporting trade promotion activities.

Matters of good governance and the rule of law

Finally, it is worth noting that some FTAs (primarily those entered into by the EU) include provision for cooperation with respect to matters of governance and democracy. The *EC–Chile FTA* provides that

> the Parties shall establish close cooperation aimed at: strengthening the institutional capacity to underpin democracy, the rule of law, and respect for human rights and fundamental freedoms; and promoting social development, which should go hand in hand with economic development and the protection of the environment.[83]

It also provides for cooperation in the area of public administration which shall aim at 'the modernisation and decentralisation of public administration and encompass overall organisational efficiency and the legislative and institutional framework'. This cooperation involves programmes such as modernisation of the State and of public administration, strengthening of civil society and its incorporation into the process of defining public policies.[84] These types of provisions are essentially based on political rationales; an attempt to induce countries to conform to the values of democracy, good governance, and human rights.[85]

Fitting FTAs into a global governance framework

In the previous section, I identified examples of regulatory cooperation provisions in a number of FTAs. These examples are not exhaustive. The US Chamber of Commerce has noted that products and services that cross borders continue to face a growing array of regulations in multiple countries that can range from opaque to duplicative to conflicting. It found that this growth of disparate regulatory regimes creates uncertainty, high costs, and inefficiencies. It has therefore argued that the Trans-Pacific Partnership (TPP) Agreement should 'go further and farther than previous trade negotiations to ensure that regulatory coherence is a strategic and political imperative within the TPP agreement and wherever possible binding commitments are sought and made'.[86]

Where do the regulatory cooperation aspects of FTAs that we see to date fit into the international governance framework that was discussed in the first section? On the whole, the provisions discussed can be seen as creating informal networks within a formal framework. FTAs are formal government-to-government treaties that in many cases contain legally binding enforcement mechanisms. However, within those treaties, informal networks are being created where regulators and technical experts have the authority to come together to establish regulatory cooperation agendas on a flexible and as-needed basis. Rather than attempting to detail exactly what kind of cooperation agencies ought to engage in, these FTAs devolve responsibility to the agencies themselves – often through the means of a subject area Committee (such as an SPS Committee or a TBT Committee) that is charged with developing a work programme and overseeing cooperative activities. The extent to which 'networks' are created will depend on the extent of the cooperative activities undertaken. Where regulatory networks do result, they are composed of sub-state actors and it is likely that they will have many of the characteristics described by Slaughter in her characterisation of transgovernmental networks. However, unlike in Slaughter's model, networks established through FTAs are not fully informal in the sense that they are established under the direction of a constitutive treaty. Examples of networks successfully developed under the umbrella of a treaty include those under the Trans-Tasman Mutual Recognition Agreement (TTMRA). The TTMRA provides for regulatory cooperation, stating that for certain specified goods, 'programmes for trans-Tasman cooperation will be undertaken'.[87] Under this arrangement, a wide discretion is given to regulatory agencies to develop such programmes. Effective programmes of regulatory cooperation include the Gas Regulators Technical Committee and Electrical Regulatory Authorities council which are responsible for liaising between technical and electrical safety regulatory authorities in New Zealand and Australia, and the Trans-Tasman Equipment Energy Efficiency Programme which is responsible for the development and implementation of regulation on the Trans-Tasman Minimum Energy Performance Standards and Mandatory Energy Performance Labels for energy-using products.[88]

Despite the legally binding nature of the FTAs, in many instances, the obligations concerning the development of regulatory cooperation activities (and thereby, networks) are 'soft' obligations – they require governments to use best endeavours rather than obliging them to undertake certain activities. In other words, while the overarching FTA is a formal legally binding treaty ('hard' law), the regulatory cooperation aspects have 'soft' law characteristics. Further to the non-binding nature of the obligations, in many cases they are also very flexible in that governments have significant discretion in how to implement them. Often, it is agencies that will exercise this discretion rather than central government, and officials will meet as representatives of their respective agencies rather than of their nations. As noted, there is much debate about the benefits of soft law versus hard law, but in the context of regulatory cooperation, surely the test is whether that cooperation is effective and achieves the objectives for which the regime was designed. The effectiveness of the regulatory cooperation agenda in FTAs is a question that both requires and deserves investigation. Clearly, the regulatory cooperation provisions in FTAs are designed to take advantage of the perceived benefits of informal networks – such as flexibility and the capacity to respond quickly to new and emerging issues that the negotiators of the FTA could neither foresee nor negotiate in sufficient detail.

An important advantage associated with informal networks is their flexibility and capacity to respond quickly to needs and issues as they arise. The discretion in the provisions means that officials are enabled to take certain actions under the auspices of the FTA, but without having to amend the FTA itself. This can be far more effective than requiring an amendment of the agreement. It is much easier for officials in the agriculture departments of two countries to come together and make a quick decision – for example, to undertake a collaborative project in the light of an emerging risk to health, or to determine new criteria for recognition of pest-free areas in the light of new scientific information about certain pests – than it would be for such decisions to have to be made at the central level of government and for the agreement to have to be amended to address these situations.

It was noted in the first section that informal arrangements for regulatory cooperation are more likely to stimulate experimentation with policy making, which has the potential to lead to improved regulation. The framework provided in FTAs in many cases would appear to provide the possibility for such experimentation, as well as proactive and anticipatory actions. For example, the provision in the *New Zealand – China FTA* that requires the Parties to establish work programmes to, *inter alia*, cooperate on good regulatory practice and the development and implementation of risk management principles would appear to provide plenty of scope for officials from the two countries to be innovative and develop concepts to drive improved regulation.

The key disadvantage identified with respect to informal regulatory networks was a possible lack of accountability to the public, with a concern being cited that too much power in the hands of 'technocrats' can marginalise governments and the political accountability to which governments are held.[89] Any charge of a lack of accountability needs to be assessed on a case-by-case basis to determine whether interested groups have access to the networks in question, whether the networks make good decisions, and the degree of legitimacy of the network. However, one aspect of regulatory networks that arises out of FTAs is that they continue to operate under the auspices of the FTA framework. Thus, they have certain objectives which guide their actions – even where they have considerable discretion as to the work programmes. Second, in most FTAs, there is some form of institutional mechanism whereby networks that are set up under individual chapters are required to report back to an overarching Commission made up of senior officials or ministers of the trading partners concerned. In the *New Zealand – China FTA*, the Joint TBT Committee (set up under the TBT chapter) is required to 'monitor the progress of work programmes'.[90] The Joint TBT Committee is itself made up of senior officials of the competent authorities of the Parties. However, the Joint TBT Committee has obligations to report to the Joint Commission on the implementation of the chapter. This is a way in which accountability of networks can be introduced through an FTA.

Some commentators have also raised a concern that in any given relationship of regulatory cooperation, the more powerful state will have the ability to shape the direction that cooperation takes and the decisions that are made. Kelsey, for example, argues that regulatory dialogue provides an opportunity for countries to pressure their partners on regulatory matters.[91] Zaring suggests, however, that in technical areas it is often difficult to identify national interests in unique approaches to regulation.[92] Certainly, whether regulatory cooperation under the auspices of FTAs which leads to concrete outcomes, in terms of matters such as adopted standards, is a positive development will be largely dependent on both the subject matter of the cooperation and the partners involved. It is not the case that all regulatory issues are amenable to uncontroversial technical solutions. Sometimes there are reasons why different approaches are appropriate for different countries. For example, standards relating to consumer health and safety are more likely to be approached differently across countries than very technical issues such as electrical standards. However, regulatory cooperation does not necessarily mean that the same standards are adopted across different countries. Mutual recognition agreements are an example of arrangements that involve cooperation even while countries maintain divergent regulations or standards. Further, regulatory cooperation does not necessarily have to result in a country adopting new regulations. For example, cooperative activities may be undertaken to help countries in their implementation efforts in respect of national regulations already enacted. Any regulatory decision-making process is open to influences from interested groups and trading partners. However, regulatory cooperation offers significant potential benefits, including for smaller and/or developing countries as they are likely to have greater need to leverage regulatory resources than other more highly resourced countries, and focus their own limited resources on regulatory issues that can support a comparative advantage or where potential risks to its citizens are greatest.

Conclusion

This chapter has described the role of regulatory cooperation provisions in FTAs and has suggested that they can be seen as creating informal networks within a formal framework. The previous section considered how regulatory networks established under the cooperation provisions of FTAs fit into the broader scheme of global regulatory governance. This discussion has raised a number of questions for further investigation and consideration. In particular, it will be useful to investigate the effectiveness of the cooperative activities undertaken by regulators pursuant to FTAs. There are many questions to ask. Are they achieving the goals that were envisaged by the negotiators? Are they adding to or complementing regulatory cooperation activities that were already being undertaken? Does cooperation under a bilateral or regional FTA undermine or complement pre-existing international networks? Answering these and other questions will be helpful not only to future trade negotiators but also to regulators designing international regulatory activities. For any party negotiating an FTA, it will always be important to consider what the net benefits are likely to be from regulatory cooperation. There is clearly significant potential in regulatory cooperation for overcoming regulatory divisions between countries, and for improving the efficiency and efficacy of countries' regulatory regimes. When regulatory cooperation is provided for in FTAs, there is the added benefit of facilitating trade liberalisation, promoting development, and in relevant areas, addressing possible negative externalities of trade. However, there will almost certainly be lessons to be learned from FTAs that have already been in operation for some time.

Notes

1 Tracey Epps is Senior Trade Law Advisor, New Zealand Ministry of Foreign Affairs and Trade, and part-time Senior Lecturer on the Faculty of Law, University of Otago.
2 Sunstein (26 May 2011).
3 OECD 1994.
4 See King 2007.
5 For example, the Basel Committee was formed in 1974 by the governors of the central banks of the G-10 countries and Switzerland to serve as an informal cooperation forum on issues of bank regulation and supervision; or IOSCO (the International Organization of Securities Commissions) which has members from over 100 countries and assists its members to promote high standards of regulation and act as a forum for national regulators to cooperate with each other and international organisations.
6 Biotechnology involves the purposeful transfer of one or several genes from one species to another in order to provide enhanced traits. National Research Council, 2002, cited in Mandel 2009.
7 Nanotechnology involves a variety of activities designed to manipulate matter at the atomic scale. Ratner and Ratner 2003, cited in Mandel 2009.
8 Synthetic biology involves the use of engineering techniques in biology to allow the purposeful design of new organisms 'piece by piece'. Balmer and Martin 2008, cited in Mandel 2009.
9 The most vivid example of this situation occurring is the WTO dispute between the US, Canada, and Argentina on one side, and the EC on the other. Different regulatory approaches with respect to genetically modified food products led to a standstill in trade with the issues being referred to a dispute panel under the World Trade Organization's dispute settlement system. Panel Report, *European Communities – Measures Affecting the Approval and Marketing of Biotech Products*, WT/DS291/R, WT/DS292/R, WT/DS293/R, Add.1 to Add.9, and Corr.1, adopted 21 November 2006.
10 Mandel 2009. See also Moore 2011.
11 Marchant *et al.* 2010.
12 Marchant *et al.* 2010.
13 See for example Bollyky 2012.
14 Shaffer and Pollack suggest that the US and EU are able to exercise a considerable degree of influence over regulation internationally due to the unparalleled regulatory expertise they have developed domestically. Shaffer and Pollack 2008. Citing a study by John Braithwaite and Peter Drahos which found that out of 13 areas of global business regulation, the US played a leading role, while the EU played a leading role in nine areas.
15 Mandel 2009.
16 Shaffer and Pollack 2008.
17 Shaffer and Pollack 2008.
18 Shaffer and Pollack 2008. Citing James Morrow: 'There is only one way to cooperate in prisoners' dilemma; there are many ways to cooperate in the real world'. Morrow 1994: 395.
19 Krasner 1991. Cited in Shaffer and Pollack 2008.
20 Krasner 1991. Cited in Shaffer and Pollack 2008.
21 Marchant *et al.* 2010. There are hundreds of examples of international regulatory cooperation that concentrate regulatory authority in legislative and regulatory bodies and rely on top-down legal mandates. A few examples include rules developed around the collection and dissemination of worldwide weather data (provided for by the Convention of the World Meteorological Organization and the International Telecommunication Convention); the limiting of harm to dolphins during tuna harvesting through the Agreement on the International Dolphin Conservation Programme; or the assurance of technical uniformity of railways under the 1886 Convention on Technical

Uniformity. For many more situations where regulatory cooperation has resulted in international conventions, or government-to-government agreements, see ASIL 2006.
22 Marchant *et al.* 2010.
23 Marchant *et al.* 2010.
24 Slaughter 2003.
25 Lang and Scott 2009.
26 Marchant *et al.* 2010.
27 Zaring 2005, citing Slaughter 2003.
28 Zaring 2005. As Zaring argues, concerns about a democratic deficit make little sense if agency actions are inseparable from the interests of the states to which they belong.
29 See Slaughter 2004: 48. Slaughter writes with respect to informal networks that: 'they lack a foundational treaty', 'they operate under only a few agreed upon objectives or bylaws', 'nothing they do purports to be legally binding', and there are 'few or no mechanisms for formal enforcement or implementation'.
30 Svetiev 2010.
31 See for example Lipson 1991; Raustiala 2005; Guzman 2005.
32 Abbot and Snidal 2000.
33 Abbot and Snidal 2000.
34 Zaring 2005.
35 Slaughter 2003: 49.
36 Marchant *et al.* 2010.
37 Marchant *et al.* 2010.
38 Svetiev 2010.
39 Slaughter cites three key authors of criticisms that networks lack accountability: Alston 1997; Perez 1996; and Picciotto 1996–7.
40 Slaughter 1999.
41 Alston 1997: 441.
42 Slaughter 1999. It is also worth noting the theory of the rise of managerialism in international politics. Lang and Scott discuss the idea of the 'colonization of international politics by professional experts and their technical discourses, and the hollowing out of the traditional political processes we normally associate with international institutions'. Lang and Scott 2009. 'The result is a movement towards technocratic, expert-oriented forms of governance, through the transnational consolidation of global professional cultures and transnational networks of expertise common to specific functional issue areas'. Lang and Scott continue by explaining that functional or problem-oriented governance, overt political contest is marginalised in favour of cooperation by experts, and that 'struggles over global governance are to a great extent … fought through the debates waged within and between various scientific and professional disciplines and their universalizing discourses'. For the latter quote, Lang and Scott cite Picciotto 1996–7: 1037.
43 Svetiev 2010.
44 Slaughter 1999.
45 Lang and Scott 2009.
46 Slaughter 1999.
47 Marchant *et al.* 2010.
48 The United States-Chile Free Trade Agreement, signed on 6 June 2003, entered into force on 1 January 2004.
49 Art. 1.2:1(g).
50 Agreement Establishing an Association between the European Community and its Member States, of the One Part, and the Republic of Chile, on the Other Part, done at Brussels on 18 November 2002, entered into force on 1 February 2003 (trade), 1 March 2005 (full agreement).
51 Part III: Cooperation, Art. 16.2.

52 Part III: Cooperation, Art. 18.1.
53 Nottage 2009.
54 See, for example, the Preamble to the Agreement Establishing the World Trade Organization which states that:

> *Recognizing* that their relations in the field of trade and economic endeavour should be conducted with a view to raising standards of living, ensuring full employment and a large and steadily growing volume of real income and effective demand, and expanding the production of and trade in goods and services...

However, the contribution of trade liberalisation to development is contested. See, for example, Goh 2006. Goh argues that the case for free trade in promoting development is far from clear. He suggests that it should be recognised that trade is only a means, to be used carefully and as appropriate while development is the goal.
55 Note, however, that there is a considerable body of research which suggests that globalisation and trade do not lead to a regulatory race to the bottom as some have suggested. A number of essays in an edited volume by Vogel and Kagan in fact suggest that overall, the tendency of globalisation has been towards greater rather than less regulatory stringency. See Vogel and Kagan 2004.
56 See, for example, the Citizens Trade Campaign (the CTC), a coalition in the US of environmental, labour, consumer, religious, family farm, and other civil society groups. The CTC has demanded that all future US FTAs must require signatories to enforce domestically the core International Labour Organization standards. It also demands that FTAs include provisions stating that the failure to enforce, or the weakening of such policies, would constitute a violation of the agreement. See online at: www.citizenstrade. org/ctc/trade-policies/tpp-potential-trade-policy-problems/ (accessed 11 June 2011).
57 See Epps and Green 2010.
58 'Soybean Association looks to open EU markets' (Harvest Public Media, 9 February 2012), available online at: http://harvestpublicmedia.org/article/1012/soybean-association-open-eu-markets/5.
59 Free Trade Agreement between the Government of Canada and the Government of the Republic of Costa Rica, signed on 23 April 2001, entered into force on 1 November 2002.
60 Part Four – Trade Facilitation – Section II – Additional Provisions – Article IX.5.3 (Sanitary and Phytosanitary Measures).
61 Art. IX.5.4.
62 *Tratado de Libre Comercio Chile–México* (Free Trade Agreement between Chile and Mexico), signed on 17 April 1998, entered into force on 1 August 1999.
63 Art. 7.02.3.
64 Art. 7.11.
65 Art. 7.11.4.
66 Art. 7.11.5.
67 Art. 6.3.5.
68 Treaty for the Establishment of the East African Community, signed at Arusha, Tanzania on 30 November 1999, entered into force on 7 July 2000.
69 Art. 118.
70 Free Trade Agreement between the Government of New Zealand and the Government of the People's Republic of China, signed on 7 April 2008, entered into force 1 October 2008.
71 Art. 90(2)(b).
72 Art. 96(1).
73 Art. 96(2)(a) and (b).
74 Art. 96(2)(a).
75 Art. 96(2)(b).
76 Agreement between Japan and the United Mexican States for the Strengthening of the

Economic Partnership, signed at Mexico City on 17 September 2004, entered into force on 1 April 2005.

77 See text associated with note 11 above.
78 See Art. 19.5 (Environmental Cooperation) of the *US–Chile FTA*.
79 Annex 18.5(1) of the *US–Chile FTA*.
80 Euro-Mediterranean Agreement Establishing an Association between the European Communities and their Member States, on the One Part, and the Arab Republic of Egypt, on the Other Part, entered into force on 1 June 2004.
81 See Langendorff (28 March 2008).
82 Art. 16.1(c) of the *US–Chile FTA*.
83 Art. 16(1).
84 Art. 41(1) and (2).
85 See Trebilcock and Daniels 2008.
86 US Chamber of Commerce. Online. Available at: www.uschamber.com/sites/default/files/grc/TPPRegulatoryCoherenceWorkingGroupPaper.pdf (accessed 8 June 2011).
87 Part IX, Programmes for Trans-Tasman Cooperation, Art. 9.1.1.
88 See discussion of the success of these and other programmes in: 2008 Review of the Trans-Tasman Mutual Recognition Arrangement, New Zealand Government Submission (2008).
89 See references to articles by Alston 1997; Perez 1996; Picciotto 1996–7.
90 Ch. 8, Art. 100(2)(e) of the *NZ–China FTA*.
91 She refers to the US regulatory dialogue with Japan, which became the US-Japan Economic Harmonization Initiative, and suggests that it provides an opportunity for the US to pressure Japan on a number of matters that also arise in the annual review of trade policy barriers and of alleged breaches of section 301 of the US Trade Act. Kelsey (23 October 2011).
92 Zaring 2005.

9 Implementation and monitoring of process and production methods

Sofya Matteotti and Olga Nartova[1]

Introduction

Perhaps one of the greatest challenges for trade is the way in which environment concerns and trade law are often thought to be and may in fact be in conflict. Finding ways to reconcile this conflict is arguably crucial for the future of both systems. With environmental problems moving to the centre of attention in politics in the early 1990s, the distinction between trade measures that are aimed at products and those aimed at production processes faced increasing criticism. The GATT 1947[2] and its successor the World Trade Organization (WTO) were often accused of preventing national policies directed at preserving the environment or other public goods. The illegality of production-based trade measures was one important aspect of the alleged shortcomings. The general idea and reasoning behind this criticism were increasingly met with approval;[3] however, this has not led to the multilateral solution that some had hoped for.

Underlying the debate is the presumption that trade measures can be subdivided into measures that are linked to products themselves and measures that are linked to processes of production, and that both groups of measures have a different legal status under the GATT Agreement.[4] Since the distinction between products and production has considerable logical appeal, it is often overlooked that the legal content of the concept is vague. In view of the development of tools to fight climate change some governments wish to protect domestic industry from competition in countries that do not apply the same, or equivalent, environmental standards, in particular with respect to CO_2 emissions. However, detecting differing standards is not always easy. It is often not possible for WTO Members to track methods of production for products produced outside their territory, particularly if the carbon values are not detectable in the final commercial product. Therefore, how can a country take measures to address harmful emissions produced during the product's manufacture in another country? This question is perhaps the most important legal issue as the vast majority of carbon emissions related to a product are associated with its production and transportation to the point of sale.

This chapter discusses how trade measures based on production methods can and should be implemented. First, it discusses process and production methods (PPMs) as criteria of likeness, under Article III of GATT.[5] Then the chapter engages in comparative studies on implementation of PPM-based trade measures. In the conclusion, the chapter suggests a legal framework addressing the management of PPM administration and monitoring in international law.

The principles of non-discrimination and process and production methods (PPMs) as criteria of 'likeness'

WTO rules are based upon two principles of non-discrimination, which are applicable to all WTO Members.[6] The most-favoured-nation (MFN) obligation prohibits discrimination between imports on the basis that they come from one exporting WTO Member rather than another. The national treatment obligation is applicable to foreign products; that is, upon entering the domestic market, these products must not be treated less favourably in terms of taxation or regulation relative to 'like' domestic products. In other words, all the trade measures imposed in support of, for instance, an environmental policy must treat domestic products like foreign products.

In the GATT Agreement, however, the concept of 'likeness' is not clearly defined. There are products which can be considered alike in terms of how they look and in terms of their functions and properties; however, these products may differ in terms of the methods used for production. Hence, the question arises to what extent may WTO Members differentiate between products produced by different methods in order to pursue environmental policies?

By definition, PPMs refer to 'any activity that is undertaken in the process of bringing a good to market'.[7] There are two types of PPMs that are utilised in the manufacture of goods: (1) product-related and (2) non-product-related. The latter, by contrast to the former, does not describe or affect the product's physical characteristics. In such instances, it is not possible to figure out the types of PPMs utilised based on an analysis of the product's physical characteristics. This type of PPM is of particular relevance in the climate change context and is under scrutiny in this chapter.

WTO law on 'unfair' trade and environmental protection

In its broadest sense, the national treatment principle of GATT Article III was developed to ensure that internal measures shall 'not be applied' in a discriminatory way to imported and domestic products. This is to avoid protectionism.

Today, the WTO agreements contain highly complex rules in respect to some particular forms of 'unfair' trade. Although the WTO agreements justify 'specific' violations in relation to trade, they do not contain 'higher' or universal moral principles which are common to all countries and recognised by all members of the organisation. The WTO agreements address disputes in relation to trade liberalisation including economic and non-economic societal values and interests which come in conflict with trade liberalisation.[8] In particular, these non-economic values and interests cover the environment and its protection, public health, national treasures and security.[9]

The WTO is criticised for its insufficient support for environmental policies. Environmentalists are convinced that the WTO trading system hinders environmental protection,[10] at a time when such protection has become more significant for the sake of future generations. The dilemma occurs because trade liberalisation is also needed for the welfare of an economy and for the many individuals seeking greater economic opportunities. These two opposing policy objectives and the conflicts are acquired from 'cultural differences'; that is, from different perceptions and attitudes which also can create misunderstandings. One way in which the two viewpoints might be reconciled is if the issues regarding PPMs are clarified. Issues of interpretation have emerged in several environmental cases about how products are produced.

The pros and cons of trade-related PPMs

Generally, there are three major arguments which point to the inappropriateness of trade-related PPMs as policy instruments.[11] First, the implementation of such measures may be used to promote protectionism. Second, the 'exportation' of priorities with respect to national policy through PPM-based regulations could work against other states' sovereign rights, including their respective policy priorities. Third, the geographic and temporal distance between the enforcing state and the actual application of PPMs could make enforcement unfeasible and arbitrary. In response to these arguments, the positive aspects of implementing PPMs should not be forgotten. The use of PPMs in a more conservative sense may also be part of the creation of sustainable environmental policy.

First of all, the ability to promote protectionist interests is common to all trade-related measures and thus the legality of such policy should not be based on whether the measure specifies PPMs, but on whether it is being applied in a non-discriminatory manner. Further, in pursuit of environmental policy objectives, foreign states could benefit from PPM- and non-PPM-based policy measures unless a foreign jurisdiction's ability to 'select' their respective policy objectives is hindered by such measures (e.g. restriction of market access, etc.). In response to the third argument listed above, non-product-related PPMs also trigger opportunities for the private sector to initiate the development of alternatives to physical verification requirements at Customs through the application of new technologies.

Extraterritoriality and non-product-related PPMs in relation to the environment and its protection

In 1982, the World Charter for Nature[12] sought the cooperation of governments to create standards for products and manufacturing processes which have negative effects on nature. Unfortunately, the Charter did not go further and link a PPM with the trade effects it might have.

Sovereignty is a key issue in the WTO's jurisdiction over PPMs. Some parties assert that the importer should not be able to directly influence change of the

PPMs in the exporting country just because it is one of the product's buyers. Such intervention is an infringement of the producer's right. Setting PPMs is within the prerogative of the producers. Also, some parties claim that if the environmental damage is purely local, then it is solely within the jurisdiction of the exporting, not the importing, state. This was the view upheld in several dispute settlement rulings[13] in the GATT era.

However, such an argument of purely domestic environmental impact is undermined when the environmental damage is not only local – if it involves polluting shared waters and air streams, depleting populations of species that migrate across borders, or damaging the atmosphere. There is a call for international cooperation on environmental issues because of the increasing incidence of extensive environmental damage.[14] The WTO has responded to that call. An important environmental provision in the WTO is GATT Article XX which states that trade discrimination may be justified, *inter alia*, when (1) 'it is necessary to protect human, animal or plant life and health', and (2) 'it is relating to the conservation of exhaustible natural resources if such measures are made effective in conjunction with restrictions on domestic production or consumption'.[15]

These provisions suggest that extraterritorial monitoring of PPMs must be consistent with those two conditions. Concerns about health and the environment have also been accommodated even in pre-WTO jurisprudence. The *Tuna-Dolphin I* dispute,[16] for example, and its various implications gained wide interest among environmental-legal practitioners and became a guide for future cases. In *Tuna-Dolphin I*, the panel held that the PPMs of Mexico, even if endangering dolphins, were not inconsistent with GATT. The ruling stated that the United States had to prove that Mexico's measure was inconsistent with GATT, and not just show that the United States had an environmental goal in order to justify imposing trade restrictions on Mexico.[17]

In eastern tropical areas of the Pacific Ocean, tuna is harvested using purse seine nets and as tuna is harvested, dolphins are also trapped in the nets and they often die unless released. The United States Marine Mammal Protection Act (MMPA) of 1972 imposed dolphin protection standards which included countries fishing for yellowfin tuna within that particular area. If a country (exporting tuna to the United States) failed to meet the relevant standards for the protection of dolphins, the United States government had the right to embargo all fish imports coming from that country. In 1991, Mexico, an exporting country, complained against the United States for banning its exports.

The part of the MMPA that was at issue provided that the importation of commercial fish or fish products obtained using commercial fishing technology would be banned in an attempt to stop incidental killings or serious injury of ocean mammals.[18] The relevant PPM had no effect on the products physically, but, was linked to an aspect of production. According to the panel report, GATT Article III was not applicable to the import prohibition since it only dealt with measures applicable to the product 'as such'; that is, the measure only regulated the sale of tuna which had no effect on tuna as a product.[19] Furthermore, the measure did not violate the national treatment obligation of GATT Article III:4

because it only covered and compared products' treatment and did not affect tuna as a product.[20] Thus, upon finding inconsistency with Article XI, the emphasis was placed on Article XX and on the issue of extraterritoriality.

GATT rules do not allow one country to impose its domestic laws on another country regardless of whether those measures are for the protection of the environment. The disputing countries held bilateral consultations outside GATT aiming to reach an agreement.[21] The MMPA effectively required other states to prove that their environmental regulatory systems were relatively similar or comparable to the United States law before any of them could access the United States market.[22] The panel did not accept that the United States measure fell under GATT Article XX (b) or (g). This seemed to be so as to avoid GATT parties finding non-compliance by others with their domestic standards and consequently triggering unilateral trade restrictions. In other words, this meant other states would not have to adopt similar standards imposed by the importing state, the United States, or otherwise accept trade sanctions for non-compliance.

In the *Tuna-Dolphin II* dispute,[23] living creatures such as dolphins were considered to be 'exhaustible natural resources'. In this dispute between the United States and Mexico, the Appellate Body found that the United States could not utilise Article XX to block imports from Mexico. The EU brought this complaint against the United States under GATT following *Tuna-Dolphin I*. The EC and the Netherlands complained that the embargoes (primary and intermediary nations) which the United States enforced, pursuant to the MMPA, were not covered by Article III, were inconsistent with Article XI:1 and not an exception under Article XX.

The United States argued that the intermediary nation embargo was GATT-consistent and was covered by environmental exceptions.[24] Furthermore, they argued that the primary nation embargo did not impair benefits of the EC and the Netherlands since it did not apply to these countries.

The decision of the panel was aligned to that of the decision in 1991 and pointed out the inapplicability of Note Ad Article III to the case. Although the *Tuna-Dolphin I* panel focused on the extraterritorial effects of the measure, the panel in *Tuna-Dolphin II* rejected the measures as they undermined the multilateral trading system and were consequently unjustifiable. In *Tuna-Dolphin II*, the GATT Panel claimed that the measures, forcing other states to change their policies, were not mainly directed towards the conservation of natural resources.[25] Similarly, the United States did not succeed in invoking the Article XX(g) defence. The difference in the second decision was that the panel did not disregard the possibility of adopting measures based on the promotion of non-economic goals. Nevertheless, there was no further development with respect to Article XX(g) and its interpretation. The *Tuna-Dolphin* disputes did not involve breaches of Article III, since the issue was the method by which the fish was caught, rather than any inherent – i.e. product-related – characteristic of the tuna.[26] On 15 September 2011, a WTO Panel issued a new report in this dispute, analysing the question of whether a voluntary labelling requirement can be regarded as a technical regulation with which compliance is mandatory under the Agreement on Technical Barriers to Trade (TBT Agreement); defining a legal test for the analysis of whether certain measures are more trade restrictive than necessary to fulfil a legitimate objective; and examining whether a Member may apply stricter national standards than international ones.[27]

The issue of strict national standards was also addressed in the *Reformulated Gasoline* case, where clean air was considered as an 'exhaustible natural resource'. In *Reformulated Gasoline*, the US created a national standard for reformulated gasoline to reduce pollution.[28] Imported gasoline was required to meet the US standard as well. The WTO panel maintained that such a policy of the US violated Article III or GATT's National Treatment clause because imported gasoline was adversely treated relative to domestic gasoline.[29]

A criterion about the product's health effects was added in the *EC – Asbestos* case. In this landmark case, France banned the use of asbestos-containing products because of health concerns. Canada challenged such a ban. The Appellate Body ruled in favour of France, claiming that Canada failed to demonstrate that the asbestos-containing products were like other products, especially when asbestos-containing products were associated with significant health risks not present in other products. The Appellate Body stated in its ruling that:

> '[t]he more vital or important [the] common interests or values' pursued, the easier it would be to accept as 'necessary' measures designed to achieve those ends. [Footnote omitted] In this case, the objective pursued by the measure is the preservation of human life and health through the elimination, or reduction, of the well-known, and life-threatening, health risks posed by asbestos fibres. The value pursued is both vital and important in the highest degree. The remaining question, then, is whether there is an alternative measure that would achieve the same end and that is less restrictive of trade than a prohibition.[30]

In *Shrimp-Turtle*, the United States had banned the import of shrimp acquired from processes that did not adhere to the United States environmental standards. Asian fishers use nets that prevent sea turtles from escaping, in effect killing them. The United States also claimed that in this case, the extraterritorial application of the environmental laws of the United States was justified because these were species of migrating sea turtles that lived in both the United States and Asian waters, thereby securing a strong connection between the United States and the sea turtles.[31] The Appellate Body said:

> it is not acceptable, in international trade relations, for one WTO member to use an economic embargo to *require* other Members to essentially adopt the same comprehensive regulatory program, to achieve a certain policy goal, as that in force within that Member's territory, *without* taking into consideration different conditions which may occur in the territories of those other Members.[32]

The Appellate Body also referred to the exception for the conservation of exhaustible natural resources in Article XX: if there is no express limitation to the location of the resources protected or behaviour targeted in Article XX of GATT, and no other rule of public international law governing these issues, limitations on states' sovereign right to protect resources, life and health, arguably cannot be presumed or implied.[33] Thailand commented that such a ruling from the Appellate Body could lead to a slippery slope, permitting states to discriminate against goods based on non-product-related PPMs, in violation of the WTO Agreement. Thailand also feared the implementation of a plethora of environmental and labour standards applied to products. Other developing countries such as Pakistan and India supported Thailand's position. *Shrimp-Turtle* revealed a significant development as it emphasised and applied trade measures extraterritorially. The extension of the United States measure for the protection of endangered sea turtles outside its jurisdiction, initially moved the panel to reject the measure as 'unlawful' under GATT Article XX; however, in the 21.5 compliance proceeding, the Appellate Body reversed the panel's finding that the US was not in compliance and found that the US had taken sufficient steps (e.g. negotiating with all the affected countries) to justify its measure under XX(g).[34]

Despite the emergence of some level of accommodation of environmental concerns in the WTO, there is still a lot of debate over imposing trade restrictions based on health and environmentally harmful PPMs, because member states utilise such provisions with much flexibility.

Climate change mitigation and PPMs

The WTO does not generally interfere with domestic issues such as labour or human rights in its member countries.[35] Although it allows countries to implement trade measures regulating product characteristics or their related processes and production methods, it generally does not allow trade restrictions on non-product-related PPMs.[36]

The mitigation of climate change raises many level-playing-field issues with respect to the appropriateness of non-product-related PPMs and their application as policies at the national and international levels. It has been well recognised that the cost implications of carbon constraining policies may provoke trade frictions that translate into deliberative and legal issues for the WTO.[37] WTO provisions tend to focus on physical products; on the other hand, climate change policies are concerned with production methods and processes for the reduction of greenhouse gas (GHG) emissions. Hence, countries need to take into account the WTO's treatment of non-product-related PPMs in designing their measures to address climate change mitigation. One country may in 'good faith' aim to reduce carbon emissions; however, the application of a relevant measure can create issues for other countries and their regulations on production methods.

One significant challenge is how to unify national approaches towards mitigating climate change through the adoption of policies which are compatible with WTO regulations; that is, how would countries develop mitigation efforts which are comparable to an internationally agreed policy approach without the related risks (e.g. protectionist interests, unmanageable climate change, etc.). Policies developed to address climate change might involve price and non-price interventions (e.g. GHG permits, taxes, economic incentives, emission sources such as processes and usage of equipment) and the current WTO rules are not adequately developed to cover such types of policies.

In the case of GHG emissions reduction and climate change mitigation, the production process has no effect on the determination of 'likeness' where there is competition between an imported and domestic product.[38] The GATT 1994 does not define the concept of 'like products', nor does it give any guidance as to the characteristics of products that must be examined. The interpretation of the term should be examined on a case-by-case basis. However, WTO dispute settlement reports provide that some criteria utilised for the determination of the 'likeness' of two products are as follows: (1) the products and their physical characteristics, (2) end uses, (3) preferences of consumers and (4) tariff classification of every product.[39] What is absent from this test is the ability to differentiate products with respect to the methods used in their production.[40] With respect to GATT Article III, products can be considered 'like' whether they are produced in the same manner or not. Therefore, an application of a measure addressing non-product-related PPMs is likely to be considered 'differential' treatment of that imported product relative to domestic 'like' products.[41]

This is why environmental advocates continue to consider that WTO rules with regard to climate change mitigation efforts are inappropriate.[42] Although governments may be allowed to differentiate products and the methods used for production, as long as they do not give less favourable treatment to imported products than domestic products, more related issues are bound to arise, particularly as various non-product-related measures may be frequently imposed due to incompatibility of regulations with respect to production.

The absence of unified international treatment regarding non-product-related PPMs in the determination of 'likeness' among products continues to promote uncertainties as methods of production are inseparable to the products' physical aspects.

While these issues concerning likeness remain unresolved, PPMs can be justified in terms of exceptions. Thus, specific fishing methods supporting conservation may be imposed, on the basis of GATT Article XX(g), as a condition of importation of the product itself. PPMs adopted in the context of climate change mitigation are, therefore, not excluded under GATT even though PPMs cannot serve as a foundation for discriminatory treatment under Article III of the GATT.[43]

Verification of environment-friendly production methods

WTO rules are evolving when it comes to supporting restrictive trade measures with the goal of promoting environmental protection. In recent years, the WTO has expressed that it stands for sustainable development, with reference to the reconciliation of globalisation with environmental and social protection.[44]

Some international environmental law sources point out that international trade could significantly contribute to sustainable development. Chapter 2 of Agenda 21, a non-binding action plan of the United Nations with regard to sustainable development, states that:

> [a]n open, equitable, secure, non-discriminatory and predictable multilateral trading system that is consistent with the goals of sustainable development and leads to the optimal distribution of global production in accordance with comparative advantage is of benefit to all trading partners. Moreover, improved market access for developing countries' export in conjunction with sound macroeconomic and environmental policies would have a positive environmental impact and therefore make an important contribution toward sustainable development.[45]

Also, Principle 12 of the Rio Declaration[46] states that 'states should cooperate to promote a supportive and open international economic system that would lead to economic growth and sustainable development in all countries, to better address the problem of environmental degradation.'[47] Principle 2 of the Rio Declaration also states that the sovereign right to exploit one's natural resources goes hand-in-hand with the obligation to ensure that no harm is caused to other states or the commons.

The effects of environmental destruction truly trickle down to many parts of the world. Adverse effects of climate change compromise development in the long run. Bringing more environmental considerations into the WTO might face certain limitations due to sovereignty issues. Assuming that a country will be able to justify its non-product-related PPM-based trade measures, another issue arises with regard to monitoring or utilising PPMs and implementing PPM-based policies. Such non-product-related PPMs in effect result in the extraterritorial reach of domestic production standards if foreign producers are required to comply, in order to obtain import clearances for their products.[48] Some member states of the WTO indeed see extraterritorial monitoring of PPMs as an avenue to promote sustainable development on a global scale.

The EU and PPMs: general principles and policies

In contrast to the WTO, the EU has more stringent regulatory measures on trade because of its commitment to the protection of human rights and the environment. In the public debate, the commitment to protecting human rights and the environment is given more importance than trade liberalisation most of the time. Some national laws, for example, permit the restriction of imports in virtue of the way they were produced, rather than based on the measurable characteristics of the products.[49] For instance, in its judgment in the case *Cassis-de-Dijon*,[50] the European Court of Justice (ECJ) stated that the motive of compelling public interests, specifically consumer interests, is a legitimate justification for restricting trade.

The ECJ has also legitimised PPM-based trade restrictions in a number of instances. A non-product-related PPM-based tax differentiation was legitimised in 1981. The case was about industrial alcohol where the EU imposed a higher tax on the product taking into consideration the environmental benefit of the synthetically produced over the naturally produced alcohol. The ECJ stated in the justification of the decision:

> community law does not restrict the freedom of each member state to lay down tax arrangements which differentiate between certain products on the basis of objective criteria, such as (...) the production process employed. Such differentiation is compatible with community law (...) if the detailed rules are such to avoid any form of discrimination, direct or indirect, in regard to imports from other member states, or any form of protection of competing domestic products.[51]

Moreover, in the case of the mandatory labelling of genetically modified organisms, the ECJ stated that 'the goal of informing consumers about the means of production – or, put differently, public morals – can provide a legitimate reason for distinguishing products which are physically alike'.[52] The Life Cycle Asessment (LCA) is a core element of the EU's labelling system. The LCA approach takes into account all aspects of the production, potential use and disposal of a product when it is being considered for eco-labelling. The EU treats such measures as the application of the precautionary principle, to ensure that the safety of the people and the environment are protected especially in cases of uncertainty or ambiguity.[53] There is a presumption of the existence of a hazard, which assumes a priori that specific products and activities are inherently harmful to humans and the environment, even without conclusive evidence. The EU has stated that while industry-based standards are important to facilitate trade, 'standards cannot replace government responsibility to safeguard a high level of protection concerning health, safety and the environment'.[54] All of these policies demonstrate that the extraterritorial monitoring of non-product-related PPMs acts as a tool for the EU to uphold its core principles.

The EU's stringent regulatory trade policies have at times, resulted in disputes with other countries. In the 1980s, the EU imposed a ban on the use of hormones in livestock because of the growing alarm from meat consumers over the health effects of such hormones. European consumer organisations also clamoured for a boycott on veal. In 1981, the 'Lamming Report' concluded that:

> most of the hormones would not present any harmful health effects when used under appropriate conditions as growth promoters in animals, but that control programs and monitoring systems for the appropriate use of these hormones were essential, and that additional scientific investigations were necessary to assess health effects of these hormones.[55]

The Commission forwarded to the other Member States a directive to monitor the use of three natural hormones for growth enhancement purposes and reassessment of the two synthetic hormones upon completion of scientific inquiries.[56] That proposal was rejected by the European Parliament, the EC Economic and Social Committee, and the EC Council of Ministers. Despite the release of the Lamming Report and the proposed directives,[57] the blanket ban on all beef hormones persisted and was also applicable to imported meat products. Such a ban was met with heavy protest from the exporters, especially from the US. According to the US, the EU ban on growth hormones violated the Sanitary and Phytosanitary Measures Agreement (SPS) rules. The US claimed that the ban was not a product of a thorough risk assessment and did not have any scientific basis. Moreover, the US claimed that the ban was meant to protect the EU's domestic cattle industry and was not really instituted because of actual health dangers. There were also inconsistencies in the EU's ban because the EU permitted domestic production of meat that had been treated with hormones for 'therapeutic purposes'. Such domestic meat products had even higher hormone levels than those contained in the imported meat. The EU also allowed other products that have increased hormone levels such as milk, butter and eggs into the market. The US stated that concern from consumers is not an adequate justification for imposing a ban on trade when that concern is not scientifically justified. The 1997 WTO panel report, reinforced the US position on the EU ban on growth hormones. According to the panel, the ban was not based on a risk assessment pursuant to Article 5.1, or on international standards in compliance with Article 3.1, and the EU had not provided scientific evidence to support the ban pursuant to Article 3.3. Also, the EU ban was inconsistent with the level of sanitary protection adopted with regard to different substances which posed the same health risks to humans; the EU allowed hormones to be used in specific cases, such as for pig feed and for treatment of cattle by veterinarians. This differentiated treatment was a restriction on trade and violated Article 5.5 on equivalence. Despite the panel's findings, the EU maintained that the use of growth hormones in beef products adversely affected consumer confidence and that such a ban was needed to uphold consumer protection.[58] The Appellate Body agreed with the panel's finding that the EC measures are inconsistent with the requirements of Article 5.1 of the SPS Agreement, but modified the panel's interpretation by holding that Article 5.1, read in conjunction with Article 2.2, requires that the results of the risk assessment must sufficiently warrant the relevant SPS measure. It reversed the panel's conclusion that the European Communities by maintaining, without justification under Article 3.3, SPS measures which are not based on existing international standards, acted inconsistently with Article 3.1 of the SPS Agreement.[59]

The US and PPMs: general principles and policies

The massive amount of imports entering the market of the US arguably unleashes the need to ensure quality control and consumer safety. About 20 percent of drugs in finished-dosage form generic and over-the-counter drugs and more than 40 percent of the active ingredients in United States medicines come from India and China.[60] Incidents of receiving dangerous imports have led to a call to impose more stringent requirements. Examples of such incidents include the recall of lead-containing toys from China in 2007 and the recall of a contaminated blood thinner from China that killed about 19 patients. In July of the same year, ginger imported from China was discovered to contain a dangerous pesticide only after the product was placed on the market. Such incidents heightened US safety concerns when it came to imports.[61] A major problem is that a lot of these product-related quality concerns were discovered only after consumers had negative experiences with the products. The nature of regulatory responses was merely reactive, instead of proactive, limiting their effectiveness.

Therefore, from the US's perspective the need has arisen to reduce risks and prevent harm by overseeing production processes directly through inspection, monitoring, reporting and licensing, to make sure that the products are safe even before they reach the US market. Various proposals to institute overseas production-based monitoring have emerged. FDA Commissioner Andrew von Eschenbach, for example, proposed a scheme called 'FDA without Borders', where FDA inspectors and technical advisers would be deployed in China, India, the Middle East and three other regions. A permanent FDA presence at the US Embassy in Beijing and two consulates in China was also proposed. The FDA also considered requiring inspections of foreign plants before foreign-manufactured active drug ingredients would be allowed in FDA-approved prescription medications for the US's domestic population.[62] But, why did such proposals not fully materialise? Perhaps unsurprisingly, the US encountered a lot of logistical and legal challenges when it came to implementing the overseas inspections. First, the FDA staff could not handle the very large size of the import sources. The differences in US and foreign business practices were also a significant barrier. For example, in the case of the deaths due to the contaminated blood thinner in 2008, FDA inspectors thought that they were able to inspect the Chinese plant that manufactured the contaminated drug, but they eventually discovered that they had been taken to a different pharmaceutical plant with a similar name. There was also recognition that proceeding with overseas FDA inspections would be economically inefficient and costly to the US, and such massive costs would be shouldered by the American taxpayers. This would not be politically or economically attractive for the government. Aside from such feasibility issues, there were also legal battles to reckon with. The US had no formal legal authority in the local jurisdiction. Because of this, it could not demand anything from the firms that it inspected such as access, information or responses to questions. This lack of formal legal authority also meant there could be no enforcement or adequate legal sanction. Further, because such products had not yet officially entered US territory, there is an issue as to whether a violation of US legal requirements actually took place. Also, there might not have been any violation of the local law or local authorities may not have been willing to crack down on their own local companies.[63] All of these complex issues weaken the viability of overseas inspections, arguably highlighting the need for other parties to support the US government in its pursuit of instituting higher-quality PPMs.

What then are the alternatives available to the US, or indeed other countries, to increase its level of monitoring of the production of its imports? There are three options: (1) product-based regulation by foreign governments; (2) third-party regulation by key industry groups or certifying organisations; (3) regulation by domestic private actors involved in outsourcing, motivated by product-based regulation. Cooperating with foreign governments has enabled the US to safeguard the quality and safety of PPMs even abroad. Imported meat, poultry and egg products can only enter the United States market if they come from countries certified by the United States Department of Agriculture and establishments deemed eligible by the foreign governments.[64] China's General Administration of Quality Supervision, Inspection and Quarantine (AQSIQ) is compelled to give the FDA access to records from inspections carried out by Chinese regulators and submit to the FDA a list of manufacturers who do not meet the standards based on the food and feed agreement.[65] AQSIQ also stated that they would notify the FDA within 24 hours of finding that a product exported to the US could cause grave health effects. A foundation for information-sharing and regulatory cooperation was also created through the drugs-and-medical-devices agreement.[66] The United States also signed a Memorandum of Understanding with the Chinese administration,[67] covering specific goods including children's toys, clothing, fireworks and cigarette lighters.

Aside from foreign governments, through the years, the US has also enlisted the support of third-party entities in monitoring the PPMs of companies exporting products to the US. For instance, GlobalGap, a private standards-setting organisation, certifies compliance of more than 81,000 plants and farms in 76 countries with food industry safety guidelines. Similarly, the US standards-setting group United States Pharmacopoeia oversees PPMs in China and India. Also, US law grants compliance powers to such third-party organisations. For instance, the Consumer Product Safety Improvement Act of 2008[68] requires safety certification of children's products by accredited third-party monitoring groups. Private parties with a US presence are also key partners in monitoring PPMs abroad. For instance, the FDA requires US-based drug makers to test ingredients that they buy abroad.[69] The US government also requires importers of fish and fishery products to ensure that their foreign suppliers meet US standards.[70] All of these examples show that the US utilises multiple strategies to monitor the production of their imports abroad and that this is the most effective strategy. The 2007 Action Plan for Import Safety, prepared by the Interagency Working Group,[71] highlighted the following schemes: ensuring compliance by foreign producers with US safety standards through voluntary and mandatory certification requirements; instituting good importer practices through public and private cooperation; and accreditation by third-party inspectors of products outside the US for compliance with FDA standards. Compliance with these measures is rewarded through the granting of expedited import privileges.[72] Truly, both the government and private sphere should work together in ensuring that production methods of foreign companies are at par with US standards. The incentive mechanism put in place would also help the US acquire safer and higher-quality imports.

Multisectoral implications of extraterritorial monitoring of PPMs

Many developing countries assert that the extraterritorial monitoring of PPMs amounts to restrictive trade measures because these policies effectively limit global trade. Non-product-related PPMs do not really deal with the characteristics of the products; instead, they look into the way products are made, influencing the conditions of competition in a global trading system. For instance, PPM-based standards and technical regulations may function like non-tariff barriers, distorting domestic and foreign prices. Therefore, PPMs can serve as a form of protectionism by treating imports coming from countries with different economic conditions and domestic products differently.[73] According to the Business Round-table,[74] 'Non-trade concerns (e.g. food safety, labelling, precaution, and animal welfare) threaten to negate improvements in agricultural market access negoti-ated in the Doha Round.'[75] Because of such limitations in global trade, some companies might pull out altogether, severely affecting consumer choice.[76] Some companies from developing countries are forced to comply with production methods that may have been demanded unilaterally by developed countries. Most of the time, such companies are not even given the opportunity to participate in the formulation of these standards.[77] In addition, in many cases where agricultural exports of developing countries have been barred from the EU, related biotech-nology research and development programmes have been temporarily frozen or altogether eliminated, which hampers product development. Developing coun-tries that want to be part of the global trading system, but are devoid of technical capacity to satisfy the requirements of developed countries, may experience detri-mental economic and social consequences.[78] In order to address this problem, developed countries could be asked to transfer green technology to developing countries or give them financial assistance in order to gain the ability to buy these environmentally friendly machines. In return, the developed country that made such a donation would earn credit or the cost of the donation could be subtracted from the importation cost that it is required to shoulder.[79] For instance, with support from developed nations, companies that use sulphur components as their raw material or have sulphur and carbon monoxide by-products, are asked to make the chimneys of their factories tall and install filters to remove the poison-ous gases from their by-products before they are emitted into the atmosphere.[80] Plants such as the Calcium Carbonate Generation plant that applies the Solvay process in order to reduce emissions are also being set up.[81]

Preventing trade restrictions is not an adequate justification for not allowing the extraterritorial monitoring of PPMs. Some parties, such as the EU members, believe that they are not obliged to prioritise the WTO's agenda of trade liberali-sation ahead of their domestic consumers' preferences. Other states also consider that it is within their rights to protect themselves from competition from states that do not apply adequate environmental standards. Moreover, even if extrater-ritorial monitoring of PPMs does increase the compliance requirements for trade, it could also improve the quality of global trade. Adequate incentives to achieve maximum environmental protection at each stage of the production process must be present.[82] Also, extraterritorial monitoring of PPMs could fulfil climate change mitigation and trade-enhancing goals.

The extraterritorial monitoring of production methods helps in conserving the environment of the producer country in two major ways: (1) instituting more sustainable means of production and (2) encouraging the use of more environmentally friendly raw materials.[83] Packaging and transportation methods are also important aspects of PPMs. Advocates say that the extraterritorial monitoring of production methods should also go as far as ensuring that the packages used in the packaging of a product are environmentally friendly. At the same time, the transportation process, either by land, sea or air should not lead to environmental pollution.[84] Minimising the use of chemical pollutants will also benefit the producer country because the population would suffer less from the deleterious effects of chemical pollution.[85]

Truly, extraterritorial monitoring of PPMs could have the beneficial effects of promoting environmental and consumer protection, but could also have adverse consequences for the liberalisation of global trade and social justice. The implementation of such extraterritorial monitoring of PPMs must be fair in order to avoid any negative impact arising from such initiatives.

Possible ways forward

Environmental labelling is increasingly used as an instrument of climate protection.[86] However, both mandatory and voluntary labelling schemes risk contravening WTO law, especially if they are based on non-product-related PPMs.[87]

An alternative to labelling is adapting existing quality assurance methods and the experience of international standards, such as the International Organization for Standardization (ISO).

The ISO's technical committee on environmental management[88] is responsible for developing and maintaining the ISO 14000 family of standards and working in close cooperation with the ISO technical committee responsible for quality management standards. It was established in 1993 in response to the challenges voiced at the 1992 United Nations Conference on Environment and Development in Rio de Janeiro.[89]

The committee addresses not only terms and definitions and environmental communication,[90] but a range of diverse areas that can be grouped as: environmental management, auditing and performance evaluation; environmental labelling, life cycle assessment and measuring the carbon footprint of products; and environmental aspects of product design, development and product standards.[91]

Environmental audits are important tools for assessing whether an environmental management system is properly implemented and maintained. Developed by ISO auditing principles, the conduct of audits and the competence of auditors[92] can be applied so that they are used to verify climate-friendly production methods, or at least to serve as a starting point.

Furthermore, the ISO 14051 standard aims to provide guidelines for general principles and a framework of material flow cost accounting (MFCA). 'MFCA is a management tool to promote effective resource utilization, mainly in manu-facturing and distribution processes, in order to reduce the relative consumption of resources and material costs'.[93] MFCA is one of the major tools of environ-mental management accounting and will be valuable for monitoring and imple-menting PPMs.

The ISO has also developed international GHG accounting and verification standards.[94] It is supported by a new standard, ISO 14069, that focuses on the principles, concepts and methods relating to the quantification and reporting of direct and indirect greenhouse gas (GHG) emissions. In addition, ISO 14067[95] will provide methods of calculation of the carbon footprint of products, services and the supply chain, and will harmonise methodologies for communicating the carbon footprint information.[96]

An additional tool developed by ISO/TC 207 aims to assist in addressing environmental aspects of both products and services. 'Life-cycle assessment (LCA) is a tool for identifying and evaluating the environmental aspects of prod-ucts and services from the "cradle to the grave": from the extraction of resource inputs to the eventual disposal of the product or its waste.'[97]

The use of eco-labels is increasing, and although WTO members generally agree that labelling schemes can be economically efficient and useful for inform-ing consumers,[98] the debate on legality of certain categories of eco-labels remains contentious; for instance in the *US–Tuna II (Mexico)*[99] case the panel majority concluded that requirements for a voluntary label can be a de facto mandatory regulation.[100] The Appellate Body agreed with the panel that the measure at issue was a 'technical regulation' within the meaning of Annex 1.1 to the TBT Agreement. The Appellate Body reversed, however, the panel's finding that the 'dolphin-safe' definition and certification developed within the frame-work of the Agreement on the International Dolphin Conservation Program (AIDCP) is a 'relevant international standard' within the meaning of Article 2.4 of the TBT Agreement. In particular, the Appellate Body concluded that the panel erred in finding that the AIDCP, to which new parties can accede only by invitation, is 'open to the relevant body of every country and is therefore an international standardizing organization' for purposes of Article 2.4 of the TBT Agreement.[101] Perhaps it is time to work out a common position on at least climate mitigation-related eco-labels and to conform to the same labelling stand-ards. One example could be the ISO 14020 standard, which 'addresses a range of different approaches to environmental labels and declarations, such as eco-labels, self-declared environmental claims, and quantified environmental information about products and services'.[102]

Also, the ISO 14045 standard focuses on principles and requirements for eco-efficiency assessment, which is also relevant to implementing non-product related PPMs. According to ISO, this standard 'will establish an internationally standardised methodological framework for eco-efficiency assessment, support-ing a comprehensive and transparent presentation of eco-efficiency measures'.[103]

Conclusion

Consumer and environmental protection are legitimate concerns. The goal of trade is indeed to promote sustainable development on a global level. However, any form of trade restriction must be based on actual, verifiable scientific evidence and multilaterally recognised international standards. It is important to ensure that PPM-based measures are not merely used to uphold protectionism or impede the free movement of otherwise safe goods. Fair treatment of all nations must also be observed to avoid interstate conflicts ensuing from the implementation of such monitoring.

Multiple strategies can be employed to ensure that PPMs employed worldwide uphold optimal levels of consumer safety. Internationally agreed third-party organisations could be utilised to extend the reach of such initiatives. Individual states, regional organisations and international organisations should foster transparency, openness, information sharing and cooperation in the development of more environmentally sound PPMs. Developing countries must also have a role in deciding which international standards to implement to uphold fairness in the global trading system. Through this, the benefits of extraterritorial monitoring of PPMs could be reaped on an international scale.

Notes

1 Sofya Matteotti is a research fellow at the World Trade Institute, Bern, Switzerland. Olga Nartova is a research fellow at the World Trade Institute, Bern, Switzerland and an assistant professor at the DAH School of Law. The authors can be contacted at sofya.matteotti@wti.org or olga.nartova@wti.org respectively. This paper is based upon research undertaken by the authors within the Swiss National Centre of Competence in Research (NCCR) Trade Regulation, Work Package 5, funded by the Swiss National Research Foundation and was presented at the conference of the New Zealand Centre of International Economic Law on 'Enhancing Stability in the International Economic Order', 7–9 July 2011, Wellington, New Zealand. The authors are grateful to Susy Frankel and Meredith Kolsky Lewis for their valuable comments and suggestions to improve the quality of the chapter.

2 General Agreement on Tariffs and Trade, 30 October 1947, The Legal Texts: The Results of the Uruguay Round of Multilateral Trade Negotiations (1999), [hereinafter GATT 1947].

3 For example see discussions in Holzer 2010; Bell and Ziegler 2012; Cottier *et al.* 2009.

4 General Agreement on Tariffs and Trade 1994, Apr. 15, 1994, Marrakesh Agreement Establishing the World Trade Organization, Annex 1A, The Legal Texts: The Results of the Uruguay Round of Multilateral Trade Negotiations (1999), [hereinafter GATT 1994].

5 The term 'like product' appears in several different GATT provisions. For the purposes of this chapter, the authors refer to the concept of likeness in the Most Favoured Nation obligation of GATT Article I:1, and in the National Treatment obligations of paragraphs 2 and 4 of GATT Article III.

6 Van den Bossche 2005.

7 Potts 2008: 3.

8 Wolf 2001.

9 As far as trade in good is concerned the relevant rules can be found mainly under

Articles XX and XXI of the GATT 1994 and Articles XIV and XIV bis. Also, see Potts 2008.

10 Brack 2002.

11 Brack 2002.

12 Art. 21.b, A/RES/37/7 adopted by the United Nations General Assembly at the 48th plenary meeting on 28 October 1982. Online. Available at: www.un.org/documents/ga/res/37/a37r007.htm.

13 GATT Panel Report, *United States – Restrictions on Imports of Tuna*, 3 September 1991, unadopted, BISD 39S/155 381, 447, 639, paras 5.26, 5.32 [hereinafter 'GATT Panel Report, *US–Tuna I (Mexico)*']; GATT Panel Report, *United States – Restrictions on Imports of Tuna*, 16 June 1994, unadopted, DS29/R444 447, 636, paras 5.20, 5.33 [hereinafter 'GATT Panel Report, *US – Tuna II (ECC)*']. In the latter case, the panel looked at the negotiating history of Article XX and found that 'the statements and drafting changes made during the negotiation of the Havana Charter and the General Agreement did not clearly support any particular contention of the parties with respect to the location of the living thing to be protected under Article XX (b) [and (g)]' (paras 5.20 and 5.33). It stated that it 'could not (...) be said that the General Agreement proscribed in an absolute manner measures that related to things or actions outside the territorial jurisdiction of the party taking the measure' (para. 5.16).

14 UNEP and IISD 2000: Ch. 5.1.

15 Voigt 2009: 122–30.

16 GATT Panel Report, *US–Tuna I (Mexico)*.

17 GATT Panel Report, *US–Tuna I (Mexico)*, paras 5.14, 5.15.

18 Section 101 (a)(2) of the MMPA. See also Conrad 2008.

19 GATT Panel Report, *US–Tuna I (Mexico)*, para. 5.14.

20 GATT Panel Report, *US–Tuna I (Mexico)*, para. 5.15, For a detailed discussion see Conrad 2008.

21 Conrad 2008.

22 Zleptnig 2010.

23 GATT Panel Report, *US–Tuna II (ECC)*.

24 Article XX provides the following relevant exceptions: protecting human, animal or plant life or health under Article XX(b), securing compliance with laws or regulations which are not inconsistent with the provisions of the GATT 1994 under Article XX(d), conserving exhaustible natural resources under Article XX(g).

25 GATT Panel Report, *US–Tuna II (ECC)*, paras 3.10–3.

26 Zleptnig 2010.

27 Panel Report, *United States – Measures Concerning the Importation, Marketing and Sale of Tuna and Tuna Products*, WT/DS381/R, adopted 13 June 2012, as modified by Appellate Body Report WT/DS381/AB/R [hereinafter 'Panel Report, *US–Tuna II (Mexico)*'].

28 Appellate Body Report, *United States – Standards for Reformulated and Conventional Gasoline*, WT/DS2/AB/R, adopted 20 May 1996 discussed in Vikhlyaev 2001.

29 Davey. Online. Available at: www.wto.aoyama.ac.jp/file/040526Davy.pdf.

30 Appellate Body Report, *European Communities – Measures Affecting Asbestos and Asbestos-Containing Products*, WT/DS135/AB/R, adopted 5 April 2001, paras 170–2, referring to Appellate Body Report, *Korea – Measures Affecting Imports of Fresh, Chilled and Frozen Beef*, WT/DS161/AB/R, WT/DS169/AB/R, adopted 10 January 2001, para. 162.

31 Biermann 2001.

32 Appellate Body Report, *United States – Import Prohibition of Certain Shrimp and Shrimp Products*, WT/DS58/AB/R, adopted 6 November 1998, para. 164 [hereinafter 'Appellate Body Report, *US – Shrimp*'].

33 Howse 2002.

34 Appellate Body Report, *US – Shrimp*.

35 Macrory *et al.* 2005.

36 Dankers 2003.

37 Low *et al.* 2010.

38 Low *et al.* 2010.

39 Appellate Body Report, *Japan – Taxes on Alcoholic Beverages*, WT/DS8/AB/R, WT/DS10/AB/R, WT/DS11/AB/R, adopted 1 November 1996, p. 20 [hereinafter 'Appellate Body Report, *Japan – Alcoholic Beverages II*'] agreed with the criteria for determining 'likeness' set out in the 1970 Report of the Working Party on Border Tax Adjustments, BISD 18S/97, para. 18. This approach was followed in most GATT panel reports, e.g. Working Party Report, The Australian Subsidy on Ammonium Sulphate, GATT/CP.4/39, adopted 3 April 1950, BISD II/18; GATT Panel Report, EEC – Measures on Animal Feed Proteins, L/4599, adopted 14 March 1978, BISD 25S/49; GATT Panel Report, Spain – Tariff Treatment of Unroasted Coffee, L/5135, adopted 11 June 1981, BISD 28S/102; GATT Panel Report, Japan – Customs Duties, Taxes and Labelling Practices on Imported Wines and Alcoholic Beverages, L/6216, adopted 10 November 1987, BISD 34S/83; and GATT Panel Report, United States – Taxes on Petroleum and Certain Imported Substances, L/6175, adopted 17 June 1987, BISD 34S/136.

40 Wolf 2001.

41 It should be noted that although these criteria are generally used, the AB and panels always say that other factors may also be relevant in certain cases and according to the Appellate Body, it is 'a discretionary decision that must be made in considering the various characteristics of products in individual cases.' (Appellate Body Report, *Japan – Alcoholic Beverages II*, p. 21).

42 For a discussion on a range of the political views in the climate change debate, see Giddens 2009: 49.

43 Cottier and Oesch (16 April 2011).

44 See paragraph 51 of the Doha Declaration, and more at the WTO website at www. wto.org/english/tratop_e/envir_e/sust_dev_e.htm.

45 United Nations Conference on Environment and Development Rio de Janerio, Brazil, 3–14 June 1992, Agenda 21. Online. Available at: http://sustainabledevelopment.un.org/content/documents/Agenda21.pdf.

46 Rio Declaration on Environment and Development, A/CONF.151/26. Online. Available at: www.un.org/documents/ga/conf151/aconf15126-1annex1.htm.

47 Voigt 2009.

48 Voigt 2009.

49 Davies 2008.

50 EJC C-120/78, Rewe-Zentral AG v Bundesmonopolverwaltung für Branntwein, ECR 1979 649.

51 ECJ 140/79, *Chemical Farmaceutici SpA v DAF SpA*, ECR 1981 1, para. 14.

52 Cottier and Oesch (16 April 2011): 21 discussing EJC C-132/03, *Federconsumatori*, ECR 2005 I-4167.

53 For more information on the application of the precautionary principle in the EU, referring to the existing case law see the Communication from the Commission of the European Communities of 2 February 2000 on the precautionary principle, COM(2000) 1 final – not published in the Official Journal. Online. Available at: http://eur-lex.europa.eu/LexUriServ/LexUriServ.do?uri=COM:2000:0001:FIN:EN:P DF.

54 European Commission (2001): 3. Also see Kogan 2003.

55 Josling *et al.* 1999: 5.

56 The five hormone types most widely used in meat production include three natural hormones: estradiol 17-b, testosterone and progesterone, and two synthetic sub-

stances: trenbolone and zeranol. A scientific inquiry regarding these hormones was led by Professor Lamming (the Lamming Committee) (EC Council Directive 81/602, *Official Journal of the European Communities* L222 (1981) 32).

57 See EEC publication EUR 8913; Proposal for a Council Directive amending directive 81/602/EEC concerning the prohibition of certain substances, Official Journal, Eur. Comm. (No. C170) 295/1984; Amendment of the Proposal for a Council Directive amending Directive 81/602/EEC concerning the prohibition of certain substances, 28 Official Journal, Eur. Comm. (No. C313) 4/1985.

58 Josling *et al.* 1999.

59 Appellate Body Report, *EC Measures Concerning Meat and Meat Products (Hormones)*, WT/DS26/AB/R, WT/DS48/AB/R, adopted 13 February 1998.

60 U.S. Government Accountability Office (September 2010): Appx 1.

61 Bamberger and Guzman 2008.

62 U.S. Food and Drug Administration, Generic Drug User Fee Act Program, proposed at 19 December 2011 public meeting (Docket No. FDA-2010-N-0381).

63 Bamberger and Guzman 2008.

64 United States Department of Agriculture, Food Safety and Inspection Service *Checklist for Importing Meat, Poultry and Processed Egg Products*. Online. Available at: www.fsis.usda.gov/regulations/Import_Checklist/index.asp.

65 In 2007, the U.S. Food and Drug Administration entered into this agreement with the General Administration of Quality Supervision, Inspection and Quarantine of China to enhance cooperation between the US and China on food and feed safety. Among others, the agreement covers collaboration to facilitate inspections of facilities that process and produce food and a creation of processes for FDA to accept relevant, verified information from AQSIQ regarding certification.

66 Agreement between the Department of Health and Human Services of the United States of America and the State Food and Drug Administration of the People's Republic of China on the Safety of Drugs and Medical Devices, signed on 12 November 2007.

67 Memorandum of Understanding between the United States Consumer Product Safety Commission and the General Administration of Quality Supervision, Inspection and Quarantine of the People's Republic of China, signed on 21 April 2004.

68 Consumer Product Safety Improvement Act of 2008, Public Law 110–314—AUG. 14, 2008.

69 Federal Food, Drug, and Cosmetic Act, Public Law 75–717, Chapter VIII.

70 U.S. Code of Federal Regulations Title 21, Chapter I – Food and Drug Administration Department of Health and Human Services, Subchapter B – Food for Human Consumption, Part 123 Fish and Fishery Products.

71 Interagency Working Group on Import Safety (2007). The Interagency Working Group (IAWG) on U.S. Government-Sponsored International Exchanges and Training was created in 1998 to make recommendations to the President for improving the coordination, efficiency and effectiveness of United States Government-sponsored international exchanges and training.

72 Interagency Working Group on Import Safety (2007).

73 Vikhlyaev 2001.

74 Business Roundtable is an association of chief executive officers of leading US corporations with a combined workforce of more than 10 million employees in the United States. See its website at http://businessroundtable.org/about-us/.

75 Business Roundtable (May 2003), 'A Business Roundtable WTO policy paper: a balanced approach to precaution and risk', available at http://businessroundtable.org or on file with the authors.

76 Kogan 2003.

77 Biermann 2001.

78 Kogan 2003.

79 Wolfrum *et al.* 2011.
80 Lakshmi 2010: 44.
81 Ehring 2002: 921.
82 Bamberger and Guzman 2008.
83 Tevini 2011.
84 Choi 2003.
85 Diebold 2010.
86 For a list of countries and measures see the database of the International Energy Agency available online at http://iea.org/textbase/pm/grindex.aspx.
87 Vranes 2009b.
88 ISO/TC 207.
89 ISO 14000 family of International Standards.
90 Includes communication on environmental values, actions and performance. According to ISO, it is broader than simple reporting and may take many forms and approaches, from an open house to a written report. See ISO 14063:2006.
91 ISO 14063:2006.
92 ISO 19011.
93 Draft EN ISO 14051.
94 ISO 14064 parts 1, 2 and 3.
95 Expected to be finalised for publication in March 2014.
96 ISO 14000 family of International Standards.
97 ISO 14040:2006. For a detailed analysis on LCA please see Guinée *et al.* 2002.
98 WTO 'Environment: Issues, Labelling'. Online. Available at: www.wto.org/english/tratop_e/envir_e/labelling_e.htm.
99 Panel Report, *US–Tuna II (Mexico)*.
100 Bridges Trade BioRes Review (9 November 2011).
101 Appellate Body Report, *United States — Measures Concerning the Importation, Marketing, and Sale of Tuna and Tuna Products*, WT/DS381/AB/R, adopted 13 June 2012.
102 ISO 14020.
103 ISO 14045:2012, Environmental management – Eco-efficiency assessment of product systems – Principles, requirements and guidelines.

10 The International Law Commission work on MFN clauses – a worthwhile venture

Kevin R. Gray[1]

Introduction

MFN (Most Favoured Nation) clauses have been a constant in international economic agreements for over 2000 years, guiding the relations between States by ensuring that no discrimination is afforded based on the origin of a good or service or the nationality of an investor.

The MFN obligation straddles an uneasy line between being a treaty provision appearing in thousands of international treaties and one that evinces a general principle of international law having normative status. The obligation is a manifestation of the international law principle of non-discrimination. In fact, MFN has been identified as the flip side to non-discrimination – the basis underscoring trade liberalization.[2] MFN purports to ensure fairness and prevent discrimination in the marketplace. By doing so, it sets the groundwork for a predictable business environment opening up opportunities for economic actors worldwide.

Yet, MFN obligations in international economic agreements arguably contain enough exceptions and derogations to deprive them of normative value. For instance, bilateral and regional trade agreements are founded on the derogation from existing multilateral MFN obligations so that more favourable treatment can be afforded to the goods and services of the parties to the agreements than what is provided to other trading partners. The World Trade Organization (WTO) permits such a derogation based on prescribed criteria restricting its usage, yet the importance of MFN obligations, and indeed the status of MFN as a principle under the multilateral trading system, is weakened when WTO members can exempt themselves from such obligations by entering into preferential trade agreements. This can potentially discount MFN's standing as a principle of international law.

Irrespective of the international law status of MFN, its operative importance in trade and investment agreements cannot be overstated. This is reflected in the boundless number of disputes addressing MFN claims. The resulting opportunities for international tribunals to interpret the scope and meaning of MFN clauses have cultivated its development in international law.

However, such clauses have not been interpreted consistently by dispute settlement bodies. That can be partially explained, at least in the investment law context, by the ad hoc nature of investor-State arbitration, where jurisdiction is limited to examining an MFN obligation in the context of a bilateral investment agreement (or an investment chapter to a trade agreement). Arbitral tribunals are not bound by previous jurisprudence on MFN clauses and lack any multilateral institutional backdrop (such as the WTO) that upholds the MFN obligation as a key principle. In contrast, WTO panels and the Appellate Body have interpreted MFN obligations consistently, based in part on valuing its critical importance for the international trading system.

In investment law, delineating the scope and meaning of MFN obligations has presented new challenges. Arbitration rulings have imported more favourable treatment guaranteed under other treaties into the MFN provision found in the agreement between the Parties. Consequently, more favourable rights are accorded to investors than is provided for in the treaty to which their home State is a party, regardless of any link that investor may have with the State which is party to the other treaty. This has gone beyond the substantive protections accorded to investors by a State under the other treaty to include procedural rules which can result in broadening the jurisdiction of an arbitration panel beyond what is stipulated in the original treaty.

In the light of the regular appearance of MFN provisions in international trade and, increasingly, investment agreements, and the emerging concern over the conflicting judicial interpretations of such clauses in the latter, the International Law Commission (ILC) has decided to (re)take up the issue of the MFN obligation. Following a draft set of Articles that was never adopted in the 1970s, the ILC has returned its attention to MFN.

A need to review MFN clauses is clearly warranted. Whether the ILC is well-suited for the task will be addressed in this chapter. I will first examine the ILC as an international law-making body. The chapter will then explore the MFN obligation, attempting to characterise it and determine its status in international law. A brief assessment of the role of MFN clauses in international trade and investment agreements and the associated problems with their application in those types of agreements follows, before addressing the previous experience of the ILC with the MFN topic. I argue that the ever-presence of MFN clauses in trade and investment agreements lends special importance to MFN. Further, the risks of disharmonious interpretation of MFN clauses profoundly demand greater attention by an international body that is divorced from specific disputes. The potential for fragmentation provides additional justification for the ILC's work.

The ILC

The ILC is once again undertaking an analysis of the MFN clause. A better understanding of the ILC and how it contributes to the development of international law will inform our understanding of how the ILC can address controversial topics such as MFN.

The ILC was established in 1949, in the aftermath of World War II, contemporaneous with the creation of the United Nations and the International Court of

Justice. The ILC comprises 34 individual members, representing designated regions of the world. The membership includes government officials, international law specialists in academia and members of the judiciary. Some commentators have viewed the geographical and professional diversity of the ILC as beneficial to the examination of various international law issues, offsetting the predominant influence States have in the development of international law.[3] The diverse backgrounds of ILC members can neutralize any bias – professional or national – that an individual member may have.

At the time of its inception, the ILC became a relevant source for the development of international law as the majority of international law was uncodified and thus based on customary international law.[4] Even today, international courts look to ILC studies to uncover the State practice needed to ascertain the existence of customary international law.[5]

The objective of the ILC is to promote the progressive development of international law and its codification.[6] Its work has led to several prominent international treaties (e.g. the Vienna Convention on the Law of Treaties).[7] The ILC also identifies state practice that can lead to the recognition of new customary international law.[8] Sixty years since the ILC's formation, international law has proliferated, as evidenced by the exponential growth in the number of treaties, along with the increasing number of dispute settlement bodies that interpret such instruments. Thus a question currently plaguing the ILC is whether it remains relevant. As much of the international law lacunae from 1949 no longer exists, the 'field open for new initiatives has considerably shrunk'.[9] Moreover, as public international law has become more technical and touches upon specific subject areas, the range of 'general' international law topics has diminished.[10]

The fact that much international law is now codified in treaties does not necessarily undermine the significance of the ILC. In some cases, the growing complexity of international law can establish a need to manage the related complications. Treaty provisions can be misinterpreted or raise new problems for international lawyers that were not anticipated at the time of their drafting. Moreover, the proliferation of treaties can also lead to conflicting jurisprudence on similarly drafted provisions covering the same obligation. The ILC may be better suited to undertake sober analyses of such problems, including those relating to MFN clauses, than dispute settlement bodies whose analytical freedom might be restricted by the facts and arguments before them.

Powers of the ILC

Article 23 of the *ILC Statute* permits the ILC to recommend to the UN General Assembly a draft instrument with a view to the conclusion of a convention or to convoke a conference to conclude a convention. In practice, only a few draft instruments have become conventions. The last ILC initiative that led to an international convention was the *Vienna Convention on the Succession of Treaties*,[11] following the fruits of other ILC work such as the *United Nations Convention on the Law of the Sea*[12] and the *VCLT*.[13]

Although a treaty is the most tangible way for the ILC's work to be relevant, other instruments such as draft articles or even ILC Reports can indirectly contribute to the development of international law. A treaty is arguably not the best outcome for the development of international law in every area. Tomouschat posits that an international treaty may be more useful where there is a lacuna in the law. However, a series of guiding principles or another type of soft law instrument may be more effective where the topic is politically controversial or where non-legal expertise is needed.[14] Non-binding instruments may also be more useful than an international treaty resulting from a massive compromise between States, thus watering down the purpose and intent of the ILC's initial work.[15] Consequently, ILC Rapporteurs may deliberately refrain from submitting ILC Draft Articles to a diplomatic conference, as the optimal outcome in the drafting of an ILC instrument could be compromised if it is submitted to a political body.[16]

Despite not having formal status as a source of international law under Article 38 of the *Statute of the International Court of Justice*,[17] ILC Draft Articles can still reflect what is international law when international courts and tribunals refer to them in their judgments or if States adopt aspects of them in their state practice.[18]

What the General Assembly will do with the ILC instruments is uncertain when the ILC commences its work. One result could be simply to take note of Draft Articles and/or inviting States to take them into account.[19] When the General Assembly takes note of Draft Articles, although not necessarily adopting them, it 'simply confirms that the work carried out by one of its subsidiary bodies has not been useless and that the task entrusted to it has been finalized'.[20] The ILC may also issue reports and declarations or set out guidelines and principles all of which may take on some importance as 'soft law'.[21] Examples of this include the *Declaration on the Rights and Duties of States*;[22] the ILC Draft Model on Arbitral Procedure[23] and the ILC Draft Articles on Nationality of Natural Persons in Relation to the Succession of States adopted by the ILC in 1999. In the last case, the ILC did not advocate for the conclusion of an international convention but recommended that the Draft Articles be adopted by the General Assembly as a declaration.

Historically, the ILC has been a useful body in further developing the understanding of international law in particular areas. The results of its work may vary from draft conventions to reports but its importance endures. The next section will examine the ILC's history in addressing MFN, and will analyse whether it should now be reconsidered by the ILC.

The ILC and MFN

The frequent appearance of MFN clauses in treaties raised systemic international law concerns about their meaning vis-à-vis non-party States. Being a general treaty issue, the ILC flagged MFN clauses in its work that ultimately led to the codification of the *VCLT*. MFN clauses were eventually hived off the law of treaties study, partially due to an acceptance that they required 'special consideration'.[24] MFN was initially seen as a treaty issue because of the impact MFN clauses had on third parties. Additional treaty aspects emerged during the ILC discussions which transformed the issue into one concerning general international law.[25] In 1966, the ILC agreed that MFN clauses would be an appropriate subject of a future special study.[26]

At the nineteenth session of the ILC in 1967, the MFN clause was placed on the ILC's work programme, followed by a UN General Assembly recommendation that the ILC study the topic.[27] At the 1968 session, the ILC asked the Special Rapporteur, Endre Ustor, to examine MFN not just within the domain of international trade but more broadly in other fields of international law as the scope and effect of it as a 'legal institution' was important.[28] At the outset, the ILC also agreed not to examine the interaction between the operation of MFN clauses and national treatment clauses but only to see how the right to national treatment operates under MFN clauses as well as how MFN and national treatment clauses apply with respect to the same subject matter.[29]

Of note, the ILC decided not to cover various exceptions to MFN clauses, including those for customs unions. This was a divisive issue amongst States in the United Nations 6th Committee and therefore the ILC deferred the decision to address it until a later meeting where the Draft Articles would be considered.

The Draft Articles on MFN Clauses were prepared for the twenty-fifth session of the ILC in 1973. They were adopted on their first reading and then transmitted to the Secretary-General and the UN Member States. The General Assembly welcomed the completion of the first reading of the Draft Articles and recommended that the ILC should conclude a second reading at the next session in light of the comments received from Member States, organs of the United Nations and interested intergovernmental organizations.[30]

The Draft Articles were not finalized until 1976 for the twenty-sixth session of the ILC, although they were subsequently revised in 1978. The penultimate 1978 Draft Articles on MFN Clauses[31] featured several articles defining the scope of the treatment accorded under such clauses as well as how the clauses affected the relationship between the 'granting' State, the 'beneficiary' State and third party States.[32] There are specific articles addressing the legal basis of MFN treatment[33] including the basis of such treatment found in other treaties.[34] Articles 9 and 10 focus on the scope of an MFN clause limited as such to its subject matter therein. Ascertaining the subject matter remains an interpretative challenge for investment arbitration tribunals as discussed below in this chapter. Other articles deal with conditional MFN clauses where the rights are triggered by some type of reciprocal act by the other State.[35] Finally, there are two articles covering the special situation of developing countries in international economic relations, whereby MFN clauses could not be enforced against treaty parties that accord trade preferences to such countries.[36]

At the thirtieth session in 1978, the ILC adopted the Draft Articles, including the Commentaries.[37] The ILC decided, pursuant to Article 23 of the *ILC Statute*, to recommend to the UN General Assembly that the Draft Articles be submitted to the Member States with a view towards concluding a convention. The General Assembly invited comments on the Draft Articles including the recommendation of a convention on four separate occasions,[38] from all States, UN organs having competence on the subject matter and interested intergovernmental organizations. In 1991, the General Assembly confirmed its reluctance to further address the Draft Articles due to the comments received and more generally because 'codification or progressive development of the international law on MFN clauses was a complex matter'.[39] For instance, the European Economic Community (EEC) Member States expressed strong concern about the omission of clauses relating to customs unions and free trade areas from the scope of the Draft Articles. The EEC had an obvious interest in ensuring that the benefits granted to EEC members under the Treaty of Rome[40] would not be jeopardized by any Draft Articles that did not accept customs unions and free trade areas as valid exceptions.[41] The relevance of MFN as a legal issue was diminishing in the light of the advent of more extensive customs unions and free trade areas and individual states' trading preference regimes, as well as the greater attention to MFN clauses from other international organizations (i.e. the OECD and UNCTAD).[42]

As the study of MFN clauses became more complicated over the years of the ILC's work, East-West political factors had always hindered the ILC's efforts from the start. The MFN study was immediately viewed by some ILC Members as being biased due to Special Rapporteurs Ustor and Ushako being from the Union of Soviet Socialist Republics, and thus their interests were seen as mirroring those of socialist States.[43] Other criticisms were directed at the exceptions for customs unions, free trade agreements and generalized system of preferences (GSP) schemes which were seen as being 'unbalanced' favouring the interests of developing countries.[44]

The decision to recommend a treaty may also have contributed to the cessation of the ILC's work on MFN clauses. The inherent disagreement amongst UN members regarding the true motivations for an MFN treaty, coupled with disagreement regarding exceptions for customs unions, free trade agreements and GSP schemes, impeded any consensus. Ultimately, the Draft Articles were never adopted and effectively shelved for future consideration.

Since the conclusion of the Draft Articles, there have been several developments in both the trade and investment fields which have created a new lens through which to view MFN clauses. On the trade side, the creation of the WTO and its near-universal membership displaced the relevance of MFN clauses in bilateral trade agreements. The jurisprudence from the institutionalized WTO dispute settlement system clarified the meaning of MFN obligations found in several WTO agreements. The cases have facilitated a deeper understanding of MFN clauses, including how they operate in practice.

The post-Draft Articles era also witnessed the proliferation of bilateral and regional investment agreements. These new agreements included MFN obligations which were now subject to ad hoc international arbitration procedures such as ICSID and the UNCITRAL Arbitration rules. These developments will be addressed below.

MFN in International Trade Agreements

MFN obligations in international trade agreements ensure equality of opportunity for States to import and export goods and services. Inversely, they aim to 'prohibit discrimination'.[45] Before the creation of the WTO, MFN clauses were included in friendship, commerce and navigation treaties dating back to the eleventh century.[46] They appeared more regularly in the agreements dating from the eighteenth century when States used such clauses as strategic vehicles to enhance their economic relations with some States while marginalizing others by extending MFN treatment only to the former.[47] The use of MFN clauses based on geopolitical objectives ultimately led to the breakdown of international economic relations and the peaceful coexistence of States.

Following World War II, MFN clauses were used to ensure fair treatment for all States and thus foster greater multilateral economic cooperation. States also included MFN clauses in trade treaties as a way to move, at the domestic level, towards reducing tariffs.[48]

By including an MFN obligation in the GATT[49] i.e. a multilateral treaty, States could now obtain MFN commitments from all GATT 1947 Members on an unconditional basis rather than extracting such a commitment from each party under individual bilateral agreements.[50] MFN clauses now appear in a number of different treaties, albeit in various incarnations, that form part of the WTO Agreement, as well as in bilateral and regional free trade agreements. The sheer number of MFN clauses throughout the WTO Agreement gives them a 'pervasive character'.[51] MFN clauses appear in several GATT articles including Article I:1; Article III:7 (dealing with internal mixing requirements); Article IV(b) (dealing with cinema films); Article V:2, 5, 6 (transit of goods); Article IX:1 (marks of origin); and Article XIII:1 (quantitative restrictions).[52]

The prominence of the MFN obligation in the multilateral treaty system is evident in the first article of the GATT 1947. At the time of the negotiations, the United States insisted that its inclusion was 'absolutely fundamental'.[53] The Appellate Body has referred to it as "a principle that has long been a "cornerstone"[54] of the GATT and "one of the pillars of the WTO trading system"'.[55]

MFN obligations are now included in other WTO agreements. They apply to the treatment of services and service providers (General Agreement on Trade in Services Art. II:1),[56] the protection of intellectual property (Agreement on Trade-Related Intellectual Property Rights (*TRIPS*, Article 4), as well as sanitary and phytosanitary measures (Art. 2.3) and technical regulations (Article 2.1).[57] Although the wording of the obligations will vary to some extent, they all stem from the same purpose – not to discriminate on the basis of nationality. Considering the obligation is found in a number of interacting and interdependent agreements within the WTO framework, the object and purpose of the MFN obligation perhaps has more influence on how the obligation is interpreted rather than the precise wording of the MFN clause.[58]

In the light of its prevalence and how it has been described as being a 'cornerstone' and 'fundamental', MFN has achieved normative status in the trade context. Of course, there are a number of exceptions to the MFN obligation, including measures that accord preferential treatment to certain WTO Members that are parties to free trade agreements or customs unions (pursuant to GATT Article XXIV or GATS Article V), retaliatory measures sanctioned by the Dispute Settlement Body or even anti-dumping and countervailing duties. The breadth of these exceptions might suggest that the MFN obligation may be more the exception than the rule, or at least a rule of limited application.

Yet the availability of exceptions for States to a rule in international law does not necessarily affect its status. For instance, the prohibition of the use of force has been recognized as being a *jus cogens* norm by the International Court of Justice.[59] This is so despite the number of instances where the use of force would be justified. Although MFN is not necessarily on the same plane as a peremptory international law norm, the ability to derogate from an obligation for delineated purposes does not deprive MFN its normative value to ensure non-discrimination. It can have a directed and limited purpose such as remedying WTO violations or addressing historical economic imbalances amongst States in the international trading system by promoting regional economic development. Exceptions from MFN obligations are also permitted for the granting of better treatment in regional trade agreements or customs unions.[60] This enhances the liberalization of trade between particular WTO Members and, in principle, can lead to the lowering of such barriers for all WTO Members – the purported aim of MFN clauses – once such commitments are made at the multilateral level.

Ensuring that WTO Members can act consistently with both bilateral and regional trade agreements as well as its multilateral WTO obligations is a difficult task. Special attention is needed to ensure compatibility of all of a party's MFN obligations and to pre-empt any possible conflicts. The ILC, in its 1978 Report, recognized the potential variance in approaches by WTO Members in their bilateral and regional trade agreements and thus noted the need to undertake some analytical work to compare how WTO Members respect their WTO MFN obligations in their regional and bilateral trade agreements.

However, this variance has not been a topic in the discussions of the current ILC Working Group on MFN Clauses, perhaps due to its greater focus on investment agreements and the more widely accepted practice of States to enter into bilateral and regional trade agreements. Chairman McRae expressed some concern over how WTO parties could claim MFN benefits provided by one WTO Member to another pursuant to a free trade agreement or other agreement concerning a customs union.[61] According to McRae, the majority of tariffs today are not applied on an MFN basis – the rates are set in free trade agreements and customs unions. Nonetheless, the Working Group did not see any reason for the ILC to consider undertaking a codification or progressive development exercise in respect of the WTO's interaction with customs unions and free trade agreements (Article XXIV) and the related WTO jurisprudence.

MFN in international investment agreements

MFN clauses in international investment agreements are currently controversial and thus have become worthy of the ILC's renewed attention. While MFN obligations under the WTO Agreement have been consistently interpreted by WTO panels and the Appellate Body, the same cannot be said for their counterparts in international investment agreements.

In interpreting MFN obligations under the WTO Agreement, dispute settlement panels and the Appellate Body are discharged with settling disputes and maintaining the fairness in the economic relations between the Parties. They are part of a permanent system which aims to preserve the treaty's multilateral benefits. Thus, there is a vested interest in ensuring that WTO requirements are met by the parties.

By contrast, the MFN obligation in an investment treaty is only one of a number of non-hierarchical obligations that provide protection for an investor. Investment treaties are also instruments that are interpreted according to their unique objects and purposes unlike the WTO Agreement which is one treaty to which there are a large number of parties founded on the principle of non-discrimination. MFN does not have the same prominence in investment treaties and therefore the adjudicators of investment disputes may not see an underlying systemic interest behind MFN obligations. Investor-State arbitration tribunals are only tasked with a role to determine violations based on a particular situation affecting an investor.[62] Further, there is a lesser need to ensure interpretative consistency within a particular legal regime. In the absence of any institutionalized dispute settlement system in investment law which, at least implicitly, aims to ensure consistency in its jurisprudence, MFN clauses are subject to the vagaries of ad hoc arbitral panels, none of which is under any compulsion to follow the decisions of other panels.[63]

MFN also needs to be understood in its multilateral treaty context as an obligation that is owed to all Parties, despite the limited number of Parties to a dispute. Under the WTO Agreement, MFN clauses apply multilaterally to guarantee access to the marketplace and thus preserve equal competitive opportunities for all imported goods and services regardless of their origin. The objective, being economic in nature, aims to improve the overall welfare for WTO Members and lock in trade liberalization gains (i.e. tariff reductions).[64] If such an obligation appears in a bilateral treaty, the interpretation of MFN may differ when considering the object and purpose of the treaty.[65]

MFN clauses in investment agreements share the same function as in trade agreements, i.e. prohibiting discrimination. They sanction discriminatory treatment against investors, and investments, of one party. However, they are designed to protect the rights of one particular investor from being discriminated against or otherwise subject to unfair treatment. The focus is on addressing the grievances arising from a particular circumstance rather than ensuring an institutional need for equality among parties. MFN clauses in investment agreements do not purport to preserve competitive economic conditions.[66]

The contextual difference between MFN clauses, depending on the type of agreements in which they appear (i.e. trade or investment treaties), can lead to situations where the competitive relationship between products and services is maintained but a particular investor or investment could still be subject to less favourable treatment than that accorded to investors or investments of other States.[67] MFN clauses were incorporated into investment treaties to address any discriminatory treatment between investors or investments – treatment that still might be consistent with the minimum standard of treatment obligations.[68]

A violation of the MFN obligation is normally triggered by the action of a State – that is, how it treats foreign investors and investments in practice, including through domestic measures. However, the violations thereof can also result from treatment provided to a third party State in another agreement that raises different issues in international law. A standard of treatment stipulated in one treaty can be applied to another in the absence of any privity between the investors of one party, and the third State party. Of course, this would make sense when a multilateral treaty with an MFN obligation replaces a series of bilateral treaties that include the same obligation.[69] In the absence of a multilateral treaty, the extension of MFN treatment stemming from another instrument has the same effect.

An interpretation of MFN clauses that allows for rights and obligations from other treaties to inform the content of the MFN obligation challenges the international legal principle of *pacta tetriis nec nocent nec prosunant* – 'treaties produce effects only as between the contracting parties'. Article 36(1) of the VCLT codifies this legal rule, stating that a treaty cannot create third party rights where the third party State has not assented to it. Therefore, a party to an investment treaty cannot in principle agree to a different scope of treatment (provided in another treaty) than what is contained in the original treaty unless it has agreed to this. It is problematic to assert that a party, if agreeing to a MFN clause in a particular treaty, is also consenting – as a condition to that obligation – to provide the best treatment it provides under all of the investment treaties it has with other States. Nevertheless, this is arguably what MFN clauses, at least in those investment treaties, are designed to do.

Of concern is that investor-State arbitration tribunals are now looking to other investment treaties as providing a basis to extend MFN treatment not just to the substantive benefits granted to an investor of another country but also to the more favourable dispute settlement provisions in another treaty relating to jurisdiction of an investor-State tribunal or the procedural guarantees in relation to dispute settlement.[70] The first case which sparked the controversy of looking to other treaties to delineate the scope of an MFN obligation in relation to dispute settlement was *Maffezini v Spain*.[71] This ruling deviated from the traditional view expressed by the International Court of Justice in the *Anglo-Iranian Oil Co. (Preliminary Objection)* case, in which the Court held, in respecting the privity rule in treaties, that the source of rights under an MFN clause is the treaty between the Parties.[72] Such reasoning was endorsed by the International Law Commission in the 1978 Draft Articles on the Most-Favoured-Nation Clause.[73]

Maffezini, however, and some of the cases decided after it, found MFN violations due to more preferential dispute settlement procedural rights being given to other foreign investors in another treaty.[74] In so doing, the terms describing the subject matter governed by the MFN clauses[75] in question have been interpreted widely to include matters relating to more favourable dispute settlement provisions such as the minimum time before invoking the investor-State arbitration process or a broader jurisdiction over the issues before the tribunal. One tribunal has even interpreted the MFN provision to include a type of claim allowed in another investment treaty that is not explicitly permitted in the treaty giving the tribunal its jurisdiction.[76] Thus, the third party treaty that provides for more favourable provisions to litigate the investor's rights and interests in the basic treaty, can be extended to the investor whose rights are only set out in the treaty to which their State is a party.[77]

Other cases have swung the other way, revealing a more narrow interpretation of MFN clauses that only extend the obligation to substantive rights that are given to all investors by the host State but not to procedural matters.[78] The tribunals have closely scrutinized the wording of the subject matter of the clauses – an arguably more difficult task in the context of MFN treatment accorded to investors or investments than the finite subject matters (i.e. 'goods' or 'services') in trade agreement MFN provisions.[79]

The recent spate of cases taking different approaches to the legal interpretation of MFN clauses has touched off debate about the broader role of MFN clauses, and whether they should play a 'multilateralizing role' that aims to ensure universal treatment to, and thus no discrimination against, any foreign investor in a host State, irrespective of whether an MFN obligation exists in a bilateral treaty between two parties.[80] Thus, an MFN clause can serve as a de facto multilateral agreement on MFN relating to investment in that most favourable treatment can be found in any investment agreement to which the host State is a party.

Some tribunals have raised similar existential questions about MFN clauses. For instance, the tribunal in *Renta* noted that 'the extension of commitments is in the very nature of MFN clauses'.[81] However, there is a danger that the MFN provisions may override, and thus establish a hierarchy over, other investment treaty provisions including ones that delineate the investor-State tribunal jurisdiction.[82] The inconsistencies in the jurisprudence have led to some thinking that institutional changes are needed, such as the creation of an appeals mechanism for investment law in order to ensure some uniformity in the jurisprudence.[83]

The ILC and MFN redux

After a 15-year hiatus, the MFN topic was resurrected at the ILC in 2007. At the 59th Session, the ILC considered a discussion paper prepared by Don McRae (Canada) and Rohan Perera (Sri Lanka) and concluded that it could play a useful role in clarifying the meaning and effect of the MFN clause in the field of investment agreements.[84] MFN was added to the long-term agenda of the Commission.

The ILC established a formal Study Group, with the discussion paper authors to serve as Co-Chairs. The Study Group had already conducted a preliminary assessment of the 1978 Draft Articles and agreed to submit eight papers to the ILC that would deal with specific MFN issues.[85]

The work of the Special Rapporteurs was commissioned despite some States at the UN 6th Committee expressing reservations about further MFN work. In particular, some were apprehensive about tackling the MFN topic because such clauses can vary in scope and meaning to be based entirely on their wording and the context of the treaties that contain them. The scope of such clauses, even if the wording is similar, can be modified by the context of the treaty as well as its object and purpose. Other criticisms were directed to whether the ILC should rejuvenate its efforts on MFN clauses, questioning how much further the ILC could go, considering the failed outcome of its earlier efforts.

The strongest impetus for further ILC work was the concern over the increase in differing interpretations of MFN clauses by arbitration panels. The differences in interpretative approaches were highlighted in a paper prepared by Don McRae, Co-Chair of the ILC Study Group.[86] This paper attempted to deconstruct the jurisprudence looking at whether interpreting MFN clauses is a general matter of treaty interpretation or a matter of interpretation of the jurisdiction of the tribunal. It addressed the question whether dispute settlement is part of MFN treatment, as some tribunals demanded that 'clear and unambiguous'[87] evidence is needed to demonstrate an intention of the parties that procedural rights have been incorporated within the scope of an MFN clause.[88] In reflecting on this approach, McRae noted that there has not been a 'systematic approach to interpretation that is uniform across tribunals and different factors appear to influence different tribunals'.[89]

In addition, McRae noted that some tribunals have inquired whether MFN provisions should be interpreted differently than other provisions in investment agreements. In other words, such clauses should be interpreted more restrictively due to the consequences of extending a tribunal's jurisdiction beyond what is provided for in the treaty. The need for a higher burden to justify the extension of the MFN clause to procedural and dispute settlement matters has been rejected by more recent investment tribunals despite the support of some commentators. In light of this development, McRae argued that further consideration of the matter by the ILC was warranted.

The absence of a 'consistent approach in the reasoning of tribunals'[90] concerning the interpretation of MFN clauses in investor-State disputes has created an unsettling environment for both States and investors. Some States have modified the MFN clauses in such a way as to explicitly exclude dispute settlement procedures from the scope of the MFN obligation.[91] This uncertainty has even pitted arbitrators on the same panel against each other. In a strong dissenting opinion in a case where the majority of the panel permitted the investor to invoke the dispute settlement provisions of another treaty,[92] Argentina's nominee to the tribunal, Professor Brigitte Stern, vociferously argued against this use of the MFN clause. She argued that investors should not be allowed to import more favourable dispute settlement provisions from other investment treaties, unless, in accordance with the clear and unambiguous evidence standard developed by previous tribunals, the MFN clause in the treaty in question expressly provides that its scope extends to provisions governing dispute settlement.[93] In principle, Professor Stern argued that MFN clauses cannot import a dispute settlement mechanism from another treaty as this is 'linked with the essence of international law'.[94]

Should the ILC address MFN?

Particularly with regard to international investment law, this chapter has identified considerable uncertainty over the meaning and application of MFN clauses. Lack of clarity in international law alone can warrant an ILC endeavour into new subject matter. However, as history has indicated, the ILC has failed to resolve many of the quandaries plaguing the MFN issue to the satisfaction of States. Why would a second kick at the can yield a different result?

As mentioned, MFN clauses are pervasive in both international trade and investment agreements. The extant differences of opinion regarding the interpretation of MFN clauses multiplied by the number of them in the accelerating number of trade and investment agreements justifiably place MFN within the ambit of the ILC's work. The varying and sometimes conflicting interpretations warrant, at a minimum, further assessment about whether MFN clauses require greater clarification. As an area of law whose goal posts seem to be shifting, the ILC seems to be an appropriate forum for this.

Disagreements between international lawyers that are now manifest in the decisions of tribunals involving high stakes issues – i.e. government regulatory freedom and protecting investor rights, both of which affect the freedoms and protections for individual citizens, do a disservice to the development of international law. Fragmentation in the meaning and application of MFN clauses ensues. An area of law that is prone to fragmentation provides ample support for continual ILC attention. One can look to the ILC Report *Fragmentation in International Law* to appreciate how such fragmentation can unsettle the coherence in international law.[95] The results of the ILC's study of MFN, without prejudicing the outcome of its work (i.e. a convention, draft articles, report), which might include codification of some principles and a related taxonomy of MFN clauses, can provide useful guidance to dispute settlement bodies. This may also be useful for States when drafting MFN clauses in future agreements.

Further, MFN is an obligation that resonates more than its wording might initially appear. MFN clauses represent the lynchpin in international economic relations between States. In trade, MFN clauses provide the 'cornerstone' of international economic relations,[96] being the key obligation rooted in the international legal norm of non-discrimination. Some have described MFN as the 'great collectivizing mechanism'.[97] Others have identified it as a 'regime norm'.[98] It thus can be argued that MFN constitutes a principle of international economic law within the realm of customary international law.[99] Notwithstanding any disagreement on its status outside of conventional law, MFN is an obligation that pervades both international trade and investment law. This instils MFN with salient transcendental value, worthy of further examination by the ILC.

The ILC should therefore continue to examine MFN. Of course, future work should not be seen as a panacea to problems such as fragmentation. What States do with ILC output is still subject to the decision-making of States. Any outcome that might prejudice the interpretation of MFN clauses in existing international agreements may not be desirable. However, the output from the ILC can at least assist States in drafting MFN clauses with more predictable results. Further, it might represent a neutral instrument providing guidance to international lawyers who sit on arbitral and dispute settlement panels.

As international trade and investment agreements continue to proliferate, lack of clarity in the meaning of provisions that appear in such instruments raises systemic concerns. Provisions such as MFN clauses, which aim to be the great equalizer in international economic law guarding against the forces of protectionism and discrimination, demand precision. MFN's prominence is more critical in the face of current economic uncertainty, compounded by the failure to liberalize trade under the multilateral trading system, and the parallel growth of bilateral and regional trading agreements, most of which deviate from MFN obligations in multilateral treaties.

Epilogue

At the 319th Meeting of the ILC on 8 August 2011, the Chairpersons of the MFN Study Group presented an oral report. The focus of the Study Group was on the MFN Clauses in Investment Agreements paper that was prepared by Don McRae.[100] Within the Study Group, there were divergent views about the proper approach needed in interpreting MFN clauses.[101] However, there was unanimity in agreeing that future work was needed in the light of the potential that, in interpreting MFN clauses, the 'overall equilibrium of an investment agreement between the protection of the investor and its investment and the necessary policy space of a host State' would be upset.[102] Moreover, there was a general understanding that MFN clauses should not function as an exception to the privity rule in treaty interpretation. Further study should be taken on how to interpret MFN clauses when the MFN clause neither expressly includes nor excludes treatment in relation to dispute settlement provisions (including requirements to seek domestic remedies) within the scope of the MFN treatment.

Thus, the Study Group will be attempting to assess the theoretical framework behind the differing interpretative approaches and reasoning in the arbitral tribunal decisions. This includes whether other factors are missing in a proper analysis of MFN clauses in investment agreements, including the point raised by Brigette Stern in *Impregilo S.p.A*, that the first part of the inquiry should be whether the investor or the investment met the relevant terms and conditions under the treaty which would allow it to have access and thus benefit from the MFN treatment in question. In addition, the Chairs will also turn their attention to the *VCLT* to determine, at least at the outset, the meaning of MFN clauses, including an inquiry into the intention of the parties, regarding the scope of such clauses.

The Study Group expects to finish its work in 2013. It has declared that it will not prepare draft articles. Instead, a draft report will be prepared 'providing the general background, analysing and contextualizing the case law, drawing attention to the issues that had arisen and trends in the practice and, where appropriate, make recommendations, including model clauses'.[103] According to the Chairpersons' Statement, an underlying motivation for the future work was to 'safeguard against fragmentation of international law by assuring the importance of greater coherence in the approaches taken in the arbitral decisions'.[104] Thus, the Study Group 'could make a contribution towards assuring greater certainty and stability in the field of investment law' and 'that the efforts should strive at preparing an outcome that would be of practical utility to those involved in the investment field and to policy makers'.[105] Guided by these dictates, the Study Group will be gearing its work towards an outcome that does not necessarily look to ending the debate on MFN clauses but towards infusing some clarity and cohesion to an area of international law that has been splintered through disparate endeavours in treaty interpretation.

Notes

1 The author is a doctoral candidate at the University of Ottawa, Faculty of Law. He is also counsel at the Trade Law Bureau, Government of Canada. He would like to thank Professor Don McRae and Professor Meredith Kolsky Lewis for their helpful comments on this chapter. All views expressed in this chapter are solely those of the author and do not represent any positions of the Government of Canada.
2 Australia Government Productivity Commission 2010.
3 Tomouschat 2006: 81.
4 Tomouschat 2006: 81.
5 For a recent example, see *Jurisdictional Immunities of the State (Germany v Italy; Greece Intervening)* 2012: 24.
6 Statute of the International Law Commission, GA Res. 174(II) of 21 November 1947 (ILC Statute), Art. 1(1).
7 (1969) 8 ILM 679.
8 Shaw 2008.
9 Tomouschat 2006: 78.
10 Tomouschat 2006: 83.
11 (1978) 17 ILM 1488.
12 (1982) 21 ILM 1261.
13 Tomouschat 2006: 92.
14 Tomouschat 2006: 101.
15 See Wood 2008: 373–88; See also Tomoushat 2006: 83.
16 This was the case with the *ILC Draft Articles on State Responsibility 1996*, Chapter 3. See Tomouschat 2006: 96.
17 Bevans 1179; 59 Stat. 1031; T.S. 993; 39 AJIL Supp. 215 (1945).
18 The WTO Appellate Body has repeatedly found that the *ILC Draft Articles on State Responsibility* reflect the codification of customary international law. For instance, see *US – Gambling*, Appellate Body Report, United States – Measures Affecting the Cross-Border Supply of Gambling and Betting Services, WT/DS285/AB/R, adopted

20 April 2005. See also the judgment in *Bosnia and Herzegovina v Serbia and Montenegro* 2007 at para. 385, where the International Court of Justice found that Article 4 of the *ILC Draft Articles* reflects customary international law. In Appellate Body Report, *United States – Definitive Anti-Dumping and Countervailing Duties on Certain Products from China*, WT/DS379/AB/R, adopted 25 March 2011, the Appellate Body clarified that the ILC Draft Rules on State Responsibility was an instrument that should be 'taken into account' pursuant to Article 31(3)(c) of the VCLT as being one of several interpretative elements of Article 1.1(a)(1) of the Agreement on Subsidies and Countervailing Measures.

19 See, for example, GA Res. 55/153 of 12 December 2000, where the General Assembly 'took note' of the ILC Draft Articles on the Nationality of Natural Persons in Relation to Succession of States. The General Assembly 'took note' of ILC Draft Articles on State Responsibility for the first time in GA Res. 56/83 of 12 December 2001.

20 Tomouschat 2006: 96.

21 Tomouschat 2006: 93.

22 GA Res. 178 (II) of 21 Nov. 1947.

23 Adopted in 1958.

24 Watts 1999: 1793.

25 See Murase 2010.

26 *Yearbook of the International Law Commission 1966 Vol. II*, p. 177, para. 32.

27 GA Res. 2272 (XXII) of 1 December 1967.

28 A/CN.4/L.127, para. 161. See also *Most-Favoured-Nation Clause*, A/CN.4/L.719, 20 July 2007 at p. 6. Other fields included MFN clauses as they related to treaties concerning diplomatic protection and consular relations.

29 A/CN.4/L.127.

30 Resolution 31/97. See also resolution 32/151.

31 Draft Articles on Most-Favoured-Nation Clauses with Commentaries 1978.

32 Arts. 1–6.

33 Art. 7.

34 Art. 8.

35 Arts. 11–15, 20(2–3) and 21 (2–3).

36 Art. 23–24.

37 Draft Articles on Most-Favoured-Nation Clauses with Commentaries 1978. Additional articles were proposed by individual ILC members at that meeting including ones dealing with MFN clauses related to arrangements between developing countries, commodities agreements and MFN clauses between members of a customs union.

38 These were made at the 35th, 36th, 38th and 40th sessions.

39 Watts 1999: 1795.

40 Treaty Establishing the European Economic Community, 25 March 1957, 298 U.N.T.S. 3.

41 See *Most-Favoured-Nation Clause*, A/CN.4/L.719, 20 July 2007 at 7. The Working Group also noted that the articles on generalized systems of preferences (GSP) were also controversial as many States differed on the legal consequences arising from the debate over the New International Economic Order. Murase 2010: 14 suggests that the Articles on GSP went beyond the ILC's mandate, which is to deal with matters of codification and the progressive development of international law but not extend to new rulemaking.

42 Watts 1999: 1795.

43 See Tomoushcat 2006.

44 Murase 2010: 3.

45 Appellate Body Report, *Canada – Certain Measures Affecting the Automotive Industry*, WT/DS139/AB/R, WT/DS142/AB/R, adopted 19 June 2000, para. 84 [hereinafter 'Appellate Body Report, *Canada – Autos*'].

46 See Vesel 2007: 128–9.
47 Pahre 2001: 873 notes that MFN clauses were used by France in their commercial treaties with independent states in the Americas in order to isolate Great Britain from the rest of Europe.
48 Pahre 2001: 879.
49 General Agreement on Tariffs and Trade (1949) 55 UNTS 194; 61 Stat. pt. 5; TIAS 1700.
50 See McRae 2011a.
51 Appellate Body Report, *Canada – Autos*, para. 82.
52 Appellate Body Report, *European Communities – Regime for the Importation, Sale and Distribution of Bananas*, WT/DS27/AB/R, adopted 25 September 1997, para. 191, footnote 138 [hereinafter 'Appellate Body Report, *EC – Bananas III*'].
53 See McRae 2011a: 2.
54 See Appellate Body Report, *Canada – Autos*, para. 69. At paragraph 84, the Appellate Body explained that the object and purpose of Article I:1 is 'to prohibit discrimination among like products originating in or destined for different countries'. See also Appellate Body Report, *United States – Section 211 Omnibus Appropriations Act of 1998*, WT/DS176/AB/R, adopted 1 February 2002, para. 297 [hereinafter 'Appellate Body Report, *US – Section 211 Appropriations Act*']. The Appellate Body in *US – Section 211 Appropriations Act* added that MFN treatment under Article I:1 of the GATT is both 'central and essential to assuring the success of a global rules-based system for trade in goods'.
55 Appellate Body Report, *European Communities – Conditions for the Granting of Tariff Preferences to Developing Countries*, WT/DS246/AB/R, adopted 20 April 2004, para. 101 [hereinafter 'Appellate Body Report, *EC – Tariff Preferences*'].
56 In Appellate Body Report, *EC – Bananas III*, para. 231, the Appellate Body noted that the panel interpreted the MFN obligation under Article II of the GATS in the light of panel reports that looked to the national treatment obligations of GATT Article III as well as the national treatment obligation in Article XVII of the GATS. These provisions were found by the Appellate Body to be not necessarily relevant to the interpretation of Article II of the GATS. Alternatively, the Appellate Body concluded that it would have been safer to compare the MFN obligation in Article II with the MFN and MFN-type obligations in GATT 1994.
57 In reference to how the MFN obligation has been one of the cornerstones of the world trading system, the Appellate Body in *US – Section 211 Appropriations Act* saw no reason why the same significance should not be accorded to the MFN obligation in Article 4. Thus, it was seen by the Appellate Body to be 'fundamental'. See Appellate Body Report, *US – Section 211 Appropriations Act*, para. 297.
58 McRae 2011a: 21.
59 *Military and Paramilitary Activities in and Against Nicaragua (Nicaragua v United States of America)* 1986: 90. The ICJ added that where a State acts in a way that is *prima facie* incompatible with a recognized rule but defends itself on the basis of available exceptions or justifications that are part of the rule itself, the significance of this is that the State's conduct confirms rather than weakens the rule. See para. 186.
60 Article XXIV of the GATT.
61 McRae 2011a: 22.
62 DiMascio and Pauwelyn 2008: 59.
63 The link between the multiplicity of international tribunals and the greater potential for inconsistent interpretation of the same international norms is elaborated upon by Romano 2007.
64 DiMascio and Pauwelyn 2008.
65 The basis for such distinction was alluded to in the *EC – Tariffs Preferences* case where the WTO panel gave the term 'unconditionally' in Article I:1 of the GATT its

ordinary meaning rather than viewing the term in the context of 'traditional MFN clauses in bilateral treaties' which 'relate to conditions of trade compensation for receiving MFN treatment'. See Panel Report, *European Communities – Conditions for the Granting of Tariff Preferences to Developing Countries*, WT/DS246/R, adopted 20 April 2004, as modified by Appellate Body Report WT/DS/246/AB/R, paras 759–60. The panel was suggesting that the interpretation of MFN clauses in bilateral agreements may be circumscribed by understanding the nature of bilateral treaties where states negotiate concessions and other benefits in exchange for the concessions and benefits given by the other side. In the multilateral agreement context, agreeing to an MFN obligation may reflect a larger commitment to equal treatment with fewer restrictions.

66 In the *Methanex* case, in reference to the term 'like circumstances', forming the basis of comparison in determining whether the national treatment obligation (or MFN for that matter) has been violated, the arbitral panel stated that the provisions in NAFTA Chapter 11 are about protecting individual investors from injury. The competitive relationship that is the main focus of WTO jurisprudence is therefore not the most important determinant. *Methanex Corp v United States* 2005: 34–7. See also *Occidental Exploration v Ecuador* 2004 and *Pope and Talbot v Canada* 2000.

67 DiMascio and Pauwelyn 2008: 69.

68 See Rubins 2008: 227.

69 In joining the GATT 1947, the bilateral obligation of MFN for parties to friendship, commerce and navigation treaties became multilateral, and thus a GATT party could obtain MFN benefits from all the GATT parties automatically. See McRae 2010: 3.

70 This has been referred to as 'jurisdiction-based MFN'. See Maupin 2011.

71 *Maffezini v Spain* 2002.

72 See *Anglo-Iranian Oil Co. (United Kingdom v Iran)* 1952. The majority of the Court held that the treaty with the third party, which confers rights to the beneficiary state, is independent of and isolated from the basic treaty and therefore cannot produce any legal effect as between the beneficiary state and the granting state – it is *res inter alios acta* (see p. 109).

73 Commentary to Draft Article 8, Draft Articles on Most-Favoured-Nation Clauses with Commentaries, in *Yearbook of the International Law Commission 1978*, vol. 2, part 2 at p. 26.

74 See also *Siemens A.G. v Argentina* 2004; *Gas Natural SDG, S.A. v Argentina* 2005; *National Grid v Argentina* 2006.

75 This is known as the *ejusdem generis* principle: 'general words when following (and sometimes when preceding) special words are limited to the *genus*, if any, indicated by the special words'. See McNair 1961. The principle was recognized by the ICJ Commission of Arbitration in the *Ambatielos* case, stating that MFN clauses can only attract matters belonging to the same category of subject as that to which the clause itself relates (*Ambatielos case (Merits: Obligation to Arbitrate)* 1953: 10). The 1978 ILC Draft Articles addressed how this principle applies to MFN clauses. Article 9(1) limited the benefits of persons or things in a determined relationship under an MFN clause to only those rights that fall within the limits of the subject matter of the clause. Therefore the scope of any MFN clause must be specified in the clause itself or implied from its subject matter (Article 9(2)). In turn, the granting State must extend MFN treatment to the third State treatment only what is within the limits of the subject matter of the MFN clause (Article 10(1)) – that is the same category of persons and same relationship with the beneficiary state as having with third State.

76 See *Ros Invest v Russian Federation* 2007.

77 *Maffezini v Spain* 2002: 56.

78 For example, *Plama v Bulgaria* 2005. See also *Technicas Medioambientales Tecmed*

S.A. v Mexico 2003; *Salini Construttori S.p.A. and Italstrade S.p.A. v Jordan* 2004; *Telenor Mobile Communications A.S. v Hungary* 2006; *Berschader v Russia* 2006.

79 Murase 2010: 8.
80 Schill 2009a: 56–8. The same author in his book argues that investor-State arbitration tribunals which interpret and apply the MFN clauses have therefore the potential to contribute to multilateral law-making. See Schill 2009b: 22.
81 *Renta 4 S.V.S.A et al. v Russian Federation* 2009: para 92.
82 McRae 2011b: 16.
83 See Gantz 2006; McRae 2010.
84 ILC Working Group on MFN Clauses (2007).
85 McRae (2010) 'Catalogue of MFN Provisions'; Murase (2010) 'The 1978 Draft Articles of the International Law Commission'; McRae (2010) 'The Relationship between MFN and National Treatment'; McRae (2010) 'MFN in the GATT and the WTO'; Vasciannie (2010) 'The Work of UNCTAD on MFN'; Hmoud (2010) 'The Work of OECD on MFN'; Perera (2010) 'The *Maffezini* Problem under Investment Treaties', McRae (2010) 'Regional Economic Integration Agreements and Free Trade Agreements'. These papers are informal working documents available from Professor McRae and are on file with the author.
86 McRae 2011b.
87 Paras 198, 204. See also *Telenor Mobile Communications A.S. v Hungary* 2006, and *Wintershall v Argentina* 2008: para. 167. Such an approach was rejected by other tribunals. See *Austria Airlines v Slovakia* 2009; *Suez, et al. v Argentina* 2006.
88 McRae 2011b: 11.
89 McRae 2011b: 12.
90 McRae 2011b: 22.
91 For instance, see Article 4(2) of the Protocol to the Switzerland-Colombia bilateral investment agreement as discussed in Ziegler 2010. See also UNCTAD 2010: 84–7.
92 *Impregilo S.p.A v Argentina* 2011 (Concurring and Dissenting Opinion of Brigitte Stern). The majority ruled that an Italian investor could rely on the MFN clause of the Italy-Argentina bilateral investment treaty in a way that would allow the investor to detour around a requirement in that treaty that investors resort to local courts for a minimum of 18 months before initiating international arbitration and thus rely on a more favourable six-month consultation and waiting period in another treaty.
93 Professor Stern rejected the majority's suggestion that arbitral awards have been near-unanimous in interpreting MFN clauses that refer to 'all matters' covered by a BIT as extending to provisions governing dispute settlement. On her accounting, if one takes into consideration various dissenting opinions and the repeated involvement of some arbitrators in more investor-friendly decisions, arbitral opinion can be viewed as more evenly balanced. In addition, she noted that prior arbitral awards should not be relied on as if they were binding precedents.
94 Para. 16.
95 *Fragmentation on International Law: Difficulties Arising from the Diversification and Expansion of International Law*, A/CN.4/L.682, 13 April 2006.
96 *EC – Tariff Preferences*, WT/DS246/R, adopted 20 April 2004 at para. 101.
97 Carmody 2009: 15.
98 Pahre 2001: 873.
99 The ILC in the Commentaries to the 1978 Draft Articles concluded that although MFN clauses are present in many commercial treaties, there is no evidence that MFN has become a rule of customary international law. Supporting this position, the Report referred to the League of Nations Recommendations (Recommendations of the Economic Committee relating to tariff policy and the most-favoured-nation clause (E.805.1933.II.B.1)), stating that treaties are the only foundation for an MFN obligation. See para. 3 at p. 25.
100 McRae 2011a.

101 ILC 2011: Ch. XII, paras 345–62.
102 See Co-Chairmen Statement (2011): 1.
103 ILC (2011): 288.
104 Co-Chairmen Statement (2011).
105 Co-Chairmen Statement (2011).

11 The TRIPS Agreement and cross-retaliation

Susy Frankel[1]

Introduction

Since the formation of the World Trade Organization (WTO) the failure of losing parties to comply with rulings of the Dispute Settlement Body (DSB) has raised many issues. Where a developing country succeeds in a dispute against a developed country there is often no direct economic reason why such a country does not follow the rulings of the DSB. The reason for not following the rulings is often political and so a domestic constituency might, for instance, prevent changing the domestic law which would be required for compliance with the DSB decision. When developed large country WTO members, such as the EU and the US, do not comply with a decision of the DSB, questions arise over the efficacy of the dispute settlement system. After all, the EU and the US have repeatedly told the developing world that a rules-based dispute settlement system is important. Developing countries and especially small developing countries may question that importance if developed countries use their relative positions of power to not follow the rules.

Does non-compliance put the future of effective dispute settlement in doubt? So far that does not seem to be the situation, but non-compliance has arguably led to innovative approaches to potential retaliation for that non-compliance and that in turn has led to calls for changes to the dispute settlement system.

From a legal perspective non-compliance with the DSB raises issues particularly about the interpretation of Article 22 of the Dispute Settlement Understanding (DSU).[2] This provides the means by which winning parties in disputes can enforce the rulings of the DSB. One mode of enforcement is suspension of concessions, including suspension of concessions under one agreement when another agreement has been breached. This is known as cross-retaliation. This chapter analyses the remedy of cross-retaliation under the TRIPS Agreement.[3] The purpose of cross-retaliation under TRIPS (and indeed other WTO enforcement remedies) is often said to be to induce compliance with DSB rulings.[4] In three arbitrations regarding non-compliance of the unsuccessful party the arbitrator has allowed the successful complaining party to cross-retaliate under the TRIPS Agreement. These disputes are *European Communities – Regime for the Importation, Sale and Distribution of Bananas (EC – Bananas III);*[5] *United*

States – Measures Affecting the Cross-Border Supply of Gambling and Betting Services (US – Gambling)[6] and *United States – Subsidies on Upland Cotton (US – Upland Cotton)*.[7]

Ecuador never exercised the cross-retaliation that the arbitration panel had in principle authorised in *EC – Bananas III*. Rather it appeared to use the potential of cross-retaliation as a lever to negotiate settlement with the EC. The proposed retaliation involved detailed suspension of certain copyright interests, which may be more economically feasible to suspend than patent rights because of the relative ease by which copyright goods can be reproduced or made available online.[8]

In *US – Upland Cotton* Brazil came very close to exercising the cross-retaliation. Brazil was authorised to retaliate against the US under TRIPS for breaches of the Agreement on Subsidies and Countervailing Measures (SCM).[9] This threat of cross-retaliation was particularly interesting and most probably effective in leading to a settlement because of Brazil's economic capacity to cross-retaliate. This economic capacity included its pharmaceutical industry and the possibility that cross-retaliation could be directed towards US-owned pharmaceutical patents. It is perhaps for that reason that soon after the WTO arbitrators authorised cross-retaliation of specific intellectual property rights, including identified patents, the US moved quickly to settle the dispute.

Most recently the DSB has authorised Antigua and Barbuda (Antigua) to retaliate against the US for the US's failure to comply with the rulings of the DSB regarding the GATS online gambling dispute.[10] At the time of writing the US seems less motivated to settle that dispute, even though the amount authorised is relatively small (no more than US$21 million on an annual basis), given the wealth of the US. It seems likely that the US is not inclined to pay up or respond to such threats because it may be seen as encouraging TRIPS cross-retaliation and Antigua is, compared with Brazil, not likely to be able to have a significant impact on the US economy. Such a conclusion, however, is necessarily speculative.

This chapter will first review the concept of suspending intellectual property concessions generally. It is probably more accurate to describe such a suspension as suspending TRIPS obligations from the state perspective and suspending intellectual property rights from the right holders' perspective. The chapter then outlines the rules relating to cross-retaliation and discusses each of the arbitrations that have allowed cross-retaliation and issues arising from those disputes.

Overall it seems clear that cross-retaliation has taken a course different from that which was anticipated when it was negotiated in the Uruguay Round leading to the formation of the WTO. The often stated reason for including the possibility for cross-retaliation in the DSU was that the US thought it would need such an enforcement technique when developing countries, in particular, did not comply with the TRIPS Agreement.[11] The rationale was that as those countries would not have significant intellectual property related assets to retaliate against then cross-retaliation under the GATT, or other agreements, would be needed for enforcement of TRIPS Agreement violations. However, what has come to pass is a different story. There has been no instance of a developing country failing to comply with DSB rulings in a TRIPS dispute and consequently of cross-retaliation being sought as a remedy to induce compliance. Instead, when a large developed economy does not comply with rulings found against it under other WTO Agreements, developing countries have pursued TRIPS cross-retaliation because they perceive it is most likely to induce some kind of compliance. This may be described as a case of 'be careful what you wish for'. From the developing country perspective it may be that cross-retaliation under TRIPS is a more effective remedy than raising tariffs which may well hurt the country raising tariffs more than it will be effective against the non-complying country.[12]

The nature of intellectual property obligations and suspension

Apart from cross-retaliation, the situations in which intellectual property rights can be legally and effectively suspended are arguably few. The conditions for suspension are carefully delineated in relevant domestic and international law. In part this is because international intellectual property law functions as an inter-connected web of territorialised rules. This inter-connectedness is also why cross-retaliation may be something that an intellectual property-owning nation may wish to avoid, both because it is hard to contain the effects of suspension of intellectual property obligations and because such suspension is likely viewed as setting a 'bad' precedent.

The territorial nature of intellectual property rights including patents, copyrights and trade marks is an important feature which impacts the mode and effect of suspension. Broadly, the territoriality of intellectual property rights is as follows. If an inventor wishes to patent something in, for example, the US then any patented invention will not receive patent protection in countries outside the US unless the inventor also applies for a patent in those other places. One of the functions of the TRIPS Agreement is that it requires all members to provide systems whereby patents can be registered for all inventions.[13]

An important qualification is that patenting standards are not uniform. That can mean that a patent granted in one country may not be granted under the patent law of another country. The TRIPS Agreement is a minimum standards regime. There are two key reasons that minimum standards do not lead to uniform harmonisation of domestic laws. The first is because many of the standards are not prescriptive in the detail of how national laws should be, but rather use terms that require further definition at national law, such as 'inventive step'.[14] Thus, there is considerable national autonomy over how to comply with the minimum standards.[15] Second, the TRIPS Agreement permits countries to provide a greater level of protection than the TRIPS minimum standards.[16]

Because copyright is not a registration system it works differently from patents (and other intellectual property registration systems), but copyright is also territorial. The TRIPS Agreement (and Berne Convention) copyright regime requires that all members protect 'literary and artistic works'[17] that originate in any country that is a member of the relevant Agreement.[18] The territorial nature of copyright is such that copyright protection in New Zealand, for instance, extends as far as New Zealand's territorial borders and copyright protection in France extends as far as France's borders and so on.

Although intellectual property protection functions in a territorial way, the borders of intellectual property are in reality porous. Territorial impacts on intellectual property rights in one part of the international network can have considerable effects beyond the territory in which such impact originally occurs.[19] An infringement of copyright online, for example, can originate in one jurisdiction but result in infringements in many jurisdictions; for the Internet knoweth not the copyright legal borders. Thus, if suspension of copyright involves making copyright works available online for no charge then that availability may extend beyond one territory and into others. There might be various ways in which copyright laws will block or require takedown of such material, but the point is that suspending in one jurisdiction is not always easily contained within the borders of that jurisdiction. On the one hand, that appears to make suspension of intellectual property rights 'different' from retaliation by raising tariffs or paying compensation and it certainly is. On the other hand, when a country refuses market access to foreign service suppliers (*US – Gambling*) or has been found to provide prohibited and actionable subsidies (*US – Upland Cotton*) the effects in reality flow well beyond the disputing party borders. I am not suggesting that therefore cross-retaliation should not be used, as properly defined (the parameters are discussed below), but the potential extra-territorial effects of suspending intellectual property rights do not necessarily speak against it as a remedy.

Not protecting an invention as a patent in one place can also have effects beyond that country's borders. A country that does not protect certain types of patents[20] (although these are fewer than before the TRIPS Agreement) could theoretically provide other countries with cheaper products. This would be possible in situations where the importing country either did not protect the products as patents (in the same way as the exporting country) or where the importing country does protect patents, but nevertheless allows parallel imports of patented products.[21]

Thus, the web of international protection is potentially fragile. This fragility makes suspension of obligations in one part of the world potentially deleterious to intellectual property rights in other countries, and therefore cross-retaliation under TRIPS is a potentially effective remedy to induce compliance with DSB rulings. Like a fishing net the inter-connections of intellectual property protection make it hard to pierce the net in order to extract only one or two fish, rather the potential effect of making a small hole is that the small hole expands and out of it tumbles many fish.

Outside of cross-retaliation for non-compliance with DSB rulings, there are limited circumstances where intellectual property rights can be suspended. These examples although few, however, tell us something about the nature of suspending intellectual property rights and why the rules around such actions are so tightly circumscribed.

Suspension under domestic law is likely to be rare because of the TRIPS Agreement requirements to provide intellectual property protection and the limited flexibilities and exceptions that are permissible under the Agreement. One such flexibility is compulsory licensing.[22] Under Article 31 the usual procedure is that the issuance of a compulsory licence must be preceded by 'efforts to obtain authorisation from the rights holder'.[23] If there is a 'national emergency', however, then the step of prior authorisation from the rights holder can be dispensed with before the appropriate administrative authority grants a compulsory licence.[24] Under the rules the rights holder must be 'notified as soon as reasonably practicable'[25] and paid 'adequate remuneration'[26] and the licence should not last longer than the national emergency.[27]

The step of dispensing with consent prior to the grant of the licence is effectively a legitimate suspension of an intellectual property right. It is notable that this procedure is circumscribed by a number of rules and conditions before it can be used.[28] This serves to reinforce the above point that rights holders generally try to prevent products, made even legitimately under compulsory licensing, from making their way back into the streams of commerce where the compulsory licence is not applicable. The same is likely to be true of any products made as a result of suspended intellectual property rights. The owners of the relevant intellectual property rights do not want any such products to enter markets where the rights are not suspended. This is legitimate because in those markets such products might be infringing, but the concern seems somewhat overstated. This 'fear' seems so strong that websites describe the US as having claimed that TRIPS cross-retaliation amounts to 'theft' and 'piracy'.[29]

Another illustration of suspension of intellectual property obligations is the facts behind the WTO dispute known as *Havana Club*.[30] That dispute involved a US law which barred certain nationals (Cubans) from applying for registration of trade marks or enforcing common law trade mark rights before US courts. The trade marks at issue were ones that were identical to or substantially similar to trade marks that the Cuban government had confiscated during the Castro revolution. The facts are complex and need not be fully repeated here. In summary, the law was enacted for the benefit of the Bacardi company and in particular its US subsidiary. Bacardi operations outside of the US exported rum to the US. That rum was trade marked as HAVANA CLUB. Pernod Ricard, a French company, had a joint venture with the Cuban Government that had a US registration for HAVANA CLUB, but that registration was identical to a trade mark that had been confiscated in the Cuban revolution and so Pernod Ricard could not use the mark under the US law at issue. The dispute at the WTO resulted in a finding that there was a violation of national treatment and MFN because the different treatment of the confiscated trade marks was entirely based on nationality.[31] What the dispute shows is that outside of cross-retaliation the suspension of intellectual property rights (when permitted at all[32]) needs to be done on a national treatment and MFN non-discriminatory basis. In contrast, suspension of concessions based on cross-retaliation is designed to be entirely discriminatory against the losing party.

The examples of suspension of intellectual property rights permitted outside of cross-retaliation are few and well circumscribed by the requirements of the TRIPS Agreement. In a similar way cross-retaliation circumscribes suspension both through the rules of retaliation under the DSU generally and because of territoriality and other specific issues. Before turning to those issues the next section outlines the DSU rules of cross-retaliation.

The rules relating to cross-retaliation

Retaliation under the DSU is not supposed to be a goal unto itself, rather it is a way to induce compliance. The DSU also permits payment of compensation, although it is voluntary and like suspension of concessions it too is supposed to be only temporary.[33]

Cross-retaliation is the third option, under Article 22 of the DSU. The first option requires suspension of concessions in the *same sector* in which the DSB has found a violation.[34] The second option is to suspend concessions in a *different sector* but under the same agreement.[35] Only when these options are exhausted can another agreement be turned to. Article 22.3 (c) provides:

> In considering what concessions or other obligations to suspend, the complaining party shall apply the following principles and procedures: ...
>
> (c) if that party considers that it is not practicable or effective to suspend concessions or other obligations with respect to other sectors under the same agreement, and that the circumstances are serious enough, it may seek to suspend concessions or other obligations under another covered agreement;

The DSU also provides factors that a party seeking cross-retaliation must consider if Article 22.3 (c) is resorted to. These are:[36]

i   the trade in the sector or under the agreement under which the panel or Appellate Body has found a violation or other nullification or impairment, and the importance of such trade to that party;
ii the broader economic elements related to the nullification or impairment and the broader economic consequences of the suspension of concessions or other obligations.

While there can be no real objection to these principles, they perhaps state the obvious and do not provide much guidance, one way or another, either to a party considering cross-retaliation or a panel looking at whether to authorise cross-retaliation. It seems unlikely, for instance, that a party would go as far as seeking dispute settlement, let alone cross-retaliation, if the trade were not important to it and the circumstances did not give rise to 'serious enough' economic consequences.

The reason that it may not be 'practicable or effective' for a winning party to retaliate in the same sector or in a related sector is that all the party may achieve is harming its own industries and consumers. If, for example, local businesses relied on the import of raw materials to manufacture products, then an increase of tariffs on those raw materials would result in a cost to the local industries that relied on those imports. In any event, if the theory of comparative advantage is accepted then the notion of raising tariffs is harmful to the country raising the tariffs even in the short term.[37] Even if local manufacturers or service suppliers benefit in some short-term way from tariff increases or service restrictions, consumers are likely to bear the costs that arise from reduced competition. Not all, however, are happy with this outcome. As Subramanian and Watal note:[38]

> ... the implementation of trade retaliation leads to a decline in economic welfare of the retaliating country. The fact that it continues to be the measure of first recourse is of course sad testimony to the disproportionate weight accorded to producer interests in pluralist systems. In the normal political calculus, the hurt to consumers is often overridden by the benefits to domestic producers.

Suspending concessions in services sectors is also likely to be complicated because it would require amendment of local laws or regulations[39] (a similar issue arises in the TRIPS context and is discussed below).

It may not be practical to suspend concessions in the same or related sector where there is no import of the product at issue or where the complaining country is very dependent on other imports from the respondent country. This was the situation in *EC – Bananas III*. Ecuador is not an importer of bananas and is highly dependent on imports of other goods from the EC. Similarly in *US – Gambling*, Antigua cannot effectively retaliate against US online gambling services supplied to Antigua when there are none.[40] Antigua is also highly dependent on imports from the US. In *US – Upland Cotton*, although permission for cross-retaliation under TRIPS was granted, Brazil was first required to retaliate in several goods sectors.[41]

A difference with suspending intellectual property rights might be, however, that all that is suspended is the royalty outflows to a country. That does not, however, make suspending intellectual property rights simple, as an owner may refuse to supply a market with an intellectual property product if suspension of its rights occurs. Also, some businesses may rely on imported intellectual property. After all, that is at least in theory one of the reasons to import technology-related goods and services. These problems are discussed further below in the context of the disputes that have raised such issues.

Arbitrations that have allowed cross-retaliation under the TRIPS Agreement and related issues

EC – Bananas III and the effects on other treaties and third-party markets

EC – Bananas III was the first dispute that discussed and authorised cross-retaliation under TRIPS. Ecuador was granted permission to cross-retaliate because it was able to demonstrate the importance of bananas to its economy and consequently the circumstances of the EC's non-compliance, with the rulings of the DSB, justified Ecuador suspending TRIPS obligations. In the end a settlement was negotiated with the EC and there was no suspension of intellectual property rights. One commentator has concluded that the authority to cross-retaliate not only prompted resolution of the dispute, but also helped Ecuador renegotiate its foreign debt.[42]

Several issues were raised in the arbitration proceedings, including the nature of international intellectual property obligations arising under international agreements other than the TRIPS Agreement. To suspend under TRIPS may mean that in the case of copyright there is also a suspension under the Berne Convention[43] and in the case of patents and trade marks there might also be a suspension of obligations under the Paris Convention.[44] Part of both the Berne and Paris Conventions are also incorporated into TRIPS, but the WTO is not the institution in charge of those treaties. They are treaties of the World Intellectual Property Organization (WIPO). The TRIPS Agreement incorporates the substantive provisions from Berne which forms the basis of the copyright minimum standards under TRIPS. Compared to the Berne Convention, the Paris Convention has fewer substantive minimum standards (much of its coverage is more procedural in nature). Thus, the TRIPS Agreement in effect creates substantive minimum standards for both trade marks and patents that are not found in the Paris Convention.

The arbitration panel noted that it could not authorise suspension of any obligations under non-WTO agreements. The arbitrators effectively concluded that once authorisation to suspend obligations under TRIPS was given, any inconsistency with WIPO Conventions was a matter for Ecuador and other parties to those treaties to consider. One might expect that the WTO would not presume to make decisions on behalf of other organisations; however, the overlap with WIPO treaties is not so simple, not least of all because they are incorporated into the TRIPS Agreement. First, the membership of the WTO and the WIPO treaties is very similar[45] and consequently actual conflicts of this nature may be theoretical. Members of the Berne and Paris Conventions who are also WTO members have agreed to the subsequent TRIPS Agreement and, thus, have agreed to be subject to any TRIPS dispute resolution in relation to those treaties. At least one commentator has reasoned that, therefore, any recourse to the International Court of Justice for a violation of Berne or Paris because of TRIPS cross-retaliation is both unlikely to occur and would not be sustainable:[46]

By accepting the WTO suspension rule, a state party would appear to have waived the right to independently enforce a complementary substantive obligation under the cross-referenced Paris or Berne regimes that would effectively nullify the suspension. Put another way, a WTO Member would be equitably estopped from attempting to independently enforce an obligation under a WIPO Convention as a means of preventing effective enforcement of its WTO obligation.

The arbitration panel also recognised that third-country markets could potentially be affected by cross-retaliation. The arbitrators stated:[47]

Distortions in third-country markets could be avoided if Ecuador would suspend the [intellectual property] only for the purposes of the domestic market. An authorisation of a suspension requested ... does of course not entitle other WTO members to derogate from their obligations under the TRIPS Agreement. Consequently, such DSB authorisation to Ecuador cannot be construed by other WTO members to reduce obligations under TRIPS in regard to imports entering their customs territory.

While it is no doubt correct that TRIPS suspension is only applicable in the territory of the member that is authorised to cross–retaliate and not in other countries, that is not the same as making the suspension 'only for the purposes of the domestic market'. There are two reasons for this. First, where works are legally made or distributed in one country, if such works are infringing in another territory then the laws of that other territory apply to any alleged infringement. The country where the copyright goods were legally produced or made available is not responsible for infringing copies in another territory. The copyright owner must enforce its rights in the country where there is an infringement. In some jurisdictions there may be a doctrine of authorisation or of contributory infringement that may be applicable on some facts, but having such a law is not an obligation under the TRIPS Agreement and is notoriously difficult to succeed as a cause of action where the alleged authorisation is across borders.

Second, and perhaps more fundamentally, is what sort of intellectual property imports are involved. When the intellectual property imported is embodied in a good then border measures can be applied to prevent such goods entering the market. The same is not quite true of goods that might be downloaded online. But more difficult still are copyright protected works which do not manifest as goods or even downloads, but are digital and, for example, may be viewed or streamed online. These may easily be received outside the borders of the retaliating country and reception in other countries is not necessarily within the control of the retaliating country.

A further complication is that there are some aspects of copyright works, particularly as they relate to the digital environments, which are protected through post-TRIPS agreements. The WIPO Copyright Treaty of 1996 (WCT)[48] requires protection of digital matters, including online communications of copyright works, technological protection mechanisms and rights management systems. A retaliating country may not have an obligation to protect such work in the first place if it is not a WCT member, in which case such obligations will not be the target of any suspension. But as such protections can be additional rights, rather than new copyright works as such, the suspension of the TRIPS rights may also impact these additional rights in other jurisdictions. The international obligations of the receiving state will determine the issue of any particular infringement. These sorts of issues are not theoretical, but may very well arise in the context of Antigua's proposed retaliation, reported as involving plans to launch a website to sell copyright content without paying American rights holders.[49]

US – Gambling *and the problem of a small and developing country enforcing compliance*

Some time ago Antigua was authorised in principle to cross-retaliate under the TRIPS Agreement for the US's failure to comply with the rulings of the Appellate Body when its laws were found to violate GATS commitments relating to online gambling services.[50] At issue was the lack of access for foreign service suppliers of online gambling to the US market and, in the context of the dispute, no access for Antigua. Proceedings under the DSU to authorise cross-retaliation have been drawn out and were in three stages. It is worth noting the formality around the stages, which may also act as a disincentive for an already cash-strapped nation to take the matter further, especially when they have every reason to believe they have no power to bring the non-complying party into line.

The first arbitration took place in 2005, which allowed cross-retaliation under TRIPS because same or similar sector retaliation would not be effective.[51] In 2007, the amount of value of permissible cross-retaliation was calculated to be no more that US$21 million per annum;[52] although Antigua had estimated their loss was considerably greater, at US$3.443 billion annually.

The US submitted that the government of Antigua needed to strictly supervise the cross-retaliation so as to make sure there was no abuse and Antigua needed to explain the details of how it would cross-retaliate. However, the panel did not accept the submission. When permission for cross-retaliation is granted the panel does not impose conditions as to how that cross-retaliation should be exercised. The DSU provides that:[53]

> the arbitrator shall not examine the nature of the concessions or other obligations to be suspended but shall determine whether the level of such suspension is equivalent to the level of nullification and impairment.

However, in order to effectively cross-retaliate under TRIPS a detailed plan and structure may be necessary.[54] The *US – Gambling* arbitration panel did note that suspension of obligations under TRIPS can be complex.[55]

At the DSB meeting in April 2012, Antigua informed[56] the DSB that the United States was not in compliance with the rulings made against it. This formality was made in order to seek the DSB's assistance in trying to resolve the dispute through its 'good offices' of mediation. However, no resolution was forthcoming and so in January 2013, Antigua requested the DSB authorise it to suspend US intellectual property rights.[57] The request was granted in accordance with the arbitrator's ruling. It is interesting to consider why Antigua has taken its time both because it seems to have tried to resolve the dispute and as it appears to have weighed carefully whether suspension of intellectual property rights belonging to US owners is politically and practically feasible.[58] Whether a nation as small as Antigua can hope to succeed against the US remains to be seen. Generally, this dispute raises the issue as to whether the dispute settlement system is really effective for small and developing economies in particular.[59]

US – Upland Cotton *and the 'threats' that a larger developing country can make*

In *US – Upland Cotton* the US was found to have violated the SCM in several ways, including both prohibited and actionable subsidies. The US did not remove the offending subsidies but in fact further entrenched them with the passing of new legislation to continue the subsidies, as is often done via the frequent Farm Bills in the US.[60] As a result, Brazil initiated arbitration proceedings to seek permission to retaliate. Brazil calculated harm at US$1.037 billion per annum. Brazil's calculations were based on income losses and effects caused by US products replacing Brazilian products.[61] The arbitrator held the losses were US$147.3 million based on calculations of Brazil's world cotton market share. The arbitrator ruled that Brazil could cross-retaliate under both GATS and TRIPS.

Brazil had some domestic legislation proposed which would be arguably necessary in order to effectively cross-retaliate. This legislation was to enable the suspension of identified intellectual property interests including patented pharmaceuticals.

Within a few weeks, the US and Brazil agreed to a solution. As suggested at the beginning of this chapter the haste of the settlement suggests that the relative economic power of Brazil compared to that of the very small nation of Antigua may have assisted in this comparatively speedy resolution. In particular the threat to patent industries appears to have been a substantial motivation to settle the dispute.

The parameters of TRIPS retaliation

The above discussion shows that avoiding violating other international intellectual property agreements and even perhaps authorising infringement in third-party markets may be difficulties that need to be addressed in order for a retaliating country to effectively cross-retaliate. There are other difficulties which include possible allegations of expropriation of property and how to calculate the appropriate amount of retaliation to address the sum of loss for which the panel has authorised retaliation.

Avoiding expropriation of property claims

If intellectual property rights are suspended then expropriation or some kind of unjustified taking of property could be alleged under the domestic law of the retaliating country. Granted, that may be largely theoretical because these sorts of property-related laws are less frequently found in developing countries than developed countries. Additionally, such suspension might be a violation of an investment agreement under a bilateral investment treaty, known as a BIT, where the BIT names intellectual property as a covered investment asset. These sorts of investment agreements are also found as chapters in free trade agreements. BITs obligations relating to property investments are more common in developing countries than domestic expropriation laws. The absence of domestic law property protection is a key reason that BITs were developed. The question of what amounts to expropriation or taking of property will be governed by the terms of the BIT, which may also provide for investor-state arbitration.

To date the only reported intellectual property 'asset' to have led to any BITs claims arises from the plain packaging of cigarettes disputes brought against Australia and Uruguay.[62] Those BIT disputes are pending at the time of writing. The claimed expropriation in plain packaging relates to the inability to use trade marks. The Australian plain packaging legislation prohibits the use of figurative and logo trade marks on cigarette packaging.[63] In other words, no one is able to use the trade mark and so no one reaps any associated benefits that accrue with trade mark use. This is conceptually different from cross-retaliation where the retaliating party (or its citizens) may reap a direct benefit from the suspension of the intellectual property right. Thus, if the retaliating country or its citizens stood to make a profit from the retaliation this might give rise to a different outcome than the potential plain packaging-related BIT complaints against Australia and the unsuccessful complaint under its domestic law.[64] There is no real precedent, therefore, or likely precedent about whether cross-retaliation by suspension of intellectual property obligations might infringe BITs. However, a country with BIT commitments relating to intellectual property may have to bear those commitments in mind when structuring any cross-retaliation package.

The level of suspension to address the loss

Calculation of the level of nullification and impairment and the means for rebalancing concessions is difficult in the fields of services and intellectual property. One might ask what is the value of intellectual property? There is a distinction between trying to value specific intellectual property products and the effect of suspension on the purposes of rights in the policy sense; that is the rationale for rights in the first place such as the values of innovation and creativity. The approach of dispute settlement, perhaps fairly, has to treat all trade matters as similar when it comes to retaliation – they can all be broken down to monetary losses. Whether patents, copyright, bananas, online gambling services or cotton subsidies they can all be valued to a financial sum – this is after all their only commonality. There is, however, something artificial about this (even if it is the fairest way to proceed). After all from an intellectual property perspective the value of intellectual property has something to do with knowledge, which, while related to economic gain, is universally recognised as hard to pinpoint in monetary terms.

The value of some intellectual property is hard to calculate and other aspects of it are frequently valued in monetary terms. Examples are where there is a known licensing fee, such as where a copyright collecting society exists.[65] Where royalty and licensing fees for copyright are known, the calculation of the value of suspending rights in relation to those copyrights can simply involve adding up the lost royalties. All of the cross-retaliation disputes involved copyright as one area of possible TRIPS cross-retaliation. There is some attractiveness to copyright as the target, rather than patents because if another party is to enter the resulting gap in the market, then reproducing copyright works is, compared to patented products, relatively cost-effective. It can be done without a significant industry base. Nonetheless, as discussed above, because of the territorial issues the simplicity should not be overstated. Additionally, if new markets are developed then these cannot be indefinite but rather should only last for as long as the failure to comply continues. In only one cross-retaliation situation have patents been named as a target. This was the *US – Upland Cotton* dispute. The next section discusses some ways that retaliation might be made effective using patents as an example.

Making retaliation of patent protection effective and DSU compliant

New markets in the short term

In many intellectual property industries the suspension of obligations might simply mean the suspension of royalty payments. If royalty payments are suspended the question can arise: who gets the benefit? Should prices be cheaper for consumers or does the government, or some other entity, pocket the profits? In *EC – Bananas III*, the proposed scheme had the government collecting any benefits.

A more potentially threatening type of cross-retaliation is where the retaliating country uses the suspension of intellectual property rights to compete with the imported product. If the imported product becomes cheaper because of the absence of the local protection then such competition might be difficult. What is more likely to occur, however, is that the imported product is no longer made available in the country where there is no protection. In that situation there is an opportunity for a replica product (which is legitimate and, but for the cross-retaliation, would be an infringement) or a local competing product (if one exists) gaining a greater market share.

Creating an alternative product is only realistic, however, where the local market actually is able to manufacture the substitute. This might be possible in a situation where the local market had, for example, the capacity to manufacture pharmaceuticals. If a pharmaceutical patent is suspended then the generic manufacturer might be able to fill the gap if the result of the suspended patent meant there was no supply from the patentee. Such a plan, however, is only possible where a country has such capacity. That was not an option for Ecuador, is not an option for Antigua, but was an option for Brazil.

Suspending identified patents

It is possible to identify particular patents relating to particular products and to suspend those patents rather than any general suspension of patent law. To do that may also mean that a law change is not necessary. Of course in so doing the particular patent owner may have nothing to do with the reasons for suspension. A pharmaceutical company, for example, may very well wonder why it has to bear the cost for the offending subsidy paid to cotton farmers. However, in essence that is a problem for the non-complying state to work out among its domestic constituents. It is not rationally the concern of the cross-retaliating country.

Suspending some rights

Another approach could be to suspend some of the patent owner's rights but not others. For example, the right to make the patent could remain enforceable but the right to control importation unenforceable.[66] This solution might be effective for a country that does not have manufacturing capacity, but only where there is another source for the pharmaceutical. If the pharmaceutical is patented those other sources are likely to be few if at all. But if the product is made elsewhere, either because it is not protected or because it is out of patent, suspending the importation right could work. In such a situation, however, the cross-retaliating country, while potentially benefiting, does not receive any direct payment from the suspended intellectual property rights. In fact, a third-party country may reap an economic benefit. A retaliating country may, therefore, prefer an option where the royalties flow directly to it.

Concluding thoughts

Even though Brazil was able to achieve a settlement through using cross-retaliation the result of *US – Upland Cotton* was, from the point of view of third parties and arguably the trading system as a whole, entirely unsatisfactory. Payments are made to Brazil to 'provide technical assistance and capacity-building for Brazil's cotton sector'.[67] This may represent a mutually convenient solution between the parties to the dispute, but it likely has a serious impact on other WTO members who produce cotton and cannot afford or do not have the immediate political motivation to bring the same kind of dispute as Brazil did.[68] In the area of intellectual property compliance (outside of cross-retaliation) the wealthy developed economies have also seemingly bought their way out of changing WTO-incompatible laws. In the US copyright exceptions dispute the US has either been unwilling or unable to repeal the offending provision. Consequently, it pays the EU compensation.[69]

Additionally, the position of a small and developing country like Antigua being unable to induce compliance is also unsatisfactory. It might be that in this sort of situation compensation might be more appropriate. If a losing country such as the US is compelled to pay Antigua compensation that may be a better outcome. It may also be a better outcome than having retaliation against unrelated industries to the original dispute. However, a compensation model may result in its own problems, such as only being affordable for some countries and still avoiding the optimal outcome which is changing the relevant domestic violating measures.

Notes

1 Susy Frankel is a Professor at the Faculty of Law, Victoria University of Wellington, and Director of the New Zealand Centre of International Economic Law.
2 See generally Limenta 2012.
3 Agreement on Trade-Related Aspects of Intellectual Property Rights, 15 April 1994, Marrakesh Agreement Establishing the World Trade Organization, Annex 1C, The Legal Texts: The Results Of The Uruguay Round of Multilateral Trade Negotiations 320 (1999), 1869 U.N.T.S. 299, 33 I.L.M. 1197 (1994) [hereinafter 'TRIPS'].
4 Decision by the Arbitrator, *European Communities – Regime for the Importation, Sale and Distribution of Bananas – Recourse to Arbitration by the European Communities under Article 22.6 of the DSU*, WT/DS27/ARB/ECU, 24 March 2000, para. 76 [hereinafter 'Decision by the Arbitrator, *EC – Bananas III (Ecuador) (Article 22.6 – EC)*'].
5 Decision by the Arbitrator, *EC – Bananas III (Ecuador) (Article 22.6 – EC)*.
6 Decision by the Arbitrator, *United States – Measures Affecting the Cross-Border Supply of Gambling and Betting Services – Recourse to Arbitration by the United States under Article 22.6 of the DSU*, WT/DS285/ARB, 21 December 2007 [hereinafter 'Decision by the Arbitrator, *US – Gambling (Article 22.6 – US)*'].
7 Decision by the Arbitrator, *United States – Subsidies on Upland Cotton – Recourse to Arbitration by the United States under Article 22.6 of the DSU and Article 4.11 of the SCM Agreement*, WT/DS267/ARB/1, 31 August 2009 [hereinafter 'Decision by the Arbitrator, *US – Upland Cotton (Article 22.6 – US I)*']; Decision by the Arbitrator, *United States – Subsidies on Upland Cotton – Recourse to Arbitration by the United States under Article 22.6 of the DSU and Article 7.10 of the SCM Agreement*, WT/DS267/ARB/2 and Corr.1, 31 August 2009 ['Decision by the Arbitrator, *US – Upland Cotton (Article 22.6 – US II)*'].
8 Slater 2009: 1395–408 discussing the arbitrator's allowance of copyright cross-retaliation and its feasibility.
9 WT/DSB/M/276, para. 87.
10 WT/DSB/M/328, para. 6.12.

11 See Croome 1995: 323.
12 See Basheer 2010, discussing how a detailed suspension model could help developing countries and arguing that cross-retaliation should not be the third option under Article 22 of the DSU. See also Grosse Ruse-Kahn 2008. See discussion in Part III.
13 TRIPS Art. 27(1).
14 TRIPS Art. 27(1) requires that patents shall be available for inventions provided they are new, involve an inventive step and are capable of industrial application.
15 See TRIPS Art. 1(1) which provides that 'members shall be free to determine the appropriate method of implementing the provisions of this Agreement within their own legal system and practice'.
16 TRIPS Art. 1(1).
17 The Berne Convention for the Protection of Literary and Artistic Works, 9 September 1886, as revised at Paris on 24 July 1971 and as amended 28 September 1979, 102 Stat. 2853, 1161 U.N.T.S. 3 [hereinafter 'Berne Convention']. This is the definition used for copyright works found in Article 2 of the Berne Convention.
18 TRIPS Agreement, 1.1 and 9.1 incorporating the Berne Convention, see Arts. 1 and 3.
19 Additionally, norm setting in domestic law can have impacts on norms in other jurisdictions, see Frankel 2008.
20 One example where some TRIPS members provide protection and others do not is what are known as second use pharmaceutical patents. In some countries second uses of known pharmaceuticals may not meet the standards of new or inventive step, as members are free to define the patentability criteria according to their level of development. For a discussion of different standards of inventive step between India and the United States, see Dinwoodie and Dreyfuss 2012: 51–8.
21 Article 6 of the TRIPS Agreement provides that 'nothing in the agreement shall be used to address the exhaustion of intellectual property rights'. Consequently countries can choose whether to allow parallel importation on the basis of the international exhaustion principle or to prevent parallel imports on the basis of territorial exhaustion.
22 Compulsory licensing must be done in accordance with the conditions set out in Articles 31 and 31 bis.
23 TRIPS Art. 31(b).
24 Article 31(b) provides that a party need not seek prior authorisation from the right holder in situations of national emergency, other extreme urgency or in cases of public non-commercial use.
25 TRIPS Art. 31(b).
26 TRIPS Art. 31 (h).
27 TRIPS Art. 31(c) provides that 'the scope and duration of [the licence] shall be limited to the purpose for which it was authorized'.
28 In relation to Article 31 bis, this extends Article 31 to allow for export of pharmaceuticals made under compulsory licence to countries without manufacturing capacity. The conditions of such licences include that the pharmaceuticals are differently coloured and packaged from those made by the patent owner.
29 See Palmedo (28 January 2013). Online. Available at: http://infojustice.org/archives/28373.
30 Appellate Body Report, *United States – Section 211 Omnibus Appropriations Act of 1998*, WT/DS176/AB/R, adopted 1 February 2002.
31 The case under US domestic law, however, found that Pernod Ricard could not assert rights to HAVANA CLUB because of the relevant law, *Havana Club Holding v Galleon S.A*, 203 F. 3d 116 (2nd Cir. 2000).
32 Such circumstances are likely to be rare because they must comply with the TRIPS Agreement. Nevertheless the agreement allows for such flexibilities in some circumstances.
33 DSU Art. 22.1.

34 DSU Art. 22.3 (a).

35 DSU Art. 22.3 (b).

36 DSU Art. 22.3 (d).

37 See Jackson 2000: 194, noting that the entire notion of trade retaliation undermines some of the principles of a liberal trading system.

38 Subramaniam and Watal 2000: 406.

39 In GATS there is an option to modify GATS commitments under Article XXI, see Grosse Ruse-Khan 2010: 141.

40 Decision by the Arbitrator, *US – Gambling (Article 22.6 – US)*, para. 4.49. See also Antigua's response to question No. 48 of the Arbitrator. Online. Available at: www. antiguawto.com/wto/80_AB_Responses_22_6_PanelQs_2Nov07.pdf.

41 Decision by the Arbitrator, *US – Upland Cotton (Article 22.6 – US I)*, para. 5.230. Basheer discusses the differences in approach of the panels to the calculations involved, see Basheer 2010.

42 McCall Smith 2006.

43 Decision by the Arbitrator, *EC – Bananas III (Ecuador) (Article 22.6 – EC)*, paras 148–52.

44 Other treaties incorporated into the TRIPS Agreement include the Rome Convention and the Washington Treaty on Intellectual Property in Respect of Integrated Circuits which may also be affected by the suspension of other relevant TRIPS obligations.

45 Although membership is not completely the same and thus the Vienna Convention on the Law of Treaties 1969, Article 30 rules on subsequent agreements between the same parties likely do not apply.

46 Abbott 2009 citing Panel Report, *United States – Sections 301-310 of the Trade Act of 1974*, WT/DS152/R, adopted 27 January 2000, para. 7.125 [hereinafter 'Panel Report, *US – Section 301 Trade Act*'] in support of his conclusion.

47 Decision by the Arbitrator, *EC – Bananas III (Ecuador) (Article 22.6 – EC)*, para. 156.

48 WIPO Copyright Treaty (WCT), adopted in Geneva on 20 December 1996.

49 Palmedo (28 January 2013). Online. Available at: http://infojustice.org/archives/28373.

50 For a discussion of the underlying dispute see Ortino 2006.

51 Decision by the Arbitrator, *US – Gambling (Article 22.6 – US)*, para. 4.118–9.

52 Decision by the Arbitrator, *US – Gambling (Article 22.6 – US)*, para. 6.1.

53 DSU Art. 22.7.

54 This is what Basheer recommends, Basheer 2010. See also Abbott 2009 citing Panel Report, *US – Section 301 Trade Act*, para. 7.125 in support of his conclusion.

55 Decision by the Arbitrator, *US – Gambling (Article 22.6 – US)*, para. 5.10.

56 WT/DSB/M/315, para. 57–68. This was done via a statement made by the Dominican Republic.

57 This is accomplished under Article 22.7.

58 See Abbott 2009.

59 See generally Subramanian and Watal 2000.

60 Food and Agricultural Act of 1965; Agricultural Act of 1970; Agricultural and Consumer Protection Act of 1973; Food and Agriculture Act of 1977; Agriculture and Food Act of 1981; Food Security Act of 1985; Food, Agriculture, Conservation, and Trade Act of 1990; Federal Agriculture Improvement and Reform Act of 1996; Farm Security and Rural Investment Act of 2002; Food, Conservation and Energy Act of 2008.

61 See Decision by the Arbitrator, *US – Upland Cotton (Article 22.6 – US I)*, para 4.2.

62 *Philip Morris Brand Sàrl (Switz.), Philip Morris Products S.A. (Switz.) and Abal Hermanos S.A. (Uru.) v Oriental Republic of Uruguay*, see ICSID *List of Pending Cases*. Online. Available at: https://icsid.worldbank.org/ICSID/FrontServlet?requestType=G enCaseDtlsRH&actionVal=ListPending (last updated 1 February 2013). Similarly, the

BIT between Hong Kong and Australia is the basis of Philip Morris's dispute against the government of Australia, see Agreement between the Government of Australia and the Government of Hong Kong for the Promotion and Protection of Investments, signed 15 September 1993, 1748 UNTS 385 (entered into force on 15 October 1993).

63 Tobacco Plain Packaging Act 2011 (No. 148, 2011).

64 In the case for expropriation under the Australian constitution a key reason that the trade marks were not treated as 'acquired' was that the government did not take title or any benefit of the trade marks for itself or anyone else. See *JT International SA v Commonwealth of Australia* [2012] HCA 43. By comparison the *EC – Bananas III* retaliation plan would have meant the government directly benefited.

65 Basheer recommends these be the first target of cross-retaliation because they can be quantified.

66 The exclusive rights of patent owners are found in article 28.1 of the TRIPS Agreement, which provides that a patent gives the owner the exclusive rights to prevent third parties from making, using, offering for sale, selling or importing the attendant product or process.

67 See Randy Schnepf, 'Brazil's WTO Case Against the U.S. Cotton Program', paper at www.nationalaglawcenter.org/assets/crs/RL32571.pdf, 30 June 2010.

68 For a discussion of the purpose of retaliation at the WTO see Limenta 2012.

69 Award of the Arbitrators, *United States – Section 110(5) of the US Copyright Act – Recourse to Arbitration under Article 25 of the DSU*, WT/DS160/ARB25/1, 9 November 2001.

Bibliography

International agreements, protocols, model agreements, and guidelines

Agreement between Japan and the United Mexican States for the Strengthening of the Economic Partnership, signed at Mexico City on 17 September 2004, entered into force on 1 April 2005.

Agreement between the Department of Health and Human Services of the United States of America and the State Food and Drug Administration of the People's Republic of China on the Safety of Drugs and Medical Devices, signed on 12 November 2007.

Agreement between the Government of Australia and the Government of Hong Kong for the Promotion and Protection of Investments, signed 15 September 1993, 1748 UNTS 385, entered into force on 15 October 1993.

Agreement on Implementation of Article VII of the General Agreement on Tariffs and Trade (Customs Valuation), 15 April 1994, 1868 U.N.T.S. 279.

Agreement on Trade-Related Aspects of Intellectual Property Rights, 15 April 1994, Marrakesh Agreement Establishing the World Trade Organization, Annex 1C, The Legal Texts: The Results Of The Uruguay Round of Multilateral Trade Negotiations 320 (1999), 1869 U.N.T.S. 299, 33 I.L.M. 1197 (1994).

Arrangement between the Australian Parties and New Zealand relating to Trans-Tasman Mutual Recognition. Online. Available at: www.dfat.gov.au/geo/new_zealand/ttmra.pdf.

Austrian Standards Institute/Österreichisches Normungsinstitut (ON) (2010) *Draft EN ISO 14051, Environmental management — Material flow cost accounting — General framework*, ISO/DIS 14051:2010.

Berne Convention for the Protection of Literary and Artistic Works, 9 September 1886, as revised at Paris on 24 July 1971 and as amended 28 September 1979, 102 Stat. 2853, 1161 U.N.T.S. 3.

Cartagena Protocol on Biosafety to the Convention on Biological Diversity, 2226 U.N.T.S. 208; 39 ILM 1027 (2000); UN Doc. UNEP/CBD/ExCOP/1/3, at 42 (2000).

Euro-Mediterranean Agreement Establishing an Association between the European Communities and their Member States, on the One Part, and the Arab Republic of Egypt, on the Other Part, entered into force on 1 June 2004.

Free Trade Agreement between Chile and Mexico, signed on 17 April 1998, entered into force on 1 August 1999.

Free Trade Agreement between the Government of Canada and the Government of the Republic of Costa Rica, signed on 23 April 2001, entered into force on 1 November 2002.

Free Trade Agreement between the Government of New Zealand and the Government of the People's Republic of China, signed on 7 April 2008, entered into force 1 October 2008.

General Agreement on Tariffs and Trade 1994, 15 April 1994, Marrakesh Agreement Establishing the World Trade Organization, Annex 1A, The Legal Texts: The Results of the Uruguay Round of Multilateral Trade Negotiations 17 (1999), 1867 U.N.T.S. 187, 33 I.L.M. 1153 (1994).

General Agreement on Tariffs and Trade, 30 October 1947, 55 UNTS 194; 61 Stat. pt. 5; TIAS 1700.

ISO (2000) ISO *14020:2000 Environmental Labels and Declarations – General Principles.*

ISO (2002) *International Standard 19011: guidelines for quality and/or environmental management systems auditing.*

ISO (2006) *ISO 14040:2006 Environmental Management – Life Cycle Assessment – Principles and Framework.*

ISO (2006) *ISO 14063:2006 Environmental Management – Environmental Communication – Guidelines and Examples.*

ISO (2006) *ISO 14064–1:2006 Greenhouse Gases – Part 1: specification with guidance at the organization level for qualification and reporting of greenhouse gas emissions and removals.*

ISO (2006) *ISO 14064–2:2006 Greenhouse Gases – Part 2: specification with guidance at the project level for quantification, monitoring and reporting of greenhouse gas emission reductions or removal enhancements.*

ISO (2006) *ISO 14064–3:2006 Greenhouse Gases – Part 3: Specification with guidance for the validation and verification of greenhouse gas assertions.*

ISO (2009) *Environmental Management: the ISO 14000 family of international standards.*

Marrakesh Agreement Establishing the World Trade Organization, 15 April 1994, The Legal Texts: The Results of The Uruguay Round of Multilateral Trade Negotiations 4 (1999), 1867 U.N.T.S. 154, 33 I.L.M. 1144 (1994).

Memorandum of Understanding between the United States Consumer Product Safety Commission and the General Administration of Quality Supervision, Inspection and Quarantine of the People's Republic of China, signed on 21 April 2004.

New Zealand-China Free Trade Agreement, signed 7 April 2008, entered into force 1 October 2008. Online. Available at: www.chinafta.govt.nz/1-The-agreement/2-Text-of-the-agreement/0-downloads/NZ-ChinaFTA-Agreement-text.pdf.

Olivos Protocol for the Settlement of Disputes in Mercosur, signed 18 February 2002, entered into force 10 February 2004, 42 ILM 2 (2003).

Statute of the International Court of Justice, 3 Bevans 1179; 59 Stat. 1031; T.S. 993; 39 AJIL Supp. 215 (1945).

Statute of the International Law Commission, General Assembly Resolution 174 (II) of 21 November 1947.

Switzerland-Colombia Bilateral Investment Agreement, signed 17 May 2006, entered into force 6 October 2009.

Trans-Tasman Mutual Recognition Act 1997. Online. Available at: www.austlii.edu.au/au/legis/cth/consol_act/tmra1997350/.

Trans-Tasman Mutual Recognition Arrangement, entered into force in 1998.

Treaty Establishing the African Economic Community, Abuja, Nigeria, 3 June 1991. Online. Available at: www.uneca.org/itca/ariportal/abuja.htm.

Treaty Establishing the European Economic Community, 25 March 1957, 298 U.N.T.S. 3.

Treaty for the Establishment of the East African Community, signed at Arusha, Tanzania on 30 November 1999, entered into force on 7 July 2000.

Understanding on Rules and Procedures Governing the Settlement of Disputes, Marrakesh Agreement Establishing the World Trade Organization, Annex 2, The Legal Texts: The Results Of The Uruguay Round of Multilateral Trade Negotiations 354 (1999), 1869 U.N.T.S. 401, 33 I.L.M. 1226 (1994).

United Nations Convention on the Law of the Sea, UN Doc A/CONF.62/122, (1982) 21 ILM 1261, entered into force 16 November 1994.

United States–Chile Free Trade Agreement, signed on 6 June 2003, entered into force on 1 January 2004.

Vienna Convention on Succession of States in respect of Treaties, (1978) 17 I.L.M. 1488, entered into force 6 November 1996.

Vienna Convention on the Law of Treaties, 1155 U.N.T.S. 331, (1969) 8 I.L.M. 679, entered into force 27 January 1980.

WIPO Copyright Treaty (WCT), adopted in Geneva on 20 December 1996.

Cases and judgments

GATT panel reports

US – Tuna I (Mexico), GATT Panel Report, *United States – Restrictions on Imports of Tuna*, 3 September 1991, unadopted, BISD 39S/155 381, 447, 639.

US – Tuna II (EEC), GATT Panel Report, *United States – Restrictions on Imports of Tuna*, 16 June 1994, unadopted, DS29/R444 447, 636.

WTO panel reports

Argentina – Poultry Anti-Dumping Duties, Panel Report, *Argentina – Definitive Anti-Dumping Duties on Poultry from Brazil*, WT/DS241/R, adopted 19 May 2003, DSR 2003:V, 1727.

Australia – Apples, Panel Report, *Australia – Measures Affecting the Importation of Apples from New Zealand*, WT/DS367/R, adopted 17 December 2010, as modified by Appellate Body Report WT/DS367/AB/R, DSR 2010:VI, 2371.

Chile – Alcoholic Beverages, Panel Report, *Chile – Taxes on Alcoholic Beverages*, WT/DS87/R, WT/DS110/R, adopted 12 January 2000, as modified by Appellate Body Report WT/DS87/AB/R, WT/DS110/AB/R, DSR 2000:I, 303.

China – Auto Parts, Panel Report, *China – Measures Affecting Imports of Automobile Parts*, WT/DS339/R/WT/DS340/R/WT/DS342/R/and Add.1 and Add.2, adopted 12 January 2009, upheld (WT/DS339/R) and as modified (WT/DS340/R/WT/DS342/R) by Appellate Body Reports WT/DS339/AB/R/WT/DS340/AB/R/WT/DS342/AB/R, DSR 2009:I, 119-DSR 2009:II, 625.

China – Measures Affecting Financial Information Services and Foreign Financial Information Suppliers, WT/DS378, settled or terminated (withdrawn, mutually agreed solution).

EC – Approval and Marketing of Biotech Products, Panel Report, *European Communities – Measures Affecting the Approval and Marketing of Biotech Products*, WT/DS291/R, WT/DS292/R, WT/DS293/R, Add.1 to Add.9, and Corr.1, adopted 21 November 2006, DSR 2006:III-VIII, 847.

EC – Tariff Preferences, Panel Report, *European Communities – Conditions for the Granting of Tariff Preferences to Developing Countries*, WT/DS246/R, adopted 20 April 2004, as modified by Appellate Body Report WT/DS/246/AB/R, DSR 2004:III, 1009.

EC – Tube or Pipe Fittings, Panel Report, *European Communities – Anti-Dumping Duties on Malleable Cast Iron Tube or Pipe Fittings from Brazil*, WT/DS219/R, adopted 18 August 2003, as modified by Appellate Body Report WT/DS219/AB/R, DSR 2003:VII, 2701.

Japan – Agricultural Products II, Panel Report, *Japan – Measures Affecting Agricultural Products*, WT/DS76/R, adopted 19 March 1999, as modified by Appellate Body Report WT/DS76/AB/R, DSR 1999:I, 315.

Mexico – Olive Oil, Panel Report, *Mexico – Definitive Countervailing Measures on Olive Oil from the European Communities*, WT/DS341/R, adopted 21 October 2008, DSR 2008:IX, 3179.

Mexico – Taxes on Soft Drinks, Panel Report, *Mexico – Tax Measures on Soft Drinks and Other Beverages*, WT/DS308/R, adopted 24 March 2006, as modified by Appellate Body Report WT/DS308/AB/R, DSR 2006:I, 43.

US – Section 301 Trade Act, Panel report, *United States – Sections 301-310 of the Trade Act of 1974*, WT/DS152/R, adopted 27 January 2000, DSR 2000:II, 815.

US – Steel Plate, Panel Report, *United States – Anti-Dumping and Countervailing Measures on Steel Plate from India*, WT/DS206/R and Corr.1, adopted 29 July 2002, DSR 2002:VI, 2073.

US – Tuna II (Mexico), Panel Report, *United States – Measures Concerning the Importation, Marketing and Sale of Tuna and Tuna Products*, WT/DS381/R, adopted 13 June 2012, as modified by Appellate Body Report WT/DS381/AB/R.

US – Tyres (China), Panel Report, *United States – Measures Affecting Imports of Certain Passenger Vehicle and Light Truck Tyres from China*, WT/DS399/R, adopted 5 October 2011, upheld by Appellate Body Report WT/DS399/AB/R.

WTO appellate body reports

Argentina – Footwear (EC), Appellate Body Report, *Argentina – Safeguard Measures on Imports of Footwear*, WT/DS121/AB/R, adopted 12 January 2000, DSR 2000:I, 515.

Australia – Apples, Appellate Body Report, *Australia – Measures Affecting the Importation of Apples from New Zealand*, WT/DS367/AB/R, adopted 17 December 2010, DSR 2010:V, 2175.

Brazil – Retreaded Tyres, Appellate Body Report, *Brazil – Measures Affecting Imports of Retreaded Tyres*, WT/DS332/AB/R, adopted 17 December 2007, DSR 2007:IV, 1527.

Canada – Aircraft, Appellate Body Report, *Canada – Measures Affecting the Export of Civilian Aircraft*, WT/DS70/AB/R, adopted 20 August 1999, DSR 1999:III, 1377.

Canada – Autos, Appellate Body Report, *Canada – Certain Measures Affecting the Automotive Industry*, WT/DS139/AB/R, WT/DS142/AB/R, adopted 19 June 2000, DSR 2000:VI, 2985.

Canada – Continued Suspension, Appellate Body Report, *Canada – Continued Suspension of Obligations in the EC – Hormones Dispute*, WT/DS321/AB/R, adopted 14 November 2008, DSR 2008:XIV, 5373.

Chile – Alcoholic Beverages, Appellate Body Report, *Chile – Taxes on Alcoholic Beverages*, WT/DS87/AB/R, WT/DS110/AB/R, adopted 12 January 2000, DSR 2000:I, 281.

Chile – Price Band System, Appellate Body Report, *Chile – Price Band System and*

Safeguard Measures Relating to Certain Agricultural Products, WT/DS207/AB/R, adopted 23 October 2002, DSR 2002:VIII, 3045 (Corr.1, DSR 2006:XII, 5473).

China – Publications and Audiovisual Products, Appellate Body Report, *China – Measures Affecting Trading Rights and Distribution Services for Certain Publications and Audiovisual Entertainment Products*, WT/DS363/AB/R, adopted 19 January 2010, DSR 2010:I, 3.

EC – Asbestos, Appellate Body Report, *European Communities – Measures Affecting Asbestos and Asbestos-Containing Products*, WT/DS135/AB/R, adopted 5 April 2001, DSR 2001:VII, 3243.

EC – Bananas III, Appellate Body Report, *European Communities – Regime for the Importation, Sale and Distribution of Bananas*, WT/DS27/AB/R, adopted 25 September 1997, DSR 1997:II, 591.

EC – Bed Linen, Appellate Body Report, *European Communities – Anti-Dumping Duties on Imports of Cotton-Type Bed Linen from India*, WT/DS141/AB/R, adopted 12 March 2001, DSR 2001:V, 2049.

EC – Hormones, Appellate Body Report, *EC Measures Concerning Meat and Meat Products (Hormones)*, WT/DS26/AB/R, WT/DS48/AB/R, adopted 13 February 1998, DSR 1998:I, 135.

EC – Sardines, Appellate Body Report, *European Communities – Trade Description of Sardines*, WT/DS231/AB/R, adopted 23 October 2002, DSR 2002:VIII, 3359.

EC – Tariff Preferences, Appellate Body Report, *European Communities – Conditions for the Granting of Tariff Preferences to Developing Countries*, WT/DS246/AB/R, adopted 20 April 2004, DSR 2004:III, 925.

EC and certain member States – Large Civil Aircraft, Appellate Body Report, *European Communities and Certain Member States – Measures Affecting Trade in Large Civil Aircraft*, WT/DS316/AB/R, adopted 1 June 2011.

Korea – Various Measures on Beef, Appellate Body Report, *Korea – Measures Affecting Imports of Fresh, Chilled and Frozen Beef*, WT/DS161/AB/R, WT/DS169/AB/R, adopted 10 January 2001, DSR 2001:I, 5.

Mexico – Taxes on Soft Drinks, Appellate Body Report, *Mexico – Tax Measures on Soft Drinks and Other Beverages*, WT/DS308/AB/R, adopted 24 March 2006, DSR 2006:I, 3.

Thailand – H-Beams, Appellate Body Report, *Thailand – Anti-Dumping Duties on Angles, Shapes and Sections of Iron or Non-Alloy Steel and H-Beams from Poland*, WT/DS122/AB/R, adopted 5 April 2001, DSR 2001:VII, 2701.

US – Anti-Dumping and Countervailing Duties (China), Appellate Body Report, *United States – Definitive Anti-Dumping and Countervailing Duties on Certain Products from China*, WT/DS379/AB/R, adopted 25 March 2011.

US – Continued Suspension, Appellate Body Report, *United States – Continued Suspension of Obligations in the EC – Hormones Dispute*, WT/DS320/AB/R, adopted 14 November 2008, DSR 2008:X, 3507.

US – Continued Zeroing, Appellate Body Report, *United States – Continued Existence and Application of Zeroing Methodology*, WT/DS350/AB/R, adopted 19 February 2009, DSR 2009:III, 1291.

US – Cotton Yarn, Appellate Body Report, *United States – Transitional Safeguard Measure on Combed Cotton Yarn from Pakistan*, WT/DS192/AB/R, adopted 5 November 2001, DSR 2001:XII, 6027.

US – Countervailing Duty Investigation on DRAMS, Appellate Body Report, *United States – Countervailing Duty Investigation on Dynamic Random Access Memory*

Semiconductors (DRAMS) from Korea, WT/DS296/AB/R, adopted 20 July 2005, DSR 2005:XVI, 8131.

US – Gambling, Appellate Body Report, *United States – Measures Affecting the Cross-Border Supply of Gambling and Betting Services*, WT/DS285/AB/R, adopted 20 April 2005, DSR 2005:XII, 5663 (Corr.1, DSR 2006:XII, 5475).

US – Gasoline, Appellate Body Report, *United States – Standards for Reformulated and Conventional Gasoline*, WT/DS2/AB/R, adopted 20 May 1996, DSR 1996:I, 3.

US – Hot-Rolled Steel, Appellate Body Report, *United States – Anti-Dumping Measures on Certain Hot-Rolled Steel Products from Japan*, WT/DS184/AB/R, adopted 23 August 2001, DSR 2001:X, 4697.

US – Lamb, Appellate Body Report, *United States – Safeguard Measures on Imports of Fresh, Chilled or Frozen Lamb Meat from New Zealand and Australia*, WT/DS177/AB/R, WT/DS178/AB/R, adopted 16 May 2001, DSR 2001:IX, 4051.

US – Section 211 Appropriations Act, Appellate Body Report, *United States – Section 211 Omnibus Appropriations Act of 1998*, WT/DS176/AB/R, adopted 1 February 2002, DSR 2002:II, 589.

US – Shrimp, Appellate Body Report, *United States – Import Prohibition of Certain Shrimp and Shrimp Products*, WT/DS58/AB/R, adopted 6 November 1998, DSR 1998:VII, 2755.

US – Softwood Lumber IV, Appellate Body Report, *United States – Final Countervailing Duty Determination with Respect to Certain Softwood Lumber from Canada*, WT/DS257/AB/R, adopted 17 February 2004, DSR 2004:II, 571.

US – Softwood Lumber V (Article 21.5 – Canada), Appellate Body Report, *United States – Final Dumping Determination on Softwood Lumber from Canada – Recourse to Article 21.5 of the DSU by Canada*, WT/DS264/AB/RW, adopted 1 September 2006, DSR 2006:XII, 5087.

US – Softwood Lumber VI (Article 21.5 – Canada), Appellate Body Report, *United States – Investigation of the International Trade Commission in Softwood Lumber from Canada – Recourse to Article 21.5 of the DSU by Canada*, WT/DS277/AB/RW, adopted 9 May 2006, and Corr.1, DSR 2006:XI, 4865.

US – Stainless Steel (Mexico), Appellate Body Report, *United States – Final Anti-Dumping Measures on Stainless Steel from Mexico*, WT/DS344/AB/R, adopted 20 May 2008, DSR 2008:II, 513.

US – Tyres (China), Appellate Body Report, *United States – Measures Affecting Imports of Certain Passenger Vehicle and Light Truck Tyres from China*, WT/DS399/AB/R, adopted 5 October 2011.

US – Wheat Gluten, Appellate Body Report, *United States – Definitive Safeguard Measures on Imports of Wheat Gluten from the European Communities*, WT/DS166/AB/R, adopted 19 January 2001, DSR 2001:II, 717.

US – Wool Shirts and Blouses, Appellate Body Report, *United States – Measure Affecting Imports of Woven Wool Shirts and Blouses from India*, WT/DS33/AB/R, adopted 23 May 1997, and Corr.1, DSR 1997:I, 323.

WTO arbitration decisions and awards of arbitrators

EC – Bananas III (Ecuador) (Article 22.6 – EC), Decision by the Arbitrators, *European Communities – Regime for the Importation, Sale and Distribution of Bananas – Recourse to Arbitration by the European Communities under Article 22.6 of the DSU*, WT/DS27/ARB/ECU, 24 March 2000, DSR 2000:V, 2237.

EC – The ACP-EC Partnership Agreement, Award of the Arbitrator, *European Communities – The ACP-EC Partnership Agreement – Recourse to Arbitration Pursuant to the Decision of 14 November 2001*, WT/L/616, 1 August 2005, DSR 2005:XXIII, 11669.

US – Gambling (Article 22.6 – US), Decision by the Arbitrator, *United States – Measures Affecting the Cross-Border Supply of Gambling and Betting Services – Recourse to Arbitration by the United States under Article 22.6 of the DSU*, WT/DS285/ARB, 21 December 2007, DSR 2007:X, 4163.

US – Section 110(5) Copyright Act (Article 25), Award of the Arbitrators, *United States – Section 110(5) of the US Copyright Act – Recourse to Arbitration under Article 25 of the DSU*, WT/DS160/ARB25/1, 9 November 2001, DSR 2001:II, 667.

US – Upland Cotton (Article 22.6 – US I), Decision by the Arbitrator, *United States – Subsidies on Upland Cotton – Recourse to Arbitration by the United States under Article 22.6 of the DSU and Article 4.11 of the SCM Agreement*, WT/DS267/ARB/1, 31 August 2009, DSR 2009:IX, 3871.

US – Upland Cotton (Article 22.6 – US II), Decision by the Arbitrator, *United States – Subsidies on Upland Cotton – Recourse to Arbitration by the United States under Article 22.6 of the DSU and Article 7.10 of the SCM Agreement*, WT/DS267/ARB/2 and Corr.1, 31 August 2009, DSR 2009:IX, 4083.

International arbitration decisions and awards

Aguas Argentinas, SA, Suez and Vivendi Universal v The Argentine Republic, ICSID Case No. ARB/03/19, Order in Response to a Petition for Transparency and Participation as Amicus Curiae, 19 May 2005.

Aguas del Tunari v Republic of Boliva, ICSID Case No. ARB/02/3, Letter from President of Tribunal, 29 January 2003. Online. Available at: http://ita.law.uvic.ca/documents/Aguas-BoliviaResponse.pdf.

Aguas Provinciales de Santa Fe v The Argentine Republic, ICSID Case No. ARB/03/17, Order in Response to a Petition for Participation as Amicus Curiae, 17 March 2006.

Austrian Airlines v The Slovak Republic, UNCITRAL Ad hoc Arbitration, Final Award, 9 October 2009.

Biwater Gauff (Tanzania) Ltd v United Republic of Tanzania, ICSID Case No. ARB/05/22, Procedural Order No. 5, 2 February 2007.

CMS Gas Transmission Company v The Argentine Republic, ICSID Case No. ARB/01/8, Award, 12 May 2005.

CMS Gas Transmission Company v The Argentine Republic, ICSID Case No. ARB/01/8, Decision of the Ad hoc Committee, 25 September 2007.

ConocoPhillips Company v The Bolivarian Republic of Venezuela, ICSID Case No. ARB/07/30, Decision on the Proposal to Disqualify L.Yves Fortier QC, Arbitrator, 27 February 2012.

Continental Casualty Company v The Argentine Republic, ICSID Case No. ARB/03/9, Award, 5 September 2008.

Cross-Border Trucking Services, USA-MEX-98–2008–01, Awards of the NAFTA Arbitral Panel, 6 February 2001. Online. Available at: www.sice.oas.org/dispute/nafta/english/U98081ae.asp.

Emilio Agustin Maffezini v The Kingdom of Spain, ICSID Case No. ARB/97/7, Decision on Objections to Jurisdiction, 25 January 2000.

Gas Natural SDG, S.A. v The Argentine Republic, ICSID Case No. ARB/03/10, Decision of Tribunal on Preliminary Questions on Jurisdiction, 17 June 2005.

Glamis Gold v United States, Award, 15 May 2009. Online. Available at: www.nafta-claims.com/Disputes/USA/Glamis/Glamis-USA-Award.pdf.

Glamis Gold v United States, Procedural Order No. 6, 15 October 2005. Online. Available HTTP: www.naftaclaims.com/Disputes/USA/Glamis/Glamis-Tribunal-Order-06.pdf.

Hussein Nuaman Soufraki v United Arab Emirates, ICSID Case No. ARB/02/7, Award on Jurisdiction, 7 July 2004.

Hussein Nuaman Soufraki v United Arab Emirates, ICSID Case No. ARB/02/7, Decision on Annulment, 5 June 2007.

Impregilo S.p.A v Argentine Republic, ICSID Case No. ARB/07/17, Concurring and Dissenting Opinion of Brigitte Stern, 21 June 2011.

Malaysian Historical Salvors v The Government of Malaysia, ICSID Case No. ARB/05/10, Decision on Annulment, 16 April 2009.

Methanex Corporation v United States of America, Decision on Authority to Accept Amicus Submissions, 15 January 2001. Online. Available at: http://naftaclaims.com/Disputes/USA/Methanex/MethanexDecisionReAuthorityAmicus.pdf.

Methanex Corporation v United States of America, UNCITRAL (NAFTA), Final Award of the Tribunal on Jurisdiction and Merits, 3 August 2005, 44 *ILM* 1345.

National Grid PLC v The Argentine Republic, UNCITRAL, Decision on Jurisdiction, 3 August 2006.

Occidental Exploration and Production Company v The Republic of Ecuador, London Court of International Arbitration Case No. UN 3467, Final Award, 1 July 2004.

Pantechniki S.A. Contractors & Engineers v Republic of Albania, ICSID Case No. ARB/07/21, Award, 30 July 2009.

Philip Morris Brand Sàrl (Switz.), Philip Morris Products S.A. (Switz.) and Abal Hermanos S.A. (Uru.) v Oriental Republic of Uruguay, ICSID Case No. ARB/10/7, Pending. Online. Available at: https://icsid.worldbank.org/ICSID/FrontServlet?requestType=GenCaseDtlsRH&actionVal=ListPending.

Phoenix Action Ltd v Czech Republic, ICSID Case No. ARB/06/5, Award, 15 April 2009.

Plama Consortium Limited v Republic of Bulgaria, ICSID Case No. ARB/03/24, Decision on Jurisdiction, 8 February 2005.

Pope & Talbot, Inc. v The Government of Canada, UNCITRAL Arbitration, 40 ILM 258, Interim Award, 26 June 2000.

Renta 4 S.V.S.A et al. v The Russian Federation, SCC No. 24/2007, Award on Preliminary Objections, 20 March 2009.

Ros InvestCo UK Ltd. v The Russian Federation, SCC Case No. Arbitration V 079/2005, Award on Jurisdiction, 28 October 2007.

Salini Construttori S.p.A. and Italstrade S.p.A. v The Hashemite Kingdom of Jordan, ICSID Case No. ARB/02/13, Decision on Jurisdiction, 9 November 2004.

Salini Costruttori SpA & Anor v Kingdom of Morocco, ICSID Case No. ARB/00/4, Decision on Jurisdiction, 23 July 2001.

Siemens A.G. v The Argentine Republic, ICSID Case No. ARB/02/8, Decision on Jurisdiction, 3 August 2004.

Suez, Sociedad General de Aguas de Barcelona S.A., and Vivendi Universal S.A. v The Argentine Republic, ICSID Case No. ARB/03/19, Decision on Jurisdiction, 3 August 2006.

Technicas Medioambientales Tecmed S.A. v The United Mexican States, ICSID Case No. ARB (AF)/00/2, Award, 29 May 2003.

Telenor Mobile Communications A.S. v The Republic of Hungary, ICSID Case No. ARB/04/15, Award, 13 September 2006.

United Parcel Service v Government of Canada, Decision on Intervention and Participation as Amici Curiae, 17 October 2001. Online Available at: http://naftaclaims.com/Disputes/Canada/UPS/UPSDecisionReParticipationAmiciCuriae.pdf.

Urbaser SA and Consorcio de Aguas Bilbao Bizkaia, Bilbao Biskaia Ur Partzuergoa v The Argentine Republic, ICSID Case No. ARB/07/26, Decision on Claimant's Proposal to Disqualify Professor Campbell McLachlan, Arbitrator, 12 August 2010.

Vladimir Berschader and Moise Berschader v The Russia Federation, SCC Case No. 080/2004, Award, 21 April 2006.

Wintershall Aktiengesellschaft v Argentine Republic, ICSID Case No. ARB/04/14, Award, 8 December 2008.

PCIJ and ICJ judgments

Ambatielos Case (Greece v United Kingdom), Merits: Obligation to Arbitrate, Judgment of 19 May 1953, ICJ reports 1953, p. 10.

Anglo-Iranian Oil Co. case (jurisdiction), Judgment of 22 July 1952: ICJ Reports 1952, p. 93.

Application of the Convention on the Prevention and Punishment of the Crime of Genocide (Bosnia and Herzegovina v Serbia and Montenegro), Judgment, ICJ Reports 2007, p. 43.

Jurisdictional Immunities of the State (Germany v Italy: Greece Intervening), ICJ Judgement, 3 February 2012.

Military and Paramilitary Activities in and Against Nicaragua (Nicaragua v United States of America), Merits, ICJ Reports 1986, p. 14.

ECJ judgments

ECJ, 140/79, *Chemical Farmaceutici SpA v DAF SpA* [1981] ECR 1.

EJC, C-120/78, *Rewe-Zentral AG v Bundesmonopolverwaltung für Branntwein* [1979] ECR 649.

EJC, C-132/03, *Federconsumatori* [2005] ECR I-4167.

Domestic court judgments

Associated Provincial Picture Houses Ltd. v Wednesbury Corporation [1947] 1 KB 223.

Attorney-General v Chapman [2011] NZSC 110.

Australian Pork Limited v Director of Animal and Plant Quarantine [2005] FCA 671.

Coalition for Fair Lumber Imports Executive Committee v United States, Civil Action No. 05–1366 (D.C. Cir.).

Democratic Republic of the Congo v FG Hemisphere Associates LLC [2011] 4 HKC 151 (HKCFA).

Director of Animal and Plant Quarantine v Australian Pork Limited [2005] FCAFC 206.

ETI Euro Telecom International NV v Republic of Bolivia [2008] EWHC 1689 (Comm).

Havana Club Holding v Galleon S.A, 203 F. 3d 116 (2nd Cir. 2000).

JT International SA v Commonwealth of Australia [2012] HCA 43.

Minister for Immigration v Teoh (1995) 183 CLR 273, [1995] HCA 20, (1995) 128 ALR 353.

Project Blue Sky Inc v Australian Broadcasting Authority (1998) 194 CLR 355; (1998) 153 ALR 490; (1998) 72 ALJR 841; (1998) 8 Leg Rep 41; (1998) HCA 28.

Tavita v Minister of Immigration, [1994] 2 NZLR 257 (CA).
Tiroa E and Te Hape B Trusts v Chief Executive of Land Information [2012] NZHC 147.

Domestic legislation, regulations, and policy statements

Australian Government Department of Foreign Affairs and Trade (2011) *Gillard Government Trade Policy Statement: trading our way to more jobs and prosperity*, April. Online. Available at: www.dfat.gov.au/publications/trade/trading-our-way-to-more-jobs-and-prosperity.html.
Competition Act, 2002, No. 12 of 2003; India Code (2003).
Constitution of the People's Republic of China, adopted 4 December1982, as amended on 14 March 2004.
Consumer Product Safety Improvement Act of 2008, Public Law 110–314—AUG. 14, 2008.
Federal Food, Drug, and Cosmetic Act, Public Law 75–717, Chapter VIII.
New Zealand Government Submission (2008) '2008 Review of the Trans-Tasman Mutual Recognition Arrangement'.
Provisions on Administration of Provision of Financial Information Services in China by Foreign Institutions, promulgated by the Information Office of the State Council, the Ministry of Commerce and the State Administration for Industry and Commerce on 30 April 2009, effective date on 1 June 2009. Online. Available HTTP: www.bjreview.com.cn/document/txt/2009-07/20/content_208369.htm.
Provisions on M&A of a Domestic Enterprise by Foreign Investors, No. 6 Decree of the Ministry of Commerce PRC, 22 June 2009. Online. Available at: www.fdi.gov.cn/pub/FDI_EN/Laws/law_en_info.jsp?docid=108906.
Tobacco Plain Packaging Act 2011 (No. 148, 2011).
U.S. Code of Federal Regulations Title 21, Chapter I – Food and Drug Administration Department of Health and Human Services, Subchapter B – Food for Human Consumption.
U.S. Food and Drug Administration, Generic Drug User Fee Act Program, proposed at 19 December 2011 public meeting (Docket No. FDA-2010-N-0381).

International organization and customs union documents

United Nations documents

Draft Articles on Most-Favoured-Nation Clauses with Commentaries, *Yearbook of the International Law Commission 1978 Volume 2 Part 2*.
Draft Declaration on Rights and Duties of States, General Assembly Resolution 178 (II) of 21 November 1947.
International Law Commission (2006) *Fragmentation of International Law: Difficulties Arising from the Diversification and Expansion of International Law: report of the study group on the fragmentation of international law*, A/CN.4/L.682, 13 April 2006.
International Law Commission Working Group on MFN Clauses (2007), *Most-Favoured-Nation Clause*, A/CN.4/L.719 20 July 2007, ILC Fifty-ninth session.
League of Nations *Recommendations of the Economic Committee Relating to Tariff Policy and the Most-favoured-nation Clause*, E.805.1933.II.B.1.

Most-Favoured-Nation Clause in the Law of Treaties: Working Paper Submitted by Mr. Endre Ustor, Special Rapporteur, Document A/CN.4/L.127, *Yearbook of the International Law Commission 1968 Volume 2*.

Nationality of Natural Persons in Relation to Succession of States, General Assembly Resolution 55/153 of 12 December 2000.

Report of the International Law Commission, General Assembly Resolution 31/97 of 15 December 1976.

Report of the International Law Commission, General Assembly Resolution 32/151 of 19 December 1977.

Report of the International Law Commission on the work of its forty-eighth session 'Draft articles on State Responsibility', *Yearbook of the International Law Commission 1996 Volume II Part II*.

Report of the International Law Commission, General Assembly Resolution 2272 (XXII) of 1 December 1967.

Report of the Work of the ILC Commission at its 63rd Session (2011) 'The Most-favoured-nations clause (chap. XII of the report)', A/66/10, paras 345–62.

Responsibility of States for Internationally Wrongful Acts, General Assembly Resolution 56/83 of 12 December 2001.

Rio Declaration on Environment and Development, A/CONF.151/26. Online. Available HTTP: www.un.org/documents/ga/conf151/aconf15126-1annex1.htm.

Statement by the Co-Chairmen of the Study Group on the Most-Favoured-Nation Clause, 8 August 2011.

UN General Assembly *World Charter for Nature*, 28 October 1982, A/RES/37/7. Online. Available at: www.un.org/documents/ga/res/37/a37r007.htm.

WTO documents

Australia – Measures Affecting the Importation of Apples from New Zealand (DS376) – First Written Submissions of Australia, Geneva 18 July 2008.

Dispute Settlement Body *Minutes Meeting held in the Centre William Rappard on 28 January 2013*, WT/DSB/M/328, 22 March 2013.

Dispute Settlement Body *Minutes of Meeting Held in the Centre William Rappard on 20 March 2001*, WT/DSB/M/102, 10 May 2001.

Dispute Settlement Body *Minutes of Meeting Held in the Centre William Rappard on 5 April 2001*, WT/DSB/M/103, 6 June 2001.

Dispute Settlement Body *Minutes of Meeting held in the Centre William Rappard on 19 November 2009*, WT/DSB/M/276, 29 January 2010.

Dispute Settlement Body *Minutes of Meeting held in the Centre William Rappard on 24 April 2012*, WT/DSB/M/315, 27 June 2012.

Dispute Settlement Body Special Session *Contribution of Canada to the Improvement of the WTO Dispute Settlement Understanding: Communication from Canada*, TN/DS/W/41, 24 January 2003.

Dispute Settlement Body Special Session *Contribution of the United States on Some Practical Considerations in Improving the Dispute Settlement Understanding of the WTO Related to Transparency and Open Meetings: Communication from the United States*, TN/DS/W/79, 13 July 2005.

Dispute Settlement Body Special Session *Contribution of the United States to the Improvement of the Dispute Settlement Understanding of the WTO Related to Transparency: Communication from the United States*, TN/DS/W/13, 22 August 2002.

Dispute Settlement Body Special Session *Further Contribution of the United States to the Improvement of the Dispute Settlement Understanding of the WTO Related to Transparency – Revised Legal Drafting: Communication from the United States*, TN/DS/W/86, 21 April 2006.

Dispute Settlement Body Special Session *Further Contribution of the United States to the Improvement of the Dispute Settlement Understanding of the WTO Related to Transparency: Communication from the United States*, TN/DS/W/46, 11 February 2003.

Protocol on the Accession of the People's Republic of China, WT/L/432, 23 November 2001.

Rules of Conduct for the Understanding on Rules and Procedures Governing the Settlement of Disputes as adopted by the DSB on 3 December 1996, WT/DBS/RC/1, 11 December 1996.

Working Procedures for Appellate Review, WT/AB/WP/5, 4 January 2005.

World Trade Organization (2006) *Trade Policy Review Report by the People's Republic of China*, WT/TPR/G/161, 17 March 2006.

World Trade Organization (2008) 'Trade policy review: China', PRESS/TPRB/299, 21 and 23 May.

World Trade Organization (2010) 'Trade policy review: China – restructuring and further trade liberalization are keys to sustaining growth', press release, WT/TPRB/330, 31 May – 2 June.

World Trade Organization *Australia – Measures Affecting the Importation of Apples from New Zealand Australia-Apples – Notification of an Other Appeal by New Zealand under Article 16.4 and Article 17 of the Understanding on Rules and Procedures Governing the Settlement of Disputes (DSU), and under Rule 23(1) of the Working Procedures for Appellate Review*, WT/DS367/14, 15 September 2010.

World Trade Organization *Indicative List of Governmental and Non-governmental Panelists*, WT/DSB/33, 6 March 2003.

World Trade Organization *Indicative List of Governmental and Non-governmental Panelists Revision*, WT/DSB/44rev.5, 29 January 2009.

World Trade Organization *Minutes of the General Council Meeting of 22 November 2000*, WT/GC/M/60, 23 January 2001.

World Trade Organization *Trade Policy Review Report by the People's Republic of China*, WT/TPR/G/161, 17 March 2006.

World Trade Organization *European Communities and Certain Member States – Measures Affecting Trade in Large Civil Aircraft – Recourse to Article 7.9 of the SCM Agreement and Article 22.2 of the DSU by the United States*, WT/DS316/18, 12 December 2011.

World Trade Organization *Working Procedure for Appellate Review: Communication from the Appellate Body*, WT/AB/WP/W/9, 7 October 2004.

WTO Trade Policy Body Review (2008) *Trade Policy Review: Report by the Secretariat – China (Revision)*, WT/TPR/S/199/Rev.1, 12 August.

European Union documents

Amendment of the Proposal for a Council Directive amending Directive 81/602/EEC concerning the prohibition of certain substances, 28 Official Journal, Eur. Comm. (No. C313) 4/1985.

Commission of the European Communities (2009) *Report from the Commission to the European Parliament and to the Council on the Implementation of Directive 2001/95/*

EC of the European Parliament and of the Council of 3 December 2001 on General Product Safety (2009), COM(2008)905 final. Online. Available at: http://ec.europa.eu/consumers/safety/prod_legis/docs/report_impl_gpsd_en.pdf.

Council Directive 81/602/EEC of 31 July 1981 concerning the prohibition of certain substances having a hormonal action and of any substances having a thyrostatic action, [1981] O J L 222.

Proposal for a Council Directive amending Directive 81/602/EEC concerning the prohibition of certain substances having a hormonal action and of any substances having a thyrostatic action, COM(84) 296 final, [1984] O J No. C 170/4.

European Commission (2012) *Report from the Commission to the European Council: trade and investment barriers report 2012*, COM(2012) 70, Brussels, 21 February.

European Commission Communication from the Commission on the precautionagry principle, COM(2000) 1 final. Online. Available at: http://eur-lex.europa.eu/LexUriServ/LexUriServ.do?uri=COM:2000:0001:FIN:EN:PDF.

Articles, books, chapters, theses, papers, speeches, and online materials

Abbott, F. (2009) 'Cross-retaliation in TRIPS: options for developing countries', ICSTD Programme on Dispute Settlement and Legal Aspects of International Trade Law, issue paper No. 8.

Abbot, K. and Snidal, D. (2000) 'Hard and soft law in international governance', *International Organizations*, 54(3): 421–56.

Alemanno, A. (2009) 'Solving the problem of scale: the European approach to import safety and security concerns', in C. Coglianese, A. Finkel, D. Zaring (eds) *Import Safety: regulatory governance in the global economy*, Pennsylvania: Pennsylvania Press.

Alston, P. (1997) 'The myopia of the handmaidens: international lawyers and globalization', *European Journal of International Law*, 8: 435–48.

Alvarez-Jimenez, A. (2006) 'The WTO AB report on *Mexico – Soft Drinks*, and the limits of the WTO dispute settlement system', *Legal Issues of Economic Integration*, 33(3): 319–33.

AmCham-China (2009) *American Business in China: 2009 white paper*. Online. Available at: http://web.resource.amchamchina.org/Podcasts/WhitePaper2009.pdf.

AmCham-China (2011) 'Market access: barriers to market entry', 29 April. Online. Available at: www.amchamchina.org/article/7938.

American Society for International Law (2006) *International Law: 100 ways it shapes our lives*, Washington DC: ASIL.

Anderlini, J. and Dyer, G. (2009) 'Beijing accused of attacking private enterprise', *Financial Times*, 25 November.

Andersen, S. (2005) 'Administration of evidence in the WTO', in R. Yerxa and B. Wilson (eds) *Key Issues in WTO Dispute Settlement: the first ten years*, New York: Cambridge University Press.

Asia Money (2008) 'Private equity: Foreign funds face Beijing blockade', 1 September. Online. Available at: www.asiamoney.com/Article/2055617/Search/Results/PRIVATE-EQUITY-Foreign-funds-face-Beijing-blockade.html?PartialFields=CATEGORY_313_IDS%3A5923.

Asian Development Bank (2005) 'Greater Mekong subregion flagship initiative: North-South economic corridor', 26 June.

Atkins, R. (2010) 'China confirmed as world's top exporter', *Financial Times*, 9 February.

Australian Government Department of Innovation, Industry, Science and Research (2006) *A Users' Guide to the Mutual Recognition Agreement and the Trans-Tasman Mutual Recognition Arrangement*. Online. Available at: www.innovation.gov.au/Industry/TradePolicies/MRA/Pages/Trans-TasmanMRA.aspx.

Australian Productivity Commission (2010) 'Bilateral and regional trade Agreements: research report', *13 December*. Online. Available at: www.pc.gov.au/projects/study/trade-agreements/.

Automotive World (2010) 'China: new auto policy to be implemented in H1 2010', 22 February. Online. Available at: www.automotiveworld.com/news/emerging-markets/80901-china-new-auto-policy-to-be-implemented-in-h1-of-2010.

Aziz, J. (2006) 'Rebalancing China's economy: what does growth theory tell us?' *IMF Working Paper*, 06/291. Online. Available at: www.imf.org/external/pubs/ft/wp/2006/wp06291.pdf.

Baldwin, R. (2011) 'Sequencing regionalism: theory, European practice, and lessons for Asia', *ADB Working Paper Series on Regional Economic Integration*, 80. Online. Available at: www.aric.adb.org/pdf/workingpaper/WP80_Baldwin_Sequencing_Regionalism.pdf.

Balmer, A. and Martin, P. (2008) 'Synthetic biology: social and ethical challenges', Institute for Science and Society University of Nottingham.

Bamberger, K. A. and Guzman, A. T. (2008) 'Keeping imports safe: a proposal for discriminatory regulation of international trade', *California Law Review*, 96: 1405–45.

Bandao Wang (Peninsula Website), 30 June 2009. Online. Available at: http://news.bandao.cn/news_html/200906/20090630/news_20090630_841206.shtml.

Barfield, C. (2011) 'The Trans-Pacific Partnership: a model for twenty-first-century trade agreements?', *AEI International Economic Outlook No. 2*, 1 June. Online. Available at: www.aei.org/article/economics/international-economy/the-trans-pacific-partnership/.

Basheer, S. (2010) 'Turning Trips on its head: an "IP cross retaliation" model for developing countries', *The Law and Development Review*, 3(2): 139–97.

Bath, V. (2011) 'China, international business and the criminal law', *Asian-Pacific Law and Policy Journal*, 13(1): 1–35.

Bath, V. and Nottage, L. (2011) 'Foreign investment and dispute resolution law and practice in Asia: an overview', in V. Bath and L. Nottage (eds) *Investment Law and Dispute Resolution Law and Practice in Asia*, London: Routledge.

Bell, R. G. and Ziegler, M. S. (eds) (2012) *Building International Climate Cooperation: lessons from the weapons and trade regimes for achieving international climate goals*, Washington, DC: World resources Institute.

Bergsten, F. (2008) 'China's challenge to the global economic order', in F. Bergsten, C. Freeman, N. Lardy and D. Mitchell *China's Rise: challenges and opportunities*, Washington DC: Peterson Institute for International Economics and Center for Strategic and International Studies.

Bergsten, F. (2009) 'We should listen to Beijing's currency idea', *Financial Times*, 8 April.

Bergsten, F., Freeman, C., Lardy, N. and Mitchell, D. (2008) *China's Rise: challenges and opportunities*, Washington DC: Peterson Institute for International Economics and Center for Strategic and International Studies.

Bhagwati, J. (1995) 'U.S. trade policy: the infatuation with free trade areas', in J. Bhagwati and A. Krueger (eds) *The Dangerous Drift to Preferential Trade Agreements*, Washington, DC: American Enterprise Institute for Public Policy Research.

Biermann, F. (2001) 'The rising tide of green unilateralism in world trade law: options for reconciling the emerging North-South conflict', *Journal of World Trade*, 35(3): 421–48.

Bilaterals.org (2009) ' China–ASEAN', April. Online. Available at: www.bilaterals.org/rubrique.php3?id_rubrique=95.

Blomfield, A (2005) 'Impressionist masterpieces held hostage in dispute over unpaid oil bill', *The Telegraph*, 17 November. Online. Available at: www.telegraph.co.uk/news/worldnews/europe/switzerland/1503241/Impressionist-masterpieces-held-hostage-in-dispute-over-unpaid-oil-bill.html.

BNA WTO Reporter (2004) 'EC threatens WTO suit against China unless it lifts coking-coal restrictions', 25 May.

BNA WTO Reporter (2006) 'China balked at joint statement of support for WTO talks, US official says', 19 April.

Boisson De Chazournes, L. (2005) 'Arbitration at the WTO: a *terra incognita* to be further explored', in S. Charnovitz, D. Steger and P. van den Bossche (eds) *Law in the Service of Human Dignity: essays in honour of Florentino Feliciano*, New York: Cambridge University Press.

Bollyky, T. (2012) *Better Regulation for Freer Trade*, Policy Innovation Memorandum No. 22, June, Washington DC: Council on Foreign Relations Press.

Borger, J. (2009) 'David Miliband: China ready to join U.S. as world power', *Guardian*, 18 May. Online. Available at: www.guardian.co.uk/politics/2009/may/17/david-miliband-china-world-power.

Brack, A. (2009) 'A disadvantageous dichotomy in product safety law – some reflections on sense and nonsense of the distinction food–nonfood in European product safety law', *European Business Law Review*, 20(1): 173–98.

Brack, D. (2002) 'Environmental treaties and trade: multilateral environmental agreements and the multilateral trading system', in G. P. Sampson and W. B. Chambers *Trade, Environmental, and the Millennium*, 2nd edn, USA: United Nations University Press.

Bradsher, K. (2007) 'Beijing seeks new security of investment by outsiders', *New York Times*, 28 August.

Brandt, L. and Rawski, T. (eds) (2008) *China's Great Economic Transformation*, New York: Cambridge University Press.

Brereton, P. (2011) 'Proof of foreign law: problems and initiatives'. Online. Available at: http://sydney.edu.au/law/events/2011/May/Justice_Brereton.pdf.

Bridges Trade BioRes Review (2011) 'Not-so-voluntary labelling in the WTO tuna-dolphin dispute', 9 November.

Brightling, D. and Feldman, J. (2009) 'Environment chapters and trade agreements: a passing fad or here to stay?', paper presented at the NZCIEL Conference on Trade Agreements: Where Do We Go From Here?, Wellington, 22–23 October.

Browne, C. and Lee, J. K. (2006) 'Private sector development', in C. Browne *Pacific Island Economies*, International Monetary Fund.

Buckley, R., Hu, R. and Arner, D. (eds) (2011) *East Asian Economic Integration: law, trade and finance*, Cheltenham: Edward Elgar.

Burch, M. and Nottage, L. (2011) 'Novel treaty-based approaches to resolving international investment and tax disputes in Asia-Pacific region', *Australian International Law Journal*, 18: 127–40.

Burch, M., Nottage, L. and Williams, B. (2012) 'Appropriate treaty-based dispute resolution for Asia-Pacific commerce in the 21st century', *Sydney Law School Research Paper*, 12/37. Online. Available at: http://ssrn.com/abstract=2065636.

Burke-White, W. and von Staden, A. (2010) 'Private litigation in a public law sphere: the standard of review in investor-state arbitrations', *Yale Journal of International Law*, 35: 283–346.

Busch, M. L. (2007) 'Overlapping institutions, forum shopping, and dispute settlement in international trade', *International Organization*, 61: 735–61.

Busch, M., Reinhardt, E. and Shaffer, G. (2009) 'Does legal capacity matter? A survey of WTO Members', *World Trade Review*, 8(4): 559–77.

Business Roundtable (2003) 'A Business Roundtable WTO policy paper: a balanced approach to precaution and risk', May. Online. Available at: http://businessroundtable. org.

Caijing Magazine (Financial Magazine) (2009) 'The US welcomes China's elimination of its surcharge on imported automobile parts', 29 August. Online. Available at: www. caijing.com.cn/2009-08-29/110230736.html.

Calder, K. and Ye, M. (2010) *The Making of Northeast Asia*, Stanford: Stanford University Press.

Cao Kangtai 'The Explanatory notes to submit the draft Antimonopoly Law to the National People's Congress of PRC', 25 June 2006, *Zhonghua Renmin Gongheguo Renmin Daibiao Dahui Changwu Weiyuanhui Gongbao* (Bulletin of the Standing Committee of the National People's Congress of PRC), No. 6 (2007).

Carmody, C. (2009) 'A theory of WTO law', paper presented at the ASIL International Economic Law Research Colloquium, UCLA Law School.

Center for International Environmental Law and International Institute for Development Studies (2007) *Revising the UNCITRAL Arbitration Rules to Address Investor-State Arbitrations*. Online. Available at: www.iisd.org/pdf/2008/investment_revising_uncitral_arbitration_dec.pdf.

Chen, Y. (2009) *Transition and Development in China: towards shared growth*, Farnham: Ashgate.

China Briefing (2009) 'Central bank governor proposes SDR as main reserve currency', 24 March. Online. Available at: www.china-briefing.com/news/2009/03/24/central-bank-governor-proposes-sdr-as-main-reserve-currency.html.

China Daily (2006) 'Anti-monopoly law draft provokes debates', 15 November. Online. Available at: www.china.org.cn/english/BAT/188976.htm.

China Daily (2009a) 'China all alone in Asian M&A growth', 6 January. Online. Available at: www.chinadaily.com.cn/bizchina/2009-01/06/content_7368947.htm.

China Daily (2009b) 'Country's firms surpass US rivals', 7 September. Online. Available at: www.chinadaily.com.cn/bizchina/2009-09/07/content_8660864.htm.

China Daily (2010) 'China honors all WTO entry commitments: MOC', 20 July. Online. Available at: http://news.xinhuanet.com/english2010/china/2010-07/20/c_13406665. htm.

China Daily (2012) 'Chinese man protest against World Bank', 28 February. Online. Available at: http://bbs.chinadaily.com.cn/thread-734025-1-1.html.

Choi, W.-M. (2003) *Like Products in International Trade Law: towards a consistent GATT/WTO jurisprudence*, Oxford: Oxford University Press.

Christian J. (2009) 'Sound science in the European and global market: Karl Polanyi in Geneva?', in M. Everson and E. Vos (eds) *Uncertain Risks Regulated*, Oxford: Routledge-Cavendish.

Clarke, D. C. (2007a) 'China: creating a legal system for a market economy', *The George Washington University Law School Public Law and Legal Theory Working Paper*, 396. Online. Available at: http://papers.ssrn.com/sol3/papers.cfm?abstract_id=1097587.

Clarke, D. C. (2007b) 'Introduction: the Chinese legal system since 1995: Steady development and striking continuities', *China Quarterly*, September.

Commission, J. (2007) 'Precedent in investment treaty arbitration: a citation analysis of a developing jurisprudence', *Journal of International Arbitration*, 24(2): 129–58.

Compa, L. (2001) 'NAFTA's labor side agreement and international labor solidarity', *Antipode* 33(3): 451–67; also in P. Waterman and J. Wills (eds) (2001) *Place, Space and the New Labour Internationalisms*, Oxford: Blackwell.

Connelly, R. (2005) 'Is there a need for a commission on environmental cooperation for managing AUSFTA?', *Environmental and Planning Law Journal*, 22: 409–17.

Conrad, C. R. (2008) 'The status of measures linked to non-physical aspects and processes and production methods (PPMs) in WTO law: a contribution to the debate on the impact of WTO law on national regulation pursuing social goals', dissertation, University of Bern.

Cossy, M. (2005) 'Panels' consultations with scientific experts', in R. Yerxa and B. Wilson (eds) *Key Issues in WTO Dispute Settlement: the first ten years*, New York: Cambridge University Press.

Cottier, T. (2006) 'From progressive liberalization to progressive regulation in WTO law', *Journal of International Economic Law*, 9: 779.

Cottier, T. and Oesch. M. (2011) 'Direct and indirect discrimination in WTO law and EU law', Working Paper, 2011/16, April. Online. Available at: www.wti.org/fileadmin/user_upload/nccr-trade.ch/hi/CottierOeschNCCRWP16.pdf.

Cottier, T., Nartova, O. and Bigdeli, S. Z. (eds) (2009) *International Trade Regulation and the Mitigation of Climate Change: world trade forum*, Cambridge: Cambridge University Press.

Crean, S. 'Commencement of PACER Plus negotiations', transcript-ministerial statement, 18 August 2009. Online. Available at: www.trademinister.gov.au/transcripts/2009/090818_pacer.html.

Croome, J. (1995) *Reshaping The World Trading System: A History of The Uruguay Round: A history of Uruguay Round*, Geneva: World Trade Organization.

Daboub, J. J. (2009) 'China's economy recovery is impossible without private investment', *21 Shiji Jingji Baodao (21st Century Business Herald, Chinese translation)*, 10 June.

Dankers, C. (2003) 'The WTO and environmental and social standards, certification and labelling', *Food and Agricultural Organization of the United Nations Commodity and Trade Policy Research Working Paper*, No. 2.

Davey, W. J. (2006) 'Dispute settlement in the WTO and RTAs: a comment', in L. Bartels and F. Ortino (eds) *Regional Trade Agreements and the WTO Legal System*, New York: Oxford University Press.

Davey, W. J. 'Environmental and Product Safety Cases in the WTO, WTO Research Center of AGU'. Online. Available at: www.wto.aoyama.ac.jp/file/040526Davy.pdf.

Davey W. J. and Sapir, A. (2009) 'The *Soft Drinks* case: The WTO and regional agreements', *World Trade Review*, 8: 5–23.

Davies, G. T. (2008) 'Process and production method based trade restrictions in the EU'. Online. Available at: http://ssrn.com/abstract=1118709.

De Mestral, A. L. C. (2006) 'NAFTA dispute settlement: creative experiment or confusion?', in L. Bartels and F. Ortino (eds) *Regional Trade Agreements and the WTO Legal System*, New York: Oxford University Press.

De Wet, E. (2006) 'The international constitutional order', *International and Comparative Law Quarterly*, 55: 51–76.

Dee, P. and McNaughton, A. (2010) 'Promoting domestic reforms through regionalism',

Tokyo: Asian Development Bank Institute. Online. Available at: www.adbi.org/files/2011.10.13.wp312.promoting.domestic.reforms.regionalism.pdf.

Defraigne, P. (2009) 'Opening speech of the international workshop on EU–China partnership', *EU–China Observer*, 2: 22–6.

Delimatsis, P. and Sauvé, P. (2010) 'Financial services trade after the crisis: policy and legal conjectures', *Journal of International Economic Law*, 13(3): 837–57.

Dent, C. (2010) 'Organizing the wider East Asia region', *ADB Working Paper Series on Regional Economic Integration*, 62. Online. Available at: http://aric.adb.org/pdf/workingpaper/WP62_Dent_Organizing_the_Wider_East_Asia_Region.pdf.

Desmedt, G. A. (1998) 'Hormones: objective assessment and (or as) standard of review', *Journal of International Economic Law*, 1: 695–8.

Dickie, M. (2006) 'Chinese official warns on "Malicious" foreign takeovers', *Financial Times*, 8 March. Online. Available at: www.ft.com/intl/cms/s/0/ea14a16a-ae92-11da-b04a-0000779e2340.html#axzz1wWsKulYu.

Diebold, N. (2010) *Non-Discrimination in International Trade in Services: 'likeness' in WTO/GATS*, Cambridge: Cambridge University Press.

DiMascio, N. and Pauwelyn, J. (2008) 'Non-discrimination in trade and investment treaties: worlds apart or two sides of the same coin', *American Journal of International Law*, 102(1): 48–89.

Dinwoodie, G. B. and Dreyfuss R. C. (2012) *A Neofederalist Vision of TRIPS: The Resilience of the International Intellectual Property Regime*, New York: Oxford University Press.

Dooley, M., *et al.* (2003) 'An essay on the revived Bretton Woods system', *National Bureau of Economic Research Working Paper*, 9971.

Dooley, M., *et al.* (2009) 'Bretton Woods II still defines the international monetary system', *National Bureau of Economic Research Working Paper*, 14731.

Downes, J. and Goodman, J. (1998) *Dictionary of Finance and Investment Terms*, 5th edn, Barron's.

Drahos P. 'The bilateral web of trade dispute settlement', unpublished manuscript, Paper for the workshop *WTO Dispute Settlement and Developing Countries: use, Implications, Strategies, Reforms*, University of Wisconsin at Madison, 20–21 May 2005.

Durling, J. (2003) 'Deference but only when due: WTO review of anti-dumping measures', *Journal of International Economic Law*, 6(1): 125–53.

Durling, J. and Hardin, D. (2005) 'Amicus curie participation in WTO dispute settlement', in R. Yerxa and B. Wilson (eds) *Key Issues in WTO Dispute Settlement: the first ten years*, New York: Cambridge University Press.

Economic Law Division of the Legislative Committee under the Standing Committee of the National People's Congress (ed.) (2007) *Zhonghua Renmin Gongheguo Fanlongguan Fa Tiaowen Shouming, Lifa Liyou ji Xiangguan Guiding (The Antimonopoly Law of The PRC: Annotations, Legislative Reasons and Other Relevant Provisions)*, Beijing University Press.

Economist Intelligence Unit (2008) 'Country report for China', 4 June.

Egan, M. (2001) *Constructing a European Market: standards, regulation and governance*, Oxford: Oxford University Press.

Ehlermann, C. (2002) 'Six years on the "bench of the world trade court"', *Journal of World Trade*, 36(4): 605–39.

Ehlermann, C. D. and Lockhart, N. (2004) 'Standard of review in WTO law', *Journal of International Economic Law*, 7(3): 491–521.

Ehring, L. (2002) 'De facto discrimination in WTO law: national and most-favored-nation treatment – or equal treatment?', *Journal of World Trade*, 36: 921.

Eichengreen, B., Wyplosz, C. and Park, Y. (eds) (2008) *China, Asia, and the New World Economy*, New York: Oxford University Press.

Elms, D. and Lim, C. L. (2012) 'The Trans-Pacific partnership agreement (TPP) negotiations: overview and prospects', *RSIS Working Paper*, 232. Online. Available at: www. rsis.edu.sg/publications/WorkingPapers/WP232.pdf.

Embassy of the People's Republic of China in Switzerland (1999) 'Statistics show China's 50-Year economic development', 3 October.

Ensinger, D. (2011) 'China trying to force technology transfer', *Economy in Crisis*, 7 September. Online. Available at: http://economyincrisis.org/content/china-trying-force-technology-transfer.

Epps, T. and Green, A. (2010) *Reconciling Trade and Climate: how the WTO can help address climate change*, Cheltenham: Edward Elgar.

European Commission (2001) 'European policy principles on international standardization', *Commission Staff Working Paper*, SEC(2001) 1296, 26 July.

European Commission (2006) 'Global Europe: EU-China trade and investment competition and partnership'. Online. Available at: http://trade.ec.europa.eu/doclib/docs/2006/november/tradoc_131234.pdf.

European Union Chamber of Commerce in China (2009) *European Business in China Position Paper 2009/2010*. Online. Available at: www.euccc.com.cn/cms/page/en/publications-archive/59.

European Union Chamber of Commerce in China (2010) *European Business in China Position Paper 2010–2011*. Online. Available at: www.euccc.com.cn/cms/page/en/publications-archive/58.

Evans, D. and de Tarso Pereira, C. (2005) 'DSU review: a view from the inside', in R. Yerxa and B. Wilson (eds) *Key Issues in WTO Dispute Settlement: the first ten years*, New York: Cambridge University Press.

Fairgrieve, D. (2006) 'General product safety – a revolution through reform?', *Modern Law Review*, 69: 59–69.

Fairgrieve, D. and Howells, G. (2006) 'General product safety – a revolution through reform?', *Modern Law Review*, 69: 59–69.

Farah, P. (2008) 'L'influenza della concezione confuciana sulla costruzione del sistema giuridico e politico cinese', in G. Bombelli and B. Montanari (eds) *Identità Europea e Politiche Migratorie*, Vita e pensiero.

Fearnley, C. (2009) 'WTO dispute settlement and the DSU review', presentation at MFAT Beeby Colloquium.

Financial Magazine (2008) 'Senior SAIC official arrested', 28 October. Online. Available at: http://english.caijing.com.cn/2008-10-28/110024002.html.

Fink, C. and Molinuevo, M. (2008) 'East Asian free trade agreements in services: key architectural elements', *Journal of International Economic Law*, 11(2): 263–311.

Flitton, D. (2011) 'My dream of Asia is here now, says Rudd', *Sun-Herald*, 24 July. Online. Available at: www.smh.com.au/world/my-dream-of-asia-is-here-now-says-rudd-20110723-1hu3i.html.

Food & Drink Weekly (2003) 'ADM to seek damages as a result of Mexico's soft drink tax', 27 October. Online. Available at: www.thefreelibrary.com/ADM+to+seek+damag es+as+a+result+of+Mexico's+soft+drink+tax.-a0109403971.

Foot, R. (2001) 'China and the idea of a responsible state', in Y. Zhang and G. Austin (eds) *Power and Responsibility in Chinese Foreign Policy*, Canberra: Asia Pacific Press.

Foreign Affairs (2008) 'Changing China', 87(1): 1–66.

Foreign Affairs and International Trade Canada (2003) 'Statement of Canada on open hearing in NAFTA Chapter Eleven arbitration', 7 October. Online. Avaliable at: www. international.gc.ca/trade-agreements-accords-commerciaux/agr-acc/nafta-alena/open-hearing.aspx?lang=eng.

Formacion, A. (2008) 'Philippines and Japan: moving forward with an economic partnership agreement – a legal analysis on labor standards', *Faculty of Law, Kyushu University, Working Paper*. Online. Available at: http://asia.kyushu-u.ac.jp/pandp/events/080308-09/presentations/doc_04antonio.pdf.

Frankel, S. (2008) 'The legitimacy and purpose of intellectual property chapters in FTAs', in R. Buckley, V. I. Lo and L. Boulle (eds) *Challenges to Multilateral Trade The Impact of Bilateral, Preferential and Regional Agreements*, The Netherlands: Wolters Kluwer.

Frankel, S. and Richardson, M. (2011) 'Trans-Tasman intellectual property coordination', in S. Frankel (ed.) *Learning from the Past, Adapting for the Future: regulatory reform in New Zealand*, Wellington: LexisNexis.

Freeman, R. (2009) 'The general product safety directive: a five year review', *European Product Liability Reporter (Lovells)*, 34: 2–7.

Fu-kuo, L. (2008) 'Beijing's regional strategy and China–ASEAN economic integration', *China Brief*, 8(10). Online. Available at: www.jamestown.org/programs/chinabrief/single/?tx_ttnews%5Btt_news%5D=4916&tx_ttnews%5BbackPid%5D=168&no_cache=1.

Gantz, D. A. (2006) 'An appellate mechanism for review of arbitral decisions in investor state disputes: prospects and challenges', *Vanderbilt Journal of Transnational Law* 39(1): 39–76.

Gao, H. (2005) 'Aggressive legalism: the East Asian experience and lessons for China', in H. Gao and D. Lewis (eds) *China's Participation in the WTO*, London: Cameron May.

Gao, H. (2007) 'China's participation in the WTO: a lawyer's perspective', *Singapore Yearbook of International Law*, 11: 1–34.

Giddens, A. (2009) *The Politics of Climate Change*, Cambridge: Polity Press.

Goh, C. Y. (2006) 'Trade negotiations and protectionism', in D. A. Clark (ed.) *The Elgar Companion to Development Studies*, Cheltenham: Edward Elgar.

Goldman Sachs (2007) *BRICS and Beyond*. Online. Available at: www.goldmansachs.com/our-thinking/brics/brics-and-beyond-book-pdfs/brics-full-book.pdf.

Gong, G. (1991) 'China's entry into international society: beyond the standard of "civilization"', *Review of International Studies*, 17(1): 3–16.

Goode, W. (2007) *Dictionary of Trade Policy Terms*, 5th edn, Cambridge: Cambridge University Press.

Government of India Ministry of Commerce and Industry (2003) 'India, China re-emphasise solidarity on WTO issues at Cancun', 11 September. Online. Available at: http://commerce.nic.in/pressrelease/pressrelease_detail.asp?id=221.

Greenwald, J. (2003) 'WTO dispute settlement: an exercise in trade law legislation?', *Journal of International Economic Law*, 6(1): 113–24.

Grosse Ruse-Khan, H. (2008) 'A pirate of the Caribbean? The attractions of suspending TRIPS obligations', *Journal of International Economic law*, 11(2): 313–64.

Grosse Ruse-Khan, H. (2010) '"Gambling" with sovereignty: complying with international obligations or upholding national autonomy', in M. K. Lewis and S. Frankel *International Economic Law and National Autonomy*, New York: Cambridge University Press.

Guiji Caijing Shibao (International Business Times) (2011), 29 November. Online. Available at: www.ibtimes.com.cn/articles/20111129/020921_all.htm.

Guinée, J. B. *et al.* (eds) (2002) *Handbook on Life Cycle Assessment: operational guide to the ISO standards*, Dordrecht: Kluwer Academic Publishers.

Guzman, A. (2005) 'The design of international agreements', *European Journal of International Law*, 16(4): 579–612.

Haggard, S. (2011) *The Organizational Architecture of the Asia-Pacific: Insights from the New Institutionalism*, ADB Working Paper Series on Regional Economic Integration, 71.

Hamilton, L. (2003) 'US antidumping decisions and the WTO standard of review: deference or disregard?', *Chicago Journal of International Law*, 4: 265–70.

Harland, D. and Nottage, L. (2009) 'Conclusions', in J. Kellam (ed.) *Product Liability in the Asia-Pacific*, Sydney: Federation Press.

He, L.-L. and Sappideen, R. (2009) 'Reflections on China's WTO accession commitments and their observance', *Journal of World Trade*, 43(4): 847–71.

Henckels, C. (2008) 'Overcoming jurisdictional isolationism at the WTO FTA nexus: a potential approach for the WTO', *European Journal of International Law*, 19: 571–99.

Heydon, K. and Woolcock, S. (2009) *The Rise of Bilateralism*, Tokyo: United Nations University.

Hix, S. (2010) 'Institutional design of regional integration: balancing delegation and representation', *ADB Working Paper Series on Regional Economic Integration*, 64. Online. Available at: www.adb.org/sites/default/files/pub/2010/WP64-Hix-Institutional-Design.pdf.

Hodges, C. J. S. (2005) *European Regulation of Consumer Product Safety*, New York: Oxford University Press.

Holzer, K. (2010) 'Proposals on carbon-related border adjustments: prospects for WTO compliance', *Carbon and Climate Law Review*, 1:51.

Hong Kong Trade and Development Council (2007) 'China agrees to eliminate subsidies challenged by the U.S. at the WTO', 6 December. Online. Available at: www.hktdc.com/.

Horlick, G. N. and Clarke, P. A. (1997) 'Standards for panels reviewing anti-dumping determinations under the GATT and WTO', in E.-U. Petersmann (ed.) *International Trade Law and the GATT and WTO Dispute Settlement System*, The Hague: Kluwer Law International.

Hornby, L. 2009 'China's provinces trot out "buy local" campaigns', *Reuters*, 18 February.

Howells, G. G. (2000) 'The relationship between product liability and product safety: understanding a necessary element in European product liability through a comparison with the U.S. position', *Washburn Law Journal*, 39: 305–46.

Howse, R. (2002) 'The Appellate Body rulings in the shrimp/turtle case: a new legal baseline for the trade and environment debate', *Columbia Journal of Environmental Law*, 27: 491–521.

Huang, Y. (2008a) 'Just how capitalist is China', *MIT Sloan School Working Paper*, 4699–08. Online. Available at: http://ssrn.com/abstract=1118019.

Huang, Y. (2008b) *Just How Capitalist is China?*, New York: Cambridge University Press.

Hudec, R. (1992) 'The judicialization of GATT dispute settlement', in M. M. Hart and D. P. Steger (eds) *In Whose Interest? Due Process and Transparency in International Trade*, Ottawa: Centre for Trade Policy and Law.

Hudec, R. (1999) 'The new WTO dispute settlement procedure: an overview of the first three years', *Minnesota Journal of Global Trade*, 8: 1–53.

Hufbauer G. C. and Schott, J. (2005) *NAFTA Revisited: Achievements and Challenges*, Washington DC: Peterson Institute.

Hufbauer, G. C., Wong, Y. and Sheth, K. (2006) *US–China Trade Disputes: rising tide, rising stakes*, Washington DC: Institute for International Economics.

Hughes, V. (2004) 'Arbitration within the WTO' in F. Ortino and E. U. Petersmann *The WTO Dispute Settlement System: 1995–2003*, The Hague: Kluwer Law International.

Interagency Working Group on Import Safety (2007) *Action Plan for Import Safety: A roadmap for continual improvement*, a Report to the President, November.

International Centre for Settlement of Investment Disputes (2007) 'Bolivia submits a notice under article 71 of the ICSID Convention', *News Release*, 16 May. Online. Available at: http://icsid.worldbank.org/.

International Centre for Settlement of Investment Disputes (2009) 'Ecuador submits a notice under article 71 of the ICSID Convention', *News Release*, 9 July. Online. Available at: http://icsid.worldbank.org/.

International Centre for Settlement of Investment Disputes (2009) 'Merill & Ring v Canada, public hearing', News Release, 15 May. Online. Available at: http://icsid.worldbank.org ICSID/FrontServlet?requestType=CasesRH&actionVal=OpenPage&PageType=AnnouncementsFrame&FromPage=Announcements&pageName=Announcement16.

International Centre for Settlement of Investment Disputes (2009) 'UN urges increased South-South cooperation in response to crisis', *Bridges Weekly Trade News Digest*, 13(5).

International Centre for Settlement of Investment Disputes (2009) 'India boosts Asian trade ties', *Bridges Monthly*, 13(2). Online. Available at: http://ictsd.net/i/news/bridges/48551/.

International Centre for Settlement of Investment Disputes (2012) 'Venezuela submits a notice under article 71 of the ICSID Convention', *News Release*, 26 January. Online. Available at: http://icsid.worldbank.org/.

International Centre for Settlement of Investment Disputes (2012) *The ICSID Caseload – Statistics (Issue 2012–1)*. Online. Available at: http://icsid.worldbank.org/ICSID/FrontServlet?requestType=ICSIDDocRH&actionVal=CaseLoadStatistics.

International Monetary Fund (2009) 'World economic outlook database', October. Online. Available at: www.imf.org/external/pubs/ft/weo/2009/02/weodata/index.aspx.

International Monetary Fund (2009) 'World economic outlook update', 28 January. Online. Available at: www.imf.org/external/pubs/ft/weo/2009/update/01/pdf/0109.pdf.

International Monetary Fund (2011) 'World economic outlook: tensions from the two-speed recovery: unemployment, commodities, and capital flows'. Online. Available at: www.imf.org/external/pubs/ft/weo/2011/01/weodata/index.aspx.

Jackson, J. H. (2000) 'The role and effectiveness of the WTO dispute settlement mechanism', *Brookings Trade Forum*, 179–236. Online. Available at: http://muse.jhu.edu/journals/brookings_trade_forum/v2000/2000.1jackson.html.

Jackson, J. H., Davey, W. J. and Sykes, A. O. (2002) *Legal Problems of International Economic Relations*, 4th edn, St. Paul, Minnesota: West Group.

Jackson, J. H., Davey, W. J. and Sykes, A. O. (2008) *Legal Problems of International Economic Relations*, 5th edn, St. Paul, Minnesota: Thomson/West.

Jinghua Shibao (Beijing Times), 12 October 2008.

Jinghua Shibao (Beijing Times), 5 March 2008. Online. Available at: http://business.sohu.com/20080305/n255532126.shtml.

Joerges, C. (2009) 'Sound science in the European and global market: Karl Polanyi in

Geneva?' in M. Everson and E. Vos (eds) *Uncertain Risks Regulated*, Oxford; New York: Routledge.

Joerges, C. and Vos, E. (eds) (1999) *EU Committees: social regulation, law and politics*, Oxford; Portland: Hart.

Josling, T., Roberts, D. and Hassan, A., 'The Beef-Hormone Dispute and Its Implications for Trade Policy', The Working Paper, 1999. Online. Available at: http://iis-db.stanford.edu/pubs/11379/HORMrev.pdf.

Kalderimis, D. (2009) 'Changes to Australia's and New Zealand's overseas investment regimes'. Online. Available at: www.chapmantripp.com/publications/Pages/Changes-to-Australias-and-New-Zealands-overseas-investment-regimes.aspx.

Kalderimis, D. (2011) 'Investment treaties and public goods', in J. Nakagawa (ed.) *Multilateralism and Regionalism in Global Economic Governance*, Oxford: Routledge.

Kawai, M. and Wignaraja, G. (2009) 'Asian FTAs: trends and challenges', *ADBI Working Paper*, 144. Online. Available at: www.adbi.org/files/2009.08.04.wp144.asian.fta.trends.challenges.pdf.

Kelsey, J. (2010) 'How the Trans-Pacific partnership agreement could heighten financial instability and foreclose government's regulatory space', *New Zealand Yearbook of International Law*, 8: 3–43.

Kelsey, J. (2011) 'Preliminary analysis of the draft TPP chapter on domestic coherence'. Online. Available at: www.citizenstrade.org/ctc/wp-content/uploads/2011/10/TransPacific_RegCoherenceMemo.pdf.

Kennedy, D. (2005) 'Challenging expert rule: the politics of global governance', *Sydney Journal of International Law*, 27: 5–28.

King, R. (2007) *The Regulatory State in an Age of Governance: Soft Words and Big Sticks*, New York: Palgrave Macmillan.

Kingsbury, B. and Schill, S. (2009) 'Investor-state arbitration as governance: fair and equitable treatment, proportionality and the emerging global administrative law', in A. J. van den Berg (ed.) *50 Years of the New York Convention (ICAA International Arbitration Conference)*, The Hague: Kluwer Law International.

Kinley, D. (2009) *Civilising Globalisation: human rights and the global economy*, Cambridge: Cambridge University Press.

Kirby, M. (2010) 'Trans-Tasman federation – achievable, impossible, unnecessary', *Canterbury Law Review*, 16: 1–21.

Kogan, L. A. (2003) 'EU regulation, standardization and the precautionary principle: the art of crafting a three-dimensional trade strategy that ignores sound science', National Foreign Trade Council.

Koskenniemi, M. (2007) 'International law: constitutionalism, managerialism and the ethos of legal education', *European Journal of Legal Studies*, 1.

KPMG (2009) *Infrastructure in China: foundation for growth*. Online. Available at: www.kpmg.com/CN/en/IssuesAndInsights/ArticlesPublications/Documents/Infrastructure-in-China-200909.pdf .

Krasner, S. D. (1991) 'Global communications and national power: life on the pareto frontier', *World Politics*, 43(3): 336–66.

Kuijper, P. (2009) 'WTO institutional aspects', in D. Bethlehem, D. McRae, R. Neufeld and I. Van Damme (eds) *The Oxford Handbook of International Trade Law*, New York: Oxford University Press.

Kwak, K. and Marceau, G. (2006) 'Overlaps and conflicts of jurisdiction between the World Trade Organization and regional trade agreements', in L. Bartels and F. Ortino (eds) *Regional Trade Agreements and the WTO Legal System*, New York: Oxford University Press.

Lakshmi, G. V. S. (2010) *Methods of Teaching Environmental Science*, New Delhi: Discovery Publishing House.

Lamming, G. E. (Scientific Working Group on Anabolic Agents in Animal Productions: 'The Lamming Committee') (1984) *Interim Report Submitted to the Commission of the European Communities 1982*, EEC publication EUR 8913.

Lamy, P. (2002) 'Stepping stones or stumbling blocks? The EU's approach towards the problem of multilateralism vs regionalism in trade policy', *The World Economy*, 25(10): 1399.

Lamy, P. (2006) 'China was strong when it opened to the world', speech, 6 September. Online. Available at: www.wto.org/english/news_e/sppl_e/sppl33_e.htm.

Lamy, P. (2006) 'Lamy warns bilateral agreements are not the "easy way out" from the suspended talks'. Speeches, 31 October. Online. Available at: www.wto.org/english/news_e/sppl_e/sppl46_e.htm.

Lang, A. and Scott, J. (2009) 'The hidden world of WTO governance', *European Journal of International Law*, 20: 575–614.

Langendorff, J. (2008) 'Promoting sustainable development through free trade agreements', presentation at Global Investment Forum, 28 March. Online Available at: www.oecd.org/dataoecd/49/26/40393967.pdf.

Leal-Arcas, R. (2001) 'Is the Kyoto Protocol an adequate environmental agreement to solve the climate change problem?', *European Environmental Law Review*, 10 (10): 282–94.

Leal-Arcas, R. (2008a) 'Services as key for the conclusion of the Doha Round', *Legal Issues of Economic Integration*, 35(4): 301–21.

Leal-Arcas, R. (2008b) *Theory and Practice of EC External Trade Law and Policy*, London: Cameron May.

Leal-Arcas, R. (2008c) '50 years of trade policy: good enough or as good as it gets?', *Irish Journal of European Law*, 15 (1 and 2): 157–82.

Leal-Arcas, R. (2009) 'The European Union and new leading powers: towards partnership in strategic trade policy areas', *Fordham International Law Journal*, 32(2): 345–416.

Leal-Arcas, R. (2010a) 'The European Union's trade and investment policy after the Treaty of Lisbon', *The Journal of World Investment and Trade*, 11(4): 463–514.

Leal-Arcas, R. (2010b) 'China's attitude to multilateralism in international economic law and governance: challenges for the world trading system', *The Journal of World Investment and Trade*, 11(2): 259–73.

Leal-Arcas, R. (2010c) *International Trade and Investment Law: Multilateral, Regional and Bilateral Governance*, Cheltenham: Edward Elgar.

Leal-Arcas, R. (2011a) 'Alternative architecture for climate change: major economies', *European Journal of Legal Studies*, 4(1): 25–56.

Leal-Arcas, R. (2011b) 'Kyoto and the COPs: lessons learned and looking ahead', *Hague Yearbook of International Law*, 24: 17–90.

Leal-Arcas, R. (2011c) 'Proliferation of regional trade agreements: complementing or supplanting multilateralism?', *Chicago Journal of International Law*, 11(2): 597–629.

Leal-Arcas, R. (2011d) 'China's economic rise and regional trade', in L. Ho and J. Wong (eds) *APEC and the Rise of China*, Singapore: World Scientific.

Leal-Arcas, R. (2012) "Reflections on EU international trade law: An EU introspective view', *Frontiers of Law in China*, 7(1): 1–18.

Lester, S. and Mercurio, B. (2008) *World Trade Law: text, materials and commentary*, Portland, Or.: Hart Publishing.

Li, G. and Young, A. (2008) 'Competition law and policies in China and Hong Kong: a tale of two regulatory journeys', *Journal of International Trade Law and Policy*, 7: 186.

Li, J. (2009) 'Foreign-invested companies: more risky facing up to China's antimonopoly law?', *International Journal of Law and Management*, 51(3): 179–86.

Lim, C. L., Elms D. and Low, P. (eds) (2012) *The Trans-Pacific Partnership: a quest for a twenty-first century agreement*, Cambridge: Cambridge University Press.

Limenta, M. E. (2012) 'Non-compliance in WTO dispute Settlement: Assessing the effectiveness of WTO retaliation from its purpose(s)', doctoral thesis, Victoria University of Wellington.

Lin Hua of the Research Institute of the MOFCOM (2005) '*Kuaguo qiye zhende zaigao longduan* (Are multinationals really practicing monopoly?)' *ZHONGGUO WAIZI (Foreign Investment in China)*, 1: 32.

Link, P. and Kurlantzick, J. (2009) 'China's modern authoritarianism', *The Wall Street Journal (Asia)*, 25 May.

Lipson, C. (1991) 'Why are some international agreements informal?', *International Organizations*, 45(4): 495–538.

Low, P., Marceau, G. and Reinaud, J. (2010) 'The interface between the trade and climate change regimes: scoping the issue', The Graduate Institute, Center for Trade and Economic Integration, Geneva.

Lowenfeld, A. (2008) *International Economic Law*, 2nd edn, New York: Oxford University Press.

Macrory, P. F. J., Appleton, A. E. and Plummer, M. G. (eds) (2005) *The World Trade Organization: legal, economic and political analysis*, vol. I, New York: Springer.

Malbon, J. and Nottage, L. (eds) (forthcoming) *Consumer Law and Policy in Australia and New Zealand*, Sydney: Federation Press.

Mallaby, S. (2009) 'Beijing's would-be Houdinis', *The Washington Post*, 26 May. Online. Available at: www.cfr.org/publication/19489/.

Mandel, G. N. (2009) 'Regulating emerging technologies', *Temple University Beasley School of Law Legal Studies Research Paper*, 2009–18.

Marchant, G. E., Abbott, K. W., Sylvester, D. J. and Gulley, Lyn M. (2010) 'Transnational new governance and the international coordination of nanotechnology oversight'. Online. Available at: http://papers.ssrn.com/sol3/papers.cfm?abstract_id=1597809.

Markell, D. L. and Knox, J. H. (2003) 'The innovative North American commission for environmental cooperation', *Florida State University College of Law Public Law and Legal Theory Working Paper*, 91. Online. Available at: http://ssrn.com/paper=453180.

Matsushita, M., Schoenbaum, T. and Mavroidis, P. (2006) *The World Trade Organization: law, practice and policy*, 2nd ed, New York: Oxford University Press.

Maupin, J. A. (2011) 'MFN-based jurisdiction in investor-state arbitration – is there any hope for a consistent approach', *Journal of International Economic Law*, 14(1): 157–90.

McCall Smith, J. (2000) 'The politics of dispute settlement design: explaining legalism in regional trade pacts', *International Organization*, 54(1): 137–80.

McCall Smith, J. (2006) 'Compliance bargaining in the WTO: Ecuador and the bananas dispute', in J. S. Odell (ed.) *Negotiating Trade: Developing Countries in the WTO and NAFTA*, New York: Cambridge University Press.

McCormack, B., Pick, R. and Subotic, S. (2008) 'Trans-Tasman mutual recognition of securities offerings: NZ closer economic relations act', *Allens Arthur Robinson*, 11(6): 69–71.

McGrady, B. (2008) 'Fragmentation of international law or "systemic integration" of treaty regimes: *EC – Biotech* products and the proper interpretation of Article 31(3)(c) of the Vienna Convention on the Law of Treaties', *Journal of World Trade*, 42(4): 589–618.

McGregor, J. (2011) *China's Drive for 'Indigenous Innovation': a web of industrial policy*, APCO Worldwide.

McNair, L. (1961) *The Law of Treaties*, London: Clarendon Press.

McRae, D. (2010) 'The WTO Appellate Body: a model for an ICSID appeals facility', *Journal of International Dispute Settlement*, 1(2): 371–87.

McRae, D. (2011a) 'MFN in the GATT and the WTO', paper submitted to the International Law Commission.

McRae, D. (2011b) 'Working paper on the interpretation and application of MFN clauses in investment agreements', paper prepared for the ILC Study Group.

Mercurio, B. (2004) 'Improving dispute settlement in the world trade organization: the dispute settlement understanding review – making it work?', *Journal of World Trade*, 38(5) 795–854.

Miller, F. (2006) 'Consolidating pharmaceutical regulation down under', *University of Queensland Law Journal*, 25(1): 111–30.

Mines, M. (2010) 'China fortifies state business to fuel growth', *New York Times*, 29 August.

Ministry of Foreign Affairs of the People's Republic of China (2010) 'Wen Jiabao holds talks with European Commission President Barroso', 29 April.

Mitchell, A. (2005) 'Due process in WTO disputes', in R. Yerxa and B. Wilson (eds) *Key Issues in WTO Dispute Settlement: the first ten years*, New York: Cambridge University Press.

Mitchell, A. (2007) 'China and the developing world', in F. Bergsten, B. Gill, N. Lardy and D. Mitchell (eds) *The China Balance Sheet in 2007 and Beyond*, Washington DC: Center for Strategic and International Studies and Peterson Institute for International Economics. Online. Avaialable at: http://csis.org/programs/freeman-chair-china-studies/china-balance-sheet/papers.

Moore, J. (2011) 'Is New Zealand's regulation of nanomedical products adequate?', *Journal of Law and Medicine*, 19: 112. Online. Available at: www.conferenz.co.nz/content/whitepapers/2012/Jennifer%20Moore%20paper%2023.02.12.pdf.

Morrow, J. (1994) 'Modeling the forms of international cooperation: distribution versus information', *International Organization*, 48(3): 387–423.

Mortensen, R. (2009) 'The Hague and the ditch: The Trans-Tasman judicial area and the choice of court convention', *Journal of Private International Law*, 5(2): 213–42.

Muck, S. (2009) 'Trans-Tasman imputation and the need for mutual recognition: a comparative analysis with the European Union taxation of cross-border investment', *New Zealand Journal of Taxation Law and Policy*, 15: 49–83.

Murase, S. (2010) 'Review of the 1978 Draft Articles of the MFN Clause', Paper submitted to the ILC Study Group on the MFN Clause.

Murray, P. (2004) 'Towards a research agenda on the European Union as a model of regional integration', *Asia-Pacific Journal of EU Studies*, 2(1): 33–51.

Murray, P. (2010) 'Regionalism and community: Australia's options in the Asia-Pacific', *Australian Strategic Policy Institute*. Online. Available at: www.aspi.org.au/publications/publication_details.aspx?ContentID=273&pubtype=.

Nakamura, T. (ed.) (2009) *East Asian Regionalism From a Legal Perspective*, London: Routledge.

Narlikar, A. and Wickers, B. (eds) (2009) *Leadership and Change in the Multilateral Trading System*, Dordricht: Republic of Letters.

Neumann P. A. and Zhang, T. (2006) 'China's new foreign-funded M&A provisions: greater legal protection or legalized protectionism?', *China Law & Practice*.

Ni, V. (2012) 'China to further open auto insurance market to foreign investors', *China Briefing*, 20 February.

Nixon, R. (1971) 'Address to the nation outlining a new economic policy: "the challenge of peace"', *Public Papers of the Presidents*, 263, 15 August. Online. Available at: www.presidency.ucsb.edu/ws/index.php?pid=3115#axzz1rmLDCUtw.

Nottage, L. (2004) *Product Safety and Liability Law in Japan: from Minamata to mad cows*, London-NewYork: Routledge.

Nottage, L. (2005) 'Redirecting Japan's multi-level governance', in K. Hopt, E. Wymeer-sch, H. Kanda and H. Baum (eds) *Corporate Governance in Context: Corporations, State, and Markets in Europe, Japan, and the US*, Oxford: Oxford University Press.

Nottage, L. (2007a) 'Legal harmonization', in D. Clark, (ed.) *International Encyclopedia of Law and the Social Sciences: American and global perspectives*, New York: Sage.

Nottage, L. (2007b) 'Consumer product safety regulation reform in Australia: Ongoing processes and possible outcomes', in G. Howells, A. Nordhausen, D. Perry and C. Twigg-Flesner (eds) *The Yearbook of Consumer Law* 2007, Hampshire: Ashgate Publishing.

Nottage, L. (2009) 'Consumer law reform in Australia: contemporary and comparative constructive criticism', *Queensland University of Technology Law and Justice Journal*, 9(2): 111–36.

Nottage, L. (2010) 'Law, public policy and economics in Japan and Australia: reviewing bilateral relations and commercial regulation in 2009', *Ritsumeikan University Law Review*, 27: 1–57.

Nottage, L. (2011) 'The rise and possible fall of investor-state arbitration in Asia: a skeptic's view of Australia's "Gillard government trade policy statement"', *Transnational Dispute Management Journal*, 5: 1–25.

Nottage, L. (2013) 'Consumer product safety regulation and investor-state arbitration policy and practice after *Philip Morris Asia v Australia*', in L. Trakman and N. Ranieri (eds) *Regionalism in International Investment Law*, New York: Oxford University Press.

Nottage, L. and Miles, K. (2009) '"Back to the future" for investor-state arbitrations: revising rules in Australia and Japan for public interests', *Journal of International Arbitration*, 26(1): 25–58.

Nottage, L. and Weeramantry, J. R. (2012) 'Investment arbitration in Asia: five perspectives on law and practice', *Arbitration International*, 28: 19–62.

Ochieng, D. O. and Majanja, D. (2006) 'International trade dispute resolution: case study on the possibility of Kenya utilizing the WTO dispute settlement system', paper presented at the Africa Dialogue on WTO Dispute Settlement and Sustainable Development, Mombasa Kenya, 2–3 November.

OECD (1994) *Regulatory Co-operation for an Interdependent World*, Paris: OECD Publishing.

OECD (2009) 'Guidelines for recipient country investment policies relating to national security'. Online. Available at: www.oecd.org/dataoecd/11/35/43384486.pdf.

Oesch, M. (2003a) *Standards of Review in WTO Dispute Resolution*, New York: Oxford University Press.

Oesch, M. (2003b) 'Standards of review in WTO dispute resolution', *Journal of International Economic Law*, 6(3): 635–59.

Oi, J., Rozelle, S. and Zhou, X. (eds) (2010) *Growing Pains: tensions and opportunity in China's transformation*, Stanford, CA: The Walter Shorenstein Asia-Pacific Research Center.

Ortino, F. (2006) 'Treaty interpretation and the WTO Appellate Body report in *US – Gambling*: a critique', *Journal of International Economic law*, 9(1): 117–48.

Pahre, R. (2001) 'Most-favored-nation clauses and clustered negotiations', *International Organization*, 55(4): 859–90.

Palmedo, M. (2013) 'Background on WTO rules allowing Antigua to partially suspend TRIPS as cross retaliation in a trade dispute', *infojustice.org*, 28 January. Online. Available at: http://infojustice.org/archives/28373.

Paulsson, J. and Petrochilos, G. (2006) *Revision of the UNCITRAL Arbitration Rules (not an official UNCITRAL document)*. Online. Available at: www.uncitral.org/pdf/english/news/arbrules_report.pdf.

Pauwelyn, J. (2004) 'Going global, regional, or both? dispute settlement in the Southern African Development Community (SADC) and overlaps with the WTO and other jurisdictions', *Minnesota Journal of Global Trade*, 13: 231–304.

Pauwelyn, J. (2006) 'Adding sweeteners to softwood lumber: The WTO-NAFTA spaghetti bowl is cooking', *Journal of International Economic Law*, 9: 197–206.

Pauwelyn, J. (2007) 'Legal avenues to 'multilateralizing regionalism': beyond Article XXIV', paper presented at the Conference on Multilateralising Regionalism, Geneva, September 2007. Online. Available at: www.acp-eu-trade.org/library/files/pauwelyn_EN_100907_WTO_Legal-avenues-to-multilateralizing-regionalism.pdf.

Pauwelyn, J. and Salles, L. (2009) 'Forum shopping before international tribunals: (real) concerns, (im)possible solutions', *Cornell International Law Journal*, 42: 77.

People's Daily (2009) 'China's top 500 enterprises, 500 strongest or 500 largest?' 8 September. Online. Available at: http://english.peopledaily.com.cn/90001/90778/90857/90860/6751630.html.

Perez, A. F. (1996) 'Who killed sovereignty? or: changing norms concerning sovereignty in international law', *Wisconsin International Law Journal*, 14: 463–90.

Piboontanasawat, N. and Hamlin, K. (2009) 'China passes Germany to become third-biggest economy (update 3)', *Bloomberg*, 14 January. Online. Available at: www.bloomberg.com/apps/news?pid=20601087&sid=aShY0wM1pD_Y&refer=home.

Picciotto, S. (1996–7) 'Networks in international economic integration: fragmented states and the dilemmas of neo-liberalism', *Northwestern Journal of International Law and Business*, 17: 1014–56.

Pokarier, C. (2008) 'Open to being closed? foreign control and adaptive efficiency in Japanese corporate governance', in L. Nottage, L. Wolff and K. Anderson (eds) *Corporate Governance in the 21st Century: Japan's gradual transformation*, Cheltenham: Edward Elgar.

Potter, P. B. (2001) *The Chinese Legal System: globalization and local legal culture*, London: Routledge.

Potts, J. (2008) *The Legality of PPMs under the GATT: challenges and opportunities for sustainable trade policy*, Manitoba: International Institute for Sustainable Development.

Prost, O. (2005) 'Confidentiality issues under the DSU', in R. Yerxa and B. Wilson (eds) *Key Issues in WTO Dispute Settlement: the first ten years*, New York: Cambridge University Press.

Public Citizen (2010) 'Comments concerning the proposed Trans-Pacific partnership trade agreement'. Online. Available at: www.citizen.org/documents/PublicCitizenTP-PComments012510.pdf.

Qin, J. Y. (2007) 'Trade, investment and beyond: the impact of WTO accession on China's legal system', *The China Quarterly*, 191: 720–41.

Qin, J. Y. (2008) 'China, India, and the law of the world trade organization', *Asian Journal of Comparative Law*, 3(1): 1–43.

Qin, J. Y. (2009) 'The Mercosur exemption reversed – conflict between WTO and Mercosur rulings and its implications for environmental values', ASIL Insight, January 23. Online. Available at: www.asil.org/insights070905_update.cfm.

Qingfen, D. (2012) 'China unlikely to join WTO agreement', *China Daily*, 21 March.

Quiggin, J. (2010) *Zombie Economics: how dead ideas still walk among us*, Princeton: Princeton University Press.

Ratliff, D. 'Dispute resolution in flexible mechanism contracts', unpublished presentation.

Ratner, M. and Ratner, D. (2003) *Nanotechnology: a gentle introduction to the next big idea*, New Jersey: Prentice Hall.

Raustiala, K. (2005) 'Form and substance in international agreements', *American Journal of International Law*, 95: 581–614.

Reich, A. (2004) 'The WTO as a law-harmonizing institution', *University of Pennsylvania Journal of International Economic Law*, 25: 321–82.

Roman, D. (2010) 'WTO Lamy: China "overall" abiding by WTO commitments', *The Wall Street Journal*, 25 July.

Romano, C. P. R. (2007) 'The shift from the consensual to the compulsory paradigm in international adjudication: elements for a theory of consent', *International Law and Politics*, 39: 791–872.

Rubins, N. (2008) 'MFN clauses, procedural rights, and a return to the treaty text', in T. Weiler (ed.) *Investment Treaty Arbitration and International Law*, Huntington, NY: Juris Publishing.

Runnalls, D., Ye, R., von Moltke, K. and Yan, W. (eds) (2002) *Trade and Sustainability: Challenges and Opportunities for China as a WTO Member*, Manitoba: International Institute for Sustainable Development.

Sacerdoti, G. (2005) 'The role of lawyers in the WTO dispute settlement system', in R. Yerxa and B. Wilson (eds) *Key Issues in WTO Dispute Settlement: the first ten years*, New York: Cambridge University Press.

Sandford, I. and TanKiang, M. (2011) 'Resolving and defusing trade disputes: the potential for creativity in the Australia-European Union relationship', *Australian Journal of International Affairs*, 65(4): 469–87.

Sanson, M. (2009) 'Facilitating access to dispute settlement for African members of the World Trade Organization', *Indian Journal of International Economic Law* 2: 1–51.

Saul, B. (2011) 'Human rights cooperation in the Asia-Pacific: demythologising regional exceptionalism by learning from the Americas, Europe and Africa', in H. Nasu and B. Saul (eds) *Human Rights in the Asia-Pacific: toward institution-building*, London: Routledge.

Schill, S. W. (2009a) 'Multilateralizing investment treaties through most-favored-nation clauses', *Berkeley of International Law*, 27: 497–569.

Schill, S. W. (2009b) *The Multilateralization of International Investment Law*, Cambridge: Cambridge University Press.

Schneider, A. K. (2006) 'Not quite a world without trials: why international dispute resolution is increasingly judicialized', *Journal of Dispute Resolution*, 1: 119–24.

Scollay, R. and Trewin, R. (2006) 'Australia and New Zealand bilateral CEPs/FTAs with the ASEAN countries and their Implication on the AANZFTA', *REPSF Project – Final Report*, 05/003. Online. Available at: www.asean.org/aadcp/repsf/docs/05-003-Final-Report.pdf.

Sen, R. (2006) 'New regionalism' in Asia: a comparative analysis of emerging regional and bilateral trading agreements involving ASEAN, China and India', *Journal of World Trade*, 40(4): 553–96.

Shaffer, G. and Meléndez-Ortiz, R. (eds) (2010) *Dispute Settlement at the WTO: the developing country experience*, Cambridge: Cambridge University Press.

Shaffer, G. C. (2003) 'How to make the WTO dispute settlement system work for developing countries: some proactive developing country strategies', in International Centre for Trade and Sustainable Development *Towards a Development-Supportive Dispute Settlement System in the WTO, Sustainable Development and Trade Issues*, ICTSD Resource Paper No. 5, March.

Shaffer, G. C. and Pollack, M. A. (2008) 'How hard and soft law interact in international regulatory governance: alternatives, complements and antagonists'. Online. Available at: http://papers.ssrn.com/sol3/papers.cfm?abstract_id=1156867.

Shah, C. and Long, M. (2009) 'Labour mobility and mutual recognition of skills and qualifications: the European Union and Australia/New Zealand', in R. Maclean and D. Wilson (eds) *International Handbook of Education for the Changing World of Work*, Springer.

Shaw, M. (2008) *International Law*, 6th edn, Cambridge: Cambridge University Press.

Shirouze, N. (2012) 'China sets curbs on official cars', *The Wall Street Journal*, 28 February.

Shirouze, N. (2012) 'Ford faces China hurdles', *The Wall Street Journal*, 27 February.

Simma, B. (1994) 'From bilateralism to community interest', *Recuil des Cours de l'Académie de Droit International*, 250: 217–384.

Slater, G. (2009) 'The suspension of intellectual property obligations under TRIPS: A proposal for retaliating against technology-exporting countries in the World Trade Organization', *The Georgetown Law Journal*, 97: 1365–408.

Slaughter, A.-M. (1999) 'Agencies on the loose? holding government networks accountable?', *Harvard Law School Public Law and Legal Theory Working Paper*, No. 006.

Slaughter, A.-M. (2003) 'Global government networks, global information agencies, and disaggregated democracy', *Michigan Journal of International Law*, 24: 1041–75.

Slaughter, A.-M. (2004) *A New World Order*, Princeton: Princeton University Press.

Snyder, F. (2001) 'The origins of the nonmarket economy: ideas, pluralism and power in EC anti-dumping law about China', *European Law Journal*, 7(4): 369–434.

Snyder, F. (2009) 'China, regional trade agreements and WTO law', *Journal of World Trade*, 43(1): 1–57.

South China Morning Post (2012) 'Citi Bank becomes the western bank to issue a credit card in China', 7 February.

Spence, M. (2011) *The Next Convergence: the future of economic growth in a multispeed world*, Perth: UWA Publishing.

Spigelman, J. J. (2006) 'Transaction costs and international litigation', *Australian Law Journal*, 80: 438–53.

Spigelman, J. J. (2007) 'International commercial litigation: an Asian perspective', *Australian Business Law Review*, 35(5): 318–37.

State Administration of Industry and Commerce (2004) 'Multinationals' Activities to Restrict Competition in China and the Counter-Measures', *GONGSHANG Xingzheng GUANLI (Journal of State Administration of Industry and Commerce)*, 5: 43.

State Council Information Office White Paper (2005) 'China's peaceful development road', 22 December, Online. Available at: http://english.peopledaily.com.cn/200512/22/eng20051222_230059.html.

Statement of the Free Trade Commission on non-disputing party participation (7 October 2004). Online. Available at: www.naftaclaims.com/Papers/Nondisputing-en.pdf.

Subramaniam, A. and Watal, J. (2000) 'Can TRIPS serve as an enforcement device for developing countries in the WTO?', *Journal of International Economic Law*, 3(3): 403–16.

Sunstein, C. (2011) '21st century regulation: an update on the president's reform', Law and Economics Blog, 26 May. Online. Available at: www.economicanalysisoflaw. org/2011/05/21st-century-regulation-update-on.html.

Sutherland, P. (2008) 'Transforming nations: how the WTO boosts economies and opens societies', *Foreign Affairs*, 87(2): 125–36.

Sutherland, P. *et al.* (2004) *The Future of the WTO: addressing institutional challenges in the new millennium*, Switzerland: World Trade Organization.

Svetiev, Y. (2010) 'Partial formalization of the regulatory network'. Online. Available at: http://ssrn.com/abstract=1564890.

Sydney Morning Herald (2009) 'China protectionism on rise, says EU', 1 July. Online, Available at: http://news.smh.com.au/breaking-news-business/china-protectionism-on-rise-says-eu-20090701-d493.html.

Talley, I. (2011) 'U.S.-China talks make progress on market access', *The Wall Street Journal*, 11 May.

Tarullo, D. (2002) 'The hidden costs of international dispute settlement: WTO review of domestic anti-dumping decisions', *Law and Policy in International Business*, 34: 109–81.

Tevini, A. (2011) 'Article XXIV GATT' in R. Wolfrum, P.-T. Stoll and H. P. Hestermeyer (eds) *WTO – Trade in Goods*, Leiden: Martinus Nijhoff Publishers.

The Economist (2009) 'How China sees the world', 21 March.

The Economist (2010) 'Dating game: when will China overtake America', 16 December. Online. Available at: www.economist.com/node/17733177.

The White House (2006) 'The national security strategy of the United States of America', Online. Available at: http://georgewbush-whitehouse.archives.gov/nsc/nss/2006/.

The World Bank (1997) *China Engaged: integration with the global economy*, Washington DC: The World Bank.

The World Bank (2012) *China 2030: building a modern, harmonious, and creative high-income society*, Washington DC: The International Bank for Reconstruction and Development.

Thomas, K. (2011) 'China and the WTO dispute settlement system: from passive observer to active participant', unpublished paper.

Tomouschat, C. (2006) 'The International Law Commission – an outdated institution?', *German Yearbook of International Law*, 49: 77–105.

Trebilcock, M. J. and Daniels, R. (2008) *Rule of Law Reform and Development: charting the fragile path of progress*, Edward Elgar: Cheltenham.

Trubek, D. M. (2008) 'Transcending the ostensible: some reflections on Bob Hudec as friend and scholar', *Minnesota Journal International Law* 17(1): 1–6.

UNCTAD (2008–9) 'Recent developments in international investment agreements (2008-June 2009)', IIA Monitor No. 3. Online. Available at: www.unctad.org/en/docs/webdiaeia20098_en.pdf.

UNCTAD (2009) *Investment Policy Development in G-20 Countries*. Online. Available at: www.unctad.org/Templates/Download.asp?docid=11749&lang=1&intItemID=2983.

UNCTAD (2010) *Most-Favoured-Nation Treatment: UNCTAD series on issues in international investment agreements II*, New York and Geneva: United Nations Publications.

UNEP and IISD (2000) *Environment and Trade: a handbook*, Canada: International Institute for Sustainable Development and United Nations Environment Program.

United Nations (1967) *Yearbook of the International Law Commission 1966 Volume II: documents of the second part of the seventeenth session and the eighteenth session including the reports of the Commission to the General Assembly*, New York: United Nations Publications.

Urata, S. (2004) 'Towards an East Asia free trade area', *Policy Insights*, 1. Online. Available at: www.oecd.org/dataoecd/36/55/31098183.pdf.

U.S. Department of the Treasury (2011) 'Major foreign holders of treasury securities', 15 August. Online. Available at: www.treasury.gov/resource-center/data-chart-center/tic/Documents/mfh.txt.

U.S. Government Accountability Office (2010) 'Drug safety: FDA has conducted more foreign inspections and begun to improve its information on foreign establishments, but more progress is needed', GAO-10–961, September.

U.S.–China Economic and Security Review Commission (2006) 'China's role in the world: is China a responsible stakeholder?', Statement by Thomas J. Christensen Deputy Assistant Secretary of State for East Asian and Pacific Affairs before the U.S.–China Economic and Security Review Commission, 3 August. Online. Available at: www.uscc.gov/hearings/2006hearings/written_testimonies/06_08_3_4wrts/06_08_3_4_christensen_thomas_statement.pdf.

Van Damme, I. (2009) 'Jurisdiction, applicable law and interpretation', in D. Bethlehem, D. McRae, R. Neufeld and I. Van Damme (eds) *The Oxford Handbook of International Trade Law*, New York: Oxford University Press.

Van den Bossche, P. (2005) *The Law and Policy of the World Trade Organization: text, cases and materials*, Cambridge: Cambridge University Press.

Van Harten, G. (2006) *Investment Treaty Arbitration and Public Law*, New York: Oxford University Press.

Vesel, S. (2007) 'Clearing a path through a tangled jurisprudence: most-favored nation clauses and dispute settlement provisions in bilateral investment treaties', *Yale Journal of International Law*, 32: 125–90.

Vikhlyaev, A. (2001) 'The Use of Trade Measures for Environmental Purposes – Globally and the EU Context', *FEEM Working Paper*, 68.2001.

Vincentelli, I. (2010) 'The uncertain future of ICSID in Latin America', *Law and Business Review of the Americas*, 16: 409–55.

Vogel D. and Kagan, R. A. (eds) (2004) *Dynamics of Regulatory Change: how globalization affects national regulatory policies*, Berkeley and Los Angeles: University of California Press.

Vogel, D. (2003) 'The hare and the tortoise revisited: the new politics of consumer and environmental regulation in Europe', *British Journal of Political Science*, 33: 557–80.

Voigt, C. (2009) *Sustainable Development as a Principle of International Law: resolving conflicts between climate measures and WTO law*, Leiden: Martinus Nijhoff Publishers.

von Tigerstrom, B. (2007) 'Globalisation, harmonisation and the regulation of therapeutic products: the Australia New Zealand therapeutic products authority project in global context', *Canterbury Law Review*, 13: 287–313.

Vranes, E. (2009a) 'Climate change and the WTO: EU emissions trading and the disciplines on trade in goods, services and investment protection', *Journal of World Trade*, 43: 707–35.

Vranes, E. (2009b) *Trade and the Environment: fundamental issues in international law, WTO law and legal theory*, Oxford: Oxford University Press.

Walker, G. (2004) 'The CER agreement and Trans-Tasman business law coordination: from 'soft law' approach to 'hard law' outcome', *Law in Context*, 21(1): 75–108.

Wallach, L. (2005) *Public Citizen Pocket Trade Lawyer: the alphabet soup of globalization.* Online. Available at: www.citizen.org/documents/Pocket_Trade_Lawyer_January_2006_Final.pdf.

Wallach, L. and Tucker, T. (2010) 'US politics and the TPPA', in J. Kelsey (ed.) *No Ordinary Deal: unmasking the Trans-Pacific partnership*, Wellington, N.Z.: Bridget Williams Books.

Wang, G. (2011) 'China's FTAs: legal characteristics and implications', *American Journal of International Law*, 105(3): 493–516.

Wang, J. (2005) 'China's new automobile policy fails to comply with its WTO commitments', *Bepress Legal Series*, Paper 758. Online. Available at: http://law.bepress.com/cgi/viewcontent.cgi?article=3665&context=expresso.

Wang, J. Y. (2006) 'China, India, and regional economic integration in Asia', *Singapore Yearbook of International Law*, 10: 269–305.

Wang, P. (2007) 'Coverage of the WTO's agreement on government procurement: challenges of integrating China and other countries with a large state sector into the global trading system', *Journal of International Economic Law*, 10(4): 887–920.

Watts, A. (1999) *The International Law Commission 1949–1998: Volume III: Final Draft Articles and Other Materials*, Oxford: Oxford University Press.

Weiler, J. H. H. (2001) 'The rule of lawyers and the ethos of diplomats: reflections on the internal and external legitimacy of WTO dispute settlement', *Journal of World Trade*, 35: 191.

Wheatley, A. (2010) 'Communist party needs to loosen its grip in China', *New York Times*, 2 March.

Whipp, L. (2010) 'Chinese economy eclipses Japan', *Financial Times*, 16 August.

White House Office of the Press Secretary (2011) 'Fact sheet: U.S.–China economic issues', 19 January. Online. Available at: www.whitehouse.gov/the-press-office/2011/01/19/fact-sheet-us-china-economic-issues.

Wilson, A. (2004) 'Good news about AIDS', *Global Education Network News*, May–June. Online. Available at: www.peacecorpsconnect.org/wordpress/wp-content/uploads/2010/07/GTNMayJun04.pdf .

Wolf, M. (2001) 'What the world needs from the multilateral trading system', in G. Sampson *The Role of the World Trade Organization in Global Governance*, Hong Kong: United Nations University Press.

Wolfrum, R., Stoll, P.-T. and Hestermeyer, H. P. (eds) (2011) *WTO – Trade in Goods*, Leiden: Martinus Nijhoff Publishers.

Wood, M. (2008) 'The General Assembly and the International Law Commission: what happens to the Commission's work and why?', in I. Buffard, J. Crawford, A. Pellet and S. Witich (eds) *International Law between Universalism and Fragmentation: Festschrift in Honour of Gerhard Hafner*, Netherlands: Brill.

Wu, Q. (2007) 'The making of a market economy in China: transformation of government regulation of market development', *European Law Journal*, 13: 750–71.

Xin Jingbao (The Beijing News) (2008) 'The death of the division head reveals cases concerning RMB 200 Billion', 27 August. Online. Available at: http://news.mbalib. com/story/6051.

Xinhua News Agency (2006) 16 September. Online. Available at: http://big5.xinhuanet. com/gate/big5/news.xinhuanet.com/classad/2006-09/16/content_5098110.htm.

Xinhua News Agency (2011) 27 August. Online. Available at: http://news.xinhuanet. com/2011-08/27/c_121919846.htm.

Xu, M. (2012) 'Hope and fears – China's aniti-monopoly law enforcement in 2011', *Business & Law Website*, 3 February. Online. Available at: http://businesslawblog.eu/category/antitrust/.

Xuto, N. (2005) 'Thailand: conciliating a dispute on tuna exports to the EC', in P. Gallagher, P. Low and A. Stoler (eds) *Managing the Challenges of WTO Participation: 45 Case Studies*, Cambridge: Cambridge University Press.

Yanovich, A. and Zdouc, W. (2009) 'Procedural and evidentiary issues', in D. Bethlehem, D. McRae, R. Neufeld and I. Van Damme (eds) *The Oxford Handbook of International Trade Law*, New York: Oxford University Press.

Yi, G. and Baoping, R. (2009) '30 years of enterprise reform in China: review and prospect', *Guizhou Caijing Xueyuan Xuebao (Journal of Financial College of Guizhou)*, 1: 45.

Yueh, L. (2003) 'China's economic growth with WTO accession: is it sustainable?', *Asia Programme Working Paper*, 1.

Zakaria, F. (2008) *The Post-American World*, New York: W.W. Norton & Company.

Zamora, S. (2011) 'Rethinking North America: why NAFTA's laissez-faire approach to integration is flawed and what to do about it', *Villanova Law Review*, 56: 631.

Zaring, D. T. (2005) 'Informal procedure, hard and soft, in international administration', *Chicago Journal of International Law*, 5: 547–604.

Zeller, B. (2009) 'Systems of carbon trading', *Touro Law Review*, 25: 909–42.

Zhang, X. (2011a) 'China's "dual track" legislation on business organizations and the effects on the Anti-Monopoly Law', in J. Garrick (ed.) *Law, Wealth and Power in China*, London: Routledge.

Zhang, X. (2011b) 'Institutional challenges to indigenous innovation in China', *International Journal of Arts & Sciences*, 4(12): 223–8.

Zhang, Y. and Austin, G. (eds) (2001) *Power and Responsibility in Chinese Foreign Policy*, Canberra: Asia Pacific Press.

Zhao, J. and Webster, T. (2011) 'Taking stock: China's first decade of free trade', *University of Pennsylvania Journal of International Law*, 33: 65–119.

Zhao, R. (2007) 'China and India: a comparison of trade, investment and expansion strategies', *Chatham House*, 1 June.

Zhong, Z. (2011) 'The ASEAN comprehensive investment agreement: realizing a regional community', *Asian Journal of Comparative Law*, 6(1): Art. 4.

Zhongguo Jingji Shibao (China Economic Times) (2012) 'Slow reorganization of the centrally controlled enterprises', 17 May. Online. Available at: http://news.xinhuanet.com/ fortune/2012-05/17/c_123145129.htm.

Zhongguo Pinglun (China Review), 12 June 2009.

Zhongguo Wang (China Net) (2004) 'Interview with Shang Ming, the Director of the Antimonopoly Office of MOFCOM', 23 December. Online. Available at: www.china. com.cn/news/txt/2004-12/23/content_5736697.htm.

Ziegler, A. (2010) 'The nascent international law on most-favoured-nation (MFN) clauses in bilateral investment agreements', *European Yearbook of International Econ Law*, 77–101.

Zleptnig, S. (2010) 'Non-economic objectives in WTO law: justification provisions of GATT, GATS, SPS and TBT Agreements', Boston: Martinus Nijhoff Publishers.

Zoellick, R. (2002) 'Unleashing the trade winds', *The Economist*, 5 December.

Zoellick, R. (2005) 'Whither China: from membership to responsibility?' Remarks to the National Committee on U.S.-China Relations, New York City, 21 September 2005. Online. Available at: www.ncuscr.org/files/2005Gala_RobertZoellick_Whither_China1. pdf.

Zoellick, R. and Lin, J. (2009) 'Recovery rides on the "G-2" ', *Washington Post*, 6 March. Online. Available at: www.washingtonpost.com/wp-dyn/content/article/2009/03/05/AR2009030502887_pf.html.

Index